MW01067648

God Almighty Hisself

God Almighty Hisself

The Life and Legacy of Dick Allen

MITCHELL NATHANSON

UNIVERSITY OF PENNSYLVANIA PRESS

PHILADELPHIA

Copyright © 2016 University of Pennsylvania Press

All rights reserved. Except for brief quotations used
for purposes of review or scholarly citation, none of this
book may be reproduced in any form by any means without
written permission from the publisher.

Published by
University of Pennsylvania Press
Philadelphia, Pennsylvania 19104-4112
www.upenn.edu/pennpress

Printed in the United States of America
on acid-free paper

1 3 5 7 9 10 8 6 4 2

Library of Congress Cataloging-in-Publication Data

Nathanson, Mitchell, 1966– author.
    God Almighty hisself : the life and legacy of Dick Allen / Mitchell Nathanson.
      pages cm
    Includes bibliographical references and index.
    ISBN 978-0-8122-4801-2 (alk. paper)
    1. Allen, Dick, 1942– 2. Baseball players—Pennsylvania—Philadelphia—Biography. 3. African
American baseball players—Pennsylvania—Philadelphia—Biography. 4. Discrimination in
sports—United States—History. I. Title.
GV865.A35N37 2016
796.357092—dc23
[B]
                                                                                                    2015033020

For Joanne, Alex, and Jackie

"I believe God Almighty Hisself would have trouble handling Richie Allen."

—George Myatt, Phillies' interim manager

Contents

Contents

Baseball's Way

"I WOULDN'T SAY that I hate Whitey, but deep down in my heart, I just can't stand Whitey's ways, man."[1] Dick Allen, in repose, at last, with a reporter of all people, spoke freely and held nothing back. A confluence of factors unburdened him for what seemed like the first time in years, maybe the first time ever, or at least since anybody outside of Wampum, Pennsylvania, had become aware of the bespectacled Superman with the seemingly never-ending litany of first names (Dick? Rich? Richie? Sleepy?). He was finally rid of both Philadelphia and the Phillies after six-plus years of torment on both sides of the equation, having settled tranquilly (although not wholly without incident) in St. Louis with the Cardinals, an organization known as much for its acceptance of its black ballplayers as its on-field success. He was now just one of the guys on a team replete with future Hall of Famers, such as Lou Brock, Bob Gibson, and Steve Carlton, and no longer the athletic fulcrum of an entire city. And he was rapping with a member of the black media for a change—speaking with someone who perhaps was more likely to understand who he was and where had been—someone who knew what it took to have to deal with those who assumed that the issue of equality had been solved years before with the abolition of "separate but equal" and the segregated lunch counters and water fountains that went with it. For a moment at least, Dick Allen was at peace.

The *Ebony* reporter tried to get it all down as Allen went on: "I get to reading those novels and things and get right mad." Here now a revelation—Dick Allen, the man reviled by so many in Philadelphia, the man thought by so many in the stands as well as a share of the media to be witless and clueless, saw truth in fiction, saw himself and all that he had been subjected to, in the characters and progression of a novel. "I just got through reading—what was it—[*The*] *Greengage Affair*, I think it was, about the life of a black cat who lived in Mississippi." Written by Linda Du Breuil, who would later be known as the Queen of Pornography for such sex-soaked paperbacks as *The Teeny-Boffer*, *Peter Powers*, and *Sex on St. James Street* (written under one of her many noms de plume, D. Barry Linder), *The Greengage Affair* was something else altogether—outside of a solitary (albeit simmering) sex scene, a meditation on race relations in both the Deep South as well as the supposedly more enlightened North.[2]

Chronicling the emergence of black consciousness in Lex Morrow, the novel's protagonist, *The Greengage Affair* resonated with Dick for its asides on the ugly truth of contemporary race relations, be they in the backwater of the fictional Greengage, Mississippi, the real-world Little Rock, Arkansas, where Dick endured a minor league trial by fire in 1963, or the large, allegedly progressive northern cities such as Detroit or even Philadelphia. "It's a good book," Allen continued, sharing a thought that would no doubt get lost, get jumbled, get misconstrued by a different audience, "but, you see, all this type of stuff makes me mad. And then I'm really aware of Whitey, man, really aware of Whitey. Philly taught me that people can be the cruelest things in the world."[3] Philly wasn't Little Rock, but as Lex's father explained in *The Greengage Affair*, that wasn't saying all that much if you really thought about it: "Sure, they ain't no signs up in the rest rooms, ain't no WHITE LADIES tacked on the restroom door and COLORED WOMEN on the others but . . . they don't *need* signs up here. We got Negro juke joints and Negro restaurants and Negro churches and Negro schools. Ain't a bit of difference. Not when you get right down to the gritty end, they ain't."[4]

"In Philly," Dick remarked, "white barbers won't even let you in their shops, and [then] whites were hollering from the stands, 'Get your hair cut!'"[5] Confusion and mixed messages seemingly reigned throughout his tenure in the city, but eventually Dick became resigned to it: "Even if they gave me an opportunity to tell all of my side of the story, I wouldn't take it because I just don't trust the white press in general. There may be some exceptions, but I don't trust the white press in general."[6] And so he took a different path, one he saw reflected in *The Greengage Affair*. As Lex Morrow put it, "there's a difference between [simply] wanting to get out of something and refusing to participate."[7] A subtle, yet strongly defiant message is sent when the former route—perhaps the easier, clearer route—is forsaken for the latter. Something is said through the mere act of refusal that cannot be uttered otherwise, something that brings a measure of dignity to what might otherwise be a situation devoid of any. And so Dick Allen refused to participate, first in little ways and then in greater ones. And a message was delivered. And a message was, ultimately, received.

Through the course of his major league career, Dick Allen was without doubt recognized for doing a lot of things. He was the 1964 National League Rookie of the Year and the 1972 American League Most Valuable Player. His 351 home runs are more than those of Hall of Famer Ron Santo and trail those of Hall of Famer Orlando Cepeda by only 28 despite the fact that he accumulated nearly 1,400 fewer plate appearances than Cepeda. His three slugging titles dwarf the lone title claimed by the prototypical slugger of the era, Harmon Killebrew, and his lifetime .292 batting average tops Killebrew's by 36 points. And for those who pray to the altar of sabermetrics, his "adjusted OPS+" is higher than that of the greatest slugger of all time, Hall of Famer Hank Aaron. Because of all that he did, the MLB Network in 2012 ranked him as a member of its "Top Ten Not in the Hall of Fame" (he placed ninth). However, despite all that he did, Dick Allen is remembered more often for the myriad ways he refused to participate: in pregame batting and fielding practice most obviously, but in other ways more subtly. He refused to pander to the media, refused to accept management's time-honored methods for determining the value of a ballplayer, and, most explosively, refused to go along with and kowtow to the racial double standard that had evolved within Major League Baseball in the wake of the game's integration in 1947.

Because of all that he did as well as all that he refused to do, Dick became one of the most controversial players in the history of a game replete with them. As *Sports Illustrated* summed him up in 1970, "He is

known as a man who hits a baseball even harder than he hits the bottle.
. . . Allen shakes the game's Establishment and stirs up its followers as no
other player can."[8] Accordingly, nearly every baseball fan with an opinion
had a strong one when it came to Dick Allen and today, many still do.

Throughout the arc of his productive yet strange and oftentimes mad-
dening career, and in the decades thereafter, the debate over who was
ultimately to blame for the controversy that seemingly followed him wherever he went raged on, and rages still. Was Dick the cause of his problems
or merely misunderstood? Were they contrived by a media and fan base
that resented what was perceived as his assertion of Black Power, or were
they grounded in and simply the inevitable fallout from a player who just
refused to be a team player in the most basic sense of the term? Who is
responsible for the tragedy that was Dick Allen? For all of his talent, and
despite how much his teammates seemed to like him wherever he went,
who is to blame for the fact that no matter where his travels took him
over the arc of his fifteen-year career—Philadelphia, St. Louis, Los
Angeles, Chicago, Philadelphia again, and Oakland—disharmony, dissension, disagreement, and disruption invariably came along for the ride?
Why is it that one of the most talented players of his generation was
ranked by the preeminent baseball historian Bill James as not only the
second most controversial player in baseball history (behind only Rogers
Hornsby, an accused wife-beater, inveterate gambler, and all-around
deadbeat who was continually dragged into court for his failure to pay his
taxes and other debts) but someone who "did more to *keep* his teams
from winning than anybody else who ever played major league baseball"?[9]
Good questions all.

Unfortunately, much of the reason why these questions have never
been satisfactorily answered is because they're the wrong ones. Instead,
the foundational question raised by Dick Allen's mercurial career is this:
Why wasn't a black superstar such as Dick, as difficult as he could be at
times, accorded the same deference by the working press and fan base as
were the white superstars of his era? Unquestionably, Dick both expected
and demanded treatment that was not accorded to his teammates, but in
so doing he was not alone; for decades, temperamental baseball superstars
such as Babe Ruth, Joe DiMaggio, and others made similar demands, and,
more often than not, their demands were met by a compliant media and

public that were more than willing to ignore or explain away transgressions and repeated instances of bad behavior in their zeal to immortalize and purify their heroes. Despite the newly ravenous media that emerged in the 1960s, this pattern persisted, with players such as Mickey Mantle and Carl Yastrzemski likewise reaping the benefits of the game's treatment of its luminaries irrespective of their personal foibles.

But with Dick Allen things were different. Yearning to be the beneficiary of the hallowed double standard accorded to the game's superstar elite, Dick found himself instead the victim of another double standard, one that enforced a code of conduct upon the game's black players, even black superstars, that was neither required nor expected of similarly situated white ones. This he could not fathom; this he could not countenance. And so he rebelled—not by yelling and stomping his feet but quietly, by simply refusing to go along with it all. And the game would never be the same.

For all of the ink spilled over the triumphant victory that was Jackie Robinson and the twentieth-century integration of Organized Baseball, there was a wave of black players that followed the pioneering Robinson and his cohorts—Larry Doby, Hank Aaron, Willie Mays, Ernie Banks, and so on—that began to infiltrate the game in the late 1950s, just as the Negro Leagues' short tenure as a de facto minor league was coming to an end. This generation negotiated a harrowing minor league gauntlet of segregated southern cities and towns on their path to The Show, where they would emerge not as symbols of racial progress, living monuments to the power of change, but merely as ballplayers, no different than the white ones playing alongside them. No different but yet oftentimes, in countless subtle ways, subjected to differing treatment nonetheless.

This second generation of black players has received much less attention than Jackie Robinson's perhaps because their stories are less obviously triumphant, less clearly symbolic of *something*. This was Dick Allen's generation and their stories are, in fact, no less compelling, no less triumphant. But this generation, unlike Robinson's, did not end with an exclamation mark. Instead it bled slowly and imperceptibly into the modern game, where the racial double standard finally disappeared, and if you don't look for it, you're likely to miss it. But it's there. And Dick Allen, at times unwittingly, at times quite cunningly, is a large part of the reason it ultimately succeeded.

In a way, Dick Allen's fight with baseball was like Robinson's—a fight for equality. But whereas Jackie's fight was simply for the right to play on the same field as equally talented white players, Dick's was to be accorded the same respect and deference as his white peers. Thanks to Jackie Robinson and his first-wave contemporaries, Dick was able to take the field under the assumption that he had just as much of a right to be there as anyone else, but he extended the battle into its logical next phase: the fight for equal treatment among the equally talented. He would accept nothing short of this and, eventually, baseball, its fans, and its attendant media would see things his way but not without a succession of clashes that would consume virtually his entire career. For as Dick surveyed the baseball landscape, he saw not that fans and the media were unable to appreciate and applaud black superstars; many within the first wave were rightly lauded and repeatedly so. Rather, he saw that those who expected white praise were in exchange expected to sublimate their anger just as Robinson was famously instructed by Dodgers president Branch Rickey to do, or simply not talk about the death threats, the ugliness of their minor league experiences, the callowness they were subjected to both as blacks and as ballplayers. "Richie Allen wants to be treated like Willie Mays so bad he can taste it," asserted Gene Mauch, his inaugural manager in Philadelphia. "But so far he's still trying to find out how to act like Willie Mays."[10] Dick realized very early on, however, that he was unable to abide as his predecessors had done. And he paid the price for this.

What follows is an examination of Dick Allen's baseball life and career with an eye toward explaining not only how one of the greatest natural talents in baseball history both fulfilled and frustrated expectations all at once but how he compelled fans, the media, and baseball itself to confront at last the racial double standard that had become entrenched in the wake of the game's integration a generation earlier. Herein also lies an attempt to clarify the walking dichotomy that was Dick Allen, a man who was introverted in the extreme but who spoke out frequently nonetheless, a man who routinely hid from the media but who was described by Roy Blount Jr. in 1973 as "the first black man, and indeed the only contemporary man of any color, to assert himself in baseball with something like the unaccommodating force of Muhammad Ali in boxing, Kareem Abdul-Jabbar in basketball and Jim Brown in football."[11] A man who was dismissed by even his staunchest supporters as inarticulate and confused who nevertheless sized up the inherent inequalities present in the contract negotiating process as it was then routinely conducted and became one of the first players of any color to successfully insert his agent into the deliberations: "The owner, he goes out and gets himself a qualified man to negotiate for him. He sends his man with all his experience or all his degrees to negotiate with me. Me? I've got 12 years of schooling. So, me, I get my lawyer. The first man, he's the owner's protection. The lawyer, well, he's mine. I mean the word is *negotiate*, isn't it? All right, so let's do that. Let's negotiate. But let's try to keep the sides even."[12] In so doing, this seemingly inarticulate and confused man eventually managed to make himself the game's highest-paid player of the pre–free agency era.

But he never confused being rich with being free. To Dick, being rich wasn't the point. In fact, it was nowhere near the point. All the money in the world couldn't buy a man his dignity, and he wouldn't sacrifice his for anything. Although he lived within the world of Organized Baseball, he refused to bow to its traditions, bred as they were in the game's segregated past. Two sets of rules for Dick Allen? "Yeah, but no one talked about the two sets of rules Black players faced down in segregated Clearwater, Florida. We had to stay in quarters across the tracks while the white ball players stayed in hotels. If that's not two sets of rules, what is?"[13] Even after the segregated camps were dismantled and Dick was living the life of the rich ballplayer, he saw what so many others missed: "A lot of people who run baseball still don't think of us, really, as human beings."[14]

And so, like Lex Morrow of *The Greengage Affair*, Dick Allen refused to participate. In so many ways, he simply preferred not to do what was either asked or expected of him and in the process sent a message—one that led to chaos as the traditional order of the baseball universe was at last upended. In this regard, his battles recall those of yet another literary figure, one removed in time by more than a century but one who illustrated all that could ensue as a result of a lone individual's decision to finally stop going along with it all. In Herman Melville's classic, *Bartleby the Scrivener*, the title character, a lowly mid-nineteenth-century Wall Street scrivener, one day decides that he simply prefers not to adhere to the rote expectations inherent in his professional life and ignites bedlam in the process. Dick Allen similarly threatened an establishment that feared anarchy in the wake of one man's decision to no longer accept the received wisdom merely because it had been received for as long as anyone could remember. In both instances, change finally came, but only at exorbitant cost. Herein, then, lies the story of baseball's Bartleby, the tale of a man who simply Preferred Not To. And who made baseball better because of it.

Chapter 1

The Individualist

1960: Elmira .281/8/42
1961: Magic Valley .317/21/94
1962: Williamsport .329/20/109

ASK PRETTY MUCH any fan of Philadelphia Phillies history about Tony Curry, even a hardcore one, and you're bound to be met with a blank stare. Sounds more like a dish than a ballplayer—an exotic one at that, something the coldly conservative organization steered clear of from its inception in 1883 through the 1950s. And, in fact, his tenure on the club over a half century ago largely justifies those bewildered looks—110 total games, 71 hits, 6 home runs, .253 batting average over parts of two seasons. But to a portion of the club's fans, as well as the local black press, Tony Curry would come to symbolize everything the Phillies were doing wrong when it came to race relations and would provide a telling reference point for everything that was yet to come for Dick Allen. For a segment of the Philadelphia sporting population that had their eyes closely attuned to what became the longest-running, most feverishly followed sports soap opera of the 1960s, nothing that happened between Allen and the Phillies could surprise them. Because, to them at least, all of it was preordained. For before there was Dick Allen, there was Tony Curry.

Curry, who arrived in Philadelphia in 1960, was hardly the typical ball-player of the era—he was neither white nor representative of the emerging African American presence within the big leagues. Instead, Curry was Baha-mian. And he wasn't even a baseball player; he had grown up playing cricket and never even played baseball until he was fifteen, only five years before he signed his first professional baseball contract. Yet his talent and potential were obvious to those who saw him play: "Tony was just an extraordinary player," recalled Frank Sweeting, a contemporary of Curry's who played with him as a youngster. "You could see his strength—Tony was built, and his neck was like a football player's. . . . When he played ball, it was some-thing to see."[1] The Phillies had eyes as well and signed him to a professional contract in 1957 despite his limited experience. He worked his way up through the organization and impressed on all levels, winning the class A Eastern League MVP while with the Phillies' affiliate in Williamsport in 1959, enthralling the club so much that by spring training 1960, he had maneuvered himself into a position to jump all the way to the varsity. As spring training progressed and his fellow minor leaguers were shipped out to one far-flung affiliate or another—Williamsport, Bakersfield, Buf-falo, Tampa, Des Moines, Asheville, Elmira, Indianapolis, Johnson City, Chattanooga—Curry remained, working out with the big leaguers and con-tinuing to impress. With the slow decline from the heady days of the 1950 pennant-winning Whiz Kids complete, punctuated by back-to-back base-ment finishes in 1958 and 1959, the club was looking for some new blood, a new spark, a ray of light to illuminate their entrance into the 1960s. Per-haps this Curry kid could be it.

For a while at least, it seemed as if he might be. He made the club out of spring training and was one of the few bright spots in what would quickly become another lost season for the Phils. On May 14 he was hit-ting .380 and by June the black biweekly, the *Philadelphia Tribune*, looking beyond the dismal present and toward the future, had singled out Curry (who by that point was second in the National League in hitting) and Cuban-born infielder Pancho Herrera as evidence that the Phillies had at last turned a corner when it came to signing and developing players of color: "Right now, the Phils' player development program is second to none and [Phillies general manager John] Quinn can take pride in the progress made in 1959. . . . Curry, a contender for the National League's batting title and Rookie of the Year award, and Herrera are two of the few bright spots in this year's version of the 'Whiz Kids.'"[2] Although Curry would eventually cool off and finish at .261, he was named a Topps All Star Rookie Outfielder, sharing the bill with Dodger outfielders Frank Howard and Tommy Davis. Looking ahead to 1961, Curry, along with black baseball fans who had waited for years to see a nonwhite player blossom in Philadelphia, had high hopes.

They were dashed the following spring. Although he played in only 95 games in 1960, Curry nevertheless remained on the club's big-league roster the entire season. However, in the midst of yet another torrid spring training in 1961, Curry, who expected his surprising rookie year to net him a $9,000 contract for the season, was instead presented with one that called for a salary of $6,000, a thousand dollars below the major league minimum.[3] It wasn't long before Curry and others took measure of what seemed to be going on. For while many players were often in the dark when it came to the accepted parameters of contract negotiations, Curry, because of his heritage, was perceived to be even more so. If any player was going to be taken advantage of come contract time, Curry seemed to be a prime candidate. Moreover, if any organization was going to take such advantage of a player, the Phillies, whose reputation when it came to their treatment of nonwhite players rivaled only that of the Boston Red Sox, seemed to be prime candidates here as well. Put the two together and accusatory fireworks were inevitable. As teammate Dallas Green recalled, Curry was still "learning how to play the game and . . . probably didn't know a lot of the rules and regulations about contracts. . . . Back in those days, obviously, the pendulum was really on ownership's and management's side."[4] Curry knew what the major league minimum was, however, and when Quinn offered the former cricket player a thousand dollars below that, Curry took offense at what he perceived to be the organization's attempt to snooker him. When Quinn refused to budge off his number, Curry packed up his .478 spring training batting average and walked out of camp.[5]

Although Quinn and the Phillies called the incident a "misunderstanding" and coaxed Curry back to camp, the organization never gave him another crack at the majors and, within two years, had shipped Curry out of their system entirely by sending him to the Cleveland Indians.

With the departure of Tony Curry went the corresponding incident that enveloped his tenure within the organization as well, at least so far as most fans, along with the daily media covering the Phils from the *Philadelphia Inquirer*, *Evening Bulletin*, and the *Philadelphia Daily News*, were concerned (which covered the Curry incident lightly to begin with). But for some fans, as well as for the *Tribune*, the loose ends had not been tidied up so neatly. Because just a few years later, another player of color would burst on the Philadelphia baseball scene and he, too, would quickly become engulfed in controversy, with both the player and the Phillies offering competing narratives, one alleging bias and mistreatment, the other asserting that, really, everything was being blown way out of proportion and much too much was being made of nothing at all. And in the midst of all that Tony Curry was resurrected and identified as the harbinger of all that was now coming Dick Allen's way. "Richie's trouble with the Phillies would seem to stem from a youngster wanting to move too fast for the club," wrote *Tribune* columnist Claude Harrison in 1968, as Allen and the Phils were in the midst of yet another spring training contract showdown. "And Richie isn't the first player to be faced with such a problem. Outfielder Tony Curry, who refused to play major league ball for a minor leaguer's fee, was buried by the Phillies. When he spoke up, Curry's career was over right then and there."[6] First through Tony Curry, then through Dick Allen, the Phillies showed their true colors, according to Harrison. Don't let the darker-skinned faces on the Phillies rosters of the 1960s fool you, he warned. Progress cannot be measured in sheer numbers alone. And when those other metrics were considered, the Phillies still had miles to go.

*   *   *

Ultimately the Tony Curry incident was about much more than Tony Curry. It was about the Phillies' troubled history of race relations up to that point; if the organization had integrated earlier and without as much fuss, the Curry episode may very well have been viewed by even the black press as little more than the misunderstanding Quinn alleged it to have been. That the club was seen by some as particularly intolerant even in the game's segregated era infused nearly every incident that even tangentially touched on racial issues thereafter. Although all major league clubs practiced overt racism prior to Jackie Robinson's arrival in Brooklyn in 1947, the Phillies ingloriously stood out among their peers, providing as they did professional homes for Ben Chapman and Herb Pennock. Even in an era where blacks were banned and an Italian superstar such as Joe DiMaggio was referred to within many baseball circles as "the Big Dago," Chapman was considered a bridge too far for most organizations. But not the Phillies. As a player for the Yankees from 1930 to 1936, he was both a productive hitter (averaging .305 during his seven seasons there) and an unapologetic racist and anti-Semite who would often yell anti-Semitic remarks to Jewish fans within shouting distance in the left-field stands in Yankee Stadium.[7] In 1933 Chapman, aided by teammate Dixie Walker, precipitated an ugly brawl with Washington's Jewish second baseman, Buddy Myer, which ultimately involved several hundred fans who stormed the field.[8]

Eventually Jewish fans tired of Chapman's goading and petitioned the Yanks to peddle him, which they did.[9] He bounced around thereafter until finally finding a home with the Phillies in 1945, first as a player and then as their manager, when he was appointed as such by general manager Herb Pennock, the Hall of Fame pitcher who had an unerring eye for talent (his signings and acquisitions would build the pennant-winning Whiz Kids) but was hardly progressive when it came to racial issues himself (he was said to have attempted to dissuade Dodgers' president Branch Rickey from bringing Robinson to Philadelphia in April 1947 by threatening a boycott of his Phillies should Robinson take the field).[10] Indeed, Robinson later remarked that he came closest to breaking his vow to Rickey to "turn the other cheek" that April afternoon in Philly when the Phillies, led by Chapman and at least implicitly sanctioned by Pennock, hurled one brutal remark his way after another: "For one wild and rage-crazed minute, I thought, 'To hell with Mr. Rickey's noble experiment.' . . . To hell with the image of the patient black freak I was supposed to create. I could throw down my bat, stride over to the Phillies dugout, grab one of those white sons of bitches, and smash his teeth in with my despised black fist. Then I could walk away from it all."[11]

This (well-publicized) incident aside, the Phillies got off relatively easy with regard to the race issue for many years simply because most sportswriters refused to bring it up. In this respect the organization was not unlike its counterparts throughout the majors in that its prejudiced nature was something that was hidden away, out of public sight. Indeed, many white fans, who received their baseball news from their local papers, were wholly unaware that their national pastime was even segregated at all given that the issue was largely ignored up through the 1930s. Black sportswriter Joe Bostic termed the white sporting press's refusal to engage its readers on this issue a "conspiracy of silence" and alleged that the game's color line could never have been maintained for as long as it was without the aid of the game's attendant sportswriters.[12] Worse, on those rare occasions in the pre-Robinson era when the issue was broached, what typically resulted was an implicit endorsement of the game's segregation through articles hypothesizing that integrated baseball would cause race riots in the stands, implying that black ballplayers were not good enough to play within Organized Baseball, and asserting that black ballplayers simply preferred to remain within the Negro Leagues and had no interest in joining white baseball.[13]

Not all sportswriters were in on the conspiracy. Black sportswriters were often left on the outside of the baseball writers fraternity, barred from joining the Baseball Writers Association for many years, which meant that they were often unable to get the press passes that would have given them access to the press boxes, dugouts, and locker rooms of the clubs they covered. This lack of access denied them the opportunity to write the stories their white cohorts were writing so they were compelled to create their own narratives of the games. These narratives were often far different than the ones found within the mainstream dailies, which likewise excluded them for many years as they toed their own color line. Even after black sportswriters finally gained the ability to obtain the press credentials they had been denied for so long, the established alternative narrative tradition continued, given that by that point it had become ingrained. Within the black weeklies and biweeklies for which they toiled, these sportswriters told their readers stories that could be found nowhere else. In Philadelphia, where the staff writers and editorial board of the *Tribune* believed that to contemplate the Phillies without considering race was like contemplating summer without considering July, readers were confronted with stories about the Phillies that were summarily ignored by the *Inquirer*, *Evening Bulletin*, and *Daily News*. These stories not only zeroed in on the seemingly racist outlook of the club's management but were often activist in nature in that they pressed the organization for answers to the questions they raised. As the *Tribune* made clear throughout the 1950s, it wasn't merely Chapman and Pennock who were the problem (and who were both out of the organization by the end of the 1948 season). Rather, the racial problems on the Phillies seemed to emanate from the very top of the pyramid.

As the *Tribune* stressed repeatedly throughout the decade, R. R. M. (Bob) Carpenter Jr., the club's owner since 1943, was hopelessly clueless when it came to race relations. Carpenter (son of Robert R. M. Carpenter, vice president of E. I. DuPont de Nemours, Inc., and who married into the DuPont family) was a college dropout with a perpetual suntan who was handed the club by his father in the hope that it would give his son something to occupy his time.[14] He fancied himself a "sportsman" and was a patrician through and through. In the course of an October 1951 interview with the *Tribune*, which pressed Carpenter on why the Phils continued to resist integration, Carpenter, the paper asserted, "admitted . . . that he has set higher standards for any Negro that might be recommended by one of his scouts than for a white prospect." *Tribune* readers were further informed that, in the course of its interview with him, "Carpenter made it as plain as possible without saying so in so many words, that it would be a long, long time before a Negro wore a Phillies uniform in Shibe Park." They also read how Carpenter's scouts routinely dismissed black prospects one after another as either "too old" or "too small," such that, in the end, the Phillies' scouts had concluded "that no player in the Negro League this past summer was good enough to be admitted to the Phillies system, even for one of their farm teams." When pushed on the issue and asked to explain why his view of the black talent was contrary to that of his fellow club owners, who were at last venturing out, albeit hesitantly, to sign Negro League players, Carpenter responded that he "was not interested in 'human relations' so far as his ball club was concerned." And if all of this wasn't enough, Carpenter shooed away the notion that, as a business proposition, signing black players simply made basic economic sense in that such a move would at last bring black fans into the ballpark when he contended that "the Phillies was [sic] not a 'business' and that people did not go in [to] major league baseball to make money." This "silly statement," as the *Tribune* categorized it, signaled to black fans that Carpenter simply did not care if they found his Phillies repugnant. He didn't want their money anyway.[15]

This article, entitled "Phils' Boss 'Seeks' Negro Super-Player" and which tackled a subject readers of the city's mainstream dailies could comfortably avoid, prompted a response by the Philadelphia branch of the NAACP, which launched a brief campaign to urge the club to integrate, to no avail. By 1956, with the Phillies still holding their nose on the integration issue, the *Tribune* attacked again, with an editorial asking why the Phillies, unlike their baseball brethren, had been unable to find any suitable black talent: "For some mysterious reason, perhaps it is the Delaware background of the Multi-millionaire Bob Carpenter who owns the Phillies, it is the only team in the National League which has not had at least one Negro player on its roster."[16] This was followed by a series of stories focusing on the club, called baseball's "Most Prejudiced" in large type on the front page of its June 26, 1956, edition, which likewise published the text of an open letter from the executive secretary of the Philadelphia branch of the NAACP to Carpenter, seeking "an appointment to discuss the 'anti-Negro' attitude of that organization." In the letter, the executive secretary remarked that he had "followed baseball very closely for the past 35 years and ha[d] never witnessed such an unfavorable situation develop between the citizen followers of the game and a local team like the one which has been developed in Philadelphia. Believe me, I am greatly disturbed when I see tens of thousands of people conditioning themselves to detest the Phillies' baseball organization." The letter went on to ask Carpenter to address the concerns of black fans who were convinced that "'there will never be a Negro player on the Phillies team as long as Bob Carpenter is president' or 'these people won't hire a Negro in any capacity at Connie Mack Stadium.'"[17]

A few days later, Carpenter publicly replied, declaring that, in fact, the Phils not only had eight black players within their farm system but had an additional thirty-five black employees who worked in and around Connie Mack Stadium.[18] Upon closer inspection, however, and as more than one

Tribune reader noted in response to Carpenter's statement, there was more to the issue than the sheer numbers: "In spite of the fact that Connie Mack Stadium is located in a predominantly Negro area, the management has obviously not seen fit to employ one Negro as a ticket taker, hot dog vendor, usher or grounds keeper; not to mention Negro ball players. Negro women and men have been seen from time to time serving as toilet attendants and some few have been noticed cleaning up the stands after games. The employment of Negroes in these lowly positions obviously intensifies the race's resentment in view of the absence of Negroes from the more conspicuous and lucrative positions mentioned above."[19] Other readers, prompted by a fan survey conducted by the NAACP in response to Carpenter's statement and published as a series of articles that ran in the *Tribune* throughout that July, remarked similarly, alleging that "Mr. Carpenter is maintaining a lily-white organization" and was attempting to "pull the wool over the eyes of those fans who are inquiring why the Phillies have failed in the past 10 years to include a Negro baseball player on their roster."[20] Said another: "today we have no home team to whom we can pledge our allegiance. We have therefore pledged ourselves not to listen to, look at on TV or go to the park; in other words, we're willing to sacrifice our baseball interest rather than support the Phillies—we prefer nothing to the Phillies."[21] And finally this: "Mr. Carpenter is right. The sort of Negro player he seeks exists only in a tale of fiction. He must be able to pitch with both hands, go from first to third on a sacrifice, steal 2nd base on one leg, and be a home run king blindfolded."[22]

Finally, in 1957, the Phillies promoted a black player, infielder John Kennedy, to their major league roster, a move that was initially applauded by the *Tribune*: "The Phillies have done it at last. When this city's representative in the National Baseball League takes the field in a week from now, there will be a Negro in the line-up and another one [Chico Fernandez] sitting on the bench. . . . We wish both young men luck and congratulate the Phillies on the move."[23] While the *Tribune* highlighted the occasion the following week as the historic moment that it was, with a banner headline ("Large Crowd Expected to Watch Phillies 'Unveil' John Kennedy") and accompanying story,[24] the *Inquirer*, true to Bostic's accusatory "conspiracy of silence," ignored the event altogether, focusing exclusively on the action taking place on the field rather than the more significant change made to the complexion of the Phillies.[25] Regardless, progress had been made and, the *Tribune* assumed, more was to come in short order. When Kennedy proved to be a bust on the field (appearing in only five games, batting twice without getting a hit), and the club's pipeline of black talent produced only a trickle thereafter, the amount of progress made through Kennedy's debut was reassessed.

All of which led to the high hopes pinned to the back of Tony Curry, a player who, the *Tribune* initially and optimistically believed, might have a legitimate chance of becoming the organization's first superstar of color and who might at last provide concrete proof that the Phillies were committed to progressing on the racial front after all. By 1961, however, the *Tribune* had soured on the Phillies once more, pointing not only to Curry's spring training contract squabble but also to the fact that the club persisted in maintaining its spring training headquarters in segregated Clearwater, Florida, where the Fort Harrison Hotel refused lodging to the club's black players and instead entrusted its bell captain with "the job of locating appropriate lodgings" for them. Prior to the Curry incident, the *Tribune* made the point that the club "sought to have all 40 players located at the Fort Harrison Hotel but the manager said no,"[26] but by the following spring training, in 1962, its edge had sharpened as it remarked that the Phillies "are among the last four ball clubs which provide segregated housing quarters for Negro players." As the *Tribune* reported and as the Philadelphia branch of the NAACP noted in its call for a boycott of the Phils throughout the 1962 season, "It is obvious that the Phillies could obtain desegregated housing facilities for its Negro ball players if they were willing to fight for them just as the other ball clubs have."[27] Finally, after the pressure applied to the club by both the *Tribune* and the NAACP had proven too much to ignore, the Phillies relented and became the last club in the majors to insist on integrated facilities for its players. Unlike its reaction to Kennedy's debut, here the *Tribune* was far from sanguine: "First in alibis and excuses but last in the National League—last of the NL clubs to sign Negro ball players—the Phillies Sunday became the last of the clubs training in the Florida area to throw off the yoke of training camp segregation and move to a site where all Phillies players could eat together, sleep together and act like members of the human race."[28]

It was in the midst these hostilities, perhaps ignored within the main-stream dailies but highlighted in painful detail by the *Tribune* and deeply felt within its readership, that Dick Allen emerged—the closest approxi-mation of that fictional "Negro Super-Player" the organization would ever develop. Here, at last, was not another John Kennedy, not another Tony Curry. Here was unlimited potential just waiting to be unleashed. Here as well was the test case the *Tribune* and many black fans had been waiting for—presented with a talent like Allen, how would Carpenter and the Phillies respond? For over a decade, Carpenter had brushed aside the race issue by proclaiming that the organization had simply been unable to find a talent comparable to Willie Mays of the Giants and Hank Aaron of the Braves. Now, at last, it found one. From here on out, there could be no more excuses. And so, from the outset, Dick Allen would be not merely a player but a measuring stick for black fans and the black press with regard to the Phillies and race relations—how far had they come, if at all? Given all that was piled on his shoulders before he even saw his first major league fastball, it was inevitable that he would become something else as well: a lightning rod.

*   *   *

Born and raised in Chewton, Pennsylvania, across the street from a baseball diamond and across the Beaver River from Wampum (population 1,189), Richard Anthony Allen knew about authority—how it was wielded, what it meant, and how to skirt it when necessary—before he knew how to walk. His mother, Era, a God-fearing Christian and strict disciplinarian whose "truth [was] in the Bible," as her son recalled in his autobiography, and who "ruled the family with an iron hand," according to Willie King, a family friend who chauffeured her to the First Baptist Church in Chewton each and every Sunday, exerted an overarching presence not only on her children but on a significant swath of Wampum proper as well; more than two decades after her death, those who knew her still refer to her only as "Mrs. Allen," such was the respect she commanded and reverence with which they recall her today.[29] In large measure she's not etched but carved into the granite of Wampum's collective memory, embedded within the mountaintop, all rough edges and imperfections smoothed and polished by the sands of time until what remains is more monument than mortal. His father, a truck driver with a trash-hauling business that carried him in and out of town on a regular basis, was likewise in and out of Dick's life (mostly out) until he abandoned the family for good when Dick was fifteen, leaving Era to raise her gaggle of children: three girls and five physical, athletically inclined boys—Coy, Caesar, Hank, Dick, and Ron—in a home with outside plumbing. "We had air conditioning," Dick recalled. "[T]he kind that comes in through the walls."[30] As her sons grew and negotiated their way through Wampum, doing the things that physical, athletically inclined boys are apt to do, Era would exhort: Don't embarrass us, don't embarrass the family. Act your age and act yourself.[31] As they grew, she provided, taking on whatever domestic tasks—sewing, washing, cleaning the homes of other Wampum families—that would put food on the table. As Dick remembered it, she "almost worked herself to death taking in washing to feed us."[32]

School was never a priority for Dick; from the time he was little he told anyone who would listen that he was going to play professional baseball when he grew up. Guy Demaio, his American Legion manager, recalled that "he never really worked hard at getting his grades and so on and so forth; it was just something he did in order to get by . . . it was like he knew baseball was going to be his life."[33] In high school, one of his coaches, John Swogger, using the carrot of athletics as motivation, attempted to goad him by admonishing him ("Sleeper, if you don't work on your grades and get to class like you should, you're not going to amount to a hill of beans"), to little effect. (Dick knew better; the day he signed with the Phillies, he drove up to Swogger in a new car filled with new baseballs and bats and did a little admonishing of his own: "Well, what do you think now?")[34] Eventually he did graduate, on time in 1960, somewhere toward the bottom third of his class at Wampum High School, and later estimated that he had "about an eighth-grade education. I figured I could count well enough to tell who won the game."[35]

Despite Era's firm hand and imposing presence, or perhaps because of it, Dick discovered early on that authority was something not only to respect but, when the situation called for it, to challenge as well. "I was always in the most devilishment. One of my brothers, he'd get up in the pear tree and get a licking once. I'd keep on doing it. And I'd be batting stones—cut the handle off Mom's old broom and throw 'em up and hit 'em—till all the windows would be broken out."[36] Batting stones, catching balls, running bases. In the end, that diamond across the street proved to be Dick's salvation. "That ball field helped me raise my boys," Era surmised several years later. "They lived on the ball diamond 365 days a year, and I spent lots of days sitting on the porch watching them and I'd have to call them in for dinner. That ball field kept them out of trouble."[37]

Lacking a traditional male role model for much of his life, Dick sought out substitutes and found an early one in his oldest (half) brother, Coy. A superior athlete himself, Coy Craine was, like Dick would one day become, a standout basketball and baseball player. After starring both on the court and on the diamond at Wampum High in the early 1940s, Coy joined a black barnstorming baseball outfit that toured Pittsburgh and its environs during the waning days of the game's segregated era: "At home we were the Pittsburgh Stars, but all we did was change jerseys on the road, and we were the Grays. Believe me, that was baseball . . . I played a pretty good second base, and possibly I might have gotten into the majors, but I knew that I would have had to spend some time down south in the minor leagues, and I wasn't about to do that. So I went into the service, and shortly thereafter, the Negro league had all but disappeared." After his army discharge, Coy joined the Philadelphia-based Harlem Hobos barnstorming basketball team that traveled throughout the country. Once his playing days were through, he took to mentoring his younger brother: "I tried to do what big brothers are supposed to in Dick's case. I taught him what I knew about the game when he was a kid."[38]

Coy would manage Dick's professional development for the early portion of his career, becoming his de facto representative (one of the first in Organized Baseball) and negotiating his first professional contract for him. "Coy was basically his agent," said Ron Galbreath, an Allen family friend for decades. "How many black athletes had agents back in that day?" After the contract was signed, Coy put Dick on an allowance, making sure that the majority of his paycheck was squirreled away for the rainy days that were sure to come once baseball was out of the picture. According to Galbreath, Dick "made a lot of money and went through a lot of money. . . . Dick still has money today because he had a brother way back when" who looked out for him.[39] Coy's money management lesson was something that would stick with Dick for the duration of his professional career; cognizant of the limitations of his formal education and aware that he most likely was not the best person to make the financial decisions in his life, he made sure that he always employed a financial advisor he could trust. First it was his brother Coy, later it would be a Philadelphia baker named Clem Capozzoli. Although Capozzoli was not blood, Dick drew close to him as though he was. When Capozzoli died in March 1976, newspaper accounts referred to him as "a father" to Dick, "never more than a phone call away."[40] The grieving Allen would pay tribute to his honorary father by affixing a black armband to the left sleeve of his uniform. It remained there the entire season.

Allen went by many names throughout his life—Dick, Richie, Rich—a matter that would become somewhat contentious once he became a professional, but as a child he was known mostly by none of these but, rather, as Sleepy, a moniker that grew out of the residue of a childhood accident. "There was this old hut that us kids played in," said Dick in 1964 of the incident that had occurred twelve years earlier, when he was ten. "We decided we needed a spring for the door and we dug through the town dump till we found an old rusty one. One of the older boys put it up with a couple of nails. He warned us to get back while he tried it out and I backed up maybe ten feet. When he opened the door, that old spring came flying off the nails and I got it smack in the left eye. Reflex action brought my eyelid down before it hit and maybe that helped save my eye. Notice that my eyelid still droops . . . I was blind in the eye for a couple of weeks and I thought I was all through with baseball and basketball. But then it cleared up. It hasn't bothered me since I started wearing glasses [in 1959]."[41]

Or at least that's how Dick recalled the incident at that time. Eight years later he contended that the injury had a different origin: "The scar over my left eye came after I fell out of a tree when I was a kid. The scar over my right eye came when one of my sisters was swinging me around by my heels when I was a kid and I hit my head on the furniture."[42] And seventeen years after that, in his autobiography, he claimed that the injury was the result of being hit in the eye with a tin can.[43] Regardless of its origin, the droopy eyelid gave him a sleepy look, hence the nickname, although some who played with or against him in high school or American Legion ball found the nickname apt given that he seemed to walk a bit more slowly than everyone else.[44] While they may have attributed his gait to laziness, those who knew Allen understood that he was anything but lazy. And in Wampum, pretty much everybody knew Sleepy Allen.

Racially, Wampum was either typical or atypical midcentury small-town America, depending on one's perspective. Although the region was overwhelmingly white, the few black families who lived there were ingrained in the community's fabric—to a point. White residents such as Ron Hughes, who crossed paths with Dick while both played with the Tri-County Baseball All Stars in the late 1950s and who lived nearby in Ellwood City, remembered a wholly integrated community: "I didn't know there were African American people. I just thought that they were people."[45] Ron Mazzano, another Tri-County All Star, had similar memories: "there were only a couple [of black] families, so we were not integrated that much, but yet we didn't think a thing about playing with anybody else. . . . [Race] was never an issue."[46] Guy Demaio, Dick's Legion ball manager, recalled that in Wampum "the Allens were accepted. They could come in and go eat sundaes with us and go eat milkshakes with us at the confectionary store and we never had a problem. . . . You know, you just look at them [the Allen boys] and you didn't look at them as black kids. You looked at them as friends."[47]

Black residents remembered things a bit differently, a bit less rosily, but still recalled a generally warm, inviting community: "Just to be frank," intoned Willie King, "African Americans always were, I don't know, [thought to be] inferior to some of the white people, let's put it that way, but in Wampum it was different. We all knew each other, we went to the small school down there and we all had a good relationship with one another. . . . It was a close community . . . everybody liked each other. Whether they were putting on airs or not, I kind of doubt it."[48] Dick had similar recollections but understood that even Wampum was not without its limits: "Compared to many places, Wampum is about as racially tolerant as anywhere I've been. But there were things you just didn't do . . . I could never think about dating a white girl."[49] As Demaio recalled, the Allen boys got along in and around Wampum largely because they "knew what they could do and they knew what was accepted. . . . There were places they could go and places they couldn't." Dick "was never [the] kind of person who would try to go places where blacks weren't supposed to go. . . . That wasn't the way he was brought up and his mother would have had a fit if he [did]."[50]

Traversing the social fabric of Wampum in the 1950s could be tricky, and the lack of a reliable male authority figure in the Allen household didn't make things any easier. Coy did what he could, and although he was significantly older than Dick, he was still a brother and could only push so much. At Wampum High Dick came under the influence of a sterner tower of authority who would help guide him as well. In Lawrence County, Pennsylvania, there exist few historical figures that loom larger than Wampum High's longtime basketball coach, L. Butler Hennon. Running the tiny school's basketball program from 1933 until the school closed in 1961, Hennon gained a national reputation as a basketball innovator who somehow managed to lead his perennially outmanned teams to one state title after another. At one point, beginning in 1950, Wampum High won a dozen straight Section 20 basketball championships, often led by one Allen or another: first Coy in the 1940s, then Caesar, then Harold (Hank), Dick, and baby brother Ron in the mid- to late 1950s. This success brought national attention, culminating in a glowing *Life* magazine portrait in January 1958, which highlighted Hennon's unusual training techniques: players wearing weighted jackets, heavy gloves and boots, and vision-limiting eye goggles. "When they take the weights and galoshes off, they move like elves," he told *Life*, which spread Hennon's gospel.[51] The *Life* article drew international attention to Hennon and his program, including a write-up in a widely distributed Soviet magazine that took Hennon's techniques behind the Iron Curtain; eventually they would find a home in the training center of the Soviet Union's Olympic basketball program.[52]

The Soviet style likewise appealed to Hennon. "He'd throw me right across the basketball court when I made a mistake," Dick recalled years later. "I used to shake out there, afraid I'd make a wrong move." For the shy, introverted Sleepy Allen, who dreaded even practicing in front of others, being called out in front of his teammates was particularly painful. Yet he persevered. Testament to the coach's influence on Dick, as well as the lack thereof from his father, Dick claimed that Hennon was "the last man I was afraid of."[53] From Hennon's perspective he offered his players a square deal: "I made the boys behave, but I also let them know I cared about them."[54] When it came to Dick, Hennon knew he had someone special, calling him "one of the best I ever coached," something he was aware of from nearly the moment he first laid eyes on him.[55] While coaching Dick in a youth baseball league, Hennon singled him out in front of the other nine- and ten-year-olds, pointing at him and proclaiming that "this guy will be in the major leagues someday."[56]

Dick and Hennon's relationship persisted and was, for the most part, productive until a disagreement during Dick's sophomore year at Wampum High led Dick to finally consider quitting Hennon and the program for good. Era stepped in, however, and compelled him to tough out what for Dick had become a trying, turbulent situation. It would not be the last time she would do so. Perhaps the fallout explained Hennon's conclusion later on that, while Dick was a good kid and meant well, "he was easily led. There were times when he was thrown out of class and sent to my office. (Hennon was likewise the school's principal.) It always happened that the kid with him was the one who got Richie in trouble. I'd tell Rich how much he had to lose and how little the other fellow did."[57] Looking back on Dick's career, Hennon concluded regretfully that "I just don't think Rich was prepared for professional sports, where they seem to treat the individual as a chattel."[58]

Despite his eventual distaste for Hennon, Dick thrived on the Wampum High basketball court as well as on the neighborhood playgrounds. "He could've played NBA basketball," contends Mazzano. "He was such an athlete. He was able to jump so high. My first recollection of him was when we went into a state championship game in Pittsburgh and the other team had a center who was 6′9″. [Hennon] put Dick against this 6′9″ center and I remember at one point in the game where he elevated above this [guy] and actually dunked the ball over the back of his head and into the basketball net. It was just amazing to see."[59] In the summer he and his friends would take off to the gym; Dick dominated there as well. "Sleep was just way ahead of everybody," recalls Demaio. "He was a terrific basketball player—so quick. He had a future ahead of him in whatever sport he chose."[60] Although his brothers Hank and Ron would go to college, Dick, despite his ability on the court and the opportunity for a scholarship, never got the chance. "Hurts me sometimes to think about it," said his brother Ron a few years later, "that Dick never got to go to college.

He was the greatest basketball player I ever saw. He got 140 offers that I know about. But we were a hardship case. When the Phils offered that money, Dick had to take it for our mother's sake."[61] He wouldn't abandon basketball despite spurning it, out of necessity, for a game that offered him more immediate material rewards; he and Phillies pitcher Dallas Green often took their teammates and coaches to school during spring training: "he and I would team up and play guys like Robin Roberts and Granny Hamner and those kind of guys and we'd end up winning because Richie was such a great athlete."[62] Former *Daily News* columnist Bill Conlin recalled that "before the Phils had a minor league complex, Mauch let the ballplayers play basketball at the National Guard armory across the street from Jack Russell [Stadium] on rainy days. Dallas Green was a high school star. Johnny Briggs was an All-State star in New Jersey. There were nine guys playing a game resembling basketball and Allen. He was five feet eleven and the first player that size I ever saw finish a fast break with a 360 dunk. He turned Briggs inside out."[63]

As dominant as he was on the court, Dick was more so on the diamond. Mazzano, a catcher, still remembers the specifics of a pitch he called that then took flight as he watched, helpless, from his crouch behind the plate: "I remember a ball we threw to Dick: outside corner, middle in, and he hit the ball over right-center—the farthest ball I've ever seen hit."[64] Primarily a shortstop, his right arm was a weapon: "he had a terrific arm," said Demaio. "If he picked the ball up and you weren't at first base yet it meant that was it." As his Legion manager, Demaio knew where his bread was buttered: with Dick and his brothers Hank and Ron. "I'll never forget the day we were supposed to play New Castle, which was going to be a terrific baseball game because they were the big power and my chance of winning rested with the Allen boys. If I didn't have them, there was no sense in me even going to New Castle. So I went over to see them [the Allen boys], and Mrs. Allen was sitting out on the porch in her rocking chair. I think they were supposed to have gone to church and they disobeyed, so she said that they were inside scrubbing the stairwell. And there they were, scrubbing away. She wasn't going to let them go. I begged her, explained to her that there was no point in us going to New Castle; it wouldn't even be a ball game without them. Finally, she consented to let them go."[65] Demaio and the Allen boys returned home later, victorious.

Era, though, was rarely such a pushover. Ron Galbreath recalled: "We were in seventh or eighth grade and Hank had done something in school, whether it was grades or whatever, but [Era] held him out of a junior high basketball game and, being his best friend, he asked me to go talk to Mrs. Allen for him, which I did. I got nowhere. And anybody who knows Mrs. Allen knows that you wouldn't get anywhere."[66]

As Hennon witnessed in basketball practice, and as Mauch would soon learn in various ways, Dick was both shy and an introvert. He feared public embarrassment, which fueled his preference for solitary practices in high school as well as his later refusal to practice his defensive skills at third base unless nobody else was around while he was doing it; but he also understood his need for quiet and spent much of his professional career seeking out an atmosphere that would provide him the comfort level he required in order to perform at his best.[67] As shy and introverted as he was, above all else Dick was loyal. As Demaio recalled, "He was quiet, he was never outgoing, but if he was your buddy, if he was your friend, you had a friend for life."[68] Never were all of his personal traits more clearly on display than in the weeks leading up to the fiftieth reunion of Wampum High's class of 1960. Dick, through an anonymous donation, footed the bill for all of his classmates; it was important to him to take care of those with whom he first bonded a half century earlier, developing a closeness that, to him at least, had not dissipated despite the passage of time. Then, on the night of the big event, he was nowhere to be found.[69]

The shy, introverted, otherworldly talented Allen soon began to draw the attention of scouts—a few at first, then hordes—and whenever they came to see him, Dick almost always delivered. "I remember he hit a ball," said Demaio, "there was a pole in right-center, right at the base of the railroad tracks. Sleeper hit that ball up over the top of that pole and over the tracks, if you can believe that. Well, the scouts that were there to watch him play met him coming around third base. It was, 'when can we meet you, sir,' and 'when can we talk to you about signing with us,' and so on and so forth."[70] When indeed. The race for Dick Allen was on, in earnest. And from the start, this was a race that the Phillies, for so many reasons, knew they had to win.

* * *

The wooing of Dick Allen was managed by Coy, who arranged everything on his brother's end. For the Phillies John Ogden led the campaign to sign the young superstar. A scout who had only recently been hired away from the Milwaukee Braves, Ogden knew from the moment he first saw Dick on the ball fields of Wampum that he had to have him: "I told myself that if we lost him I'd be sick for the rest of my life. I decided right then and there I'd camp out at his home until he graduated." This was in 1958; it would be two long years before Ogden could get Dick's signature on a Phillies contract. "He was only a boy, a sophomore . . . [but] you could see the muscles ripple through his uniform. Jim Gallagher (then chief of Phil scouts) came out to see him once and he hit two long homers. Gallagher was out there the next day with a tape measure. They each went 400 or 500 feet . . . I didn't want to lose that boy."[71] Later, the Phils added scout and former Negro League star Judy Johnson to their pursuit, hoping that he could help assuage any reluctance Dick might have in signing with a club that had such a prickly record when it came to race relations.

In many respects, the game, when it came to wooing and signing black talent such as Dick Allen, was entering a new phase. The amateur draft was still several years away, and with the slow, steady demise of the Negro Leagues, which limped through the 1950s until fizzling out all but completely by the early 1960s, came an increase in signing bonuses for black ballplayers. The death of the Negro Leagues would have many negative repercussions for blacks working their way up to the majors, but one positive consequence was that money previously paid by major league clubs to the Negro League club owners for their black talent now went directly to the players themselves.[72] The elimination of the Negro League middlemen meant that by the late 1950s, signing bonuses for black players shot up, with the Dodgers, as usual, leading the way. In 1957 they gave Earl Robinson, a collegiate multisport star from Cal-Berkeley, a previously unheard-of signing bonus of $65,000. Other clubs, including the Phillies, followed. In 1958 they gave the promising Haines brothers (Richard and Robert) $40,000 each, and now they had their sights set on another set of talented brothers, Dick and Hank Allen.[73]

At the time, Dick had no opinion when it came to his professional destination: "I didn't care what team I went with. . . . My mother and oldest brother handled it."[74] And so Dick (along with Hank), who grew up idolizing and channeling Jackie Robinson and the Dodgers as he batted stones through one Wampum window after another with Era's old broom handle, wound up signing with the Phillies instead, largely because Era trusted John Ogden. "He backed up everything he promised," she later said.[75] Coy likewise found himself in the employ of the Phillies; the club signed him as a scout of an undetermined nature. In the midst of this flurry of Allen signings, Coy was seen driving around Wampum in a new car. Suspicions were raised by some of the other clubs that were wooing Dick at the time, convinced that the Phils were funneling gifts to the Allens under the table to curry favor. Commissioner Ford Frick eventually ruled that the Phils had done nothing wrong; Frick determined that the car was merely on loan from the Phils, who rented it for Coy so that he could carry out his (still undetermined) scouting duties.[76] For his own part, Dick received a signing bonus of $70,000—the largest ever for a black prospect at the time—$40,000 of which he signed over to Era without first paying taxes on it, a transfer the IRS would take issue with in the coming years.

After the signing, Coy came to his brother's aid in talking the club out of sending him south to the minors.[77] (At the time, the Phils had two class D affiliates: one in Tampa and one in Elmira.) And so he debuted instead with Elmira where he played shortstop, the position he played almost exclusively as an amateur, and adjusted to life as a professional rather well, hitting .281. The following season the Phils switched him to second base when they moved him up to the class C Magic Valley (Idaho) Pioneers. He excelled there at the plate, hitting .317 but struggled at his new position, committing 27 errors in only 117 games.

It was here where the relationship between Dick Allen and the Phils took its first wrong turn. Concerned about his spotty defensive play as well as his potential vision problems given the glasses he was now wearing (the permanent remnant of his childhood encounter with either the screen door, a tin can, or his sister, depending on the day he told the tale), the Phillies, who had been so high on him just a few years earlier, left him exposed in the 1961 major league expansion draft; either the nascent New York Mets or Houston Colt .45's could have purchased him for a mere $50,000. Even worse, neither did. "As I recall," said John Murphy, a Mets executive at the time, "the scouting reports on him were very bad. They said he couldn't see, that if he didn't catch the ball he didn't see well enough to find it and pick it up." Further sullying Dick's image were the reports surfacing from his managers at Elmira and Magic Valley that he was strong-willed and independent and, as such, a handful to deal with. In two short seasons it appeared as if the Phillies had soured on their prized prospect. "OK. We didn't take him," said Murphy, rationalizing the Mets' decision to pass on what would have been one of the few legitimate talents to join the woeful organization. "But the Phillies put him on the list."[78]

In later years, when the media would become fascinated with Dick's tortured relationship with the Phillies, most would point to his year in Little Rock in 1963 as the fulcrum and in many ways it was. But the more perceptive among them, such as *Daily News* columnist Stan Hochman, pointed to the "dreadful mistake" made in 1961 when the Phils effectively told the hypersensitive Allen that they thought he was worthless.[79] Whenever Dick remarked that "the Phillies didn't really want me from the beginning," a theme he'd return to repeatedly later in his career, this is what he was referring to.[80] Little Rock would be traumatic. But exposing him in the expansion draft set the table for everything that would transpire later on.

But that was in the future. For now, Dick, a Phillie by default if no longer by choice, was promoted up the ladder once more, this time to Williamsport in the class A Eastern League. Here he endured yet another position change, to the outfield where he primarily played centerfield. Defensively he continued to struggle, but offensively there was little question that he was a major league–caliber hitter: he finished with a .329 average and 20 home runs. Despite the organization's second thoughts, the bonuses given to both Dick and Hank appeared to have been money well spent: at one point in mid-June, the brothers each led their respective league in hitting (Hank was with Magic Valley in the Pioneer League). Regardless, Dick's Williamsport manager, Frank Lucchesi, still had reservations, opining that he didn't believe Dick could "make the grade" as a centerfielder.[81]

On top of his defensive struggles, Dick and the Phils became involved in a second incident that would further strain their relationship. During the season, a woman he had briefly dated claimed that she was carrying his baby. Despite Dick's assertions that this was highly unlikely (the woman had scant proof), Carpenter and Quinn intervened and paid the woman $5,000 to go away. Although the organization may have thought it was doing Dick a service by stepping in and removing a potential distraction, Dick read the situation differently. As he recalled the incident in his autobiography, he believed that by paying off the woman, Quinn and the organization had made not merely a payment but a value judgment: "Quinn decide[d] I'm guilty." To Dick, it was proof that the organization saw him as a troublemaker and a liar to boot. Worse, he believed that the club had an ulterior motive in making the payment: "The Phillies, to their way of thinking, have bailed me out of a jam, and in their eyes I'm beholden to them. A lot of guys would have been, but then a lot of guys aren't Dick Allen."[82]

The nature of the payoff also became an issue because, though Dick stated in his autobiography that the Phillies absorbed the cost of the payoff, in an earlier interview with the *Daily News'* Stan Hochman he implied that the club merely fronted the money but then took it out of his paycheck; in 1976, Dick told Stan Hochman that "[m]y first year they paid me $7,000. . . . Some gal came up with a story that wasn't true and they gave her $5,000. Then Uncle took $2,800. I played for nothing that year."[83] Although Hochman noted that "Dick Allen does not forgive, does not forget," it was oftentimes difficult to reconcile his shifting memories of past events and transgressions. This would make it challenging for even his staunchest supporters to fully defend him against his accusers; he seemed to contradict himself at every turn. Indeed, a multipart refresher on his life that ran in the *Daily News* upon his return to the Phils in 1975 was headlined "Dick Allen Might Not Be His Own Best Historian."[84] Be it the nature of a childhood injury, a minor league payout, or virtually any number of topics, Dick's stories often changed with the seasons. And then they'd change again.

Journalists, both local and national, would often come to Dick with a sympathetic ear only to leave confused and disenchanted, so much so that they sometimes became hardened and impervious to the real wounds that had been inflicted upon him regardless of the vagaries of his ever-shifting interpretations of them. "He has so many versions of so many stories," concluded *Daily News* columnist Bill Conlin,[85] an early Allen supporter who painstakingly demonstrated that very point in a 1968 column that tried to make sense of an alleged bar fight between Dick and a Germantown bartender. In his column, Conlin catalogued the various responses Dick gave to similar questions posed by different reporters at different times.[86] The variety was impressive. Conlin was in the midst of a tiff with both Dick and his mother (whom Dick was fiercely protective of) at the time, so perhaps that particular column could be written off as a case of momentary bitterness. However, it was indicative of Dick's shifting realities, something a *Life* magazine reporter would conclude as well. In 1969, Dave Wolf, the magazine's sports editor, was dispatched to Philadelphia to examine what by that point had become a war between the city and its cleanup hitter. In the process, he became enamored with Dick and his resulting article was practically reverential. Talks ensued and soon Wolf was working with Dick on his autobiography. By 1974 he gave up. "He (Allen) would tell me stories one day, terrific stuff. And the next day, the supportive facts would change completely. There was no way we could produce a libel-free book." Eventually Wolf threw up his hands and walked away from both Dick and the project. Said Wolf, "I was emotionally wiped out."[87]

By the conclusion of the 1962 season, at least Dick considered himself the organization's top prospect. After his successes at the plate he expected two things from the Phillies in 1963: a raise and a promotion to the big leagues. He got neither, a slap of baseball reality that opened his eyes even wider to both the nature of the business and his relationship with his employer. In an interview with Hochman during spring training 1964, Allen displayed his disillusion with the professional game in a way that was stunning both for what he said as well as for the fact that he, still an unproven prospect, did not hesitate to speak his mind: "I found out [when shipped back to the minors in 1963] there's nothing cut and dried in baseball. Even in Triple-A ball, a guy goes into a slump, and bam, he gets shipped out."[88] In an era where even veteran players were expected to say little of substance beyond the rote pablum that they were grateful for the mere opportunity to play baseball for a living, Dick's candor was a shock to the system. Here was a player, more a prospect than anything else—and a black prospect at that—who was simply not going to abide by the time-honored conventions of the game. Here was something different.

Here as well, for those protective of the game's wholesome image, came trouble.

When the raise didn't materialize of its own accord, Dick sought out GM John Quinn to rectify the situation: "I wanted a fifty-dollar raise. I'd hit .329 for Williamsport . . . the team finished with a fourteen-game lead. Where I come from, western Pennsylvania steel country, a man makes sure he gets a raise for work well done." Quinn was not persuaded; he told Dick that if he persisted in hounding him he'd spend the 1963 season in the minors. Dick held his ground and, at least the way he saw it, "Little Rock was the result."[89] From Quinn's standpoint, Dick Allen was bucking the system, rocking the boat, demanding what he, an unproven prospect, had no right to demand. To Quinn, a traditionalist who felt quite at home within an organization as conservative as the Carpenter-led Phillies, there was no room for such obstinacy. The organization was simply not going to bend to the whim of any one player, no matter how talented he might be. A lesson had to be taught, and taught now, or things would only spiral out of control. And so Little Rock it was.

In effect, Quinn was processing Dick through the organization's "Conveyor Belt." As journalist William Rhoden describes it, "the act of 'processing' athletes along the Conveyor Belt involves a significant and often subtle element of 'deprogramming' potential troublemakers—black athletes who might be tempted to think of themselves, or their situations, in racial terms and who might want to use their prominence in the service of something other than enriching the institution. . . . On the Conveyor Belt, young athletes quickly learn that easy passage through a white-controlled system is contingent upon not 'rocking the boat,' not being a 'troublemaker.'"[90] Indeed, according to Rhoden, "the ultimate effect of the Conveyor Belt is not so much to deliver young black athletes to the pros [or, in Dick's case, the majors], but to deliver them with the correct mentality . . . the black athlete learns early on that the best way to continue the trip on the Conveyor Belt is to accept the power structure as it is."[91] Given Dick's history with the organization in the few years he'd been there, as well as the growing perception from those in management that he was an independent thinker and a headache, Quinn's decision to ship him off to Little Rock rather than give in and promote him made perfect sense: better to make his point with Dick now rather than let things fester.

Of course, there were perhaps baseball-related reasons as well to send him down for another year of seasoning, but it certainly wouldn't hurt to kill two birds with one, particularly sharp-edged stone.

And there was a third bird as well. Prior to the 1963 season the club switched its Triple-A minor league affiliate from the Buffalo Bisons to the newly reconstituted Arkansas Travelers, an organization that in its previous incarnation was a segregated outfit that would no longer do for an organization looking, at last, to progress on the racial front. Somebody had to be the one to break the color line down there; it might as well be Dick Allen. Times were changing and the Travelers were going to have to change with them, like it or not. The demise of the Negro Leagues only accelerated this process.

When Organized Baseball integrated in the 1940s, not everyone believed that the Negro Leagues would crumble as an aftershock. Effa Manley, co-owner of the Newark Eagles, was convinced that integration would only spur interest in her league: "If our men make good in the majors, fans all over the country would want to see the teams that they came from. Just as Joe Louis made other Negro fighters popular, so would Negro big-league stars increase interest in other Negro players."[92] She doubted very much that the long-segregated white baseball clubs would ever undertake the effort to scout and develop their own black talent, particularly given that so many minor league affiliates were located within the South; they would forever look to the Negro Leagues to do this for them. But the Negro Leagues never formalized any sort of working agreement with Organized Baseball and, rather quickly, the white clubs began to see the value of cultivating their own talent rather than paying Negro League club owners for theirs. This was the case even though such a commitment would involve negotiating the tricky politics of southern racial segregation. Throughout the 1950s, many southern-based minor leagues desegregated, something they had to do if they were going to maintain their affiliations with the big-league clubs that were now seeking placement for their homegrown, developing black talent. By the time of Dick's signing in 1960, the Negro Leagues were all but dead, squeezed out by Organized Baseball and choking to death.

Coy might have managed to temporarily spare his younger brother the cruelty of southern segregation upon negotiating his initial contract, but by 1963 the Phils had only two minor league affiliates above the class A level, and they were both located within segregated cities (the other being the class AA Chattanooga Lookouts). If Dick was going to spend another season in the minors, he was going to have to confront the ugliness of segregation at last. (Hank would have to do this as well; he, along with Bobby Gene Sanders, broke the Lookouts' color line in 1963.) When he received the news, Dick immediately understood that he was being thrust into something he wanted no part of: "In Wampum we were welcome anywhere. I had heard about all that stuff [down South] but I never dreamed I'd be involved in it. I was scared."[93]

Chapter 2

————— ❖❖ —————

The Double Standard

1963: Little Rock .289/33/97

ONE OF MANAGER Gene Mauch's core beliefs was that when it came to the special players, the ones that organizations built around, the players like Dick Allen, there was no choice—they had to be homegrown: "You can't ever trade for a player like him. He's the type of fellow you must develop in your farm system."[1] In the process of minor league development, young players learned more than baseball, particularly in the 1950s and 1960s and especially if a player was black: "I didn't know anything about racism or bigotry until I went into professional baseball in 1953," recalled Frank Robinson.[2] As for Arkansas, Hall of Famer Lou Brock, who was born in El Dorado (about two hours south of Little Rock), liked to say that he was true to his home state's official motto, "the land of opportunity," in that he took the first opportunity available to get the hell out.[3] Dick Allen would experience all of this and more, before he even arrived in Little Rock. "I remember my first year," Dick recalled near the end of his career of his initial spring training experience in Clearwater in 1960. "Tony (Taylor) was cooking for 18 of us in one room. We [the 18 black players invited to spring training] each put in five dollars." Taylor's efforts to help the

organization's younger black players navigate the cruelty of southern segregation stuck with Dick and would lead to an unbreakable bond between
the two men. Still, nothing could make him immune from all he saw
around him and experienced firsthand: "Nobody knows how hard it was
then."[4]

From the start, Dick never had a social agenda; he simply wanted to
play baseball: "I didn't want to be a crusader. I kept thinking, 'Why me?
Why do I have to be the first black ballplayer in Little Rock?'"[5] Regardless,
there was nothing he could do about it. He was going to be the face of
change in a city that by that point had become the epicenter of the civil
rights movement, a reality he couldn't escape even during the lazy days of
spring training. "There were some old guys who lived in Little Rock but
who were down [in Clearwater] looking at the talent of the people who
were going to be playing for the [Arkansas Travelers]," recalled Jim Bailey,
sportswriter for the *Arkansas Gazette* who covered the Travelers and Allen
in 1963. "They especially wanted to look at Allen. A little old guy, about
80, was standing there, looking at him, and said something to him, not
anything bad, and they started a conversation. At one point Dick said to
the little fellow, 'All I wanna do is play ball and not be bothered.' This
meant something to the little fellow, and he says, 'Well, Stevie [there was
another young black phenom on the verge of taking the country by storm,
Little Stevie Wonder, whose first major hit, "Fingertips," was released the
previous June], you got to re-uh-lize that Little Rock has been an ole
Southern city for many, many years.' That pretty well chilled 'Stevie.'"[6]

Upon his arrival in Little Rock, things would not get any better. On
the field, Dick was introduced to yet another new position, left field, in
the organization's ongoing quest to find a place to hide him defensively.
At Travelers Field, this would prove to be a monumental mistake. According to Bailey, "Left field just kept climbing. They called it 'the dump.'
Allen had a lot of talent but he couldn't handle the dump. There were all
kinds of potholes all over the place. It was a disgrace of a baseball field."[7]
After his visit to the dump in 1963, the *Daily News*' Stan Hochman wrote:
"If you can play in Little Rock, with the rubble of an outfield slanting
upwards towards a tin fence, and the rabble in the bleachers shouting
insults at you, you can play anywhere."[8] Historically, clubs identified their
best defensive outfielders and assigned them to "run up and down the

dump" on the theory that they were the only ones who had even a remote chance of success under those conditions.[9] The Phillies put their shakiest defensive outfielder out there on the theory of, well, who knows—perhaps on the theory that he couldn't be any worse there than he had been in centerfield the year before. Whatever the theory, Dick would struggle out there all season.

On opening night, April 17, the first game for the Travelers since the end of the 1961 season, the stands were full. The club's moniker, taken from an Arkansas folktale involving a lost traveler and the fiddle player he encountered on his journey, suited Dick as he fidgeted in left field; above and beyond all else, he surely felt lost as well. "There I am," he recalled nine years later, "looking around the stands and praying, 'Please God, don't let the ball be hit to me.' The pitcher cranks up and—whoosh!—a line drive right at me, no more than a foot over my head. I couldn't raise my arm. I couldn't even chase the ball. I was scared to death."[10]

That morning, Little Rock residents read in the *Gazette* about the continuing incarceration of Martin Luther King Jr. and Ralph Abernathy in Birmingham, as well as a voters' rights march taking place there in their absence. Now, in the evening, they were presented with a black face in the outfield for the first time.[11] Throughout the game, Dick was dialed into the hatred spewed at him from the stands and beyond. Before the game even started, the Capital Citizens' Council (CCC), a local white supremacist group, picketed outside the stadium, holding up signs saying "Nigger Go Home" and passing out leaflets to fans entering the stadium detailing what the CCC alleged was a "conspiracy" among the Travelers and the Little Rock media to "Negro-ize" the local baseball club along with the town's hotel and coffee shops.[12] "I thought Jackie Robinson had Negro-ized baseball sixteen years earlier," said Dick.[13] Apparently not in Little Rock. For a man who just wanted to play baseball, Dick was getting a helluva lot more.

Throwing out the first ball that evening was none other than Arkansas governor Orval Faubus, the same man who, six years earlier and in defiance of the U.S. Supreme Court, had called in the National Guard to stop the desegregation of Little Rock's Central High School. "I knew who he was," said Dick, "and I sure as hell knew what he was famous for."[14] Opening night would set the tone for the entire season, one in which Dick

Richard Anthony
Allen, 1963—
the lone black
Traveler.
(Arkansas Travelers
Baseball Club, Inc.)

thought seriously about giving it all up and going home to Wampum. Joe
Lonnett, the Travelers' third base coach who grew up in nearby Beaver
Falls, Pennsylvania, and even officiated some of Dick's high school basketball games, talked him off the cliff by presenting him with the cold reality
of the next forty years of his life should the young slugger call it a career
in Little Rock: "His bags were packed and he was ready to leave . . . I told
him to hang on . . . that it was either this or a lunch bucket in the coal

CONSPIRACY AT LITTLE ROCK TO NEGRO-IZE TRAVELERS BASEBALL TEAM

Censorship and news suppression by the Little Rock Press Media, kept the following news from you. BELOW ARE THE "CHAMPIONS" OF THE SO-CALLED "FREE PRESS" WHO STAGED A NEWS "blackout" on the apparent plan to integrate our Travelers Baseball Team, Travelers Field, our Hotels and Coffee Shops.

UNITED PRESS INTERNATIONAL
ARKANSAS DEMOCRAT
ARKANSAS GAZETTE
COMMERCIAL APPEAL
HERBIE BYRD, KLRA
ASSOCIATED PRESS
KARK-TV
KTHV
(Each of the above received a copy of this letter as a news release nearly two weeks ago— But "Killed" IT.)

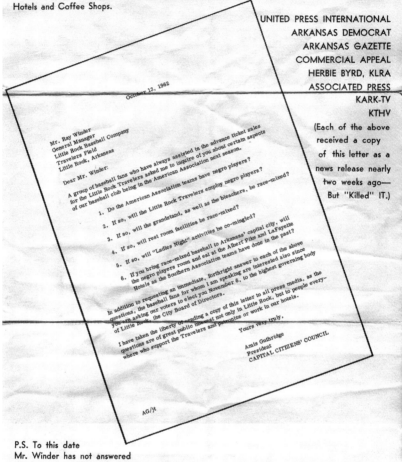

October 13, 1962

Mr. Ray Winder
General Manager
Little Rock Baseball Company
Travelers Field
Little Rock, Arkansas

Dear Mr. Winder:

A group of baseball fans who have always assisted in the advance ticket sales for the Little Rock Travelers asked me to inquire of you about certain aspects of our baseball club being in the American Association next season.

1. Do the American Association teams have negro players?

2. If so, will the Little Rock Travelers employ negro players?

3. If so, will the grandstand, as well as the bleachers, be race-mixed?

4. If so, will rest room facilities be co-mingled?

5. If so, will "Ladies Night" activities be race-mixed?

6. If you bring race-mixed baseball to Arkansas' capital city, will the negro players room and eat at the Albert Pike and LaFayette Hotels as the Southern Association teams have done in the past?

In addition to requesting an immediate, forthright answer to each of the above questions, the baseball fans for whom I am speaking are interested also since you are asking our voters to elect you November 6, to the highest governing body of Little Rock, the City Board of Directors.

I have taken the liberty of sending a copy of this letter to all press media, as the questions are of great public interest not only in Little Rock, but to people everywhere who support the Travelers and patronize or work in our hotels.

Yours very truly,

Amis Guthridge
President
CAPITAL CITIZENS' COUNCIL

AG/jt

P.S. To this date Mr. Winder has not answered this letter but he stated over the telephone Definitely and Emphatically to a Little Rock Minister that he was bringing NEGRO BASEBALL to Little Rock.

Published and Distributed by the Capital Citizens' Council, P. O. Box 1977, Little Rock, Ark. Amis Guthridge, President

Leaflet distributed by the Capital Citizens' Council to fans entering Travelers Field for the first integrated baseball game in modern Arkansas history, April 17, 1963.

(Butler Center for Arkansas Studies, Central Arkansas Library System, Little Rock, Arkansas)

mines." And so Dick hung on. "If it wasn't for Joe Lonnett I might not be in baseball today," said Dick in 1972.[15]

There would be a price to pay for his persistence that season. Little Rock was certainly not the first traumatic incident in Dick's career, but it was far and away the most resonant, the one he'd refer to over and over for years afterward. The one that shaped him and his vision of professional baseball, as well as its role in American society, more than any other. More than anything else in his life, Little Rock was the lens through which he, along with his admirers and detractors, would frame his career and personality going forward. Which begs the question: What was *really* going on in Little Rock?

*   *   *

Whatever was going on there, it traveled. Arkansas historian Bob Razer recalled that, as a child, seemingly whenever he and his family left the state, questions and implied accusations followed them: "I remember a car vacation trip my family made to visit relatives in Ohio in the summer of 1958 or maybe 1959. Nearly every time we stopped for gas or checked into a motel, people would see our Arkansas license plate and ask about the school integration in Little Rock."[16] For the African American writer Hoyt Fuller, who had never even been to Arkansas, the stench of Little Rock reached across the Atlantic, something he discovered in the course of his travels throughout Europe in the late 1950s and early 1960s: "People from Sweden to Spain have found it necessary to tell me they think Little Rock 'such a terrible thing.' . . . I might be able to say I have heard Little Rock and American race prejudice abhorred in a dozen different languages."[17]

Indeed, the racial turmoil in Little Rock, and throughout the South, led directly to the demise of a previous incarnation of the Travelers and the Southern Association in which they played.[18] As the majors integrated during the 1950s, tensions rose between the major league organizations and the southern minor league towns in which their affiliates played over the issue of the placement of black ballplayers. Many towns had entrenched policies prohibiting integrated audiences or athletic teams and were, for a time, unwilling to budge. The New Orleans Pelicans, founded in 1887 and a charter member of the Southern Association (which started up in 1901), folded first, followed by the Memphis Chicks, another charter member. Soon other clubs either folded, relocated, or switched leagues. In Little Rock, civic concern over losing the beloved Travelers led the club to issue public shares of stock in the franchise (Governor Faubus purchased some himself) so as to quell fears that it might relocate. However, although the Travelers were now anchored to Little Rock, by the completion of the 1961 season they were one of only three surviving Southern Association clubs—not enough to comprise a league. The Southern Association folded and in 1962 the city of Little Rock was left without a ball club anyway. Everything, it seemed, was coming apart.

At the same time, things were also starting to come together. As a result of forces from both within and outside the city, Little Rock, at last, began to take affirmative steps to improve its image. In October 1962, Bill Hansen, a Student Nonviolent Coordinating Committee (SNCC) worker, arrived in Little Rock to establish SNCC's third major regional project. The first two, in Mississippi and Georgia, focused primarily on voter registration; in Little Rock, however, the goal was broader: the overall desegregation of an entire city.[19] Hansen believed that in Little Rock, the conditions were right for such an ambitious project to succeed and, in his November 1962 field report, noted, "Since 1957 the city has been laboriously trying to rebuild its completely shattered image. There is indication that they might consider capitulating to demands rather than suffer through another outbreak of racial trouble."[20] Little Rock might also have been so amenable to change because, prior to the Central High debacle, it was thought to be, if anything, a broad-minded southern city. Bob Razer recalled, "Little Rock was considered a progressive city in racial relations prior to 1957. That's one of the reasons Little Rock was selected as the site to integrate southern public schools. Arkansas was a border state and not part of the Deep South. Faubus was considered a progressive governor, or at least left of center. His overall record as governor is rather progressive if you ignore the integration issue, which is rather hard to do of course."[21] At least two public facilities had been desegregated prior to Central High: the public library in 1954 and the city bus system.

Hansen and SNCC went to work and very quickly saw results: on January 2, 1963, the lunch counters at Woolworth's and Walgreen's, along with those at two local department stores, desegregated. By February, all public facilities within the city were integrated by court order (including Travelers Field). Rather than fight the ruling, many among the business elite, who were desperate for a revived downtown, cajoled others into not only complying with it but peacefully integrating much of the private sector as well. In the end, large swaths of the city integrated with surprisingly little unrest. The resurrection of the dormant Travelers was part of the revitalization effort. Ray Winder, a longtime executive with the club, saw the handwriting on the wall. Bailey recalled that he "was an old, grouchy guy but he wasn't a dummy. He knew he had to do something. The Marion Hotel had most of the business from the baseball people, and I don't know if he went in there himself but if he didn't, he sent somebody" to ensure that, going forward, it would house and feed all of the visiting players who came through, black and white alike.[22]

When it came to the arrival of the integrated Travelers themselves in April 1963, both local papers, the *Gazette* and the *Arkansas Democrat*, took pains to ease the tension; fearful of rousing up any racial unrest that would further tar the city's image, the papers made the editorial decision to downplay the racial aspect of the upcoming opening night by not mentioning it at all. "The editors decided we'd be better off not getting things all stirred up again," remembered Bailey.[23] A conspiracy of silence, perhaps, but one with at least a tangible antecedent. Throughout the season, Dick's race was mentioned from time to time; the fact that he was the first black Traveler never was, although that detail was one few Traveler fans missed. Moreover, although, as Dick recalled so vividly in his autobiography, Governor Faubus did indeed attend the opener and threw out the first ball, his presence was most likely not an implied threat. Rather, he was there to signal the birth of a new era. As the *Sporting News* reported on the event, the mood in the stands was, for the most part, celebratory, at least as far as it related to the presence of Faubus at the game: "Little Rock baseball officials, who have done a tremendous job in rebuilding interest in the game, also had a big hand in helping the integrated program work. That Governor Faubus attended the opener is a tribute to the job Little Rock baseball officials did. They are to be congratulated for a giant progressive step, not only in baseball, but in the general area of civil rights."[24]

It's possible that the *Sporting News*, historically tone-deaf when it came to the nexus of baseball and race relations, misinterpreted the mood at the ballpark on opening night. If it did, however, then so did the *Philadelphia Tribune*. Below a banner headline proclaiming "Richie Allen Breaks Baseball Color Barrier in Little Rock, Ark.," the *Tribune* reported to its readers that opening night went surprisingly smoothly with Dick well received: "Playing before a roaring crowd of 7,000, the Arkansas Travelers brought Triple-A baseball, International League-style, to Little Rock this season—desegregated club, grandstand, hotels, and all. . . . Each of the [game's] heroes shared the enthusiastic applause of the crowd and the 21-year-old Allen, the first Negro ever to don a Traveler uniform, received even a bit more of the glad hand than his mates." As for Dick's misplay in left field in the first inning, the *Tribune* reported that "the fans forgave him quickly. As he came to bat in the last of the first, there was a round of hand clapping. In the fourth, he was greeted by more applause and immediately doubled to right-center. The tension was over and Allen doubled again in the sixth."[25]

Razer, who was in the stands that evening, likewise recalled the enthusiastic reception for Dick, something that, in his experience as a Travelers fan, meant more than mere appreciation for yet another new face in the lineup: "I thought the fact that Allen received applause from the fans his first time up was interesting. That would have been unusual, I think. Travelers today don't get applauded their first at-bat—I don't ever remember that—and we've had some big-name prospects pass through. People know they are big-time prospects, but they don't applaud them, as I recall, on their first at-bat."[26] The *Tribune* made note of Dick's reluctance to play in Little Rock given all that had gone on before but pointed out that "[Travelers'] club officials went out of their way to make Allen and two other Negroes, Ferguson Jenkins and Dick Quiroz, feel they were welcome. The team was met at the airport by a group of fans, ushered into convertibles and paraded down Main Street to their hotel."[27]

In the stands, things went smoothly as well: "several hundred Negro fans crowded into the grandstand for the first time, sitting where they could find space," reported the *Tribune*. "There were no incidents." As the season wore on, Traveler fans became acclimated (some more comfortably than others) to the new open seating policy. "Early in the season," recalled Jim Bailey, "somebody in the press box handed me a pair of binoculars—he wanted to show me something. So I took a look and there were about twelve people sitting more or less side by side down in the middle of the stands, and about ten of them were black and two old white folks, about seventy years old, were in the middle of them, and they didn't look too happy. I doubt they came back that year." Regardless, the old days were over: "if you bought a ticket, you could sit where you wanted to."[28] Wadie Moore, a young black fan and future *Gazette* staffer, remembered Dick's arrival as signifying much more than simply the start of the new season: "it was an exciting day for black people. Allen didn't just integrate baseball in Little Rock, he integrated life. Before he got here, black folks who went to the ballpark sat together in a separate section. . . . After him, we could sit anywhere we wanted, and believe me, we did just that."[29] Technically, Dick took no steps to integrate Little Rock; if anything he wanted no part of baseball or life there. The integration of the stands and the city had more to do with the work of SNCC and the prodding of local business leaders than anything else. But those people were largely unknown figures. Dick Allen was front and center—the symbol of all of the work these other folks had done. And as such, and not for the last time, he stood for something that reached well beyond the ball field. For many people the story was self-evident: before Allen there were segregated stands, hotels, and an entire ball club; after Allen everything changed and Little Rock moved forward. It was an awful lot to put on the shoulders of a twenty-one-year-old kid.

This was particularly true given that Dick's reality differed from the one experienced by all those who were looking for signs, any signs, of progress. For Dick, who grew up amid at least a modicum of racial tolerance, all he saw in Little Rock was regression. Despite the widespread desegregation, some private businesses held out, clinging to the old ways for as long as they could. "The first day I got to town," Dick recalled in 1964, "I asked somebody where I could eat, and they pointed out a place across from the Marion Hotel. So I went in and sat at a table, but when nobody waited on me, I, finally, went to the counter and asked the man if I could get something to eat. He said, 'Go in the kitchen and tell the cook what you want.' Well, I gave him some choice words, all right. I told him 'I'm no animal.' I just couldn't understand this." At the ballpark, not everyone was applauding. One fan in particular liked to position himself behind the Travelers' dugout and yell "Hey Chocolate!" whenever Dick approached.[30]

After the games, Dick found negotiating the reality of Little Rock, irrespective of its evolution, daunting and confusing. "Coming from Wampum, it was a cultural shock to him," said Ron Galbreath. "He didn't leave his [home in the black section of town] hardly at all. He was afraid for his life. Imagine: you're coming out of [Wampum] and you're a high school phenom—you're loved, you're revered. Now—boom!—you're in Little Rock, Arkansas, and you're black."[31] As Dick remembered it in 1964, he and his wife spent almost all of their time in Little Rock at home: "we went out twice all summer." While there was one integrated movie house in town, Dick recalled that many blacks were nevertheless afraid to go there. "And the Negro movie house wasn't air-conditioned, you sit there and roast."[32] The integrated grandstands at Travelers Field, the integrated Marion Hotel, the burgeoning integration of Main Street businesses— lilies in a field of bull thistle—were all peripheral to Dick, whose reality was rooted instead within the black neighborhood in which he and his wife lived (in an apartment within a house owned, no less, by a couple whose daughter was one of the three black students involved in the Central High integration debacle) not by choice but by a deeply ingrained, rigidly enforced tradition.[33]

Just like Curt Flood (who received his indoctrination in Tampa, Florida, during spring training 1956) wrote in his autobiography, the black experience in the South during the era was one of sharp contrasts: "white law, white custom and white sensibility required me to remain offstage until wanted. I was a good athlete and might have an opportunity to show it, but this incidental skill did not redeem me socially. Officially, and for the duration, I was a nigger."[34] A 1968 *Sports Illustrated* article summarized the dichotomy facing black athletes in the South by observing that "the white American was able to compartmentalize his attitude toward the Negro, to admire his exploits on the field but put him on the back of the bus on the way home. The white American expected the Negro to perform, to put out, but after he had showered and shaved, he was supposed to know his place."[35] Dick noticed this as well: "When the game was on, everybody was for you. When the game was over, everybody walked away from you and you were on your own."[36]

Further isolating to Dick in Little Rock was the quick demotion of Ferguson Jenkins to the club's class A affiliate in Miami. And then there were his difficulties in confronting and navigating "the dump," which often left him frustrated and upset during what would otherwise be the only hours of the day where he could seek respite: on the ball field. One spectator reflected upon Dick's time in Little Rock by observing that he was "the worst outfielder I've ever seen."[37] All of these factors made an already difficult situation even more so.

On top of everything else was the continuing resistance from the hard-core segregationists who were determined to fight SNCC and the local business elite in their efforts to fully desegregate the city. Amis Guthridge, who organized the picketing of Travelers Field on Dick's opening night, was on the forefront of this charge.[38] To call Guthridge an extremist would be to understate his worldview: he considered FDR a traitor and believed that his election in 1932 was the year when "communists actually took over the operation of the government of the United States from the inside." Guthridge had a long and checkered history as a race-baiter in Little Rock (he worked as state secretary for Strom Thurmond's 1948 presidential run as a "Dixiecrat"), becoming, in 1954, counsel for White America, Inc., an organization created "to help white people to organize to fight legally and morally for their rights." He fought desegregation for decades, eventually becoming an attorney, advisor, and spokesman for the CCC, which organized much of the terroristic opposition to the integration of Central High in 1957. In 1961 he was elected president of the CCC and the following year launched "reverse freedom rides" where the CCC attempted to mock the Freedom Riders by sending thirty-four black Arkansas residents (fourteen unemployed adults and twenty children) to Hyannis Port, Massachusetts. Although Guthridge was a failure in many ways, he did succeed in making Little Rock "an international symbol of racist resistance to integration."[39]

Though he was not representative of the majority, Guthridge had no shortage of sympathizers within Little Rock. Plenty of people, even those who would never go so far as to support the CCC, were, as Bailey recalled, nonetheless "cranky" when word spread that the Travelers were going to return as an integrated outfit in 1963.[40] Although a majority of fans at least accepted the integration of the club as an economic and functional necessity for the city to be able to maintain a minor league franchise going forward, there were marchers, led by Guthridge, who picketed and protested Allen's arrival for days. The stress on Dick was overwhelming and, he admitted a few years later, he began drinking regularly during this time.[41] Through it all, the Phillies remained mum, never making any attempt to ease his transition to Little Rock or taking any steps to ameliorate it in any way. Decades later, this perceived indifference still burned. "Maybe if the Phillies had called me in, man to man," Dick wrote in his autobiography, "like the Dodgers had done with Jackie, and said, 'Dick, this is what we have in mind, it's going to be very difficult, but we're with you'—at least then I would have been better prepared. I'm not saying I would have liked it. But I *would* have known what to expect."[42] Combined with the organization's exposing him in the expansion draft, Quinn's paternity payoff, and the annual on-field position changes, Little Rock only added to Dick's growing cynicism toward the folly of "benevolent paternalism" that had ruled Organized Baseball for decades. For what did this concept mean if he was left out to dry by the organization once again, left to fend for himself amid the catcalls and worse? From where he stood, the club clearly wasn't looking out for him and his best interests. If it were, the string of indignities he was suffering wouldn't be taking place; somebody from the Phillies would have stepped up to straighten things out. Just as he was literally on his own in Little Rock, he saw that he had no one to turn to within the organization to help him manage his professional career and development. If he wanted out of Little Rock, he'd have to negotiate his release without their assistance.

To do so, he relied on the bedrock of Wampum: Joe Lonnett, who painted for him a grim portrait of the remainder of his life in western Pennsylvania without baseball; his brother Coy, who told him that "if you want out of there, you beat that ball. Beat your way out of there"; and his mother, Era, who administered a bracing dose of tough love that shook her son to his core: "Dick, if you come home, if you quit, if you leave there and come here, you can't live with me. . . . Now, if you're going to leave baseball, you'll leave because you just don't have the talent. Don't let them drive you out." Dick recalled that after that conversation with his mother, "I went home and cried like a baby, I'll never forget it. I just cried and cried."[43] Then he stopped, wiped himself off, and beat the hell out of the ball until the Phils had no choice but to promote him.

*   *   *

One year, one player, one city, two realities. Which one hews closer to "the truth"? As with most things, it all boils down to perspective. Even accounting for Dick's ever-shifting recollections, both are grounded in verifiable fact; the one that predominates depends greatly upon the lens one chooses to view the situation. Unquestionably there was significant impetus for change in Little Rock during the early 1960s, and there was in fact substantial progress. At the same time, the city presented black residents with a nightmarish existence as they had little choice but to confront and navigate the lingering realities of a well-entrenched segregationist mind-set. The Phillies, along with much of the white media, only acknowledged the reality they encountered and had great difficulty imagining that for blacks, life in Little Rock behind the banner of change could be something else altogether. Orville Henry, sports editor at the *Gazette* and perhaps the most influential sportswriter in all of Arkansas at the time, made it a hobby to counter Dick's Little Rock recollections whenever possible. From where he sat, Dick was treated "as well as any baseball hero in town since 1901," an opinion he liked to share with the national and Philadelphia media whenever they came around inquiring about Dick's Little Rock experience.[44] In 1964 he told a *Sports Illustrated* reporter that "by the end of the season, Richie Allen was one of the all-time favorite ballplayers at Little Rock."[45] He could point to several factors to support his contention: the cheers he received on opening night, his productive season (his 33 home runs were a Travelers' record and would remain one for a right-handed hitter for the next four decades), his selection to the International League's All-Star squad, and, perhaps most significant, the fact that he was voted, by the fans, the Travelers' most valuable player at the conclusion of the season. But all of these things could be deceptive. Years later, Jim Bailey offered a corrective to his editor's sunny declarations. To Bailey, Dick's MVP award hardly signified everything that Henry claimed. Rather, it was merely an acknowledgment that Traveler fans recognized his talent and didn't let his race obscure all they were seeing on the field. "They didn't embrace him, but they didn't reject him either," he concluded.[46] And that was about as far as it went.

Yes, there were cheers, but there were also the catcalls, the segregated housing, and everything else. *Inquirer* columnist Bruce Keidan would later write that in situations presenting "a mixture of hostility and loyalty, anger and sympathy," almost certainly "the boos will register louder than the cheers in Allen's delicate psyche."[47] So it was in Little Rock. His manager, once again Frank Lucchesi, struggled for many years to understand Dick's alternative take on Little Rock: "Richie was upset one night because one person said, 'Come on, Chocolate Drop, hit one out. . . .' That's not in taste but the fan didn't realize it. They say worse things to white ballplayers. Richie is sensitive and self-centered."[48] Throughout the 1960s, Lucchesi would proclaim to anyone who asked that, contrary to Dick's contention, Traveler fans loved him: "I dispute his claim that the fans mistreated him in Little Rock. He was voted the club's most valuable player by fan vote. Do fans who hate a player give him a new suit?"[49] Decades later, Lucchesi had a deeper appreciation for what Dick endured: "the one thing I regret in [my] forty years of professional baseball was that I did not talk to Dick about what he was going through . . . I would often give him a pat on the back for his great performance and for being a good teammate but never did I give him a pat on the back for doing it all under the conditions he faced."[50]

Once he finally escaped Little Rock, Dick's experience there would be viewed through various prisms—whichever one best served the narrative of the moment. In 1964 Gene Mauch contended that, if anything, Little Rock was a positive experience for Dick, something that would only help him become a better ballplayer: "We knew, on the basis of his record at Little Rock, that pressure wouldn't bother him in the majors."[51] Later, when he was scuffling with the organization as well as various members of the media, Little Rock would be invoked again, this time to bolster allegations of Dick's poor character. In 1969, *Inquirer* columnist Allen Lewis, who was in the middle of such a skirmish, fell back on Lucchesi's and Henry's perspective of Dick's season in Little Rock and proclaimed him "A Con Man with Muscles."[52] "Richie Allen speaks softly and he looks at you with those sleepy eyes and you just know he's telling it like it is. It's possible he believes everything he says and doesn't even know he's a con man. . . . His tales of racist threats and notes left in his car at the ballpark and of the treatment accorded him by the baiting fans made you ashamed to be white. There was anger in your heart when you wrote that story, and disbelief when you were told a day or two later by someone who was there that it wasn't that way at all. Little Rock manager Frank Lucchesi and respected newsmen indicated that Richie's accounts were, to say the least, exaggerated."[53] The *Sporting News*, likewise, invoked the integration of the Travelers to serve its own ends: "the people of Little Rock solved their own problem," read the paper's editorial in May 1963. For the "baseball bible," as it was referred to in those days, it was important that Dick's experience in Little Rock be an example of the power of baseball to facilitate social change: "If they had not wanted integration, they would not have permitted the Little Rock ball club to acquire three Negro players. If the people of Little Rock had not wanted this, they would not have cheered the Negro Outfielder Richie Allen. . . . It can be said that baseball provided the means for making [integration] work in Little Rock as it has in almost every section of the country since integration became a reality after World War II . . . baseball has shown the way."[54]

The black press viewed Dick's year in Little Rock through a prism as well, but there the light was refracted much differently. In the *Baltimore Afro-American*, Sam Lacy wrote in 1972 that "although he didn't realize it at the time, [Dick's] personal education was progressing in step with his baseball indoctrination." Speaking with a member of the media whom he felt could relate to him and what he had been through with the Travelers, Dick told Lacy that "with mom's ultimatum on the one hand and the crack phone calls and other things there with me, I decided that Dick Allen had to harden up . . . and [go] about my business. . . . At the end of that season, by ignoring everybody and sticking to doing my thing, I got the overwhelming vote as Little Rock's most popular player—and without even trying." Lacy identified Little Rock as the experience that "firmed Dick's resolution to be himself." Dick confided in Lacy that Little Rock taught him something about the business of baseball as well as the men who ran it, something he would later confirm in his travels and travails throughout the majors: "to them (the owners), it is a business which they operate as a fetish . . . I've been traded four times, not because I couldn't produce, but because I wouldn't dance to their tune."[55] Little Rock changed him, contended the *Chicago Defender* in 1964, altering his worldview forever after. "You know," Dick told the *Defender* reporter, "if it hadn't been for Little Rock I might not be in the majors today. That is something to be thankful for."[56] As for the overarching lesson he took from Little Rock, it was most likely this: "There were two sets of rules in Little Rock, one for the Arkansas Travelers and one for Dick Allen, the black left fielder for the Arkansas Travelers. That didn't go with me. From that day on, I decided if there was ever a double standard again, I would be the beneficiary, and not the other way around."[57]

A Job, Not a Game

1963: Philadelphia .292/0/2
1964: Philadelphia .318/29/91

IN SEPTEMBER 1963, Dick was liberated from Little Rock at last: he was promoted to Philadelphia to play out the final month of the season with the big-league club. In his memory, his relationship with the city and its fans was contentious from the start: Dick always claimed that he was booed in his very first at bat as a Phillie.[1] However, if there were any boos, they were most likely not directed at him personally; he began his career in Milwaukee and there is no record of him being booed there. Perhaps there were a few boos hurled in his direction, but if so, they were most likely of the sort reserved for opponents of any stripe. When the club returned to Connie Mack Stadium on Friday, September 6, he did not play. The following evening, when he made his debut in front of the hometown faithful, 11,589 fans welcomed him much as they would any other new arrival. Although he went 0 for 4 and struck out twice, contemporaneous newspaper accounts do not mention any unusual booing or other negative crowd reaction. Although one might argue that the boos could perhaps have gone unreported within the white press (although such an oversight would have been unlikely given how prominent a prospect Dick was), the *Tribune*, which covered the game as well, and with a sensitive and astute eye and ear when it came to race relations, likewise made no mention of any negativity toward Dick.

Although Dick struggled to impress that September, hitting a respectable .292 but without any home runs (and only three extra-base hits) in limited action, he was nevertheless the locus of attention for the upcoming 1964 season. The *Tribune* pinned all of its hopes on the rookie, remarking that while other clubs had a "banner crop of [black] prospects," the Phils had only Allen: "The supply line of talent from the minor leagues to . . . Connie Mack Stadium is just about ready to run dry," leaving Dick as the club's only hope to improve upon what had been a surprisingly competitive 1963 season.[2] Clearly the *Tribune* was going to watch him, and how the Phils treated him, closely and with great interest.

When he arrived in Clearwater the following spring, Dick learned that he was about to switch positions yet again, this time to third base—a position he had never played before. If he was going to learn how to play it, he was going to have to learn it at the major league level, in front of thousands of discerning critics every night. Teammate Dallas Green recognized the folly of this move from the start: "He was very suspect defensively so third base was not a [viable] option. If he couldn't play second base, he certainly wasn't going to play third base."[3] And yet he was going to play it nevertheless. Gene Mauch wasn't worried: "When I was managing Minneapolis [in the Red Sox farm system], I was impressed by a shortstop the Red Sox sent me, the kid named Carl Yastrzemski. One thing struck me about him. As a fielder at short he was at least three or four years away from the major leagues. So I switched him to the outfield because he had a bat that was this close to being of big-league caliber."[4] The results spoke for themselves. Mauch expected nothing less here.

There was another reason for the switch as well: the club had an everlasting hole at third that was crying to be filled with something other than yet another stopgap. Third base had been a revolving door for years: since 1959 twenty-five players had given it a shot at Connie Mack, with little success. As *Sports Illustrated* summed it up in 1964: "Every year there are two big parades in Philadelphia. One is the Mummers . . . [t]he other is the one to third base in Connie Mack Stadium."[5] In 1963, the club

The Phillies' rookie third baseman, 1964.
(© 2014 Legendaryauctions.com)

acquired veteran Don Hoak but he struggled, hitting only .231, so Mauch was considering his alternatives. Perhaps Dick could be a permanent solution to a perpetual problem. The black press was excited about the position switch for other reasons: "While Junior Gilliam, Jackie Robinson and Hank Thompson had solid seasons at the hot corner . . . the fact remains:

no tan third baseman has ever been tapped for either the All Star game or the annual BBWAA (Baseball Writers Association of America) All Major League team. . . . [Black fans] are licking their chops and exclaiming with glee: 'He's here!' They have waited 16 seasons for a tan hot corner ace who can swat 40 homers, bat .315, and field like the fabled Ray Dandridge."[6] Everybody, it seemed, had their hopes pinned on Dick Allen making it at third.

Don Hoak realized this as well. As spring training progressed, he became convinced that the fix was in. Everyone—management, Mauch, and especially the media—wanted to see Dick open the season at his position. Initially Hoak took his frustration out on Dick himself: he liked to position himself on the third base dugout rail and stare his rival down as Dick took infield practice, attempting to unnerve him. *Daily News* reporter Larry Merchant wrote that the scene "seemed eerie, Hoak sitting there steel-eyed by the hour."[7] The *Daily News'* Stan Hochman also remarked on the curious dynamic between Hoak and Dick: "Nobody can figure out how you get ready for a season by standing with your arms folded staring at Richie Allen's back."[8] Later, Hoak directed his ire at the media, and in the process, Dick bore witness as a teammate schooled him on the perceived evils of the working press. "Stan Hochman, Ray Kelly [of the *Bulletin]* and Allen Lewis [of the *Inquirer*] have written me out of the game," Hoak protested, "and they can't do it. You can't write a man out of baseball. . . . You have to play yourself out. That's the only way."[9] To Hoak, Hochman, Kelly, and Lewis were trying to subvert the natural order of the game by declaring him dead before his manager did. Through the power of the pen, they were, he believed, transitioning him out of baseball; rather than merely bearing witness to history they were attempting to make some themselves. And he wouldn't stand for it. Always a willing interview subject throughout his career, now Hoak glowered whenever a reporter dared to approach, hoping to intimidate him.[10] Dick, as both subject and witness, had a front-row seat for all of this.

On Opening Day, Dick was at third and Hoak on the bench. (His career wouldn't survive the season; he was gone and out of baseball by mid-May.) Very quickly, Dick made sure that everyone knew he had arrived: he told one reporter that if Hoak was making $40,000 then he was worth double that. (He later denied making that comment, at least for publication. "You only tell that to your wife," another player said.) Before the first pitch of the season, he issued a warning to opposing pitchers, including a future Hall of Famer: "[Warren] Spahn has to be as careful with me as he'd be with [Hank] Aaron."[11] And it wasn't only baseball immortals like Aaron that Dick saw as instructive models for those seeking to understand him and his abilities more fully: "I won't say like Cassius Clay that I'm the greatest but if a pitcher makes a mistake against me I might drop one out of the park."[12] At one point during the season a veteran black player pulled Dick aside and told him that, irrespective of his true personality, he needed to cultivate a fan-friendly public façade, something that management and the public would be comfortable with; bravado, particularly from a black man, was certainly not the image that would breed acceptance within Organized Baseball and the white fans who followed it. Dick bristled at the very thought. A few years later, he reflected on this player's suggestion: "I can't have one face for the public and one for Dick Allen. When I do wrong, it's right out in the open. . . . I was alive 22 years before I got here. Why do I have to undo what I am—or keep it under cover—just to suit them? I don't owe the ball club anything but the best nine innings I can play."[13]

Sensitized to the issue of race through his experience in Little Rock as he never was growing up in Wampum, Dick now was more aware than ever of both the overt and the more insidious instances of racism present within the orbit of Organized Baseball. On the club's trek up from Clearwater to Philadelphia in the spring of 1964, he and the Phillies were the opponents of the Pirates in an exhibition game held in Asheville, North Carolina, where Pittsburgh manager Danny Murtaugh attempted to field the first all-nonwhite lineup: "Before the game," Dick recalled years later, "Murtaugh gets in the middle of a big argument. Now, Danny was the kind of guy who just sat in the dugout chewin' his tobacco. Every once in a while he'd spit. . . . But this argument was really ragin', right out where we could all see what was goin' on. It was between Danny and this guy from the Chamber of Commerce. I can still see tobacco juice flyin' out of Danny's mouth and goin' all over this guy's shirt. What Danny had done was, he'd penciled in an all-minority lineup. And the guy from the Chamber of Commerce was out there to tell him he couldn't do that. At first Danny said that he didn't know it was an all-black lineup till they told him. But he didn't want to change it, and that's when the tobacco juice started flyin'."[14] Eventually Murtaugh backed down and inserted an injured Bill Mazeroski at second so that the game could go on as scheduled. (Mazeroski batted once and then left the game.) In the process, Dick received another example of just how deep-seated racism could be. And he would not keep quiet about it.

Before Opening Day Dick told Larry Merchant that he clenched his teeth whenever teammates referred to the black left fielder Wes Covington as "Kingfish," a cutting reference to one of the characters on the old and infamous *Amos 'n' Andy* show. He also said that he didn't appreciate the new nickname that some teammates were attempting to pin on him: "Sammy Davis." "I'd get out of baseball rather than put up with that," he said.[15] In what was supposed to be a puff piece in the *New York Times*, Dick told columnist Arthur Daley that while in Little Rock, "It was as if I were playing baseball in a prison. A fellow who does that loves playing ball while he's at it, but he never can forget entirely that he's locked up."[16] From the outset, Dick made it clear to anyone willing to listen that, unlike those who came before him, he would not follow Branch Rickey's directive to "turn the other cheek" and accept subordinate racial status.

Though blacks were now permitted to play within Organized Baseball, as Dick surveyed the game's landscape, he saw that that was about as far as it went. For the most part, although black players dominated the major awards and the game overall throughout the 1950s (particularly in the National League, which embraced integration more readily than the American), they were largely invisible before the games started and after the last out was recorded: between 1954 and 1964, in the era of Robinson, Mays, Banks, Aaron, and on down the line, 90 percent of *Sports Illustrated* covers featured white athletes.[17] Blacks could play the games, but they were ancillary actors at best in the media's creation of modern-day heroes and role models. Little Rock drove this reality home to Dick.

Regardless, and despite his boasts and frank talk to Merchant and Daley, Dick was warmly received by the fans as well as the local and national media—at least at first. Mauch gushed whenever his name came up, raving that Dick was "a pleasant mixture of man and boy. I mean, there's enough man within him to know what he's doing up there at the plate and enough kid in him so that he's refreshingly wide-eyed about being around these other major leaguers."[18] When asked to put Dick's skills in context, Mauch shooed away the offered analogies to Banks, Aaron, and Roberto Clemente, choosing for Dick instead the company of the ballplayer occupying the rarest air of all: Ted Williams.[19] Above and beyond the comparisons, Mauch would tell anyone within earshot that Dick was, more than anything else, a "winning player" both in attitude as well as in his general approach to the game.[20]

By July, Dick had won over nearly everybody. Larry Merchant raved that "among active players only Vada Pinson, Frank Robinson, Orlando Cepeda and Mickey Mantle have had major league debuts as impressive" as Dick's, and most effusively, *Sport* ran a breathless article on the young phenom complete with a title that, if it were used only a few years later, could only have been interpreted as sarcastic: "The Cheerful World of Richie Allen." Describing Dick's admiration for Ernie Banks, author Myron Cope wrote that "Richie Allen likes cheerful people because he himself is so downright cheerful, and so ready with crackerbarrel wit, that men who have met him for the first time go away a little warmer in the heart." Cope stressed that Dick was refreshingly uninterested in his press clippings: "[The box scores] don't mean a thing to me. They're history. We can't get it back." Lurking beneath the surface was a man more complex than the two-dimensional caricature drawn by Cope, but whenever it threatened to expose itself, Cope tamped it down, choosing instead to paint the portrait he knew his readers wanted to see. At one point in the interview, after professing that he didn't have a temper, Dick told the story of beating up a schoolyard bully who was picking on his younger brother, Ronnie: "I got him down and just wouldn't let him up and beat him in the face and kicked him in the head . . . that boy was beat up pretty bad." Yet even this story ended cheerfully; Cope reported that later, Dick and the bully became best friends.[21]

As the 1964 season kicked into gear, baseball writers and fans everywhere were fascinated by everything Allen-related. Even his clothes became a topic of conversation; Stan Hochman in the *Daily News* made his sartorial flair the focus of an entire column: "A guy who wears four-button suits and orange shoes and sport coats with buckles in the back either craves attention or has way-out taste in clothes. . . . If you're a rookie and you wear four-button suits and orange shoes, you had better hit .500 or you're going to take a wicked needling from your teammates." In the article, Dick responded that "I wear them [the clothes] because I like them, not to attract attention."[22] And as for the shoes, Dick later set the record straight: "[Hochman] exaggerated. Those shoes weren't orange. They were olive."[23] Regardless, and as he made clear from the start, Dick was an individual who was not afraid to stand apart. On the field, he preferred to stretch his stirrup socks to their yawning limit in order to expose as much sanitary hose as possible: "the higher the better," he liked to say.[24] It didn't matter how everyone else wore theirs, when it came to his socks, much as when it came to his life, he was going to do things his way. The initial returns were overwhelmingly favorable; within a few short months, plans for Richie Allen days in both Pittsburgh and Philadelphia were already being made. But the initial returns were just that. Final judgment was still out there, waiting to be rendered. Those returns would come in as well, some of them much sooner than expected.

*　*　*

In truth, when it came to his press clippings, as well as so much else that Cope buffed to a shine in his article, there was much more to the story. Dick wasn't so much unfazed by his clippings because he was humble but because he wasn't playing professional baseball for the glory; he was in it primarily to put food on the table and to provide for a lifestyle he believed his talent entitled him to. "Shucks, that eight and ten cents I put into a newspaper, I might save it and buy me a Cadillac."[25] "You see," he would say whenever the issue of baseball and money was broached, "that's my job—to take care of my mom."[26] It was a theme he'd repeat for years: "I play baseball for two reasons: one, because I love it, and two, because I have to feed my family."[27] As for his love of the game, Dick always made clear that things were different in the professional game than they were on the sandlots: "[Professional] baseball is not a game for kids. It is a game for grown men, professionals. If they're kids, they don't belong here. . . . These guys have families to feed and they intend to keep feeding them."[28] This was not a perspective on the game that was his alone; Era stressed it as well. Whenever reporters would seek her out, prodding her to offer a corrective to her son's viewpoint on the nature of professional baseball, she would instead reinforce it by admonishing them that "this is a job. Not a game."[29] Indeed, it was the sort of job that would make it possible for an eighteen-year-old to buy his mother a house with the bonus money he received simply because of his ability to hit a baseball more consistently, and consistently farther, than practically anybody else on earth. It was a means to an end. The Allen family understood that as well as anybody.

This was a view of the game that was foreign to most fans, and one that was almost never stated publicly by the athletes themselves no matter how much they felt as Dick did on the matter. Sportswriters as well typically steered clear of the topic, choosing instead to focus their readers' attention on the perceived glories of the games themselves. White players of the era were tuned into what their fans wanted to hear so they repeatedly chirped the familiar bromides about being grateful for the mere opportunity to play a child's game for a living. Black players of the late 1940s and throughout the 1950s repeated them as well but, given the game's recent integration, were also able to speak of their presence as significant steps in the burgeoning civil rights movement. By the early 1960s, however, the first wave of integration had passed; every team had, at least technically, integrated. The connections between baseball and civil rights were no longer as obvious as they once were; for the second generation of black players, playing professional baseball was more of a job than a statement. While black players of the early 1960s typically kept these thoughts to themselves, Dick did not. This was a shock to both the sporting public and those within the business of professional sports, which, according to journalist Bill Rhoden, "ran on the fuel of strong bodies— black or white . . . —and an overdeveloped sense of gratitude."[30]

When he surveyed the baseball landscape through this lens, Dick saw plainly how much more difficult things were for black players than they were for their white teammates. Expectations were different, endorsement opportunities were fewer, careers were shorter. But things, as he saw them, weren't so great for white players either. Rather than see professional baseball as an Eden, he saw it as a plantation. Few white players saw themselves as farmhands or, worse, chattel. Black players, descendants of a legacy of both, oftentimes saw things more starkly.[31] Dick, in particular, was attuned in this manner. He saw how the plantation mentality filtered into nearly everything associated with the game; how athletes, particularly black ones, were often seen as something less than human. In the course of tripping over themselves while writing about his impressive physique, journalists, although attempting to be flattering, oftentimes delivered the message that Dick was more animal than man. Even the most complimentary articles, such as Cope's, dehumanized him by referring to him as "racehorse-sleek."[32]

Dick refused to see himself as chattel and prickled at the comparisons between himself and farm animals, no matter how well-intentioned. He was a man, a professional, who possessed talents that, to him at least, merited commensurate compensation and respect. There was a market for this ability and, despite the game's reserve clause (that bound players to their clubs in perpetuity, thereby eliminating the marketplace for athletic talent), he was determined to make sure that he received market value. In the pre–free agency era, this was blasphemy. Even the most liberal-minded sportswriters were so heavily indoctrinated into the plantation mentality of professional baseball that they were unable to acknowledge, much less appreciate, an athlete's desire to seek financial security for himself and his family. When Curt Flood refused to accede to a trade (to the Phillies, of all teams, and for Dick Allen, of all players) and unilaterally declared his free agency in 1969, *New York Times* columnist Red Smith exonerated the system that artificially depressed players' wages and uprooted them from their homes, communities, and business interests without notice and instead placed the blame on players like Flood who had the audacity to even consider anything beyond the game on the field: "After two pennants and one world championship, [Cardinals' manager Red] Schoendienst found himself managing a band of fat cats who had lost the incentive to win. Their salaries were well above the major league standard and many had outside sources of income."[33]

From the start, Dick was up-front with anyone who would ask with regard to his professional motivations. Nobody—fans, sportswriters, management—wanted to hear that the national pastime, at least at the professional level, was about more than the pure, undiluted love of the game itself. All of them knew it, but the illusion was powerful and overarching nonetheless. If there was one thing Dick was *not* about, it was protecting and promoting illusions of any stripe. He was who he was, and his opinions were not only his own but free and available for public consumption—on this topic as they would be on nearly anything else. Bob Carpenter was perpetually vexed by his star third baseman's concern for his finances: "Richie's a peculiar boy," he once said. "He has some strange feelings about money."[34] To a man who once proudly told the *Tribune* that he didn't consider his Phillies to be a business and that he didn't care if the club ever turned a profit, perhaps Dick's pecuniary sensitivity would seem peculiar. But Carpenter, of the DuPonts, could afford such a luxury. Dick, of Wampum, could not.

Very quickly, the sportswriters from the local dailies noticed that Dick was a sharp break from the past, so, even while praising him, they urged him to conform to the traditional model of the superstar black athlete. As Dick tore through the National League in the early months of the 1964 season, Larry Merchant of the *Daily News* wrote that if Dick was looking for role models, he'd already found them: "Hank Aaron and Ernie Banks have shown him the best attitude—loose, even-tempered, businesslike."[35] This would become a theme—(white) writers and club management urging Dick to follow in the steps of the first generation of black players in terms of temperament and demeanor, such as when Mauch called him out later on for not properly emulating Willie Mays. Dick bristled at such suggestions because he understood early on that continuing down that path would only strip him of whatever leverage the uneven playing field of the business of baseball provided him. He knew that it was his talent that gave him a bargaining chip even in the era of the reserve clause and that it would bring him the salary that would ultimately bring him the respect that he otherwise stood little chance of receiving. And he knew that these things were crucial because, as he later said, without them, "I'd be just another black man that nobody would want anything to do with."[36]

The divergence in perspectives on the professional game came into sharp focus in August 1964. With the Phillies cruising to what seemed to be a certain National League pennant, and Dick inspiring awe wherever he went, talk of postseason honors was everywhere, with outfielder Johnny Callison rumored to be the front-runner for league MVP, pitcher Jim Bunning in the discussion for both MVP and the Cy Young Award, and Dick the odds-on choice for Rookie of the Year honors. While Callison and Bunning expressed the expected gratitude for even being considered,

Dick's take was markedly different: "Let them put up $1,000 for the rookie of the year and it would be worthwhile. I have a family to support. As it is, rookie of the year doesn't mean a thing."[37] This was the first of many public statements he would make regarding the financial worth of various honors and activities associated with professional baseball. He later remarked that, unlike the Rookie of the Year award, earning an All-Star berth was something to strive for because "Willie Mays told me that that's an automatic $5,000 raise."[38] And in 1969 he walked off a postgame radio show in San Diego when he learned that he would be paid in trading stamps rather than cash: "I'm not doing any interview for trading stamps," he said. "We have to have a certain standard."[39] Standing around after a long game and chatting with a broadcaster merely for the alleged honor inherent in the request itself hardly met it.

Sports Illustrated picked up Dick's comments and ran with them, concluding that they indicated "a most unbecoming indifference to fame."[40] And just like that, a national controversy was born. Very quickly, things spun out of control. "I didn't see the story when it first came out," Dick said a few days later, "but my mother saw it. When we got to Pittsburgh she gave me heck. She said I sounded money hungry and greedy and she knew I wasn't that way." While the national media interpreted Dick's comments to mean that he was demanding a cash prize for the award, Dick responded with resignation that "the whole thing has been twisted around."[41] A few months after bearing witness to Don Hoak's battle with the media, Dick was now in the middle of one himself and claiming, just as Hoak had, that the media was unjustly trying to bury him.

That fast, the honeymoon was over. As July melted into August boos began to waft above the crowd, a few at first but increasingly more as the month progressed, whenever Dick misplayed a ball at third (he'd finish with 41 errors at the position he was still learning how to play) or struck out at the plate. For a while at least, he claimed that the booing didn't bother him, alleging that even at its worst it was more benign than what he endured in Little Rock. "It doesn't bother me a bit," he said. "The only time I'll worry is when No. 4 [Mauch] starts booing me."[42] But things were about to get much worse in a hurry.

*   *   *

Fans booed for various reasons: some booed out of resentment of the bonus money Dick had received upon signing with the club; others booed because they sensed ingratitude as highlighted by the Rookie of the Year flap; and still others booed because, what the hell, it just made them feel good. "The thing is," said teammate Bob Uecker a few years later on the general tenor of the crowds at Connie Mack, "they work in sewers for eight hours, then come out to this sewer and all their emotions are expressed—boooo."[43] Beginning in September, however, the booing of Dick intensified even as the club continued its march toward its seemingly inevitable pennant (the infamous collapse would not occur until the end of the month), this time not for anything Dick had said or done but, in the wake of a brutal riot in the North Philly neighborhood surrounding the stadium in late August, for what at least some fans believed he represented.

The politics of the neighborhood, as well as the stadium, were complicated and reached back to the turn of the century. First, the stadium. Upon its completion in 1909, Shibe Park (as Connie Mack Stadium was initially called) was considered a palace. Built and financed by Ben Shibe, the owner of the Philadelphia Athletics, his namesake stadium was as much a statement as it was a ball field. It was the world's first concrete and steel stadium and was designed to be a showstopper. It had an ornate façade with columns, arched windows and vaultings, and a domed tower. There were also "Ionic pilasters flanking recessed arches on either side of the building," which was sheathed in brick with terra-cotta ornamentation.[44] As for the neighborhood, referred to at the time as Swampoodle, it was sparsely populated around the time the stadium project was in the works as the city existed mainly as starts and stops that far north, with some of it merely a plan that could be found only on architectural drawings. Indeed, some residents of the area kept chickens and pigs in their yards.[45] As the neighborhood developed it became largely white working class, dominated by various ethnic groups, the Irish mainly, but there were also Italians, along with American-born families of Germans, Irish, Jews, and English Protestants. By World War II, the area was still white working class and predominantly populated by Irish Americans.[46]

By the time of Dick's arrival in 1963, both the stadium (which was renamed after Mack, the Athletics' manager and part owner, in 1953) and the neighborhood were vastly different. In his reminiscence of a youth spent at the stadium in the 1960s, musician and writer Lee Vilensky recalled Connie Mack as "dark, cool, and damp, and smell[ing] of mustard, urine, stale beer, and cigar smoke."[47] Caught in the middle of a tussle between Carpenter, who wanted the city to build him a new stadium, and the cash-strapped city, which had bigger problems to deal with, the stadium fell apart and was maintained only to the crudest, most bare-bones degree. In this way it reflected the surrounding neighborhood, which likewise seemed to have been abandoned by those with the means to improve things. Racially, the neighborhood became predominantly black and was considered dangerous by the white fans who trekked into it for Phillies games. As Vilensky recalled, the area was "solid ghetto, no artists' lofts in sight. There was no stadium parking, so you had to find a spot on the street and then give the neighborhood kids some money so they wouldn't break your windows."[48] Crime in the area shot up such that by the early 1960s, police reported an average of five complaints per game concerning damage done to cars.[49] The stew of a predominantly white team, owned by a white man historically indifferent to black players and fans, in the middle of a black neighborhood only accentuated the racial chasm that defined the area. Added to the mix was Dick Allen, whose arrival brought a modest influx of black fans, and tensions only increased.

Philadelphia was in many ways as segregated as southern towns, although the similarities were often hidden beneath a veneer of inclusion. (Stan Hochman once wrote that "there are parts of this town that make Alabama look liberal.")[50] Although there were no signs posted throughout the city designating certain drinking fountains "colored" or "white-only," the city was largely segregated nonetheless, although here, as was the case throughout much of the North, segregation was de facto rather than de jure.[51] The North Philadelphia neighborhood encompassing Connie Mack Stadium was routinely referred to as "the jungle," and racial mixing, outside of the uncomfortable walk by white fans from their cars to the ballpark, was largely kept to a minimum. In so many ways, North Philadelphia was a cauldron just waiting to explode.

And then it exploded.

On August 28, after an altercation between a black woman and two Philadelphia police officers, which attracted a large crowd and resulted in the arrest of the woman along with a bystander who attacked one of the officers, rumors spread that a pregnant black woman had been beaten to death by the police. Three days of rioting ensued, during which protestors torched several white-owned businesses along Columbia Avenue and other environs near the stadium. Along with the fires, looting became uncontrolled as well (in the end, 225 stores were destroyed or damaged in the course of the riot) and gunshots pierced the air. In the end, two people were dead, 339 were wounded, 308 arrested. Very quickly, the event became a political symbol.

While the mayor's office (most vocally a rising young police division captain named Frank Rizzo) along with many white residents (particularly those who had recently absconded to the suburbs) saw only chaos and disorder in the riot, many black residents saw something else. On September 1, a *Tribune* editorial declared, "The rioters and hoodlums . . . are American citizens. That fact should be driven home to all and sundry. These people are American citizens. They are what they are because America made them that way."[52] Other stories that ran within the paper over the ensuing days focused on how such an outbreak, horrifying as it may have been, was nevertheless "insignificant when measured against centuries of injustice. This is only one explosion of the social dynamite that will continue to lie ready for a spark."[53] To the *Tribune*, the rioters (which, the paper took pains to emphasize, did not constitute a majority of the city's black residents) were making a statement. One statement, however, was not made: "The only thing I regret about the riot," said one of its participants, "was that we didn't burn down the goddamn stadium. They had it surrounded by cops, and we couldn't get to it. I just wish we could've burned it down and wiped away its history that tells me I'm nothing but a nigger."[54]

By the luck of the schedule, the Phillies were out of town during the riot. When they returned on September 1, Connie Mack Stadium rattled with the aftereffects of what had just occurred. Sports journalist Arnold Hano had been commissioned by *Sport* magazine before the riot to spend a week with the club that was racing toward the National League pennant and to document what it was like to spend time with the freewheeling front-runners.[55] The agreed-upon week was to be that of September 1, the official beginning of the season's home stretch and, for the Phillies, the start of what was most likely going to be their month-long victory lap. What he saw was something else altogether: "The aftermath of a riot is, in a sense, almost more tragic than the night of violence itself. The streets had a forlorn look, empty, broken. People stayed indoors. Red police cars quietly patrolled the streets. Boards had replaced broken windows. It looked as if man had been evicted from his dwellings. The city—here—was a silent bomb shelter."[56]

Crowds, he noted, were noticeably smaller than they had been before, and beer sales were banned—in the stadium as well as in the taverns and liquor stores throughout the area. These were unfortunate developments but hardly unexpected in the aftermath of what had just occurred. Something else struck Hano, however—something he had not thought he'd see: the vicious treatment of the club's young superstar. "Every time a ball was hit to Allen, fair or foul, every time he came to bat, the crowd booed. It was not just a few hundred people, but many thousands, perhaps ten or eleven of the twelve thousand people at the game. A bellowing sound in the Philadelphia night, deep-throated, almost frightening." Sitting in the press box, Hano overheard the beat writers debate the meaning of the crowd's reaction: "Maybe," said one, "we are seeing—hearing—baseball backlash."[57] Although he quite obviously played no role in the riot himself and had been up to that point silent when it came to the city's racial politics and dynamics, Dick Allen, through the color of his skin and the way he spoke his mind, had become the symbolic face that unleashed white anxiety and discontent with the changing complexion of the city in the wake of the riot.

Everything about Dick, it seemed to many people, screamed dissent. In so many ways, he struck a stark contrast to those who occupied Connie Mack's hallowed ground before: his race, most obviously, but there was more. His socks were pulled up higher, his way of speaking was different ("new hipster" as it was called by *Sport*), and his clothes were "way-out" according to Hochman and others.[58] He exuded "black cool"—the desire to express individuality and creativity and to make a performance out of everyday acts—and it frightened white fans who saw this instead as evidence of "attitude," which was unwelcome in the homogeneous world of sports in the postwar era.[59] In the white-bread world of the 1950s and early 1960s, free expression of any sort, particularly by blacks, was synonymous with surliness, with having a chip on one's shoulder toward American morals and values. This was considered a threat, particularly in the rigidly hierarchical world of professional sports: ownership and management ran things, and strict compliance and uniformity were expected (at least publicly).[60] White superstars such as Mickey Mantle could bend the rules but that was about it. Black players, superstar or otherwise, were expected to conform, no exceptions. Dick's display of black cool was perceived as an attempt to upend the established social order, and after the riot, Connie Mack fans let him know what they thought about this every time he came to bat or when a ball was hit his way.

Dick's style of play further alienated many white fans. "Sleepy" Allen just didn't approach the game the same way his white teammates did. One teammate alleged that "it looks like he doesn't care, the way he never changes expression when he strikes out. Maybe we're jealous of his talent and expect too much. But I still feel he doesn't care about us."[61] "He had a languid look about him," Hano recalled,[62] and in a 1967 article that ran under the headline "Sleepy-Time Super-Star," the *Daily News'* Hochman wrote that Dick "marches to a mournful tune that only he hears, moving with an insolent grace." Hano and Hochman both understood, however, that looks could be—and in this case were—deceiving: "People mistake the droopy posture of his eyelids for boredom," Hochman wrote. "People think the slouch in those enormous shoulders means he doesn't give a rap."[63] Jim Murray of the *Los Angeles Times* later alleged that it was clear from Dick's demeanor both off the field as well as on it that he didn't sufficiently love the game because he didn't express himself, through words as well as actions, as the archetypical baseball icon Babe Ruth did.[64] Although Murray claimed that there was "nothing racial" about his conclusion, in fact it was all about race, although he never realized this; what turned Murray off was Dick's expression of black cool, which he interpreted as a lack of love or passion, as Murray defined those terms.

Dick wasn't the only player on the club to suffer for his individualized approach to the game that season. Vic Power, a dark-skinned Puerto Rican known for a flashy style that garnered him the nickname "the Showboat" (and who did not identify himself as black), heard it from the Connie Mack faithful as well after he was picked up in a trade with the Dodgers in early September.[65]

In actuality, beyond his clothes and manner of speech, Dick was hardly a radical. He was, as *Ebony* characterized him a few years later, a "regular brother."[66] He wasn't active in the civil rights movement, he took few if any political stands, and he almost never spoke out on issues that did not affect him personally. Yet he exuded an aura of someone who would, and he paid a heavy price for this. Though the accepted wisdom as it developed in subsequent decades asserted that Dick was publicly well received as both a player and a person for the better part of a season and a half, until his infamous run-in with teammate Frank Thomas in July 1965, the reality is that many Phillies fans developed a distaste for him much sooner. In a town that Murray once claimed would "boo a cure for cancer," none of its wrath was spared on Dick and all of it was on display during the games that followed the riot.[67] The Houston Colt .45 players who were in the visitors' dugout for that first series were appalled by what they witnessed. "I never heard anything like it," said shortstop Eddie Kasko. "What have the Philadelphia baseball fans got against Richie Allen?" asked another.[68]

Mauch claimed to be confused by the venom: "I don't understand—he has such exceptional talent and I guess they expect him to be exceptional all the time."[69] The booing and viciousness became so constant and, very quickly, so accepted that eventually it became a headline when the Phillies managed to make it through nine innings at Connie Mack *without* Dick being booed.[70] Once beer sales resumed, fans seemed to let up a bit. But then, starting on September 21, came the club's infamous collapse, and the booing returned, although this time, the fans were more democratic in their targets. Despite hitting .330 during a month when the club overall slumped to .240, Dick remained the primary target, but now his teammates were no longer spared. By the end of the month, as they were completing the infamous ten-game losing streak that would seal their doom, several players spoke openly about wanting to play anywhere but in front of their home fans: "I think everybody wants to get out of this place," said infielder Ruben Amaro. "Some of the things that happened these seven days were unbelievable. I think if we stayed here five more days—forget it. The people will be hollering here 10 years after we're gone."[71]

In the aftermath of the collapse, at least some questioned what had just occurred. "You know what I think?" asked a waitress of a *Bulletin* reporter shortly after the season ended. "I think this town doesn't deserve a pennant. I think the fans in this town are lousy. The way they booed, I think they might have caused the team to lose three or four of those games." Turning her attention to the two men standing nearby and who continued, unabated, to rain their scorn upon the club, she admonished, "You don't deserve a winner."[72] When it came to assessing fault for what was considered at the time to be the biggest meltdown in baseball history, few were spared. Seemingly everyone—management, Mauch, pitchers, relievers, starters, benchwarmers, fans, and the city as a whole—took some of the blame. In the end, it was Mauch, whose decision to overwork starting pitchers Jim Bunning and Chris Short spectacularly backfired, who bore the brunt of the blame. But over the course of the second half of the season nobody suffered the city's wrath more than the person most responsible for the fact that the club was even in contention at all: Dick Allen.

Chapter 4

What Fight?

1965: Philadelphia .302/20/85

THE 1965 SEASON was weighted down almost immediately by the simmering resentment that had fouled the second half of the 1964 campaign. For, even before the start of spring training, Dick Allen announced that he wasn't reporting to Clearwater until he received a contract to his liking. This, by itself, wasn't unusual; players had been holding out for as long as there had been spring training. And when they did, fans as well as the media often sided against the player, disparaging and ridiculing the recalcitrant holdout until he was shamed into accepting whatever meager compromise management offered (oftentimes little more than a few thousand dollars above the initial offer). Curt Flood recognized the dynamics of the holdout as elements that perpetuated the players' subjugation to management. As he wrote in his 1970 autobiography, "Baseball has managed to persuade its public that *good* players are superhumanly selfless. . . . Accordingly, a player becomes suspect when he postpones his arrival at the spring training camp while attempting to negotiate an equitable contract for himself. The delay in his conditioning supposedly endangers the Club. This betrays him as more concerned with his own good than with the Good of the Game. No *good* player behaves like that. Players who do can count on getting the works from the press."[1]

Worse, for decades, the players themselves had bought into this rhetoric (or "fable," as Flood termed it). Marvin Miller, the executive director of the Players Association, summed up the genesis of this mind-set: "From time immemorial, the baseball powers-that-be force-fed the players propaganda: The commissioner (although appointed and paid by the owners) represented the players; players were privileged to be paid to play a kid's game; and (the biggest fairy tale of all) baseball was not a business and, in any case, was unprofitable for the owners."[2] When he arrived on the scene in 1966, Miller stressed that "when a player feels that a contract offer is less than he deserves, the only recourse he has is to hold out."[3] It was all he could do to convince the players that their union was "not a social club."[4] Miller believed that an adversarial relationship was not only inevitable but necessary if the players were going to break the cycle of being pushed around every year come contract time.

As for the media, Flood realized that they were largely ignorant as to the realities confronting the professional athlete: "An astonishingly high proportion of our sports reporters become incensed when a young man with a career expectancy of five years undermines the Good of the Game by holding out for a $25,000 salary."[5] Although, at the time, most reporters earned significantly less than this, Flood pointed out that "a young reporter's career expectancy might well be forty years. If he decides to leave newspapering, or is discharged, his education and experience qualify him to enter a related field at no loss of pay. . . . the washed-up player often confronts a dead end."[6] All of this explained why a player such as Joe DiMaggio might hold out, as he did in 1938, as well as why he was eviscerated in the press for doing so. (As a further insult, DiMaggio's holdout yielded him nothing: he eventually signed for $25,000—the same amount offered to him initially.) In this respect, Dick's holdout was a continuation of this tradition.

In a larger sense, however, Dick's holdout was a sharp break from the ones that preceded it, in that he was not merely seeking more money, he was calling into question the entire salary structure of Major League Baseball. After winning the Rookie of the Year award in 1964, Dick attempted to monetize it via the Phillies come contract time. When General Manager

John Quinn mailed him his contract for the upcoming season (for $10,000—no more than he made as a rookie),[7] Dick refused to adhere to even the time-honored negotiation pas de deux of returning it unsigned; he tossed it in the trash instead. "I gave him my figure," he said. "That's all I can do, tell him what I want. The general manager has all the moxie, from years of experience." After being informed that baseball tradition (to which an old-school type like Quinn stridently adhered) frowned on large salary hikes for younger, less experienced players, Dick was hardly swayed: "Why separate me because it's my second year? Why should they deal differently with guys up here 10 years? It's the big leagues, isn't it?" As he was coming to realize, baseball executives were preaching a never-ending waiting game for players with the expectation that most of them would be washed out of the majors before ever cashing in. "In the minors, when I asked for a raise they'd say 'Wait until you get to the majors . . . that's where you'll make the money.'"[8] Now that he had arrived, he saw that things hadn't changed. "Well, I made it. I had a good year and I want to get what I think I'm worth. They say I should wait some more."[9]

Very quickly it was clear that Quinn and Dick were talking at cross-purposes. While Quinn, who had "the reputation of dealing sternly with young players and generously with veterans," repeatedly harped on "baseball tradition" as it applied to player contracts, Dick focused instead on the realities of the game's economics. "I have tried," said an exasperated Quinn, "to explain to Allen that consistency and experience are needed to get the kind of salary he's asking for. We don't think that happens after one year. We think he's asking too much after one year."[10] Dick disagreed: "You get paid on performance and value to the team . . . they drew 1,000,000 people. I know that one or two of those people came to see me."[11] As for the errors and strikeouts that detractors claimed devalued his accomplishments, Dick replied pragmatically: "They didn't hurt the gate."[12] Presaging Flood, he spoke of the injustice of the game's salary structure: "He [Quinn] talks about being paid for experience. You see guys sit round for six, seven, eight years and never have a .300 year. Yet they're getting $30,000 just for being around. I can't agree with that. It's a fight to get to the top. If you have a good year, you're supposed to get paid for it. He says a career isn't made in one year and I say it can all end in one day." From Dick's perspective, while he was trying to speak rationally about baseball and finances, Quinn refused to budge from his dusty script. "I gave him my figure," said Dick, "and he gave me the old rigmarole."[13]

Reporters and Dick's teammates alike criticized his holdout and leaned on him to return. Fellow infielder Cookie Rojas complained that the holdout was hurting the club's chances of getting out of the gate quickly in 1965, while old-school beat writer Allen Lewis of the *Inquirer* stoked public resentment by writing that the holdout "may affect the Phillies' pennant chances in the National League race."[14] An unnamed older pitcher claimed to speak for the club's veterans when he suggested that Dick had been "given some bad advice" with regard to holding out. "You just can't expect to jump that far in one year," the pitcher said. "Rich is trying to buck a system which has been around a long while—that you're underpaid on the way up and overpaid on the way down. It's a system which has worked pretty well for a long time."[15] Despite the mounting pressure as the days passed, Dick would not give in. "My family has set the price," he said, "and Mr. Quinn won't meet it. I can't back down because it's out of my hands. I guess I'll just sit here and grow my beard."[16]

That Dick's black teammate Wes Covington joined in the holdout—they were the only two holdouts that preseason—exacerbated the matter of race. Although Covington never claimed to have a higher purpose in his dealings with management ("Look man, I'm not out to start a civil war. All I want is a fair shake"),[17] whispers out of the Phillies' camp hinted of a "Negro conspiracy" and suggested that Covington was orchestrating Dick's holdout from behind the scenes.[18] "Sure I give the kids advice," Covington said later. "I've learned a lot of things, a lot which have helped me stay in the majors. . . . Today, because of the experience I have picked up no manager can bother me."[19] Although considered the de facto team captain of the club's black players, Covington (along with Dick) denied that any such conspiracy or backroom maneuvering ever took place.[20]

In truth, like Covington, Dick simply wanted what he thought was his. Not only did he see professional baseball as a job, he saw it as one with some unsettling historical parallels. For decades, management and (white) players alike compared baseball's labor relations under the game's reserve clause, oftentimes jokingly, with slavery. However, given that salaries were involved and the labor at issue was baseball and not field work, the connection was always made benignly: "You do not hear many of the players complain of being bought and sold, do you?" said Connie Mack in 1912. "They seem pretty happy in their so-called slavery."[21] White players might not make the connection in real-world terms, but many black players saw things through an altogether different lens.

When it came to salary and slavery, black players such as Dick, Wes Covington, and later Curt Flood recognized associations that their white counterparts and the white media missed. This was particularly true given the tenor of the times: the heart of the civil rights movement. In a meditation on baseball's salary structure a few years later, *Ebony* suggested that the modern black player was a mere rube when it came to contract negotiation and oftentimes unwittingly complicit in his own oppression: "Generally young and poor, he is the 'unsophisticate' of the pro sports world. His 'college professors' after he finished high school were the old coaches of minor league baseball back in Tidewater, Waterbury and Danville and they unfortunately had taught him how to play ball 'for' but never 'with' the front office." Aside from the few "gutsy holdouts," most players, the piece concluded, got the shaft, succumbing to management's tired refrain that it was years of service that mattered rather than the notion "of paying a baseball player a reasonable salary for what he is worth *today*." Reflecting on Dick's penchant for holding out, *Ebony* praised him as one of the few trailblazers in the game: "Allen's courage, as well as his physical talent and intelligence, enable him to say more about his professional worth than most players." Standing up for oneself like Dick did had to do with more than just money, the piece concluded. It was, underneath it all, an issue of respect, of human dignity.[22]

Rather than be recognized as heroes or role models for their willingness to stand up for themselves, black players were constantly admonished for having any opinions at all regarding their professional lives. Flood wrote that fans would stop him and lecture him on the nature of his privileged life, telling him that without baseball, he'd most likely be "chopping cotton or pushing a broom."[23] Dick heard this as well. "Listen," he once said, "[a]ny time a black guy says something about his job, they say, 'Well, it beats pushing a broom' or something."[24] In the end, wrote Flood, the prevailing opinion was that "any black hurts his people if he is other than abjectly, supinely, hand-lickingly grateful for having been allowed to earn a decent living."[25] The *Tribune* was attuned to this dynamic and took pains from 1965 onward to compare the feats of the city's recognized hero, Johnny Callison, with those of its presumed villain, Dick Allen. In May, it noted that while the black holdouts were off to fast starts, "glory boy" Callison was "having trouble getting wood on the ball." Drawing the attention of its readers to his salary, the *Tribune* story highlighted that "Callison, a $40,000 per season outfielder, is batting .188, with four home runs and 11 RBIs."[26]

Finally, after several weeks of contentious back-and-forth, Quinn threw up his arms in mid-March and bowed out of the negotiations, turning them over to owner Bob Carpenter. Dick responded to the switch immediately: "It was the first time I've talked to him [Carpenter] since I signed. I felt sort of honored, like I meant something to them."[27] The next day he agreed to terms on a contract for approximately $20,000—double his 1964 salary. Still, he was not happy. "My mother wanted me to do it for Mr. Ogden," he said. "Mr. Ogden is the best friend I have in baseball. He calls me every day during the season, writes me letters a couple of times a week. He kept telling me I shouldn't miss any more spring training. So I came down here for him."[28] He chafed at any suggestion that his shortened spring training might affect his preparation for the season: "I'm in shape. I've been riding my quarter-horse Angel. It will take me four days to get my eye in shape and I'll be okay. Spring training is too long anyway. Back in '38 and '39, spring training only lasted three or four days."[29]

Although Dick had returned, he made it clear that not all was well; a rift had opened up between him and Quinn that was not likely to be repaired soon: "Quinn said I was getting bad advice when I told him what I wanted. Huh. I haven't had bad advice in 23 years from my family. . . . the man holds on to the money like it's his. I'd rather talk to Mr. Carpenter. He's fair."[30] So as to make it clear to anyone who didn't fully grasp the extent of his pique, Dick arrived thirty-five minutes late to the official contract signing the following day.[31] When asked to explain how he felt upon finally agreeing to terms, he challenged the premise of the question itself: "My mom agreed to terms, not me."[32] As for how he felt, he said he was beaten down: "I understand now about the 'sophomore jinx.' They

Dick and John Quinn in Clearwater, March 15, 1965,
shortly after Dick's return from his holdout.

(© 2014 Legendaryauctions.com)

get a man down where he don't really care. It's not the sophomore jinx, it's the general manager's jinx." He also reiterated once more his stance on the nature of professional compensation: "If you worked for me all week and sold meat at a pretty good clip, you'd expect the 'dust' on Fridays—not three days from Friday or three months from Friday."[33]

Although the saga was now over, Dick made it clear that it was only over for now: "This is the last time I let my mom and Mr. Ogden set the figure.[34] . . . If I have a good year and we win a pennant, I'm not taking anybody's advice. Rich Allen will make up his own mind and stick with it."[35] By this point, nobody doubted his resolve. The battle lines had been drawn and Opening Day was still three weeks away.

* * *

All of this—the Rookie of the Year flap, the reaction to him in the after-math of the riot, and the bad blood caused by his holdout—were just the warm-ups for the main event: Dick's July 3 batting practice altercation with teammate Frank Thomas and the fallout that ensued. The incident is bathed in the half-light of the recollections of those who saw only pieces of it, those who saw none of it but claim that they did, and those who saw all of it but didn't understand what they saw until years later. The Phillies' beat writers, who were all congregated in Mauch's cramped Connie Mack Stadium office at the time, were most assuredly in the second category.[36] Regardless, many of them wrote about it afterward as though they had had ringside seats. Whatever happened around the batting cage as the Phils were taking their pregame hacks, it did not occur out of the blue, as the white press would contend in the immediate aftermath.

Frank Thomas was, at this stage of his career, a utility infielder/out-fielder who had been picked up by the Phillies during the 1964 stretch run. He provided a valuable bat off the bench, but there was much more to him than that. *Bulletin* sportswriter Sandy Grady wrote, "They called him the Big Donkey because Frank Thomas has always owned two spec-tacular talents. He could hit a baseball out of any ball yard yet invented by man. And he had an uncanny knack for saying the wrong thing at the wrong time to the wrong guy."[37] Thomas's second talent was on display more often during his short tenure with the Phils than was his first. Affec-tionately termed a "needler" by some, others, such as teammate Ryne Duren, considered him to be flat-out obnoxious: "When he gets on a guy he never knows when to stop. . . . Thomas doesn't seem to realize how he rubs people the wrong way."[38] Catcher Pat Corrales remembered him as a "tough bully type," and even Thomas himself freely admitted that "I'm one of the biggest agitators around, always have been."[39] He was also a reliable interview, recalled the *Daily News'* Larry Merchant, who remem-bered him as "a loosey-goosey, happy-go-lucky, go-to guy for quotes."[40] Although he claimed that "I never try to hurt anybody" and that he nee-dled merely in an attempt "to try to keep the club loose," some, particu-larly Dick, perceived a darker motivation. "He would pretend to offer his hand in a soul shake to a young player on the team," Dick recalled later, "but when the player would offer his hand in return, Thomas would grab the player's thumb and bend it back hard. To Thomas this was a big joke.

But I saw too many brothers on the team with swollen thumbs to get any laughs."[41]

Thomas managed to get under Dick's skin with his thumb-bending act, and he pierced it during a road trip to Chicago in early June. As Corrales recalled it, "He [Thomas] had been picking on Johnny Briggs [a twenty-one-year-old black outfielder], saying 'Boy this' and 'Boy that.' Dick didn't go for that, and there were some words between them."[42] Dick himself had been on the receiving end of similar barbs and had warned Thomas to lay off: "The needling by Thomas went way back," Dick recalled shortly after the altercation itself. "Frank said, 'Boy, pick up my bat for me,' 'Boy, shine my shoes for me.' Things like that. I warned Frank to stay off my back."[43] The Big Donkey didn't get the message.

Twelve days after the Briggs incident, the club landed in Los Angeles. At the airport, Thomas started up again. "We were at the airport in Los Angeles," recalled Dick, "Thomas flipped me a quarter and said, 'Hey, boy, take my bags!' He was only joking and didn't really mean any harm. But I was only 22 and I wasn't ready yet for that kind of humor."[44]

Two weeks later, on Saturday, July 3, Thomas was in Big Donkey mode yet again, and this time, Dick erupted. As for precisely what happened, nobody can be certain; there were few non-uniformed witnesses, and the players who were there, outside of Thomas, clammed up initially and refused to provide specifics. But the basics of the altercation eventually emerged. In his autobiography, Dick recalled that Thomas was in the cage after what had been a tough night for him: he failed three times to get a bunt down with runners on first and third. When he swung and missed during his turn at batting practice, Callison took the opportunity to needle the needler: "Hey Lurch!" said Callison, referencing Thomas's unfortunate resemblance to the manservant on *The Addams Family*. "You rang?" replied Thomas. "Why don't you try to bunt instead?"[45] Although Thomas liked to disparage those who "can dish it out but can't take it," on this occasion he was in no mood to let the comment pass.[46] Rather than respond to Callison, however, Thomas turned his gaze toward Dick and challenged him. As Dick recalled the exchange in his autobiography, Thomas yelled: "What are you trying to be, another Muhammad Clay, always running your mouth off?"[47] Earlier, though, Dick had spoken to Bill Conlin about the incident, and while the basics of the exchange were the same, the specificities of the language were different. "He told me," Conlin recalled, "Thomas triggered the actual fight itself by yelling from the batting cage, 'Mind your business you Black Mohammedan Son of a Bitch.' I have also read or heard Thomas yelled, 'What are you trying to be, another Muhammad Clay.' While a brilliant malaprop, that hardly has the ring of something that would start Allen running toward the batting cage."[48] Dick also intimated something similar to *Jet* in 1972: "Whether he called me a 'nigger s.o.b.' or not, the fact is, I'm not going to be an s.o.b. for anybody."[49] The most contemporaneous account of Dick's version of what was said probably came from Era. A few days after the fight, she (after presumably speaking with her son) told Ric Roberts of the *Pittsburgh Courier* that Thomas twice called him a "black bastard."[50]

Thomas's take on the incident was markedly different. The day after it occurred, he gave his version to the *Inquirer*'s Lewis: "When I went into the batting cage, Richie yelled from down around third base, 'Do what you did last night.' I missed a pitch and he's laughing at me. Then I fouled off a bunt, and then bunted down the third-base line. At that, he yelled, 'That's 21 hours too late.' They were laughing just like a while back when I was at third base and somebody hit one at me in batting practice just as I turned around. It hit off both my legs as I reached down for it. They're laughing like anything. I had to go in and put ice on my legs, though I wouldn't give them the satisfaction of rubbing them out on the field. . . . He started calling me 'Lurch,' and we yelled back and forth, and that's when I said, 'You're getting just like Cassius Clay—Muhammad Clay— always running your mouth off.' "[51]

Whatever Thomas yelled, it set off what was to come next. Dick recalled that Thomas thought Dick had made the Lurch reference as well as the disparaging comment that followed it.[52] Although Callison was standing next to Dick, he kept mum after hearing Thomas's response directed toward Dick rather than him. John Ogden recalled that "when [Callison] wouldn't own up, Allen didn't say anything. He refused to point the finger at [him]."[53] Instead, things escalated between Thomas and Dick within seconds. As Dick remembered it, Thomas followed up with "There's no fence around me, 15. You may get a meal out of me, but I'll get a sandwich out of you."[54] So, after being compared to Ali, Dick "tried to mimic the world heavyweight champion by throwing some combinations at the utilityman," wrote Claude Harrison.[55] Unfortunately for Dick, because this was batting practice and because Thomas was still in the cage, he had his bat in his hand. After Dick hit Thomas in the chest, Thomas swung the bat and connected with Dick's left shoulder. "I was surprised," Thomas told Lewis. "I had the bat in my hand and I hit him in the left shoulder. It was just a reflex action."[56] The blow struck Dick in more ways than one: "Thomas," he said later, "broke the ballplayers' rule by hitting me with a bat."[57] Dick then flew into a rage and responded with a barrage of punches. Eventually he was wrestled off of Thomas by several of his teammates (one of whom, Ruben Amaro, took a punch himself in the chaos). Whatever the specifics of the blow-by-blow, it was "a helluva fight between large and powerful men."[58]

In the aftermath, most of the local daily and national media painted Dick as the aggressor and expressed sympathy for the quotable journeyman Thomas, who was placed on irrevocable waivers by the Phils after that evening's game (in which Thomas pinch-hit and hit a home run). Despite categorizing Thomas's swing at Allen as "vicious," the *Bulletin* contained an emboldened subheading stressing that "Allen Lands First Punch."[59] Dick was further characterized by the papers as a poor sport in that much was made of the fact that he refused to accept Thomas's apology.[60] Although he later claimed to have made up with Thomas and said that he and Thomas even exchanged Christmas cards for a while many years later, at the time, Dick was not in a forgiving mood. "When he walked into the dressing room at Connie Mack Stadium and apologized," Dick said a couple of weeks after the fight, "I was hurting. He hit me on the shoulder with the bat and to tell you the truth I was hurting so I had to restrain myself to keep from going after him again."[61] At one point after the game a *Bulletin* photographer entered the clubhouse and asked Mauch if he could get the two men together for a picture. Mauch replied: "If you've got enough guts to get those two together, you're welcome to try."[62]

As bad as the fight was, it was, above all else, simply a fight between teammates, perhaps a particularly ugly one given the racial undertones, but such fights had occurred before. What separated this one from all those others was what the club did in the aftermath: it not only released

Thomas (along with a statement from Quinn asserting that doing so was "in the best interests of the ball club"), it placed a gag order on Dick (along with the rest of the team), threatening him with a substantial fine if he spoke to the media about it (any Phillie caught speaking to the press about it would be fined $1,500; if Dick were caught, his fine would be $2,500).[63] Perhaps, after witnessing the media backlash after his comments concerning the Rookie of the Year award as well as the very public tussle between Dick and Quinn over his 1965 contract, the club was concerned that anything Dick might say this time could blow the incident into an even bigger event. As such, and claiming to act in his best interests, it instructed him to sit back and say nothing, no matter what.[64] Thus, after the fight, while the newly released, media-friendly Thomas, unencumbered by any gag orders, was giving, and tweaking, his version of the altercation over and over again, all Dick would say in the immediate aftermath was "what fight?"[65] Very quickly, Dick realized that just like its decision to place him in Little Rock two years earlier, the organization was hardly capable of looking out for him. Rather, and as he learned once more, it was not to be trusted.

In the ensuing days and weeks, Thomas spoke to anyone who would listen, demonstrating contriteness and stressing his attempted apologies. Later he began lashing out, claiming that Dick "cost me my job."[66] He also claimed, somewhat remarkably for the Big Donkey, that he had attempted to apologize to Dick before the physical altercation even started.[67] Over and over he claimed that his release was unfair and that Dick had simply taken his comments "the wrong way."[68] Meanwhile, as Thomas recast himself as the victim, Dick stood by, mute. Even as he said nothing, however, the public perception grew that Dick had said quite a lot behind the scenes.

Many white fans suspected that Thomas's release was not the decision of Phils' management. If it had been up to Quinn and Carpenter, they believed, Thomas, the club's valuable pinch hitter, would still be on the roster. Indeed, the *Bulletin*'s Sandy Grady—the most authoritative journalistic voice in town—was adamant that, as a baseball move, it was foolhardy to say the least: "The needle is gone, but the bat went with it. Frank Thomas may not be the only one in this untidy scene who will regret a flash reaction."[69] Since the move made little baseball sense, these fans concluded (without any hard evidence) that it must have been dictated by Dick himself, who, they were convinced, obviously had made an ultimatum to management. Letters and phone calls poured into the Phillies' offices, complaining of Thomas's release and blaming Dick for the move that put the club's pennant hopes in jeopardy. "Out of a population of six million," Quinn remarked to Grady in an attempt to put the avalanche of protest into perspective, "it is a small percentage."[70] Dick's continuing silence only served as confirmation of their suspicions.

It didn't take long for these fans to reach all of these conclusions. The very next night, Dick was greeted with a chorus of boos. Some fans were more specific, yelling "Nigger" and "Go back to South Street with the monkeys."[71] Others threw things at him from the stands.[72] A few days later, as the booing, name-calling, and pelting continued, Dick expressed concern and dismay: "I don't know why they're booing. I don't want to know . . . I didn't cost [Thomas] his job. I'm not the general manager."[73] Grady wrote: "Some men draw drama to themselves as the lone tree pulls lightning. Allen has the knack. For four evenings in the humid shoebox, the clients booed his every move."[74] They booed him as he took the field only a few hours after being named to the All-Star team; they booed him every time he stepped up to the plate or when a ball was hit his way. For several days the onslaught slackened only briefly—they cheered when he doubled and tripled during a July 7 game against the Pirates and when he smashed a mammoth grand slam off the scoreboard the next evening against the Giants—but then quickly and ferociously resumed as though it had never abated.[75]

The intimidation was not limited to the ballpark; Dick and his wife, Barbara, also experienced it at home. A couple of days after the fight, while Dick was riding his horse in Fairmount Park, Barbara picked up the phone and listened as an anonymous voice threatened: "We're going to get your husband. We know where he rides his horse and we'll wait for him. When we get through, he'll never play baseball again."[76] Other fans threw chicken bones on his lawn and tore up his grass with their cars.[77]

Even with the passage of time, Dick was never able to process the source of the fans' anger. This was particularly true given that only a month after his altercation with Thomas, there was another baseball altercation involving a bat that played out quite differently. As Dick viewed it,

"A month or so after the Thomas thing, Juan Marichal [of the Giants] hit Johnny Roseboro [of the Dodgers] with a bat at home plate and they damn near ran Marichal out of baseball. But in my case, Thomas's decision to use his bat as a weapon was *underplayed*. Instead Mauch silenced me with the threat of a fine."[78] A couple of years after the incident Frank Bilovsky of the *Bulletin* wrote: "In any other city, people who hit other people with baseball bats are ranked near criminals. In Philadelphia, Thomas was a hero."[79]

For several days, Dick followed club orders and remained silent, even as Era pleaded with him to speak out: "Let the booing Philadelphia fans know that Frank Thomas twice called you a 'black b......d' before you found it impossible not to strike back," she told the *Pittsburgh Courier*.[80] The most Dick would do was appear on Pittsburgh television with Pirates' broadcaster Bob Prince after the club's July 7 game and tell the folks back in Wampum that "I'm sorry about the whole thing. I'm really sorry. I should have thought it over. . . . In the heat of a pennant race tempers flare. I know it won't happen again." He also said that he didn't accept Thomas's apology "because I was still mad." As for the published accounts of the incident, he contended that they were inaccurate but he refused to correct the record: "I don't want to say anything that might hurt him to get a job."[81]

Although Dick refused to comment, the *Tribune* did not: the paper ran an editorial a week after the fight, reminding its readers of the point Dick had made earlier: "Allen did not fire Thomas." The editorial concluded that "the constant booing of Allen by the fans indicates a deep-seated feeling that some people have against Negroes having complete equality. It is questionable that Thomas would have been so severely booed as is Allen."[82] Claude Harrison tackled the issue more directly, noting that the fans' reaction in this instance was in keeping with historical precedent: "PHILADELPHIA is the city where Roy Campanella's bid to sell his catching wares to the Phillies was rejected. Not because his ability was short of major league standards but because he was a Negro. PHILADELPHIA is the city where Jackie Robinson, in his first season with the Brooklyn Dodgers, was hooted and booed by the biased fans at Connie Mack Stadium, then Shibe Park. PHILADELPHIA was the last National League city to hire Negro ballplayers." As a direct consequence of all of this, Harrison contended, "PHILADELPHIA, I'm willing to bet, is the only city where heaven and earth are being upended in an effort to make a super star out of an average player [Johnny Callison]."[83]

As sobering as Harrison's and the *Tribune*'s words were, they swayed few because the limited circulation of the paper meant that it was largely preaching to the choir. Its readers already knew of the club's troubled racial past; it had been covered, almost exclusively, within the *Tribune*'s pages a decade earlier. And many of them had long since suspected Callison of being yet another in a long line of average white ballplayers trumpeted as something else altogether by the club and the daily press. They weren't the ones most in need of a counterbalancing viewpoint. Unfortunately, diversity of perspective on matters of race was impossible to achieve given the racial demographics of the newsrooms of the era. "There were very few black sportswriters during my time," Dick told the *Tribune* many years later. "A lot of misconceptions stemmed from the sportswriters. They were young and they were trying to make a name for themselves. The '60s were a changing time and here I come after Jackie Robinson and the print media went and took after me; they did everything except respect my playing dignity."[84]

Those in the stands booing and throwing things were receiving their information from the daily press and the national media, which were insistent that a racial angle did not exist at all, or at least nothing that required much introspection. Sandy Grady quickly and lightly brushed over the racial issue and concluded that releasing Thomas was a mistake merely because the loss of his bat might hurt the Phils' chances down the stretch. The message that might be sent to the club's black players by keeping Thomas on the roster in the incident's aftermath (to say nothing of the potential damage to the organization's already tenuous stature within the black community) did not enter into his calculation. Nationally, the *New York Daily News*' Dick Young concluded bluntly that when it came to baseball fights, irrespective of race, all that really mattered was who was the star and who wasn't. Add in the racial element and Young conceded that "racial undertones" could be at play but to him, all of the problems stemmed from the "ultra-sensitivity" of black players. In assessing a similar altercation, this one between a white coach and a black player, Young contended that although the white coach, Houston's Clint

Courtney, called outfielder Lee Maye a "black unprintable," it was not the "unprintable" that was the problem. "The key word was not the unprintable one; the key word is black." White players, Young felt, were as they always were. Black players such as Dick were a break from the black players who came before. Accordingly, Young preached to his readers, the fault for any interracial altercation had to lie solely with the new generation of black players.[85]

Years afterward Dick would look back at the fight and lay the majority of the blame for how he was treated in its aftermath with the press, which he claimed incited the fans to boo him.[86] Although there was not an outright campaign by the beat writers, along with the national press, to encourage readers to torch the young third baseman, they did seem to take pains to present a portrait of the incident that left fans few alternatives other than to blame Dick, although they perhaps painted this portrait only inadvertently. Leading the charge was Larry Merchant of the *Daily News*, an original Chipmunk reporter—an informal consortium of new-age sports journalists who were upending the sports pages of the era through their reporting of more than simply the goings-on between the foul lines. "We tried to show the human side of the game," Merchant recalled. "Or the complexities or controversies that would sometimes arise within the game. A lot of writers back in the day wrote as fans—happy when the team won, angry when the team lost. We were determined just to be reporters."[87] In their reporting of the Thomas incident, part of the story eluded them, however. Immediately, Merchant supported Mauch's view of the altercation and claimed that on a club such as the Phillies, "as harmonious a melting pot of people as there exists in sports," Thomas's "Muhammad Clay" reference "had no racial connotation whatsoever."[88]

As for where the blame lay, Merchant was acerbic and confident in his columns, positive that he had the story and that it was that Dick was a temperamental man-child; the Thomas incident only exposed him for what he was: "The irony of Thomas' dismissal is that it probably will have the opposite effect as intended. Far from protecting Allen, it exposes him nakedly as a kid who caused a veteran to lose his job. . . . Allen resents authority, and he admits it." Regarding Thomas, Merchant portrayed the bat-wielding benchwarmer sympathetically: "To his credit, Thomas had the grace to apologize for wielding the bat. Allen has coyly denied that anything even happened. Kids will be kids."[89] To Merchant, the incident revealed more about Dick than it did the man who came at him with a bat.

After Dick spoke to Pirates' broadcaster Bob Prince, Merchant rebutted him, claiming that Dick was being disingenuous when he alleged that Thomas's account of the fight was inaccurate. Merchant countered that "[e]yewitnesses have substantiated Thomas' version" without expanding on who these additional eyewitnesses were or providing confirmatory details.[90] A couple of days later, he refused to accept responsibility for playing at least some role in the booing, name-calling, and strafing of Dick that was now occurring nonstop at Connie Mack Stadium: "It wasn't the sportswriters who started the brawl. If anyone hurt Richie Allen's reputation it was Richie Allen."[91] Other writers, while not going to the lengths Merchant did, similarly downplayed the racial component of both the fight and the public reaction to it, contending that it was a baseball issue more than a social one. On the surface, it might have appeared to have been exactly that. "Dick Stuart once said that in Philadelphia they boo parades," Merchant recalled. "There was [just] a sense of the angry Philadelphia fan."[92] But in this instance there were additional layers that informed everything: the fight as well as its aftermath. It was here where the daily press swung and missed.

As for why, in the middle of the civil rights movement, the daily press repeatedly brushed aside the racial component inherent in the incident is anybody's guess. The old-school writers such as Ray Kelly of the *Bulletin* and Allen Lewis of the *Inquirer* were merely doing what they had always done: focusing on the game itself and ignoring locker room politics and broader social context. This was the tradition handed down to them from the sportswriting icons of their youth and which they proudly carried into their professional careers. But the younger generation, Chipmunks such as Larry Merchant and Sandy Grady, prided themselves on reporting more than simply the goings-on between the white lines. Here, however, they held back. Perhaps they simply did not see the racial issue. But perhaps they did and were frightened by the implications. Coming on the heels of the 1964 riot, along with the recent outbreak of racial violence in many other cities (Rochester, New York, Jersey City, Paterson, Elizabeth, and Chicago in 1964 alone), perhaps they decided that playing up the racial angle here was the equivalent of playing with gunpowder—one spark could blow everything right to hell. Given the racial tensions that still simmered across the nation (indeed, only a month later, the Phils would land in Los Angeles in the middle of the Watts riots; Mauch ordered his players to crouch below the windows as the team bus passed through Compton on its way to the Ambassador Hotel as snipers had been spotted on the overpasses[93]), perhaps they concluded that it was their job, seeing as they did their job as more than mere ink-stained fans, to keep a lid on things. And so they did. Or at least they tried. For sure, Merchant was no neophyte when it came to the intersection of sports and race and was not one to view the sports world as an insular one, untouched by societal issues: "A couple of years before I went to the *Daily News*, I was the sports editor—a one-man sports staff—of the *Wilmington* [North Carolina] *Daily News*," Merchant recalled. "It was my first professional job. Some months into my time there, I was told that if Jackie Robinson hits five home runs in a game, I could use his photo. Otherwise, they didn't put photos of black people in the paper. And I quit."[94] Here, though, he either didn't see the racial angle or didn't want to see it.

In avoiding it, however, and by refusing to acknowledge the racial implications and undertones of the incident, Merchant and his cohorts only succeeded, ironically, in making them more pronounced. For if Thomas's remarks to Dick in the batting cage were not racially charged, then the subsequent confrontation between them made no sense whatsoever; removing the racial undertones left no rational explanation as to why Dick charged Thomas and hit him in the chest. Without the perceived racial barb, all the public was left with after digesting Merchant's columns in the days following the fight (along with Dick Young's national diatribe) was an image of a crazy, irrational, hypersensitive black man attacking a white man for no reason. And this as well was racial to the core.

From their perches on the beat, the baseball writers of the city's three dailies presented to their readers a simplified, blinkered explanation of what occurred on July 3. Reflecting back, from a half century's distance, Merchant spoke as a man resigned to the reality that perhaps there was more to the story than what he and his colleagues stressed at the time. "Ali was in the air. The women's movement, the anti-Vietnam movement, the civil rights movement, all of that was percolating at the time. I don't know how you directly connect all those dots . . . but Thomas's comment to Allen that he was becoming another 'Muhammad Clay' was a way of saying 'You're a black loudmouth.' Is that racial? Yes. Is it racist? I don't think so, but it's racial. How can you deny that?" Fifty years later, with all of the background now filled in, Merchant had come to understand that Thomas's "Muhammad Clay" reference was not benign after all, concluding, "There was a racial element involved in that."[95] In retrospect, perhaps on this occasion it was a matter of things spiraling out of control, not only for those at the center of the story but for those covering it as well. "It all seemed to happen so quickly," Merchant recalled. "In a flash. Virtually overnight. As far as we knew, we knew the story. The subtexts, the background, came out piecemeal over the years."[96]

While it is perhaps unfair to look back a half century hence and lament what was not written, it is fair to note that in the black press, the altercation was viewed quite differently and, in some quarters, was believed to constitute proof of long-awaited racial progress in light of the event's immediate aftermath. In his column in the *Chicago Defender* ten days after the fight, A. S. Doc Young wrote: "As shoddy as was the incident, however, one discerns some good. It proved once more that sports are way ahead of the rest of the country when in the area of working democracy. A Negro slugged a white man, was slugged back, and the white man got fired. It would never have happened in the South; at least, not outside sports."[97] Given how the sports departments of the *Inquirer*, the *Daily News*, and the *Bulletin* were staffed at the time, and notwithstanding Merchant's experience at the *Wilmington Daily News*, such a perspective was unlikely to be expressed within their pages. The three dailies were monochrome outfits and would remain that way for decades; Thom Greer, at the *Daily News*, became the city's first black sportswriter at any of them in 1978 although he was never assigned the prestigious baseball beat. The *Bulletin* was shuttered in 1982 without ever assigning a black writer to cover the Phillies. The *Daily News* broke ground in 2002 when Marcus Hayes became the city's first black writer on the Phillies' beat. As of 2015, the *Inquirer* had yet to follow suit.

Dick came away from his altercation with Thomas a changed man. In following the club's orders not to speak, not to give his version of the incident itself, along with the long and ugly backstory, Dick found himself at the mercy of the beat writers whose stories only encouraged a fan base already angry and bitter over the changing face of their city. Dick would often reflect on the machinations of this incident and would invariably come to the same conclusion every time: "The Phillies," he would bemoan, "have done nothing to help me."[98] In the end, and as he came to learn, it wasn't the fight itself that was the problem: "Hell, Willie Mays has had fights with guys. Hank Aaron and Rico Carty got in a fight in a plane and nobody says nothing. Man, Gene Mauch actually called players into his office and invited them to rumble with him. Thousands of other ballplayers have had disagreements. But my thing went on for some six or seven years."[99] The fight lasted all of a few seconds; the aftershocks never seemed to subside.

On the field, the altercation seemed to have had an impact as well. Batting a league-leading .341 at the time of the fight, Dick cooled considerably over the season's final three months. Still, he ended the season at .302—ninth best in the National League. More important, he remained as he was: the club's best chance for victory on most nights. With the pennant all but lost by September and a first division finish the most Phillie fans could wish for, Mauch understood that the only way to get there was to ensure that Dick stepped up to the plate as often as possible; he moved him up to second in the order and then, finally, into the leadoff spot. Both the club and Dick thrived for a time (Dick hit .333 as a leadoff hitter), but it was too little too late—the club finished in sixth place anyway. Regardless, fans treated to an extra at-bat by what was now unquestionably one of the game's most dynamic players were able to experience something during his plate appearances that was receding rapidly whenever his teammates dug in: hope. The fog of the Thomas fight and its repercussions settled in nevertheless, straining an already stressed relationship that would ultimately culminate in the exit of the club's most exciting player. If only, he said upon reflection years later, "they would have let me clear the air around here . . . maybe I never would have had to leave."[100]

Chapter 5

Rules

1966: Philadelphia .317/40/110

DESPITE THE THOMAS incident and the shoulder bruise that went along with it, Dick played out the season, establishing himself along the way as one of the game's premier tape measure sluggers with several of his moonshots over the first two years of his career traveling farther than 450 feet.[1] He also cemented his early reputation as a "gamer," compiling a consecutive game streak that reached 317 (all 162 games in 1964 plus the first 155 of 1965) before he finally begged off in late September. Although the *Tribune* reported that the streak's end was caused by an "upset stomach,"[2] the dailies dug deeper, with the *Daily News'* Stan Hochman reporting that Dick "showed up late" to a late September game against the Cubs, "got dressed and went out to take batting practice. Then came a closed door conversation with Mauch. Then he changed clothes and left." Though Mauch did his best to provide cover, saying, "He felt kind of funny when he got here, and he didn't feel good after he hit. We decided it was best that he see a doctor and get some rest. I think it's just an upset stomach," Hochman wasn't convinced. "If it took Allen 14 minutes (the length of his meeting with Mauch) to describe the symptoms to Mauch, it is liable to be a lot more serious than a tummy ache."[3] This would be the first indication that the lingering effects of the Thomas fight resonated deeper within Dick than his shoulder tissue.

The season's end brought little respite. In November Dick had a run-in with the police in West Philadelphia, an incident that this time was reported lightly within the dailies but was covered breathlessly within the *Tribune*. The official story offered up little mystery and died for lack of oxygen in the *Bulletin, Inquirer,* and *Daily News*: Philadelphia police reported that two of its officers pulled over a 1959 Chevy for a defective muffler and thereafter detained the driver, Richard Anthony Allen, for an hour because he was unable to produce the registration card for the vehicle. The police captain termed the incident a "misunderstanding," acknowledged that Dick and the arresting officers exchanged words, but concluded that apologies followed all around "and all parted friends."[4] The *Tribune*, however, dug up two eyewitnesses to the incident who claimed otherwise—that Dick was in fact beaten by one of the officers. "We saw the policeman shove a man against the vehicle," said one of the witnesses. "The officer straightened up and then I saw him strike the man in the face." She also claimed that at that point a second officer (a black officer) got out of the squad car and attempted to restrain his (white) partner. At that point "all three men got into a struggle." She also claimed that a woman was in the car with the victim, holding a baby in her arms, screaming, "These policemen are trying to say Richie attacked them!"[5]

Neither the Phillies nor Dick would confirm the eyewitnesses' report (Dick initially skipped town in the days immediately following the incident), leading the *Tribune* to speculate that "the player's silence about the incident and his unavailability have led to speculation that he may have decided to forget the incident or not press charges." Eventually he was spotted riding his horse in Fairmount Park, where he denied that an altercation had occurred at all.[6] The Police Advisory Board, under pressure from the *Tribune*, announced that it would have investigated the case but for the fact that nobody involved in the incident had filed a complaint: "Unless someone files a complaint, our hands are tied."[7] Later, the chief of the board amended its position, acknowledging that an investigation could be undertaken even if Dick never filed a complaint, provided that the two witnesses came forth and supported their stories before the board.[8] He announced that he stood ready to conduct a "sweeping probe," but none ever commenced and the incident faded into the dark of December.

Shortly thereafter more surprising news surfaced: Dick had signed his contract for the 1966 season and it wasn't even February yet. "That's good," remarked pitcher Jim Bunning. "He'll be in a much better frame of mind than he was last year after that hassle about salary in the spring."[9] Dick claimed to be "very satisfied" with his new deal, which called for a $10,000 raise over his 1965 salary.[10] The good vibes didn't last long, however; he reported late to spring training, and this time the Phillies claimed that he was overweight. After refusing to step on a scale, Dick sloughed off the club's concern, asserting that "I've got no problem. I'll be ready in a week and a half."[11] After reiterating his claim that spring training was too long anyway and that a day here or a day there didn't really matter in the long run, he insisted that when it came to his weight, perception had trumped reality. "I weigh 196," he said. "It's just that I wear all those clothes under my uniform"—that was what caused him to look puffy. Because, he alleged, "I don't sweat down here unless it's humid," he had recently taken to wearing long johns under his uniform to get a sweat going.[12] Soon the extra layer became a permanent part of his game-day attire regardless of the weather. "He never wore a short-sleeve shirt, ever," recalled Ken Henderson, who played with Dick on the White Sox in 1973 and 1974. "And he would wear thermal underwear under his long-sleeve sweatshirt. He would go out and play in ninety-degree weather with [high] humidity like that. It was unbelievable. I tried that in batting practice once and I almost fainted." As for why he donned his billowy attire no matter what (indeed, there are few photos or baseball cards of Dick after 1965 that show him sporting anything other than long sleeves, or even a jacket, under his jersey), he claimed that his sartorial practice was rooted in historical precedent: "If you look at people in Egypt and India or any of those warm places," he once told Henderson, "they keep their bodies covered. By wearing the thermal underwear, it cools my body under the sweatshirt." Henderson recalled a player who dressed as if he were going hunting rather than playing baseball: "from pants to the shirt, it was all thermal. . . . Whether it was sixty degrees or ninety-five degrees, he wore the thermal underwear. And this was under a double-knit uniform, which doesn't breathe."[13]

Although not a fan of spring training in general, Dick was nevertheless looking forward to working on his game at third base, where he continued to struggle, although he did cut down his errors in his second season (from 41 in 1964 to 26). Claude Harrison was perhaps a bit overenthusiastic when he proclaimed that "[i]f Richie continues his astounding improvement he will eventually become as good a fielding third baseman as there is in baseball,"[14] but Dick had improved and he thought he could improve even more in 1966. Mauch wasn't convinced and, a few weeks into spring training, began raving about Tony Taylor's play at third: "Nobody can play it any better," he crowed. Soon Mauch floated the idea that Dick might move to left field to make room for Taylor at third: "I like the way Taylor plays baseball and I like the way Cookie Rojas plays baseball and I like the way Allen plays baseball. I'd like to have all of them in the lineup if I can. I talked to Allen about it, and he said, 'I'll still get to hit, won't I?'" Dick's take was somewhat different: "I don't think I'll be playing out there. I feel like I won the third base job and I want to keep it."[15] Much to his dismay, the positional roller coaster appeared to be restarting once more—Dick played third base one day, left field the next. As the shuffling continued throughout the spring, Dick grew agitated: "I've been shoved back and forth before but then it was from year to year. Not from game to game."[16]

Worse, his pleas appeared to be falling on deaf ears. Recalling his earlier stints in the outfield, he reminded anyone who would listen that "I had a tough time out there [in center field] in Williamsport and it wasn't the sun out there, it was me."[17] As for left, that only brought up yet another unpleasant Little Rock memory of being defeated by the infamous "dump": "I was a terrible leftfielder at Little Rock," he reminded the press corps.[18] Presently, he claimed that he was "scared and awkward" in left field. "I'm a third baseman," he pleaded.[19] If Mauch wanted Taylor in the lineup so badly, Dick saw a way for him to make that happen: "I'd like to see Tony out there," he said.[20] Finally, two days before the season opener, Mauch relented and announced that Dick would once again be his full-time third baseman (Cookie Rojas opened the season in left and Taylor at second). The opportunity for him to hone his defensive skills at that position before the season began was gone, however.

Very quickly, the 1966 season introduced Dick to two things that would follow (and in many ways define) him throughout the remainder of his career: the accumulation of disciplinary fines and the accumulation of injuries. As for the fines, the first one—for breaking curfew—came quietly and went unreported. His compatriot in the incident that led to the fine, *Daily News* beat writer Bill Conlin, recalled it vividly:

> The club was in Chicago in late April 1966. Every major league club stayed at the famed Edgewater Beach Hotel. It is where Eddie Waitkus was shot by Ruth Steinhagen. And it closed forever in 1967. The ball clubs were housed in the south wing of the sprawling landmark. I took a nap after the game and with my 5 A.M. deadline took my time writing. I ordered room service, watched TV, and around 1 A.M. felt like a drink. There was a bar about three blocks down the street called Mr. & Mrs. T's. Closing time in Chicago was around 3 A.M. Dick Allen was at the bar in a Nehru, chatting up the bartender. I joined him. About an hour in, an inebriated patron who knew that ballplayers hung out there started in on Allen. The guy got more and more insulting and when he used the words "Uppity Nigger ballplayers," Allen turned to me and said, "I'm gonna pop him." I could see the headline. . . . So I slid off the stool, moved in front of Allen, and I popped him. The guy was drunk, so it didn't take much to drop him. The bartender knew Allen and said, "You guys get the hell out of here; I'll handle this." Dick left a couple of twenties on the bar and we left. It was about 3 A.M. We were laughing about the incident when we saw flashing red lights up by the hotel. Fire trucks. When we got within a block we noticed a crowd of hotel guests in assorted nightclothes or hastily donned pants had gathered in front of the South Tower entrance. Including the entire Phillies ball club. Including Gene Mauch. We tried to blend in with the crowd, but Mauch had seen us crossing the street. He smirked at Allen and held up two fingers, signifying a $200 fine. There had been a small fire in the main building that had been extinguished before firemen arrived, but the alarms had gone off.[21]

As for the injuries, Dick experienced his first major one in late April when he severely bruised his right shoulder during an attempted stolen base (he was safe). Subsequent x-rays also revealed a slight dislocation, torn tissues, and an old football break that had never been treated and had healed on its own. Although he was initially expected to be out for approximately half a month, Dick countered that he thought he'd be back in "less than a week."[22] Though he claimed he could hit even though he was unable to throw, Mauch was reluctant, at least initially, to even allow him to dress for the games. "I want him back in the lineup healthy," he said. "I'm afraid to sit him on the bench. I'm afraid to have him in a uniform. I'm afraid I'd see his big bat sitting there in the late innings of a game and I'd make an unwise move with him."[23] He wouldn't be afraid for long.

On May 20, about three weeks after his injury, Mauch sent Dick up as a pinch hitter against the Cardinals. He hit a long fly, over 400 feet to dead center, which floated into Curt Flood's glove for what the *Daily News* described as "the most exciting out of the season." Tantalizing as it was, Mauch tried to tamp down expectations in its aftermath: "as of now, his return to the lineup is not in sight. I wish I could say it were. He can lob the ball, yes. But if he had to put something on it in a hurry . . . there's no way he can do anything but throw it away, and possibly hurt it worse."[24] The fans, though, had seen enough and rendered their judgment: anybody who could hit a ball like that must be okay to play. They cheered wildly as he strode to the plate, concluding that the long wait (one week more than had initially been predicted) was finally over; their cleanup hitter was back. "The applause," Frank Dolson of the *Inquirer* wrote, "the wild, animal yells began the moment Richie Allen, bat in hand, stuck his head out of the Phillies dugout. No announcement was necessary. Some of the people, nearly half it seemed, stood and clapped. Two or three grown men, occupying front-row box seats in the upper deck near home plate, pounded their fists against the roof of a photographer's booth as their hero advanced to home plate. It was the kind of emotional outburst Mickey Mantle creates at Yankee Stadium when he limps into sight as a pinch hitter." As for what it all meant, Dolson surmised that "Richie apparently had to get hurt to be appreciated."[25]

Mauch refused to concede as much, choosing instead to provide cover for his young third baseman: "I've always felt that part of the treatment the fans have given Richie was because they were mad at me. They couldn't see me all the time, so they were booing Richie Allen. They thought I didn't handle the Frank Thomas incident well and they were

Master manipulator Gene Mauch among
the scribes: Ray Kelly (left, with cigar) and Ritter Collett (right).
(Bill Conlin)

taking it out on him." All Dick would say about the at-bat was that as he
strode to the plate, "I felt like an Academy Award winner."[26]

A week later, Dick was finally back in the lineup—but in left field
rather than at third base. For his quick return he credited Era's home
remedy, a salve that Stan Hochman alleged "smelled stronger than a team

of mules."[27] Dick pressed to return out of fear that if he didn't, "People will think I'm faking." "I can sympathize with the guys in prison," he said. "Not playing is like being in solitary confinement for three or four days and then having them put a tray of food in front of you, just out of reach."[28] Because Dick still could not throw, Mauch devised a scheme that called for the third baseman or shortstop to sprint out to meet him on any ball hit his way, thereby limiting Dick's throws to "the short relay variety."[29] Dick found the relay system humiliating ("they've got me out in leftfield, making an ass of myself, lobbing the ball in underhand"), but he consented to it nevertheless.[30] Five weeks after the injury, with short-stop Bobby Wine running out to meet Dick in left on a regular basis, the whispers that Dick was a malingerer got louder. In all, he spent six weeks in left field before his arm permitted him to return to third base at midseason. Recalling the initial diagnosis and the long pinch-hit fly ball in May, some fans wondered what had taken so long. If nothing else, Dick knew his audience—it didn't take much for at least some of them to question his dedication.

Dick's commitment to the club was called into question once again shortly after his return to third when he was fined, this time publicly, for breaking curfew in San Francisco. Dick seethed and insisted that he in fact had done nothing wrong: "The bus got back to the hotel at 11:30 P.M.," he said. Given that the club's curfew was two and a half hours after a night game, he had until 2 A.M. to make it to his room. "I don't see where I broke the curfew," he said, claiming that he was in his room at 1:50 A.M.[31] Conlin, for the most part, supported him, this time in print, concluding that the fine "sounds ridiculous. Allen was at a restaurant adjacent to the Jack Tar Hotel having a sandwich and a beer. It was only a few minutes after curfew when he was apprehended. Rich was on the way IN, not OUT."[32] Regardless, the optics were not good: a publicly debated curfew violation coming directly on the heels of an injury that took much longer to heal than expected. And in baseball, optics are everything.

"A lot of baseball is show," contended former teammate Bill White as he reflected on Dick's career in Philadelphia. "Look at Pete Rose. Helluva player but he let you know he was a helluva player, and they [the fans] loved him. Larry Bowa showed his emotions; they loved him. If you look at [Mike] Schmidt, you look at Dick, they didn't show much emotion.

They just hit home runs and drove in a hundred runs." The problem with Dick, according to White, was that "he looked lackadaisical—in the field and at bat." However, "I've never seen Richie give less than 100 percent on anything—on pop ups, on taking a guy out at second base, on going from first to third. . . . I've never seen him not hustle on the field. Once he got on the field, he gave 100 percent."[33] Dick's 100 percent came packaged with a healthy dose of black cool, and when his style was contrasted with that of players like Rose, who exuded none of that, the differences were obvious to anyone looking to make a point. Although those who played with both often contended that their hustle and dedication to the game were similar, they just *looked* so different that if you weren't careful, you could be fooled. Most were. Ron Hughes, Dick's Tri-County All Stars teammate and, later, Rose's teammate in 1960 during his minor league stint in Tampa, said that, at least visually, Rose "was the opposite of Richie. He ran everywhere, he had his pitchers stay afterwards and hit ground balls to him."[34] Throughout the careers of both ballplayers, many within the media, along with some players, would draw the contrast; catcher John Stearns later remarked that, unlike Dick (who at the time was being eviscerated in the press for skipping a workout before the 1974 All-Star Game), Rose exemplified everything that was right with the game: "Nobody does as much with what he's got as that man right there. That's what it's all about."[35]

Many black players approached the game differently than did their white teammates and suffered the wrath of the media for doing so. Curt Flood openly disdained Rose as well as how he was interpreted by fans and many within the press box: "The dumb show of racing full tilt from the outfield to the dugout when teams change sides is regarded as the sincerest possible sign of competitive integrity. And is publicized as such. . . . The showmanly, stereotyped hustler may or may not be a good team man. His colleagues may despise him if, like one or two famous hustlers, he races to and from the dugout, tears to first base after being walked, yet sometimes shows no enthusiasm about chasing a batted ball that has gone through his legs. His moments of immobility may go unnoticed in the grandstands, but are conspicuous on the field. They betray him for what he is—a self-seeking, self-absorbed hot dog and, as such, an unreliable competitor."[36] Add in the fact that Dick was always uncomfortable and guarded with the media, and the impression was made worse. "Everybody loves an extrovert rather than an introvert," Ken Henderson recognized after spending a career observing the relationship between the press and the players they covered from his locker.[37] Introverts like Dick were destined for punishment by a press corps that relied on quips and quotes for their seemingly endless coverage of the games on their beat.

As the whispers questioning Dick's dedication grew louder, Conlin, for one, attempted to tamp them down, writing that Dick was doing all he could on the field. The problem, as Conlin saw it, was that he refused (or, more likely, given his nature, was unable) to crow over his feats or accentuate them in ways other ballplayers liked to do: "Dick Stuart and Bo Belinsky . . . lived by the quote and died by the quote. . . . The Rich Allen who comes across as something less than brilliant when men with pencils hover around him is a façade, his way of protecting who he is. . . . What he wants to do is let his bat do the talking. The way he wants to be judged as a baseball player is by his performance, not on his ability to say shallow things."[38] Unlike Rose, who, talented as he was, never tired of informing all those around him of his accomplishments and demonstrating his hustle whenever possible, Dick's makeup was such that he was incapable of putting on a show for the fans and the media. He wouldn't spew forth a platitude or two, which might have defused speculation that he was malingering; wouldn't run on and off the field between innings just to give the impression of hustle; and wouldn't, as that fellow black player encouraged him to do in 1964, construct a public image that conflicted with his private self. "The real Rich Allen," Conlin concluded in his column, "is . . . well . . . real."[39]

Dick—reserved, haughty, aloof—paid a heavy price for the way he carried himself, as would many black players following him who conducted themselves in similar fashion. MLB Players Association director Marvin Miller, after decades of dealing with management and the baseball media, became convinced that "those in positions of authority in baseball have a tendency to assume that a black player is more likely to 'jake it' than a white player."[40] Miller's supposition echoed that of the writer Donald Hall, who noticed that up through the 1970s, various lists (unscientific as they were) of the most unpopular sports figures were oftentimes dominated by black athletes.[41] To the untrained eye, Dick often looked like he just didn't care. But looks could be deceiving. One afternoon in 1968 Dick was stretched out in the Dodger Stadium dugout, apparently checked-out as to the game taking place on the field. "He was just lounging there," said Bill White the next day, "and after I came in [from the field] one inning I threw a ball at him. I figured he was sleeping . . . but he caught the ball. Just as it was about to hit him in the stomach, he caught it with one hand. That's got to tell you something. Maybe he's a little more alert than we think he is."[42]

On the base paths, few were better. "He could steal a base anytime he wanted to," recalled Ken Henderson. "If [his team] needed a run, he could get into scoring position better than anyone I've ever seen other than [Willie] Mays. He was that good. He had this unique way of lowering his shoulder when he rounded [the] bases. Most runners just touch the bag kind of straight up and make the big wide turn but Richie could cut the corners of the bag and he could take off five feet getting from first to third." Years later, while with the White Sox, he taught this skill to his teammates: "First thing we'd often do in spring training, [manager] Chuck [Tanner] would talk about how we could run the bases more effectively and he would involve Richie in coaching the other players in how to run the bases."[43] Still, as far as many were concerned, Dick was a malingerer and his delayed return to third base was proof positive of this. As such, he soon developed a reputation as a "slacker"; even those who considered themselves in his corner could often only find backhanded ways to compliment him: "Rose hustles all the time," wrote a Chicago columnist attempting to defend Dick in 1974, "Allen hustled only when he thought it would do some good."[44]

Dick's shoulder injury and the drama that surrounded it provided further confirmation to him that the only way he stood a chance of earning enough money to enable him to get what he wanted out of baseball was by extracting as much of it as possible from the Phillies—and doing it now, while he was still young and at least relatively healthy. The end, as he saw (and now he could speak from experience and not merely theoretically), could come at any moment, on any play, and once that happened, that would be it. He had little goodwill with the public and, for many reasons, had little hope of building any. No, if he was looking for money (and all that it could bring him, as he would demonstrate once he finally had enough of it), it would have to come directly from his employer, no one else.

Flood noticed this as well—that, regardless of personal characteristics, black players of the era had little hope of landing anything more than the endorsement scraps that remained after their white teammates took their pick. Even though Bob Gibson's Cardinals had defeated Carl Yastrzemski's Red Sox in the 1967 World Series, Flood noted that Yaz bankrolled approximately $200,000 in endorsements and speaking fees in the aftermath while Gibson netted all of $2,500: "Commerce had not yet conceded that blacks use razor blades, automobiles and deodorants. . . . Gibson's sole problem with Madison Avenue was his blackness."[45] Dick was more hard up than Gibson in this regard; the offers he received prior to 1973 (in the afterglow of his MVP season with the White Sox) could best be described as the scraps of the scraps.

Beyond endorsements, black players faced longer odds of even collecting their big-league paychecks for a significant number of years (and thereby reaping the benefits of the game's seniority-based pay scale) because they were more likely to be cut and ushered out of the game as soon as their performance declined. Although black players often earned more than their white counterparts of the era, this was because almost all black players were, if not stars, then at least everyday players; few blacks rode the pines in the majors. As soon as their performance declined, however, they were less likely than their white counterparts to age gracefully within the game by taking on a part-time role or specializing as a pinch hitter. Instead they were often released. "One possible interpretation of this finding is the possible existence of a quota on black players," concluded a study that focused on the racial dynamics within the game between 1971 and 1985. (Although baseball as it existed in the 1960s was not analyzed in this study, it likely speaks to the racial dynamics that existed during that era as well.) "Perhaps motivated by the concern that white fans will not support a predominantly black team, management has silently placed an 'invisible ceiling' on the black percentage. When coupled with the desire to have a winning team, this ceiling would generate strong pressures to (a) employ as many black players as possible in order to capitalize on their performance, but (b) in order to remain under the ceiling, to eliminate black players as soon as their performance declined, and (c) to retain white players of declining but similar ability."[46] All of these later studies merely demonstrated what Dick knew in his heart to be true in 1966: that his financial options were limited, not only by the reserve clause but by public perceptions driven by racial factors. And there was little he could do about it: "You have to get it while you are producing, not when you are nearing the end of the road. I am producing now and I want to be paid now. My career could end tomorrow and where will I be then?"[47]

Though Dick was not the first to recognize these issues, few others spoke so freely about them. "They call it a baseball team—one big happy family," Dick said in 1971, reflecting on his early career. "But they still don't room Black and White together. There are so many little things that have gone on in the game from way back that just haven't been changed. In race relations, basketball and football are way ahead of baseball."[48] The mythical "big happy family" was even more of an illusion once a player's skills declined. And he didn't need academic studies to tell him that this was particularly true for black players. He was resolved not to wind up like so many others—homeless and destitute. "One Black player, now deceased, once called me for a loan of $50," Dick recalled. He was determined to never place such a phone call himself one day. If Carpenter and Quinn thought they were going "to boost their earnings at my expense," they had another thing coming; he was going to demand his share.[49]

Dick was especially vocal when it came to the absence of black managers—yet another potential stream of baseball-related income shut off to him. In 1970 he laid it on the table as clearly as anyone ever had: "Look at managers," he said. "We have black ballplayers today who are capable of managing in the big leagues. Frank Robinson [who would, in fact, become the game's first black manager, albeit not until five years later] has more qualifications than most of those white cats managing. You never heard of some of [the white managers] because they barely, or maybe never, played the game. But then Whitey blows the whistle and calls a 'tech' on the brothers with that qualifications bull."[50] "If baseball isn't racist," he said years later, "why are there no black managers?"[51] Was it because, as Claude Harrison opined in a 1969 *Tribune* column contemplating the musings of Giants' manager Alvin Dark, the perception of black athletes was that they were "all brawn and no brains"?[52] Dick thought so, and he said so as well.

Although he'd be criticized throughout his career for flouting the rules, starting with his 1966 fines, Dick's understanding of rules differed from that of most of his peers and certainly that of management. Certainly there were rules, but as Dick understood them, some were enforced and some were blithely ignored: "Yeah, there are rules. If everybody followed them, maybe we'd be all right."[53] Given that they weren't, he was determined to look out for himself. Within a few months, he'd be earning more than double what Mickey Mantle had earned at the same stage of his career, having also gained the reputation of being "as adept at extracting money from the tight-fisted Bob Carpenter . . . as a professional shucker is at opening clams."[54] And he'd do it by driving home his criticism of seniority as often as he drove in runs. "Say you're buying a 1955 Cadillac," Dick observed. "You won't pay the price just because it's been around. In '55 when it was qualified to do the job you paid full price for it. Now it's not worth it. A ballplayer should be paid for his production, not seniority. Seniority don't drive in any runs. If it did Ty Cobb would still be playing."[55] It would not be easy, however, and yet another spring training drama would ensue before things would settle down once more, at least for a few months.

Chapter 6

❖

Seniority Don't Drive in Runs

1967: Philadelphia .307/23/77

EVEN THOUGH HIS shoulder injury cost him 21 games in 1966, Dick put up the best numbers of his career: 40 home runs and 110 RBIs to go along with a .317 batting average. Although advanced metrics did not exist at the time, in retrospect they illuminate the otherworldly season he had just completed: Dick led the National League with a 1.027 OPS (on-base percentage plus slugging percentage) and, in this category, was second in all of baseball only to Frank Robinson of the Orioles—and Robinson won the American League's Triple Crown. Other advanced metrics (offensive WAR [wins above replacement], runs created, adjusted batting wins, offensive winning percentage, at-bats per home run, and so on) likewise ranked Dick at the top of the list. He might not have been aware of his offensive WAR ranking, but he knew that he had excelled amid difficult circumstances and a painful injury and was determined to be compensated accordingly. "I figure on being a little higher-priced next season," he informed *Sports Illustrated* in January 1967.[1] Not surprisingly, the *Tribune*'s Claude Harrison was in his corner immediately: "How much is a fourth-year major league player worth? . . . if your name is Richie Allen and you can play your third base position as well as any man in the league in addition to hitting the ball a country mile, the answer may range from $50,000 on up. [Phillies' GM John] Quinn can no longer tell Allen to wait and prove himself to be a major leaguer. He's here. An established star, everything the club hoped outfielder Johnny Callison would be, Richie is."[2]

Because everybody knew what was coming long before it arrived, no one was stunned when Dick officially held out in spring training. Repeating his mantra "Seniority don't drive in runs" like a meditative chant, he was resolute that, unlike in 1965, this time he would get what he wanted or he wouldn't play at all. The *Tribune* reported that Dick was seeking the unthinkable for a fourth-year player—$100,000—although given the tight-lipped nature of contract negotiations of the era, it was never precisely clear exactly what he was demanding. All Dick would say was, "I talked with him [Quinn] and I gave him my figure. I do not plan to do anything until they meet it."[3] Unlike Harrison, the daily beat writers met Dick's holdout with wry and weary resignation, as confident that the Phils wouldn't meet his price as they were that he would ask for the moon in the first place. Ray Kelly of the *Bulletin* wrote that despite Dick's outstanding 1966 season, "There is no precedent for this sort of thing. Joe DiMaggio, Ted Williams and Stan Musial, along with present day 100 granders like Willie Mays, Hank Aaron and Roberto Clemente all reached the top wage bracket on a much more gradual scale."[4] The *Daily News*' Bill Conlin wrote, with tongue in cheek, that although Dick was reportedly seeking $100,000, "He'll settle for $85,000."[5]

As for how he arrived at the reported $100,000 figure, Dick refocused everyone's attention on his shoulder injury: "Adhesions had formed," he told Stan Hochman of an off-season checkup he had recently undergone at Temple University Hospital. "The reach in the right arm was four inches shorter than the left. The injury made me think . . . what if I had been messed up so I couldn't play anymore? I didn't have a job, no college education. How would I take care of my family? . . . I love to play baseball but I don't like to dicker. I told them a figure and that's what I've got to get. I've just got to." As for why he was seeking such a sharp increase in salary, he said it was only fair: "I always felt if I doubled my production my salary ought to be doubled. Because if I go the other way, I know I'm going to be cut that much." And as for Mays and Aaron? "If I'm the only one who handles it this way I can't help it. Maybe that's why Aaron was underpaid for so long. He should have made $100,000 a few years ago. If I'm worth $100,000 then I want it when I'm worth it, not when I'm an old-timer on my way down."[6] A few days later, when he was asked how he felt when he read that his more experienced teammate Jim Bunning had just signed for $80,000—$20,000 less than what he was allegedly demanding—Dick replied, "I wish it had been $500,000. Isn't anybody on the club overpaid."[7] He didn't trust management even a little, certainly not enough to bank on the promise that eventually he'd get what was coming to him: "They treat us like guinea pigs," he said the following spring. "They tell a guy 'run into that wall.' If he does and gets hurt, they look for somebody else."[8]

As always, Quinn appeared lost when it came to negotiating with Dick: "I've been dealing with player contracts since 1945 and this is the first time a player has told me he wouldn't negotiate." He was confounded when Dick told him that he had no desire to exchange figures with him and engage in the traditional salary negotiation dance (which almost always ended with the general manager stomping on the toes of the player). "Why should I have to give figures?" Dick wondered. "The man was there every day, watching every game. Why should I have to tell him I did this or I didn't do that?" Regardless, Quinn was confident that, eventually, he'd emerge victorious in this battle of wills: "I have said before that Eddie Roush is the only player I know of who stayed out for one full season," he said resolutely.[9] Surely Dick wouldn't be the second. Quinn found solace in the beat writers who were solidly behind him. (The *Inquirer*'s Frank Dolson suggested that Dick's insistence on upending the game's salary structure could very well compromise the integrity of the game itself, while the *Bulletin*'s Sandy Grady denigrated Dick's stance via barbed sarcasm.)[10]

Dick held firm, and to demonstrate his determination to hold out until he got what he thought he deserved, he took a job selling cars at Kardon's Chevrolet in Mt. Holly, New Jersey. When Hochman showed up to discuss his holdout, Dick brushed aside Quinn's Eddie Roush anecdote: "Didn't Joe DiMaggio stay out 'til July one year? Me and Joe." Then he turned the tables on Hochman as he had more pressing matters to discuss: "Hey, how about swapping that heap of yours for a new Caprice?" Later he reasserted his position that he was staying put until he got what he asked for. "I'm not budging for love or money," he said. "Well, anyway, not for love."[11]

Very quickly things devolved to the point where once again the exasperated Quinn was pushed aside and Carpenter interceded in an effort to end the stalemate. Quinn tried to save face, reminding the beat writers that his track record remained impeccable: "I think the longest [a player had ever personally held out on him] was Lew Burdette [two weeks] the spring after he won the Corvair in the World Series for winning three games." As spring training had not yet reached the two-week mark, his record was, at least in his mind, intact. Besides, he suggested, "Carpenter's liable to tell Allen that the figure I'm offering him is too high."[12]

As the media buzzed about this most recent takedown of the club's general manager, Carpenter agreed to sit down with Dick and lay it all out for him, to explain the rationale behind the byzantine customs that governed baseball's finances. Conlin wrote that Carpenter gave Dick "some fatherly instruction about baseball tradition." Quinn added that "Bob went over the Seniority System in baseball. He produced some figures we've reached about the salary progression of about ten star players in the league who had Allen's ability at this stage of their careers. Then he broke down for Rich how much money is involved in getting a player through the minors."[13] Money, as it applied specifically to Dick, was not mentioned. Instead it was the system that was explained to Dick—what it was, why it existed, and why it couldn't be compromised, not even for Dick Allen. All of this was done in the hope that by providing clarity, peace would inevitably ensue, and under the assumption that Dick's pique was grounded in a mere ignorance of the system itself rather than his conclusion that the system was designed to thwart his financial aspirations. The possibility that Dick understood the system all too well—to the point that he saw clearly just how it artificially suppressed the wages of players like himself—was never considered. Consequently, the sit-down was not only doomed to fail, it could only make matters worse.

Which it did.

In essence, what Carpenter tried to explain to Dick was the folly of his position, one that assumed a relationship among equals. Such an assumption was naive, explained Carpenter, in terms both technical and opaque, as ballplayers were hardly partners. Rather, they were property, to be bought, sold, valued, and discarded by the owners and at their whim. It was this very idea that Dick bristled at and that motivated him to become ever more resolute in his subsequent refusals to acquiesce to the demands of Phillies' management. In the short term, however, Carpenter's talk did succeed in at least greasing the wheels: "I would say we reached the negotiating stage," Quinn announced after Dick's sit-down with Carpenter. "I told him our figure and he gave us a figure that was under his original demand."[14]

If Carpenter and Quinn thought they had softened Dick, they were mistaken. This was particularly true because now, unlike in 1965, other players were finally starting to question baseball tradition as well. Marvin Miller had assumed the helm of the Players Association in 1966 and immediately began asking the same questions of the game's time-honored salary structure that Dick had asked the year before. Now, in 1967, there was at least a small but gathering chorus of players, along with rogue former (and future) owner Bill Veeck, who were less dismissive of Dick's logic than they had been before. "Don't tell me about $100,000 salaries," said Veeck. "When I started drinking beer it was 10 cents a bottle. Now, you go into some fancy place and it's a buck a bottle. The value of the dollar has changed. Allen deserves what he can get. And what difference does it make if he's up for two years or four years or 10 years? If seniority is the thing, then Dick Groat ought to be paid $250,000."[15] One Phillie player confided to Sandy Grady (anonymously, out of fear of retribution) that "we all hope Allen gets as much as he can—it means bigger salaries are easier for us later." Grady reported that Dick's older teammates were "dazzled" by his salary demand while the younger ones "talk of it like a voyage to Mars"—something that was unfathomable just a few years earlier but now seemed to be at least faintly visible on the distant horizon. Still, one of them said, "nobody wants this thing to last too long."[16]

Finally, in mid-March, the holdout ended. Dick signed a one-year contract that made him "one of the highest paid four-year players in the game," according to Quinn.[17] He didn't get his $100,000 but he got a lot: $85,000. This made Dick many things: the highest-paid player in the history of the franchise up to that point; the highest-paid fourth-year player in the history of the game; the highest-paid twenty-five-year-old in baseball history; and the highest-paid infielder in the majors.[18] In the end, what drove Dick was not so much the $100,000 plateau as his determination that his salary be doubled given his increase in production. While some articles preened that Dick's signing was "not for the $100,000 for which he was holding out," in the end it was the Phillies who gave more, who bent in order to bring the game's most exciting young hitter back to camp.[19]

Technically, Carpenter did not have to give an inch in his negotiations with Dick—the reserve clause ennobled him to stare down any recalcitrant player with steely resolve if he so chose. That he not only engaged Dick but in fact doubled his salary said a lot: that the club needed Dick's bat in the lineup, that the club hoped that by doing so his mind would be free of distractions, and that Dick was no ordinary player. Above all else, at least to Carpenter, his doubling of Dick's salary was testament of his benevolent nature—he didn't have to do anything but, on his own volition, did. Even more so than in the act of signing Dick to the largest bonus ever paid to a black player back in 1960 (which, at least partially, could be explained as a necessity given the risk of losing him to another club if he did not), here there were no obvious competitive pressures; certainly Dick could sit out the entire 1967 season and sell Chevys, but if nothing else Carpenter and Quinn understood history and recognized that this was highly unlikely to occur. At some point, and despite all his rhetoric, Dick would most likely break and sign on for the best deal he could get. That Carpenter refused to let things devolve to that point marked him, or so he hoped, as a charitable man—someone quite different than the ogre demonized within the pages of the *Tribune* for so many years. Once Dick saw this as well, things would not only improve between him and the organization but also between the club and black players overall. Carpenter was sure of it. This would turn out to be a serious miscalculation.

That Dick was not going to be cowed by the mere acceptance of $85,000 became apparent immediately: he arrived at spring training with bushy hair, a fuzzy mustache (facial hair had been verboten on major league faces for decades), a gold bracelet, and smoking a cigarette (he would shave the mustache before taking the field; the other accoutrements would remain with him the remainder of his career).[20] Mauch would later describe his third baseman as someone who "wants independence . . . not acceptance," and his aura upon arrival to Clearwater signaled as much.

While one teammate later complained that "when Carpenter came in and gave him that $80,000 [*sic*] contract everybody lost authority over him,"[21] to Dick that was precisely the point—he finally had the resources to afford to do things his way and on his clock. And although he might not be completely free under the rules as they existed, he realized that he nevertheless could purchase at least a modicum of freedom given enough money. Carpenter had just provided him that money. And now he was free. A few years later he would crow with pride that "I wouldn't change a thing. I'm 30 years old and I'm still my own man. I call my own shots. How many people can say that?"[22] In the general population, very few. In professional baseball, almost nobody. Except Dick Allen.

With his newfound wealth came a new favorite slogan: "Seniority don't drive in runs" was replaced with "I only do what my pocketbook can stand"—meaning, to Carpenter's chagrin, that if he could afford the fine, he could own his time.[23] No longer was the choice before him a false one: one of either conforming and feeling powerless or rebelling and threatening the financial well-being and security of his family. Given his newly stuffed coffers, a third option was now available: Dick could simply "prefer not to" do those tasks or conform to the rules he found distasteful. He could buy his way out of seemingly anything he preferred not to do merely by paying the fine. As his career progressed, Dick increasingly resisted by preferring not to participate in what he saw as the cruel order dictated to him without his consent. Here was how money could buy power, how money could buy freedom. Simply pay the fine and move on. If Mauch's fines were the price of freedom, so be it. He could finally afford it. And the more money Carpenter threw his way, the more freedom and independence Dick would have.

With his heavier wallet came more opportunities for Dick to assert his independence. "I hate to have a hammer over my head," he said blithely after another fine for arriving late to the ballpark in July 1967. "That's why I couldn't have an 8-to-5 job."[24] If Mauch thought he could use his power to issue fines as a means to mold Dick's behavior, Dick quickly disabused him of that idea: "My mom raised me, see? I'm raised now. I know my own responsibilities. I gotta do things as I see fit. I gotta do them myself. I know lots of times when I'm late for anything it costs me. I know it costs me. But I'd rather pay than worry about some minutes here and there."[25] His indifference toward the game's entrenched disciplinary system mystified nearly everyone in the press. Arthur Daley of the *New York Times* couldn't figure it out: "Not only has he missed curfew, he also has missed the start of ball games. It hasn't seemed to bother him especially. He paid his fines without complaint and Mauch probably slapped more plasters on him than on all the other Phils combined."[26] Even some in the black press questioned Dick's unprecedented approach to the issue of fines; Doc Young of the *Chicago Defender* categorized his "casual attitude" toward the game as "unprofessional" and, quoting an "insider," wrote: "Richie seems to feel that if he misses a game and pays a fine, everything is all right. He doesn't think anyone should say anything about the incident after he has paid the fine."[27]

Dick responded to the mystification with yet another verbal shrug: "I've done things that were bad, but the things I've done bad I've paid for."[28] He was well aware that there was a price for his freedom; if he was willing to pay the fare, so be it. "What have I ever done that I wasn't willing to pay for?" he would incredulously ask an equally incredulous audience, reminding them that "If I wanted to take some time off I was also willing to pay top rates."[29] Transaction completed. End of story. At least from Dick's standpoint. Eventually Mauch understood this as well. The thing to do with Dick, he said years later, was to "play him, fine him, and play him again."[30] The fines might be necessary to send a message to the rest of the club that Dick wasn't receiving special treatment, but they were wholly useless when they came to Dick himself. Play him, fine him, and play him again. Even in the age of the reserve clause, Dick discovered that there were limits to a club's authority over its personnel. He could "prefer not to" and, given his salary, there was little the organization could do about it.

For the most part, his teammates were unfazed by it all. A few, such as catcher Clay Dalrymple and pitcher Dick Ellsworth, took offense, with Ellsworth declaring after the season that "Allen's behavior on and off the field [was] disgusting."[31] Although Ellsworth alleged that many of his teammates felt similarly, in fact most professed to have no opinion and some were at least mildly amused, particularly at the interplay between the tyrannical manager and the sovereign star. A few, such as Bill White and Tony Taylor, were staunch supporters.

The beat writers were another story. Dick's independent streak infuriated many of them, who had no choice but to somehow deal with the increasingly autonomous slugger. For decades the relationship between the press and the players was one of mutual dependence: the players submitted to interviews, the writers filed their stories, replete with the pre- and postgame comments of the players fans wanted to hear from, and everybody was (seemingly) happy. Dick, however, was always uncomfortable speaking with the press and, as the years went on, grew to distrust much of it. By 1967, he realized that there was no reason why he had to speak to reporters if he didn't want to. So increasingly he didn't. To some of the beat writers, this was a sin far worse than missing batting practice; now, in their eyes, he was compromising *their* livelihoods. According to Dick's friend Bill White, "If you get a guy who just goes out there and does his job and is quiet, unless he's a DiMaggio, most [of the press he gets] is negative . . . [Dick] didn't trust too many writers in Philadelphia and when that happens, you only get one side. The writers don't like that because they don't have a source of good material and so they go negative."[32] Pitcher Larry Christenson, Dick's teammate during his return to Philadelphia in the mid-1970s, marveled over how "at every ballpark, he seemed to know how to get in and out without being noticed. He had friends on the grounds crew at every stadium who helped him [navigate the tunnels and passageways]. In the locker room he'd be there and then you'd turn around and he'd be gone."[33] While he was negotiating the bowels of the stadium the beat writers were left staring into the abyss of his abandoned locker, their notebooks unfilled.

To Dallas Green, Dick's refusal to play the games that occurred before and after the game on the field was at least one reason why he never achieved superstar status in the eyes of many: "He really didn't want to pay the dues, didn't want to accept the responsibility of being a superstar. He just wanted to play the game. . . . He didn't like all the preliminaries, all the battles outside of baseball that came with the business. . . . He had a chance to be [a superstar]. He never became one, unfortunately, in my opinion, but if you look at his numbers, they're not too shabby."[34] "He had a hard time dealing with the notions of stardom and celebrity and fans who can be fickle," added Larry Merchant.[35] Perhaps this was because, as Ken Henderson remarked, he was introverted in the extreme: "if you could get two words out of him you were lucky. . . . The media loves a story. The personalities in sports are so important to what the writers and the broadcasters can contribute to the sport. Richie just wasn't the type of guy that could be [such a personality]. He was just more private and to himself."[36] To some writers, this amounted to treason.

When he did talk to the press, Dick occasionally tried to play mind games with them, infuriating them even more. Sometimes he bragged about his skill in this regard: "Those guys would come around and mess up my concentration with all their questions. So I just did the same to them. If I was in the mood, I would sit down and answer whatever they asked me. The next day, I would tell the same guy to get out of my face. It threw them off their stride. They resented the lack of control—and they'd get back at me in print."[37] And on top of that, at times he would downright lie in an effort to embarrass a gullible writer. Bill Conlin recalled a perennial Allen favorite:

Early in spring training 1967, AP Philly sports editor Ralph Bernstein showed up at Jack Russell Stadium for a scheduled 9 A.M. player interview. Dick Allen was in a batting cage hitting against a machine, and what was unusual besides the early hour for him, he was hitting left-handed. And really pounding the ball. Ralph asked him about it. "I think I'm going to try it, Ralph. It feels comfortable and I think I see the ball a little better." Excited, Bernstein interviewed the player then dashed upstairs to the press box and pounded out an exclusive that would flash around the country on the "A" sports wire. "Phillies slugger Richie Allen said today he was working on becoming a switch-hitter," et cetera. Ralph put a 6 P.M. embargo on it so the other writers in camp would not be able to react until the next day. When the story broke that night, their phones were ringing off the hook as sports editors informed them of the AP scoop. Neither Gene Mauch nor any of the coaches knew anything about it. Allen had a permanent "No Calls" order on his Jack Tar Hotel room.

Next morning, the scooped scribes confronted Allen at his locker. Was he really planning to switch-hit? Allen laughed. "Just kidding around with Ralph," he said. "I thought you guys always liked something different to write in spring training so you didn't all have the same story every day. I always mess around with some lefty swings when I hit off the machine. Helps me loosen up both sides. No, I'm not gonna switch-hit." Everybody got a good laugh but Ralph Bernstein, who had to follow his scoop with a "Never Mind. . . ." And just to keep the joke going, Allen took his first three or four BP swings that day left-handed.[38]

All of this contributed to the increasingly adversarial relationship between Dick and much of the media. "He takes orders from no one," wrote one scribe a few years later. "He submits to no formalities. He is subject to none of the normal niceties that go with being a public figure."[39] Consequently, he became their enemy. "Richie Allen's sin," wrote a *Tribune* columnist, "was to be black and independent. . . . The tragedy of the Philadelphia writers is in their seemed willingness to take a Black player apart when he threatens the establishment."[40] Dick's theories regarding salaries and fines certainly threatened the established order of things, at least as they existed within the world of professional baseball. Throughout the 1967 season, he would continually clash with those writers, young as well as old, who struggled with how to respond to one man's attempt to dismantle baseball's hierarchy. Some might cheer and urge him on in certain respects but, still, they had reason to be concerned overall. Because they were part of the hierarchy as well.

For despite their insistence that they were independent and incorruptible, most beat writers were company men—on the dole from the clubs they covered in many ways. Writers rode the team bus, flew with the team from city to city, and saw most of their expenses picked up by the club even though they were officially paid by their newspapers. "My first two years on the beat," Conlin recalled, "the Phillies picked up all media spring training and regular season travel expenses. This included spring training rental or hotel expense, meal money and 'Murphy Money' [daily expenses] for laundry, etcetera. In [the] regular season, the club provided hotel, transportation, and meal money. In addition each member of the media with any connection to Phillies' coverage received four choice season tickets to all home games."[41] Although technically free to write it as they saw it, for some it was difficult to see things from any perspective other than that of the people who were supporting their lifestyles.

In July 1967, one such writer, Allen Lewis, had seen enough.

In bold type, asserting that Dick "Lacks Complete Dedication," Lewis proclaimed that despite his numbers, Dick was not a "super-star." For support, he dismissed the three seasons Dick had put together prior to 1967, along with the .319 batting average he carried into midseason, and asserted that he fell short: "The Phillies' disappointment over Allen is not with his game performances—he never fails to hustle and give all-out effort—but with [a] lack of dedication to excellence." This lack of dedication showed itself, Lewis alleged, in his spring training holdout, his practice of being "habitually late in reporting to the park before the Phillies' games," and in his skipping a recent photo shoot for the team picture. In sum, Lewis asserted, "A major league ball club cannot win when all 25 players are not governed by the same rules."[42] Although numerous teammates throughout his career praised Dick as a solid teammate and, in his own way, a mentor, Lewis's article implied otherwise and asserted that his individuality was threatening the club's cohesion. The article made little sense when read as a referendum on Dick's on-field accomplishments—even Lewis conceded that there wasn't anything there that supported his contention. But like many of his fellow writers, Lewis saw the model ballplayer as one who sublimates individual wants for the good of the organization. Under that definition, an individualist could never be a good teammate. Rather, he could do nothing other than tear a team apart.

The article caused the expected stir and soon other writers piled on. Sandy Grady suggested that Dick was responsible for the treatment he was receiving from the Connie Mack faithful: "[Del] Ennis heard the sour Meistersingers here for years, yet there is no record that he ever complained."[43] In a game driven by statistics like no other, sportswriters—first local and then national—began spearing Dick by suggesting to their readers that they didn't mean all that much after all. Ignore the numbers, they told their readers, pay no mind to the performance on the field, Dick Allen was worthless nonetheless. In 1970 *Baseball Digest* ranked him first in an article on the game's most overrated players: "Neither batting average nor runs batted in take the measure of a man . . . Richie Allen . . . has been nothing but trouble for the Philadelphia Phillies. . . . Not even if he gives . . . peak production—as he did with the Phils in 1966 . . . —will

Allen be a useful player."⁴⁴ Conlin, perhaps the most internally conflicted writer of them all, who could never decide whether Dick was ultimately more worthy of his admiration or his disdain, chose a tone of acid contempt at the close of the 1967 season:

Poor, beleaguered misunderstood Rich Allen. Whopping five figure bonus out of high school. . . . Salary doubled after each of his first three big league seasons, escalating last spring to the $80,000 plateau. . . . Beautiful home in Mt. Airy. . . . Sleek new Cadillac. . . . Flashy $200 suits and custom-tailored $20 shirts. He is almost 26 now and at that age, maybe life in the public eye has become too tough for him. Maybe he should wrap up his suspicions, his peevish attitude, his sullen disregard for sportswriters and fans and the organization that pays his handsome salary. Maybe he should take them all and do the thing he always threatens. Maybe he should quit baseball and go to work selling used Chevrolets. Maybe he should take up exercising horses full time. Maybe he should go down to Champs gym and volunteer as an all year punching bag. A man who is tortured by phone calls, interviews, newspaper criticism and uncharitable fans deserves a more anonymous line of work.⁴⁵

Professional baseball, suggested the writers, was best left to those who conformed to traditional expectations, who possessed the ever-elusive "intangibles." Players such as Johnny Callison, who finished 1967 with a .261 batting average and 14 home runs (three more than the previous season).

Two days after Lewis's article appeared, it was cap day at Connie Mack Stadium. The previous day Dick had been benched for arriving at the ballpark during batting practice (it was his first benching of the season). "Seldom has a story received quicker confirmation," wrote Lewis's fellow *Inquirer* sportswriter Frank Dolson. But today was Sunday and the fans donned their club-issued caps and pronounced their allegiance; Johnny Callison signs were everywhere. "Phillies No. 7, Callison No. 1," read one. "Callison Is the Greatest," proclaimed another.⁴⁶ There wasn't a single Dick Allen sign to be found. All, it seemed to the sporting literati, was right with the world.

Clearly the fans' brief respite in their treatment of what was unmistakably by now the club's only remaining star was over. The ovations that greeted Dick upon his return from his shoulder injury were long gone. For a brief moment early in the season, Mauch attempted to capitalize on the ripple of goodwill and tentative détente by suggesting that he might anoint Dick team captain. For a while he asked Dick to carry the team's lineup card out to home plate as team captains are traditionally expected to do, and Dick was thrilled by the possibility that his appointment was perhaps imminent: "I'd consider it quite an honor," he said.[47] But nothing ever came of it. "I've thought about it," said Mauch, "but we've got a lot of ballplayers on this team who don't need a captain. Does Groat? Does White? Does Callison? Do the four starters? But I've thought about it."[48] That was all he was prepared to do; Mauch soon dropped the idea. Allen Lewis, in the middle of his article detailing why Dick was not a superstar, contended that Dick "never made the sacrifices necessary to earn the captain's position," validating Mauch's decision.[49]

Though Dick might have considered it an honor, the captainship would not have prodded him to arrive at the ballpark any earlier. (Mauch insisted that his players arrive at the stadium by 5 P.M. for a 7:30 game.) "I guess the club was trying to give me responsibility," Dick said as he reflected upon his near-captaincy. "I told Mauch the players didn't like being treated like kids. He said that for every day I wasn't in position at five he would fine me $150. It was principle with me. I didn't show up—and I paid."[50] Dick wasn't the only player who was rubbed raw by Mauch's militancy: Johnny Callison found his nitpicking to be so incessant that "it makes a guy want to give up."[51] He fumed when Mauch fined him $1,000 merely for criticizing him: "I'm not a kid any more. I don't need that kind of treatment. . . . I don't need a kick in the pants from him."[52] If anything, the captaincy might have empowered Dick to lead a full-scale revolt against Mauch's rules. Without it, he soldiered on alone. Jim Murray of the *Los Angeles Times* later observed that, to Dick, baseball was a "hard-hat" job: "You and I might look around [the stadium] and see glamor [*sic*] and romance and pleasure. To Richie Allen, it's just another rolling mill, a lunch pail, time-clock, wait-for-the-whistle job." Which was why, Murray concluded, Dick arrived at the ballpark "about the same time as the box-seat holders."[53]

On time is game time, as Dick would say. When the whistle blew, he'd be there. But not before.

In many ways, 1967 wore Dick down. The boos got louder, the fines became more frequent, the benching discussed and debated ad nauseam. Though he continued to pay the fines without complaint, he became more dour and melancholy, sometimes quite publicly: "I think baseball players should be nice to fans, but not because he owes them anything . . . I don't mind the fans out here at the park. But when I'm with my family they bother me."[54] Even at the park, though, he often refused to sign autographs. The day after his July benching he was bombarded by reporters who wanted to know every detail. Sitting there, in his damp long johns, sipping a beer, "He looked uncomfortable and confused and miserable. Sports writers were grilling him, managers were benching him, fans were booing him." Finally Dick looked up at them and pleaded, "I don't want to be a super-star."[55]

Too late. In the media's opinion Dick was either thought to be a superstar but shouldn't be or wasn't one but should be. Wrapped up in this debate was the issue, raised (not for the first time) in Lewis's article, of whether he was subject to, or demanded, a separate set of rules. Dick responded to Lewis's allegation in the *Sporting News* (in a piece written by Allen Lewis of all people): "There aren't two sets of rules on this club," he said. "I wear the same uniform as the others and I expect the same treatment. I'll admit it's a little difficult to live within the rules. . . . I know my responsibilities, though, and I'll live up to them. I expect to be fined. But don't get me wrong. I want to be a good player. If the club doesn't believe I deserve the salary I'm getting I'll give it back."[56] When it came to discussing rules, Dick and writers were speaking at cross-purposes. They were focused on the minor ones people like Mauch taped to the clubhouse door; he had his eyes trained on the big ones organizations like the Phillies enforced for years, such as their unspoken color line, separate spring training living arrangements for black players once they finally did integrate, and refusal to integrate their front office. "Two sets of rules?" he said years later, "Baseball set the tone."[57]

Even when it came to those smaller rules, the Phillies sent mixed messages. Responding to Lewis's article (as with all things Allen, nearly everyone felt the urge to chime in), Mauch initially insisted, "There are not two sets of standards on the Phillies. And there never will be."[58] Five days later he said that "[a]ny player on my club who wants to produce the way Richie Allen produces will receive the same privileges [he receives] gladly."[59] Amid the confusion, the crowds at Connie Mack grew increasingly more hostile. During one 29-game stretch where he hit well but failed to homer, Dick was subjected to a public evisceration every time he stepped on the field. At one point in the season, the club, overall, was hitting so poorly that when Mauch simply eliminated from consideration those hitting below .200 he barely had enough players left to make out a lineup for a game against the Giants.[60] Yet it was Dick, hitting above .300 and leading the club in nearly every offensive category, who was their target. Though Dick had been booed before, Hochman recognized that in Philadelphia, boos were like wine—each year's harvest had its own unique characteristics. As a connoisseur, Hochman noticed that the 1967 vintage was noticeably thicker, with a longer finish than those of prior years: "There is a different tinge to the jeers this year, a sullen, envious grumbling noise because Allen held out for a huge raise, and people expect him to hit baseballs over tall buildings."[61] Although he led the club in home runs, runs, and hits at the All-Star break, the booing not only continued, it intensified.

By August Dick led the majors in triples, was among the league leaders in runs, doubles, home runs, RBIs, and stolen bases, and, as Conlin pointed out while in a fit of admiration, "is only the fourth major leaguer in baseball history to reach double figures in doubles, triples and homers in each of his first four years. He is tied with Lou Gehrig at four. Ducky Medwick did it in each of his first five and Stan Musial holds the record with seven. Select enough group for you?" As his article suggested, for most fans it wasn't. "We know, we know. Booooooooooo!"[62] Writers from other National League cities were uniformly appalled whenever their beats took them to Connie Mack Stadium. "The Phillies are baseball's orphans," wrote a *Houston Post* reporter. "It's all because the fans back home treat their team like prisoners of war."[63] The folks in the visitors' dugout were similarly stunned. "[T]his is the worst I've ever seen," said Cubs' manager Leo Durocher of the venom directed toward Dick. "You're not talking about an average ball player— you're talking about one of the great players. Holy cats! I've been around a long time, but this is the worst."[64]

Philadelphia fans booed Dick during infield practice, they yelled things from the stands, they sent him letters calling him a "dirty, black nigger." Bill Campbell, the Phillies' play-by-play announcer, somehow managed to coax him onto his postgame show one evening and was rewarded the next day with three letters calling him a "nigger lover." Finally Dick had had enough. "I'd just like to go somewhere else to play," he said after an August 17 game where the crowd booed him all night until it cheered him when he won the game with an extra-inning home run. "I just want one thing right now—that's to get out of Philadelphia."[65] The next evening he was greeted at third base by more boos, catcalls, and a smoke bomb that landed and smoldered only twenty feet from where he was positioned.

Years later Dick would reflect upon this tumult as the moment when things changed for him: "I'm no psychiatrist, but I believe it was during those '67–'68 seasons that I first began to act the role that Philadelphia had carved out for me. I'd been hearing I was a bum for so long that I began to think maybe that's just what I was. I began to hit the sauce pretty good, and I didn't care who knew it."[66] In retrospect, Larry Merchant acknowledged the human tinderbox that resided within the Phillies' clubhouse: "Allen didn't have the temperament to deal with the downsides of being a superstar—with the expectations of the crowd, with the temptations to become a prima donna. You mix that up with what apparently was a more serious drinking problem than we knew about, that was an explosive cocktail."[67] Still, there were limits to his drinking. "To be honest, I was nervous under all that pressure, and a couple of drinks before a game would settle me down. The press would smell liquor on my breath, and, bam, I'm supposed to be a drunk. But I never walked on a field where I couldn't do the job better than anyone else. Ain't nobody ever seen me fall and stagger around a ball field. No man, not even me, can hit two home runs in a game drunk."[68] But Dick didn't make things easy on himself in that regard: not only did he keep a bottle of Jack Daniels in plain view on the top shelf of his locker, he often invited writers waiting to interview him to "have a taste."[69] Here, as elsewhere, the optics were terrible. But Dick didn't care at all about such things. Not surprisingly, he soon developed a national reputation for being "more thirsty than hungry."[70]

Shortly after taking the field the day following his pronouncement that he wanted out of Philadelphia, Dick hangs his head as a smoke bomb explodes behind him, August 18, 1967.

(Temple University Libraries, Special Collections Research Center, Philadelphia, PA)

One week after he suggested that his time in Philadelphia might be coming to an end, Dick's career was placed in peril. While working on his stalled Ford, he severed two tendons and the ulnar nerve in his right hand. The accident occurred at approximately 8 P.M. on a Thursday—normally around the second inning or so of a game. It was raining that night, however, and the Phils' game with the Pirates was postponed, leaving Dick with time to kill. He decided to fill it by tinkering with his 1955 Ford. (He had recently purchased a new Cadillac but loved to tinker with the Ford when he had free time.) "Blood spurted from a three-inch cut on the heel of his hand," Conlin reported the next day, "two inches above the wrist and in a line beneath his little finger. Another, more serious, cut traversed his wrist on a three-inch diagonal from left to right."[71] Minutes later, Dick Allen Jr. watched his dad rush into the house, gushing blood from his hand and wrist. "Where's your mom?" Dick said to his son. "I got to get to the hospital."[72]

His Mt. Airy neighbor and friend, a fender and auto-body mechanic, was with Dick when the accident occurred. "I spent about two hours helping Rich carpet the floor of the car," he said the following day. "Then we drove it around the neighborhood to build up charge in the battery. It was a new battery. We were driving on Mt. Airy Avenue, across the street from Rich's house, when the car stalled. Rich headed it toward the curb and [it] climbed over the curb. The right front wheel got stuck in the muddy grass." When the car wouldn't start, Dick and his friend began rocking it back and forth so as to maneuver it back into the street. Dick was on the driver's side of the car, his friend on the other. As they attempted to push the car back into the street, Dick's hand slipped off the wet headlight and was sliced by the razor-sharp bumper mechanism.[73]

The trip to the hospital was harrowing. "I didn't want to pass out. I was fighting it in the car. My wife was driving and my Mom was watching the blood soak through the towel she'd wrapped around it tight. I saw the tendons and they looked like wires."[74] In the wake of Dick's earlier shoulder injury, Mauch suggested that "the only man strong enough to hurt Rich Allen is Rich Allen." "That aphorism was disproved last night on a rainy street in Germantown," Conlin wrote the day after the accident. "The only thing that could hurt Philadelphia's most controversial athlete was a $50 Ford."[75]

Dick was shaken by the episode: looking at his wrist "was like looking at strands of spaghetti," and the doctors refused to speculate as to whether he would ever play again.[76] Nevertheless, Quinn was quick to conclude that he'd be okay: "The doctors explained to me that the injuries are quite severe. Rich will wear a cast for six weeks," he lectured the assembled throng at Temple University Hospital shortly after the completion of the five-hour surgery to repair the damage. However, he assured them, "they told me that if his recovery is normal, the injury probably won't affect his grip on a bat or ability to throw a ball."[77] In this case Quinn, as in seemingly everything else that involved Dick, badly misjudged the situation. "The hand/wrist injury was a game-changing event in his career," Conlin asserted, "and he was never the same ballplayer after it." Without a doubt, it was "the unkindest cut of all."[78]

Unlike what occurred in the aftermath of Dick's earlier shoulder injury, this time few fans took the occasion to reassess their opinion of him. There were a few reasons why, including the way Dick handled the injury from his hospital bed. Initially he was depressed, but a visit from boxer Joe Frazier lifted his spirits and caused him to dart out of the hospital, to disastrous effect. "Frazier may have saved my career," he said a few years later. "I was down and depressed and Joe came to see me. He had also once hurt his hand. He said it didn't do any good to feel sorry for yourself. He said 'Man, you can't lay around, you've got to fight this thing.' Well, I don't know, but it was just the way he said it. I called my mother and told her I'd be right home. I got up and walked out of the hospital."[79] Although he did stop to appropriately secure a medical discharge from the hospital before leaving, he failed to inform the Phillies of his early departure; they assumed that he was leaving later in the day and had scheduled a news conference to brief the media on his condition and to allow them to ask Dick questions. The news conference went forward as scheduled, only without the star attraction.[80] Once again, Dick appeared to be a no-show.

Then a rumor began spreading that the whole stalled Ford story was simply a cover for the real story—that Dick's hand had been sliced open in a bar fight. The rumor gained credibility when it turned out that one of the people spreading it was none other than Judy Johnson—the old Negro Leaguer who helped sign Dick back in Wampum and who was considered to be a good friend of Dick's. "Judy Johnson told me for sure Allen was razor cut in the bar down 21st Street after the game was rained out early," recalled Conlin.[81] Indeed, the injury seemed to mark a break in the relationship between Dick and Johnson. Later Johnson reflected on his relationship with bitterness: "I don't know how many times I was sent to straighten him out. He was just a wild something from up in Wampum, Pa. He was the best player from up there and it just went to his head. The liquor just went to his head. I loved his mom and she loved me. But I said the hell with Richie Allen. I just got sick of him."[82] Everybody, it seemed, was getting sick of him. So the "Richie Allen bar fight" story took root, even without any supporting evidence. (Nobody ever stepped forward to substantiate or corroborate any of Johnson's allegations.)

A few weeks later, Dick visited his teammates and showed them just how long his road back was going to be. He was wearing a full cast from fingertip to shoulder and had no feeling in his pinkie—a fact he illustrated by lighting a cigarette lighter and holding it under the finger for several seconds.[83] He was largely unable to care for himself; his wife had to dress and shave him. He let his mustache grow back, however, for practical reasons: "If you think I'm letting her get above my upper lip with a razor in her hand, you're crazy."[84] Despite some moments of levity, Dick was deeply depressed over the situation as well as his future; his doctors refused to speculate on his prognosis until they could examine him without his cast. In the meantime, he was left to brood. "One Sunday [Bill] White had a bone to pick with me over something I wrote he didn't like," Conlin recalled. "I was the only writer left in the clubhouse and White was airing his gripe at his locker when Allen came lurching into the clubhouse in khakis and a Ban-Lon looking like he had slept in a stable. He was drunk and he burst into tears, told White the hand wasn't getting any better and he was going to announce his retirement the next day. Bill calmed him down and told me to wait. They talked in private. After Allen left, White said, 'Don't even think about writing what you just saw and heard. He's drunk and he didn't mean any of it. If you write it you'll make a fool out of yourself. Just let me take care of him.'"[85] The story was never written and Dick eventually pulled himself together. Still, there were an abundance of unanswered questions as the off-season approached.

One of the main questions had to do with his seemingly never-ending contract situation: what would happen now, given that his status for the 1968 season was so much in question? Despite missing the final six weeks of the season, Dick once again put up impressive numbers before the injury—a .307 batting average along with 23 home runs and 77 RBIs. And in December he received good news from the doctors: his ulnar nerve seemed to be healing.[86] Still, nobody knew precisely what that meant; he still hadn't swung a bat at live pitching. But a new contract had to be negotiated. Claude Harrison suspected that the Phils might "make Richie an offer which could be re-negotiated when and if the hand heals," although whether he'd settle for something like that, "no one knows but Allen."[87] Everybody else would find out shortly. And loudly.

First, however, Dick was adamant about demonstrating to everyone—the Phillies, the media, the fans—that he was in fact largely healed and ready to play ball out of the chute in 1968. On January 30, he found an opportunity to do so. That evening, the annual Philadelphia Sports Writers Association dinner was held at the Sheraton Hotel, and Dick was determined to use it to prove a point. Although he had previously shied away from such events, this time he not only showed up, he glad-handed everyone he could find, squeezing their hands tightly within his newly reconstructed right hand so as to illustrate just how well he had healed. He also took the occasion to announce that he, of all people, was heading down to Florida—a full month early—to begin his preparations for the upcoming season. "I think working out under the sun in Florida will give me the opportunity to do something with the finger," he said. "This is my own project. I want to play this season and I think an early start will aid me."[88] For a player whose past holdouts were suspected to be, at least in part, fueled by his disdain of preseason workouts, this announcement caught everybody pleasantly off guard.

While everything seemed smooth on the surface (there were even rumors—false ones—that he had signed his contract quickly and without complaint), beneath it things were roiling.[89] The awards dinner was a case in point. Although it was not reported at the time, while Dick was smiling and glad-handing, his agent, Clem Capozzoli—the "chubby, bespectacled Philadelphia baking executive," as described by Sandy Grady—spent the better part of the evening sparring with Quinn. Quinn, who was the one who had started the rumor of the signed contract a month earlier, took umbrage at Capozzoli's refusal to engage him in contract negotiations and his insistence that he and Dick deal with Bob Carpenter directly. Quinn, in turn, refused to recognize Capozzoli's role as Dick's agent and the result was a loud disagreement backstage at the banquet.[90]

Nobody knew quite what to make of Capozzoli. The writers rarely portrayed him generously; Hochman described him as "a short, plump man with a face like a dinner roll." He was an executive at the American Baking Company who spent much of his time, according to Hochman, "at the Latin Casino or the ballpark or the racetrack or the golf course." He never played golf, though. "I've got enough bad habits without taking up golf," he said. "But I go out on the course with the stars. When they're in town I set up golf games for them." Hochman couldn't figure him out: "He is not funny enough to serve as court jester, nor deep enough to provide meaty conversation, nor rich enough to open locked doors. Why then do the stars want him around?" Capozzoli got a particular rush out of hanging out with ballplayers: "Being around baseball players puffs him up like yeast in a biscuit," wrote Hochman. He hooked up with Dick shortly after Dick arrived in Philadelphia: "I showed him how things worked in business. He doesn't know about those things. When you're young, you eat, sleep and drink baseball. He won't need any help in three years or five years. He won't need me or anybody else." Until that time, Capozzoli would be there and serve as the conduit through which Dick operated. "John Quinn is dealing with a different breed of players now," Capozzoli told Hochman. "He has to put up with stuff he didn't have to put up with years ago."[91] Some of that stuff involved having to put up with agents like Clem Capozzoli. Quinn couldn't stomach that and let Capozzoli know it at the banquet.

Contrary to the stories published the next day, Dick was not all smiles at the event either, as he was involved in a row that evening with Conlin. Theirs was a confrontation that had long been simmering. It began shortly after the season ended when Conlin attempted to contact Dick to check on the condition of his injuries and who appeared to have gone into hiding: his home number had been changed, and the Phillies claimed to have no idea where he was. Conlin called Quinn, who suggested that he call Era in Wampum, which he did. Era refused to tell him where her son

Dick, Clem Capozzoli, and Joe Frazier enjoy a night out
on March 7, 1967, during Dick's March 1967 holdout.

(Temple University Libraries, Special Collections Research Center, Philadelphia, PA)

was (he was on the West Coast at the time) and pleaded with Conlin to leave Dick alone. Conlin attempted to curry favor with her by informing her that, of all things, he withheld printing the story about Dick's inebriated locker room retirement confession a few weeks earlier, but it got him nowhere; she insisted that Conlin "was just another one of those writers who wouldn't give her son any peace." When Dick got wind of Conlin's conversation with his mother, he was outraged, thinking that Conlin had insulted her and called her a liar for claiming not to know that he was on the West Coast.[92] To a man who was particularly sensitive about anything having to do with his mother, Conlin's phone call with Era had little chance of ending well; Dick responded by confronting him at the banquet and announcing that "the next time he upsets my mother I'm going to punch him."[93]

But all of that was behind-the-scenes. Publicly, at least, the evening had been a success: Dick had demonstrated his fitness and, as promised, followed up by heading down to Florida with a jockey friend of his to prepare for the season. Before he arrived in Clearwater, he stopped off at the Gulf-to-Bay Batting Range: "I was driving my car towards Clearwater when I noticed a lot of nets. It reminded me of a batting cage. I looked twice. It was a batting cage. All of a sudden I had the urge to do some hitting. I was a little scared, too, because I didn't have the faintest idea what kind of swinging I'd be able to do. But it was something that had to be done sooner or later and I figured this was as good a time as any." He popped the trunk of his Cadillac, pulled out a leaded bat—one much heavier than even the 41-ouncers he swung in games—and started hacking. Luckily he had several quarters to feed the machine—ten balls per quarter plus a free game if he hit seven balls out of the cage itself—because he missed nearly everything at first. Soon he loosened up and began to make contact. He still had some numbness in his hand but could hit nevertheless. "It was actually the first time since I've been playing baseball that I really was pleased with myself," he said afterward. "For me, it was a great moment—after all those months of wondering." He quickly made a visit to the Gulf-to-Bay Batting Range part of his daily routine, and word spread that Dick Allen, of all people, was feeding quarters into the machines there while learning how to get his groove back. Soon there was a crowd of kids waiting for him every morning as he pulled up to take his swings. "I'm getting there," he told them.[94]

Quinn wasn't interested in a ballplayer who wasn't all the way there yet; he offered Dick a conditional contract for 1968, one that required Dick to demonstrate his fitness for baseball activities before the contract would fully kick in. "I can't understand that man," Dick said. "He wanted me to sign a restricted contract that won't mean anything if I didn't show I could play in March. I asked him what happens if I can't hit and throw right. He told me 'Well, you can catch a bus home.'" Because, Quinn claimed, Dick's injury had occurred in a non-baseball-related context, the conditional contract was appropriate. "He had a piece of paper signed by a doctor," Dick told Sandy Grady. "It wasn't my doctor but some man who didn't even know my injury. Quinn had this paper that said I would be 50 percent recovered opening day, and 70 percent recovered eventually." Dick found the discussions with Quinn, along with the contract offer itself, demeaning: "I was burned up. I didn't want any more to do with him. I didn't like the way he treated my manager [Capozzoli] either. . . . I don't want to have anything to do with that man. I just want to stay away from him."[95] From then on, he would.

To Dick, a contract that tied his salary to his health so crudely only reinforced his suspicion that to management, he was less a man than a piece of property—when he wore down physically he would lack any value at all in their eyes. Although salaries were inevitably tied to performance (indeed, Dick had spent the previous few years making this very point to anyone who would listen), it seemed that here, with Quinn's conditional contract, the human element—compassion—had been stripped from the equation. Worse, Quinn didn't even have any hard evidence that Dick's performance would in fact decline. Instead he identified a weakness in Dick's bargaining power and jumped on it—and after years of scolding Dick for attempting to tie salary to performance himself.

"No play, no pay" was how he recalled Quinn's conditional contract. "No job to get me through. It made me stop and think: Even if you hit 95 home runs, they say 'See you' if you can't produce." If it hadn't crystallized before, by now he had hard evidence that irrespective of the rhetoric, a ball club was not a family, or at least not one worthy of emulation. Quinn's negotiating style drove home to him the reality that in management's eyes, ballplayers were less like family members than widgets, to be swapped out when they inevitably wore down. "From then on," he decided, "it was 'I'm for Dick.'"[96] This would only further pique his succession of employers who could never understand why, despite the relatively large salaries they gave him, and the other perks and indulgences they provided him, he only seemed to become even more insolent and ungrateful in return.

Although Carpenter refused to concede that Quinn had presented Dick with a conditional contract, he interceded and re-signed Dick for a contract that called for him to receive his full salary ($85,000) regardless of how well he swung the bat in March. But things would never be the same. "God gave me a warning," Dick recalled a few years later of the freak injury and its aftermath. "He took some of it away from me. But He left me enough."[97] Now he knew without a doubt that it was up to him, and only him, to look out for his best interests. His employers, he understood now more clearly than ever, could only be counted on to look after themselves. Through his assignment to Little Rock, the constant shifting around the diamond defensively, the gag order in the wake of the Thomas affair, and now this, he understood that, as it applied to management's relationship with their players, the notion of benevolent paternalism was simply that—a notion. Reality was something else altogether.

Consequently, Dick thought little of it when, after he felt some additional pain in his hand in early March, he skipped out of camp without bothering to inform the club and hopped on a plane back to Philadelphia to have his personal physician take a look at it: "When I decided to have the hand examined, I called my wife and had her make the appointment. It didn't occur to me to tell anyone."[98] Quinn dutifully announced that Dick's continued absence would cost him $500 a day, to which Dick acquiesced: "I guess I'll be fined $500 a day while I'm away—it's in my contract—but I won't fight it." And why should he? In his eyes, this was merely the price of freedom. He paid for this. And so the time was now his. Mauch was all but resigned to this reality: "Richie evidently has made up his mind he's going to live his life the way he wants it," he said when asked for his opinion on his missing third baseman.[99] While he chafed at this latest rebuke of his authority, he knew that, ultimately, there was little he could do about it. Dalrymple, however, had other tactics in mind: "I think if it were up to me, I'd suspend him for two months and [see] if that didn't change his attitude."[100]

A few days later Dick returned, complete with a heated batting glove (powered by two small batteries taped to his upper arm and connected to the heating mechanism by wires) to help reduce the pain that intensified in colder weather.[101] He was still unable to fully close his hand and could not cross his fingers, but he could hit well enough to return to the lineup for yet another season.[102] Although barely two years had elapsed, the drama of spring training 1966 and Dick's subsequent shoulder injury seemed like a lifetime ago—a more innocent age, at least in retrospect. Amazingly, however, despite all that had occurred in his short career up to this point, it was nothing when compared with what would come next: the succession of incidents and dramas that took place throughout the 1968 and 1969 seasons, culminating, at last, in his departure from Philadelphia.

Chapter 7

When I Don't Like Something, I Rebel

1968: Philadelphia .263/33/90

OVER THE NEXT two seasons, the walls came crashing down at last. In certain instances, Dick acknowledged at least loosening some of the bricks himself, in others he claimed to have played no role in the destruction whatsoever. Legal troubles led the way, including an IRS ruling against him involving his 1960 signing bonus, an issue that stubbornly refused to go away, and another bar fight, this time in his Mt. Airy neighborhood, for which he was eventually exonerated but not before several weeks of bad press.

Dick's legal battles were merely the sideshow, however. The real drama in 1968 and 1969 took place at ballparks throughout the National League. "By the '68 season," he recalled in his autobiography, "I had my mind on only one thing: getting the hell out of Philadelphia. . . . The fans were no longer just booing—it was open warfare. I had security people checking my mail, which was almost always nasty and usually threatening. Some of my teammates suggested that I hire protection. My family was scared and unhappy. And the Phillies were a lousy team. I wanted out. I decided to get myself traded. This time the double standard would work in my favor.

A clean-shaven Dick Allen in a 1969 publicity still.

(National Baseball Hall of Fame and Museum, Inc.)

I began to set my own rules. Before ballgames, instead of going straight to the ballpark, I started making regular stops at watering holes along the way."[1] In theory, this plan would at least land Dick at the ballpark by game time. In practice, things sometimes worked very differently. Before April was out he was in hot water with Mauch again: he arrived late to a game against the Mets at Shea Stadium and found himself both fined and benched. "I stopped off at Aqueduct," the left fielder (he was moved, again, for the 1968 season, this time to the outfield) quipped to one reporter when asked how he managed to delay his arrival until twenty minutes before the game's first pitch; to another he claimed that he had gotten lost on the Long Island Expressway.[2] Although several of his teammates had sought and received permission to travel on their own to the series in New York, Dick hadn't bothered to ask; he just hopped in his car and decided he'd meet the club at Shea.

What piqued the beat writers even more than the late arrival was Dick's reaction to it all: "He looked so casual," the *Inquirer*'s Frank Dolson wrote after the game, which the Phils dropped, "so unconcerned. Outwardly, the loss hadn't bothered him. Or the fine."[3] He wasn't groveling, wasn't repentant. This, above all else, constituted baseball blasphemy. Teammate Larry Jackson likewise arrived late to the ballpark. He, however, showed remorse—he was "thoroughly disgusted with himself," wrote Ray Kelly.[4] So he received journalistic absolution.

Although few believed it possible, Dick's relationship with Mauch was by now deteriorating even further. A few years later, Dick reflected on his unpleasant relationship with his manager: "He would call us all kinds of names. Nobody should be called what he called us but I was the only one who would stop and say: 'Hey, you can't call me that.' "[5] Mauch fancied himself a master manipulator—of both games and people—something that was bound to rub Dick the wrong way. Pete Rose recalled a time when Mauch instructed catcher Mike Ryan to tip Rose off to his pitch selection in an attempt to get inside the great hitter's head: "Ryan says, 'Pete . . . Mauch told me to tell you what's coming.' Jim Bunning was pitching. Ryan says, 'Here comes the curve.' Then he says, 'Here comes the fastball.' Shag Crawford was the ump. I said, 'Make him quit telling me what's coming next. I hate that. I don't want that.' Anyway, they get me out three times. I come up in the ninth, one on, two out. Ryan says,

'Here comes the curve.' Strike one. I step out and start thinking, he's told me right the whole damn game. Now he says, 'Here comes another curve ball.' Sure enough, he throws a curve. I hit it off the scoreboard at Connie Mack Stadium, the guy scores and we win it 2–1. The next day, Ryan says, 'Gene Mauch told me to tell you to go to hell.'"[6]

Mauch firmly believed that he knew baseball players better than they knew themselves and, as such, knew what was best for both them and the club. His theories and tactics seemingly knew no bounds: he once cut a relief pitcher (Joe Verbanic) for being "too polite" for the job and was said to order the team trainer to give tranquilizers disguised as aspirin to a jittery pitcher.[7] In retrospect, there was little chance that a manipulator like Mauch and a free spirit like Dick would ever see eye to eye. "Gene was one of the best tacticians," recalled Dallas Green. "He understood the rules better than anybody, he was a good teacher of fundamentals, but he was an ogre when it came to handling people."[8] Dick wasn't amenable to being handled by anyone, even on a good day. On a bad day, all hell was liable to break loose if anyone tried. And the next few months would see far more bad days than good ones. "When I don't like something, I rebel," Dick liked to proclaim.[9] Nearly every day, Mauch gave him something to rebel against.

Mauch's dictum, "play him, fine him, play him again," was something he arrived at after the dust had settled, when he looked back and tried to figure out how things could have possibly gone as wrong as they did. Before he came upon his Zen-like resolution, he tried to manipulate Dick as he would anyone else. In the wake of Dick's late arrival in New York, Mauch instituted a new rule: mandatory afternoon workouts before night games. On his 25-man club, it was obvious that the rule was directed primarily, if not solely, toward Dick, something Bill White pointed out, with a smile, to the media shortly thereafter: "It's the only way he can be sure of getting Richie Allen to the ball park on time for our games."[10] If Mauch thought that the fear of a fine would alter Dick's behavior, he, like Carpenter before him, was misguided. "I fined him probably more than the minimum salary over times he got to the park late," Mauch recalled years later.[11] Indeed, he fined him seven times within a two-month span in early 1968.[12] To his shock and amazement, things only got worse—Dick was buying his freedom and he was intent on demonstrating to anyone who dared challenge him just how unencumbered he was. "Just have someone put the envelope [for the fine] in the box in the hotel," he once told Carpenter. "Just don't give me any lectures."[13]

As tensions mounted, it became increasingly obvious that something was going to burst soon. Unable to influence Dick through fines, Mauch began to attack his work ethic. In mid-May he held him out of a pair of games and suggested that perhaps he should work harder in practice. The daily scribes, as well, began questioning his dedication. Sandy Grady summarized the growing criticism when he wrote, "The rap by literati and fans has been that Allen was loafing. He is an $82,000 athlete accused of half-hearted practice, of lackadaisical work in the outfield, and of dim-headed moves on the bases."[14] Dick denied the charges, saying, "Listen, this is my living . . . I'd be crazy not to give it everything. I've played sports all my life and never been told that I wasn't going all-out."[15] The *Daily News'* Hochman could feel the anxiety every time he wandered into the locker room: "There is a feeling of discontent boiling in the clubhouse like a smog. Allen spends the pre-game practice lobbing a ball at the yellow circle that dots the 'i' in the Wise potato chip sign. Mauch sits in the dugout staring at Allen and wondering what is going on inside that muddled head. . . . The whispers get louder: someone's gotta-go, someone's gotta-go."[16]

A couple of weeks later, on May 25, Dick showed up to a game with the Cardinals in St. Louis well after Mauch's posted arrival deadline (Dick arrived at 6:35 for a 7:05 game). This time, the frustrated Mauch decided to take no action—Dick started the game and helped the Phils to a victory—but warned him that if he was late again, he'd be suspended indefinitely.[17] Dick called him on his threat four days later when he showed up late for a twi-night doubleheader against the Cubs at Connie Mack Stadium. This time, Dick offered an excuse—he had pulled a groin while riding his horse a few hours earlier in Fairmount Park, claiming, "I was hurt. What was the use of getting there early?"[18] Mauch took no action and, instead, inserted him into the lineup as he had four days earlier. Dick played through game one, and to what extent the injury affected him was unclear—some reports concluded that he showed no symptoms of his injury, while others observed that runners were taking extra bases on balls hit to him in left.[19] But in game two, he limped badly on the bases and was pulled after one at-bat. Making matters worse, reports surfaced later that on the afternoon Dick alleged he was riding his horse in the park, he was spotted at Garden State Park cashing in a winning ticket at the $50 window. (He bet on Bogue Island, which paid $38.)[20] Dick then admitted that, in fact, he hadn't injured his groin horseback riding at all; rather, "it's something that had bothered me ever since spring training."[21] He also told Hochman, "I didn't hurt it falling off a horse. You fall off a horse, you hurt something else, but you don't pull a groin muscle. I hurt it at a horse farm in Jersey. I went over there to look at some horses."[22] Somewhere along the way, his groin was pulled. Again, conflicting reports, conflicting statements. Through it all, Mauch seethed.

By the next day, Mauch was ready to make good on his earlier promise. When Dick arrived, Mauch informed him that he "could cool his heels on the bench until he decided he was going to conform to club discipline."[23] Not only that, every game it took him to figure things out was going to cost him. Dick responded by informing Mauch that "You can take my money. But after you take that, what else can you take? You'll have to get rid of me."[24] A couple of days later, on June 1, Dick was still fuming—fines he could deal with, attempts to control and coerce him were something else altogether. According to coach George Myatt, Dick approached Mauch with the intention of fighting him right then and there. On top of that, Myatt smelled liquor on Dick's breath. Myatt promptly interceded and sent Dick home.[25] What ensued was a bizarre showdown between Dick and Mauch where Mauch was determined to break his star left fielder once and for all but equally determined not to signal as much to the press. For the next two weeks, Mauch would announce before every game that Dick was not in the lineup because of a medical condition that was "day-to-day." However, trainer Joe Liscio rebutted the manager when he told Ray Kelly two weeks into the showdown that Dick hadn't been to see him.[26] Moreover, after Myatt sent Dick home, Mauch addressed the clubhouse by announcing that "I'm afraid we're gonna have to get along without Allen for a while. But as long as I'm here things are going to be run my way."[27] After the meeting concluded, Mauch blurted out to confidants, "That——will never play for me again."[28] Perhaps Dick was "day-to-day" as Mauch publicly insisted. But everyone waited to see whose days would be up first—Dick's or his manager's.

Technically Dick was never suspended (the Phillies neither filed a formal notice of suspension with the league office nor publicly announced it, as they would have been required to do). Instead it was an unofficial, spectacular showdown. On June 2, the club headed west for games against the Giants and Dodgers. Dick accompanied the club (which he would have been forbidden to do had he been officially suspended) but remained apart from it (or, more specifically, from Mauch) whenever and however possible. Mauch boarded the plane with an iron will but little more than that to buttress him: regardless of his strong words to his confidants (who then promptly leaked them to the media), he had little choice but to figure out some way to coexist with Dick. Short of a trade (and recent events had done little to enhance Dick's market value), he was either going to have to learn to live with Dick or start searching for alternative employment. Perhaps away from the blinding glare of Philadelphia he could finally make Dick see the error of his ways, he thought. It was the final gamble by a man who was all but out of options.[29] Mauch was all-in: either he'd resolve things to his satisfaction before the club returned to Philadelphia, or he'd most likely be gone. Dick couldn't possibly stare him down, he believed. Surely, at some point, either in San Francisco or, at the latest, in Los Angeles, he'd blink.

Dick was just as determined to see to it that it was Mauch who blinked. Once out in San Francisco, Dick set his own schedule: arriving at the ballpark on his clock, dressing on his clock, and ignoring batting and fielding practice altogether. Nobody knew quite what to make of it all. Conlin recalled the San Francisco leg of the trip:

[Dick] sat with the relievers on the bench. When it was time for the bullpen to report to a pen that was in the open, halfway down the left-field line, Allen went with them. This confirmed what neither Mauch nor Allen would address: a sit-down strike was in progress. In the top of the seventh, Allen walked out to Jim Ray Hart in left field while Ray Sadecki was warming up, said a few words, then proceeded to center-field where he chatted up Willie Mays, then to right field for a brief visit with Ollie Brown. From there, he vanished through the double doors down the right-field line that led to both clubhouses. After the final out of a Chris Short 1–0 victory [in the series opener], we hustled to the press elevator down the right-field line and arrived at field level just in time to have Allen breeze past us, turned out in a Nehru suit. He greeted us warmly and kept going. Mauch blew us off with a "Write what you saw" response. The same bizarre scenario was repeated the next two games. [Dick] sat with the relievers on [the] bench and in [the] bullpen, visited the San Francisco outfield on his way to the clubhouse, and was gone as soon as the final out was recorded.[30]

Years later, Giants manager Herman Franks recalled that Dick spent more time during that series in the Giants' clubhouse than in his own. He also recalled Dick lobbying for a trade to the Giants: "He always used to say to me: 'Why can't I be over here playing with you?'"[31] In fact, the Phils were making at least some effort to accommodate him, inquiring as to whether the Giants would be willing to swap left fielders. The Giants were interested and believed that their third base coach (and former Phillies' coach), Peanuts Lowrey, could get through to Dick.[32] Negotiations went nowhere fast, and the showdown plowed on, down to Los Angeles.

There, the same scenario ensued with one exception: given that the Dodger Stadium bullpens were enclosed, Dick was unable to make his nightly rounds with the Los Angeles outfielders. In all, he sat out the entire Coast trip, making a lone pinch-hit appearance (and even that was against Mauch's will) in Los Angeles. To Mauch's relief, the specifics of Dick's nightly sojourns, along with detailed descriptions of "the troubled look that haunted the manager's face," were not relayed back to Philadelphia, at least not immediately; the June 6 assassination of Robert Kennedy caused the three Philadelphia beat writers who traveled with the club on their Coast trip to conference and jointly decide to hold off on reporting on the saga until a few days had passed.[33] After their agreed-upon moratorium ended, on June 10, readers were overwhelmed by the avalanche of everything that had taken place over the previous few days. Allen Lewis, who a year earlier had contended that Dick was many things but certainly not a superstar, this time alleged that Dick was trying to force the Phils to trade him through his purported sit-down strike as well as his "lackadaisical" play beforehand.[34] For his part, Dick denied that he was engaged in any sort of sit-down strike at all: "I didn't play because my name wasn't in the lineup."[35] While he wasn't going to bend to Mauch's will, he emphasized, it was Mauch's decision to sit him throughout the Coast trip, not his. If anything, the positions of both sides appeared to be hardening.

Behind the scenes, back in Philadelphia, Clem Capozzoli was meeting with Quinn, insisting that Quinn reduce the fines that were piling up day by day. They were way out of line, the little baker argued, and Dick would never play unless and until they were reduced.[36] Quinn stood firm and a standoff ensued here, too. Capozzoli then demanded a meeting with Carpenter, which Quinn rebuffed as well. Finally, with things stalled on all fronts, Carpenter intervened again, as he had during Dick's contract holdouts, and dismissed Quinn from the negotiations. He sharply reduced the fines (yet another of his small charitable acts that he hoped would purchase the good graces of his star left fielder), got Mauch on the phone, and ordered him to play Dick that evening against the Dodgers. The beaten Mauch had no choice—in the eighth inning, he begrudgingly sent Dick up to pinch-hit for catcher Clay Dalrymple, thereby technically complying with Carpenter's mandate. Although he sat Dick again the next day (in a futile effort to preserve the illusion that Dick was still recovering from his mysterious groin pull), the battle was over. The Phillies announced that the issue had been "resolved"; Allen Lewis quipped that that was "a statement that must rank as one of the most optimistic in sports history."[37] Nobody missed the significance of what had just occurred: "Carpenter neutered general manager John Quinn's authority last spring by negotiating Allen's huge raise himself," wrote Conlin. "Now the owner appears to have severed whatever shred of shaky control Mauch had over his slugger." Going forward, he concluded, "It would appear that Mauch will control only 24 of the team's 25 players for the balance of the season. Or until a press conference is called to name his successor."[38] Lewis was incredulous over what had just occurred: "The Phillies cannot very well refuse to back up Mauch in this dispute, or it would be an open invitation to others who might dislike the way the manager runs his team."[39] Yet, to Lewis's astonishment, they just did. He also charged that "the majority of Phillies' players are fed up with Allen," a contention Bill White refuted the next day: "He hasn't affected my morale. I worry about his future because he's my roommate and I like him, but I am still playing as hard as I can. . . . To my way of thinking, this is not a divided team. That is simply not true."[40]

The club departed Los Angeles for Philadelphia for a series against the Astros at Connie Mack. In his cramped office on the day of the series opener, the media descended upon Mauch en masse, picking the final scraps off the bones of what was once the cocky authoritarian. When questioned about Dick's denial that he had engaged in a sit-down strike, all the weary Mauch could respond with was an annoyed, "What do you want me to do, call him a liar? You guys get in a hassle with him. I've had mine."[41] The game itself was a contradiction in many ways: feverishly anticipated yet sparsely attended (only 5,243 in the stands), a crowd full of venom but, to the surprise of many, replete with admiration and support as well. In all, it was one of the more confusing nights in Philadelphia sports history.

While many fans stayed away that evening, others decided that they had no choice but to be there. "I was a Phillies fan first but I absolutely loved Dick Allen," recalled one fan of his pilgrimage to Connie Mack Stadium that night. "I felt as if, being black in Philadelphia, that I had a place there that evening to show my support for him." He was not disappointed. Despite the meager crowd, "the atmosphere was electric . . . when Dick came out of the dugout and took his place on the on-deck circle, he was greeted by what sounded like a million boos and heckles. Myself and four other friends were seated on the first base side, looking right in Dick's face—he was on the third base side. Among all of these boos, we're giving Dick Allen the raised fist. And he responded in kind, from the kneeling position on the on-deck circle."[42] He then stepped up with two outs in the first inning and launched a rocket over the left-field fence off of Astros' pitcher Larry Dierker. As he rounded the bases for what would be the only run the Phillies would score that evening, both cheers and boos rained down upon him, each fan responding to whatever it was he believed Dick Allen symbolized. Some were convinced that he represented Black Power and the fight for racial equality, others were just as sure that he stood for the destruction of everything they grew up believing in, and others weren't sure which. But they knew that he represented something, even if they couldn't quite put their finger on it. For better or worse, and without even trying, he had achieved a sort of cultural significance, his every action, or refusal to act, seemingly meaningful in some larger way. For all of his energy devoted to diminishing Dick, to subjugating him, Mauch had only succeeded in making him larger-than-life. By comparison, Mauch was shrinking. Three days later, during the first game of a doubleheader against the Dodgers, Mauch received a phone call from his daughter in Hacienda Heights, California, beckoning him home to be with his wife, Nina Lee, who had suddenly taken ill and needed emergency surgery. He left the club during the nightcap, leaving Myatt in charge. It was an open question as to whether he'd ever return.

*　*　*

"Just days before Mauch was fired, I had gone to see Carpenter again," Dick recalled. "I told him that all the stories in the press about the coming showdown between me and Mauch had made me a depressed and confused ballplayer. In my mind, I told Carpenter, it was no longer a question of wanting to be traded—I *had* to be traded. Again, he refused. Instead, he told me that Mauch was going to be fired."[43] On so many levels, Dick and Mauch just didn't see eye to eye. While Mauch liked to say that Dick "lik[ed] high fastballs and fast highballs," Dick would correct the record by saying that "Oh, I've done my little bit of dirt, I suppose, but I've really honestly never done anything bad. And I carry my Bible with me and I read it—just like my mother trained me to live."[44] Responding to a reporter's suggestion that Dick was a loner, Mauch once replied, "Yeah, he's fallen in with the wrong crowd."[45] It was useless to pretend any longer that there was some way to remedy the situation. Without a doubt, these were two people who could no longer coexist.

The official end of the Mauch era came while the skipper was in Hacienda Heights, tending to his wife (unofficially, he was most likely dismissed when he sat down with Carpenter before he left for the airport).[46] At the press conference, and with Mauch in absentia, Quinn stated that "the Allen problem was a factor, but not the entire reason," he had been dismissed. He then added, mysteriously, "We know Gene had some personal problems that would have affected his managing which I won't discuss."[47] Carpenter, as well, maintained that Mauch had his own issues apart from Dick. He later said that his dismissal had "nothing to do with

Allen. If the club had been winning there wouldn't have been a change."[48] Hochman likewise tried to add clarity: "Mauch wasn't fired because he couldn't handle Rich Allen. Heck, John McGraw couldn't handle Rich Allen. Joe Frazier couldn't handle Rich Allen. Jorge Velasquez couldn't handle Rich Allen. Well, you get the idea. No, Gene Mauch was fired because he thought only about winning the next game on the schedule and wouldn't squander his time or energy worrying about the future." In short, "when it came to analyzing people in his own farm system he was brutally swift. He scoffed at Ferguson Jenkins' fast ball, he scorned Adolfo Phillips' batting stance, he mocked Alex Johnson's lethargy. Joe Verbanic was too polite. Costen Shockly was too brash. Jeff James shot pool with Bo Belinsky, and on and on." As Hochman recognized, Mauch undermined the entire organization by dismissing all of the work it had done preparing the next generation of Phillies each spring training when he "would stand behind the batting cage, sneering. Zap. In five days he'd have his mind made up. . . . Which is why Gene Mauch got fired."[49]

Regardless, Dick knew what was coming. "I'd rather not comment," he said to the media surrounding his locker in the immediate aftermath, "because I'm going to get blamed for Gene being fired."[50] Afterward, while coming off the field after practice, he was booed, hollered at, and insulted by the early arrivals along the third base stands. Several months later, he expanded on his point: "The fans and the press seemed to think that I was the one who fired him, which is really not right because if I had the power to fire him, that would give me the power to change a whole lot of things."[51] As he contemplated the recent succession of events, he understood that the idea that he, of all people, could dispose of the club's manager was preposterous. Still, for many people, that idea took root.

A couple of years later, one reporter wrote that Dick was like Vietnam: "some are for, some are against, but nobody's neutral."[52] How Dick measured up in someone's eyes largely depended on where one stood socially and politically and how one measured all of the other things that were percolating throughout the decade: civil rights, the Black Power movement, the free speech and student movements, and on and on. Dick took no formal position on any of these, yet he was somehow considered symbolic of all of them for those who chose to look for the connections—and plenty of baseball fans and sportswriters were hell-bent on looking. By the late 1960s, categorizing Dick Allen was like trying to grasp the fog—he was all-enveloping yet elusive. He was so many things to so many different people and perpetually subject to interpretation—baseball's Rashomon.

The most obvious dividing line when it came to perceptions of Dick Allen was racial; as a general proposition, many white fans and writers saw him as a controlling figure who demanded special treatment and who was emblematic of the newly emerging demands by blacks and young people for individual freedoms and rights that some believed had become extremist and were tearing the moral fabric of the country apart. Dick recognized as much: "I came along at a time when the country was in turmoil over race relations. I was an easy symbol and an easy target."[53] After the Thomas incident, some portrayed him "as a madman who'd beat hell out of anybody at the drop of a hat."[54] He was also described in *Sport* magazine as "the premier nonconformist who needled the Establishment and made it pay"[55] and in *Sports Illustrated* as a man with "radical notions."[56] Conlin even once remarked that "there are whispers that Allen is getting his advice from some black militants he's been friendly with the past couple of years."[57] In their nostalgic eyes, Jackie Robinson was baseball's Martin Luther King, and Dick was its Malcolm X. In a world where everything was seemingly coming apart all at once, Dick's mere presence appeared to illustrate that reality within the confines of the national pastime. Hochman once pleaded with him in print to "maybe, just maybe . . . bend a little?"[58] To those who saw the world through the filter of baseball, and who were horrified by what they were seeing, Dick's refusal to give even an inch was received as a militant threat.

It was hardly that cut-and-dried, however; not all white writers, or fans, saw him this way. Sandy Padwe of the *Inquirer* defended Dick to the extreme. One of his fellow newsmen described Padwe as a journalist who wore his politics on his sleeve: "He was writing and opining during the volatile Vietnam era, the civil rights movement, Woodstock, the Chipmunks era [Dick Schaap, Stan Isaacs, Larry Merchant] when modern sportswriting developed, and the assassination anger (of John and Robert Kennedy and Martin Luther King Jr.) [raged]."[59] Padwe was "brashly emotional" and part of a cadre of younger journalists who were angry at society to the point where they would write columns "that would dare their sports editors to print them."[60] To Padwe, Dick was not at all as he was being portrayed by his colleagues and the thousands who booed and hurled insults and garbage at him at Connie Mack Stadium. He often used his column as a pulpit to decry what he believed to be the societal injustice perpetrated upon Dick. To Padwe, Dick was symbolic of the future—a more promising, more enlightened future. He was "A Man Ahead of His Times," as one of his headlines read. "Allen does not accept the dogma and ancient shibboleths which govern the sporting establishment. And because he is challenging an established way of thinking, he has, in many respects, been vilified and maligned. . . . He is challenging one of the strongest, oldest, most revered portions of the establishment and is being met with a pounding, vicious counterattack."[61] As Padwe saw it, Dick was hardly a madman, hardly a radical. Instead, "Rich Allen is an individual. A powerful, brawling, let-me-lead-my-own-life individual. It is the wrong thing to be if you are public property in this city, which clings to a Victorian sense of order."[62] By late 1969, Padwe was the only local journalist Dick would even acknowledge.

And Padwe was not the only white writer to defend Dick. At times, various writers of the three dailies took up his cause; Conlin would veer from one extreme to the other while Hochman spilled several gallons of ink throughout the 1960s and 1970s trying to make sense of who he was and what he represented. And then there were the national writers who would periodically jet into Philadelphia in the hopes of sorting out just what the hell was going on both in the locker room and in the stands. Many from the glossies concluded that he was an out-of-control head case but others veered closer to Padwe, defending Dick and drawing cultural parallels between him and the changing face of America.

Things weren't any simpler when it came to the black press. Here again, whether a writer from the *Tribune*, *Chicago Defender*, *Los Angeles Sentinel*, *Baltimore Afro-American*, or any of the other black papers defended or deplored Dick Allen largely depended upon where that writer stood with regard to larger cultural issues. Those of the older generation, the generation of "turn the other cheek," often criticized Dick ruthlessly throughout the 1960s and charged him with damaging the civil rights movement with his confrontational style. "You know," Dick once said, "there's an old saying, 'You have to stand up for something or you'll fall for everything.' I just made up my mind that I wasn't going to accept some things."[63] This did not sit well with the old lions of the civil rights movement (along with the younger cubs who aligned themselves with the old guard) who believed there were boundaries when it came to how and when to push an issue, even a noble one. A. S. Doc Young of the *Defender* and *Sentinel* was, at first, a persistent critic, charging that while some of Dick's troubles were indeed created by whites, "some of those problems Rich created for himself." To Young, Dick was pressing matters to a point where he was being counterproductive. He was "convinced that Rich Allen is a man who anticipates trouble. And anticipating it, he always finds it."[64] "Fighting for rights is one thing," he wrote. "Being an obstructionist merely for the sake of being an obstructionist is another, totally another. Too many black athletes today, fired up by meaningless, phony militants, miss that point, to their own detriment."[65]

Norman Unger of the *Defender* was similarly critical of Dick through the years, charging him with "creat[ing] his own static on purpose."[66] And the *Defender*'s editorial staff strongly rebuked Dick after his tardy arrival in New York in a Sunday editorial in which it even compared Dick with President Nixon. On balance, the editorial concluded, Nixon came out on top—at least he showed up to work every day.[67] After Mauch's firing, Doc Young backed Mauch, concluding that despite all of his talent, Dick "lacked the ideal temperament."[68] With regard to Dick's place in the civil rights movement, Young wrote that it was obvious: "There is a kinship between these super-duper militants and such as Richie Allen: Neither of them is willing to pay the price off [sic] success; neither has any respect for rules; both are spoiled silly." To old lions such as Young, black militants (and Young regularly lumped Dick in with them even though there was no actual connection between the two) were blind to the realities of social change that had already occurred: "They prefer the luxury of the complaint to the open opportunity. They can't stand to admit to Negro progress in this country, because singing the blues is their game and playing the psychedelic mouth-organ is their hobby. . . . Richie Allen & Company and these people play in the same league."[69] Ultimately, to Young, Dick was, at best, a "spoiled brat."[70]

Other black writers saw Dick differently. Claude Harrison of the *Tribune* was perhaps his loudest cheerleader throughout his career, often blaming the Phillies' management for allowing the skewed portrait of Dick to emerge in the first place: "Management has been a little, no a lot, behind in its duty to build up Allen's image, one that would put him in company with the Mayses, Aarons, Robinsons, Mantles, and Bankses. The club seems to have a tell it all system for Allen and a hold it back for a while pattern for some of the other players. It's a sure thing that Allen isn't the only Phillie player who goes against house rules."[71] After Mauch was fired, Harrison provided some historical context that he noticed was missing from the "blame Allen" storyline: "Some say baseball was hurt when Mauch got the ax. Others say management was losing control of the game because a player (Richie Allen) was able to give birth to a revolt that led to the exit of Mauch. . . . All of these statements may be true. But the fact remains that baseball hurt itself many, many years ago when it refused to open its doors to Negro talent. And once the doors were opened baseball further injured itself by having two sets of standards—one for the white athlete and another for the black performer."[72] Dick was standing up to that, according to Harrison. He was saying, in effect, that the time to turn the other cheek was over. For this he was being pilloried. But, as Harrison exclaimed, it was about time somebody put a period on that era: "[L]ike everything else, time is bringing about a big change. Negro athletes are demanding their due—both on and off the field."[73]

With regard to the game's racial double standard, and as the intensifying debate over the meaning of Dick Allen revealed, it was hidden for years beneath the veneer of the black superstars such as Banks, Mays, and Aaron who emerged in the 1950s and who were both admired and well compensated. But it was there nevertheless. As Dick's troubles mounted in the late 1960s it percolated to the surface for the first time, where everybody could see it, whether they wanted to or not. In the course of the raging argument over Dick's off-field and practice habits, a few writers in both the black and white media began to recognize realities that may have passed their notice earlier, such as the fact that, like Dick, Stan Musial was often the last in uniform and on the field, yet nobody seemed to find that to be troublesome; or that Mickey Mantle had numerous off-field problems and at times was even drunk on the bench but the supposedly ravenous New York media often covered for him in order to protect his all-American image; or that Ted Williams bristled at the media throughout his career and although he was chastised for doing so was still accorded significant deference. Now that they were starting to look, some journalists noticed that even lesser white players seemed to get a pass that was unavailable to Dick: "Bo Belinsky did things that violated convention and people wound up laughing at him. Joe Namath does things that violate convention and people laud him. Richie Allen does those same things and people boo him and say things to his children."[74]

Quinn, in his typically garbled way, acknowledged the double standard but tried to defend it: "Allen is an individualist. Babe Ruth was an individual. Ruth was a showman. He pointed to the bleachers and then hit a homer there. Whenever he hit a homer that cap was sky-high the moment he got to home plate. But Ruth was such a friendly fellow. Sportswriters covered up his escapades because of his personality. I would say that a manager would have more trouble with Allen than with Babe Ruth."[75] Quinn, like many who perpetuated the double standard for years, often fumbled while trying to explain just why it was somehow okay to overlook Ruth's drinking, debauching, and paternity suits but to obsess over Dick's shortcomings. Perhaps, some on the sports beat were starting to realize, there was more to it than simply that Ruth liked to doff his cap after a dinger.

By this point in Dick's tenure with the Phillies, there was no longer any denying the fact that a double standard of some sort was at play: either Dick was demanding, and receiving, treatment and favors not accorded his twenty-four teammates, or he was representative of an unfortunate legacy of the game's integration two decades earlier, which demanded that black athletes "turn the other cheek" and assume a subservient role, unlike their white counterparts, who were more free to act as they pleased and who could expect to receive cover from club management and the press for their peccadilloes and other indiscretions. Even more confusing was the likelihood that both were occurring simultaneously: Dick very much wanted to be the beneficiary of the game's "superstar" double standard—he wanted and expected the same deference and cover provided to his elite contemporaries such as Mantle and Yastrzemski, as well as their forebears such as Ruth and DiMaggio—but became increasingly frustrated when he found himself instead the victim of its racial one, which demanded that he keep his mouth shut and his nose clean if he wanted to receive the benefits accorded to his athletic peers.

The more frustrated he became, the more he simply preferred not to go along with it all.

As both writers and players preached to him ad nauseam throughout his career, there was a path toward the perks of big-league stardom for black ballplayers—players such as Robinson, Banks, Aaron, and Mays had forged it—but as they were made to learn to their eternal consternation, Dick was constitutionally incapable of following in their footsteps. He couldn't suppress his rage as Robinson did early in his career, don "the cheery front" of an Ernie Banks, or provide "the wooden Say-Heyness" of a Willie Mays.[76] And he was unable play the role carved out for black ballplayers of the era that pressured them to, like Aaron, keep quiet about the indignities and worse they endured in the small southern towns they played in on the way up or the ugly taunts and letters they received simply because of the color of their skin. Instead, contrary to their admonitions, he spoke his mind, freely and unfettered. In an editorial shortly after Mauch's firing, the *Tribune* called out Dick's detractors and suggested what was really driving their criticism of him: "Much that Allen did, or is reported to have done, is done every week during the baseball season by other players. In Allen's case, conduct which would not have been mentioned in the newspapers if another player was involved was usually blown up out of all proportion. Could it be that, even today, years after Jackie Robinson broke the color line in organized baseball, there is a segment of the American public, including what we hope is a minority of baseball players, who still resent successful Negroes in baseball?"[77]

The expectation that he keep quiet, that he muzzle his opinions and emotions, particularly grated on him and affected his outlook on both professional baseball as a whole and his place within it. Ultimately it was this that made him feel powerless and drove his desire to achieve at least a measure of control over his professional life, in whatever way possible.

Dick experienced this sense of powerlessness in ways large and small. A case in point was the seemingly minor, yet deceptively significant, issue of his very name. Although he had always gone by "Dick" growing up (when he was not answering to "Sleepy" or "Sleeper"), he was rechristened "Richie" by the three dailies upon his signing, a nod to the club's last superstar, Richie Ashburn, and an attempt to connect the club's past with its apparent future. Upon his arrival in Philadelphia in 1964, he tried in vain to correct reporters who, in his opinion, were not only misidentifying him but belittling him in the process: "It makes me sound like I'm ten years old," he said while a rookie. "Anybody that's close to me and knows me well calls me Dick. I don't know why as soon as I put on a uniform it's Richie."[78] For a while, he'd grit his teeth and compromise, signing his name "Rich" Allen, but he never wavered as to how he felt about his name. Whenever asked, and sometimes even when he wasn't, he'd proclaim that his name was "Dick" and always had been. For years his pleas were ignored by everybody. Even within the black press, his requests went nowhere—the *Tribune* referred to him as "Richie" for years (until 1972) even as it was publishing articles pointing out how and why he preferred "Dick." Doc Young made light of his appeals, concluding that despite Dick's insistence, "I still think 'Richie' sounds better" (he did eventually accede).[79] To Dick, what he was called was important because it signified the level of respect he was being accorded—he wanted to be treated like a man, not a child. (One of the reasons he stopped speaking to Quinn altogether was because Quinn insisted on referring to him as "son.") The issue of his name was just another example to Dick of how his career was barreling onward largely without his input. In so many ways he was an involuntary participant in his own livelihood.

But it was in the big issues where he felt this sense of powerlessness most acutely—the ones that affected the arc of his career, the ones that dictated to him where he would ply his trade. Because of the shackles of the game's reserve clause, he was tied to the Phillies in perpetuity or until Carpenter unilaterally decided to either trade or release him. As things deteriorated all around him in Philadelphia, he came to the conclusion that the only possible solution to his problems was a change of scenery. However, Carpenter repeatedly refused his trade requests throughout the 1968 season. No matter how Dick framed his request— one time he even suggested that it would be in the city's best interests that he go: "I would be doing the fans a big favor by leaving," he told the *Tribune*—it was met with the brick wall that was the game's reserve clause; there was no way for him to break through it.[80] By the end of the season, he announced that if it meant getting out of Philadelphia, he'd even play again for Mauch (who had just been named the inaugural manager of the expansion Montreal Expos). When asked whether he'd take Dick if offered to him, Mauch replied, "You bet. Then I could hear him booed in two languages."[81]

Dick's frustrations carried over onto the field. After Mauch's firing he went into a prolonged hitting slump; before breaking out of it near the end of the season, he hit only .181 with 8 home runs and 24 RBIs in the first 61 games of the post-Mauch regime. At one point he was benched for an entire series against the Pirates—not because he had arrived late to the park but simply because he was having trouble putting the ball in play.[82] After the season his spirits brightened a bit when Carpenter suggested that he might be amenable to trading him ("one way or the other you'll see a new team on the field in 1969," Carpenter announced shortly after the end of the season). For once, he welcomed the criticism coming his way. It signaled, he hoped, management's determination to move him at last. Carpenter's postseason state-of-the-ball-club address to the media focused on his frustration over the Phillies' dwindling attendance as well as the factors he believed were responsible for it. "I'm disappointed in Allen's production," he said. "I think he should give you a .300 average and 120 runs batted in [he finished the season at .263/90 in those categories, to go along with 33 home runs]. He's not untouchable."[83]

So anxious was Dick to escape Philadelphia that in the season's final game he broke out of his extended funk and put on a dazzling show for the hometown Mets, who were rumored to be interested in him. He hit three home runs and drove in seven—career highs in both categories—in a 10–3 shellacking and afterward spoke effusively to the New York media (he refused comment to every member of the Philadelphia press corps) about his desire to relocate. Each of his home runs was longer than the one before it, with the final one traveling an estimated 485 feet and landing in the outfield parking lot, barely missing the Phillies' team bus.[84] Although media reports speculated that a deal with the Mets was imminent, some New York writers were skeptical. Given that the Mets' manager, Gil Hodges, was still in the hospital recovering from a heart attack, they couldn't fathom club general manager Johnny Murphy pairing him with Dick Allen. "If the Mets make a deal with Allen," one wrote, "I'm willing to bet Gil Hodges won't be back."[85] They were right; the talks soon fizzled, as did preliminary ones with other clubs.

Realizing that they were destined to spend another year in each other's company, both sides tried, at least initially, to make the best of things. Quinn, who had previously refused to recognize Capozzoli as Dick's agent, agreed to meet with him and Dick together to iron things out. In a four-hour lunch meeting at the Bellevue Stratford Hotel, they believed they had done so.[86] Afterward, the Phils tried to put a positive spin on the events of the previous few months: Quinn denied that he had shopped Dick at all, and manager Bob Skinner (who had replaced Mauch) suggested that if he had tried, Skinner would have stopped him: "I want him on my ball club. . . . I like Allen. I like what he can do. After what he went through last season I look for him to turn the corner this year. . . . I see the beginning of a new career for him. His next five years should be his greatest."[87] Dick, as well, cautiously hoped that the change in managers would at least bring him some relief from the dictatorial atmosphere that had pervaded the Mauch regime. In fact, Dick tested the waters in this regard almost as soon as Skinner assumed command of the club by wearing his batting helmet out in left field, an act that was a clear violation of one of Mauch's myriad rules. Although in later years many would claim (as would Dick, in his autobiography) that he began wearing his helmet on the field in order to shield himself against objects being hurled at him from the stands, a few weeks after he began wearing it, he told Stan Hochman, who wondered as much himself, that this was not the case. "You can't make a story out of it," Dick told him. "I wore the helmet in the minors and I've done it before up here. Then Gene (Mauch) wouldn't let me do it. It just saves stuffing your cap in your pocket and then back on your head. The cap gets all sweaty and crumpled, and then you slide and it gets full of dirt. This way I just wear the helmet all the time."[88]

Dick's contract was not the subject of the lunch meeting and everybody girded for the seemingly inevitable showdown that was to ensue on that front. However, it never happened; Dick agreed to terms quietly in late February and, at last, a peaceful spring training beckoned over the near horizon. Adding to the rapprochement was Skinner, who suggested that he, unlike his predecessor, understood Dick. Beyond permitting him to wear his helmet on the field, Skinner contended that he understood and respected Dick's individualized training methods: "I know he likes to work and I know he doesn't think very much of the amount of time wasted in past spring trainings he's been through. He likes to get his work done and leave, and that's the way it will be for him."[89] The tenuous truce was, inevitably, short-lived; when spring training officially commenced a few days later, Dick was nowhere to be found. Initially Quinn brushed his disappearance aside, telling the press that Dick would arrive at some point "early in the week." When Wednesday rolled around and Dick was still absent, Quinn was pressed as to his definition of "early in the week." "Well, I would say Monday and Tuesday are certainly early in the week," he explained. "I guess early in the week could run all the way to noon Wednesday."[90] When the clock struck noon, Quinn was officially humiliated once again. Perhaps, he then suggested, Dick would make his way to camp before the end of the week.

Instead, a couple of days later Dick's picture made its way into the *Miami Herald*, which reported on Dick's dinner with the Jets' star quarterback (and former rival on the western Pennsylvania diamonds and basketball courts back in high school), Joe Namath, at Namath's Miami restaurant/nightclub. Not to worry, wrote a mocking *Inquirer* reporter, "Driving down from his home in Philadelphia, he simply veered left where he should have veered right and landed in Joe Namath's restaurant along Florida's east coast instead of the Phillies' sweat box along the state's western shore line."[91] The next day, Dick arrived in Clearwater and met with Quinn to sign his contract while the media huddled and speculated as to whether the first fine of the season was in the process of being administered. "As far as I'm concerned," said Quinn after emerging from the meeting, "if there is (any punishment), it will never be announced." Dick, "wearing a white shirt with ruffled collar and cuffs, an Edwardian blue suit, long, thick sideburns and a mustache," then ambled down to the field to meet with Skinner. They talked for half an hour, out of earshot, but not eyesight, of the gaggle of reporters who had scurried from Quinn's office to the field to witness this very exchange. "Gee," said one, "I hope Richie isn't being too hard on him."[92] With that, the 1969 season was officially under way.

Chapter 8

A Threat to the Game

1969: Philadelphia .288/32/89

BY OPENING NIGHT of the 1969 season, hostility was thick in the Philadel-phia air; most of those who trudged toward the dilapidated ballpark in the dilapidated neighborhood did so for one reason: to boo Dick Allen. They booed him before his first at-bat of the season, they booed him when the official scorer gave Dick a hit on a ball that took a bad hop off of Mets' second baseman Al Weiss's chest, and they booed him whenever the game found him on the field or at the plate.[1] In the bottom of the third inning, however, he swatted a mammoth home run, and in the top of the fourth, after taking his position at first base (he had been moved yet again), Dick tipped his cap to the fans who, all of a sudden, were cheering him. Per-haps, some hoped once again, a whiff of détente was in the air as well.

Capozzoli suggested as much, claiming the gesture to be momentous. "He's changed," Capozzoli insisted. But Dick downplayed its significance after the game. "I'm not looking for nothing," Dick stated flatly. "I'm not trying to change my image. I've got to live my life, for my family and for myself. I can't change my way of living for some people. I don't care a thing about [the fans]. The kids, maybe. I guess I'm a little callous."[2] So why tip his cap? "I just did it," he told one reporter, "so you wouldn't have anything to write."[3]

They would have plenty to write about soon enough. Only a few weeks into the season, Dick missed the team's plane to St. Louis. Then he missed another one. And then, in an unprecedented move, he missed the game in St. Louis itself. Though Dick had missed team planes before, he'd always managed somehow to make it to the ballpark prior to the first pitch. This time he didn't. And nobody was quite sure why. Dick claimed innocence. After missing the team's 8:00 A.M. flight, he said, he arrived at Philadelphia International Airport in time to take TWA's 4:00 P.M. flight to St. Louis, which would put him at the ballpark, if all went well, just before game time that evening. He went to the wrong gate, though, "got mad and panicked," and then went home.[4] He then missed a succession of other flights and didn't make it to Busch Stadium until twenty-five minutes after the first pitch of the next day's game. New manager Bob Skinner promptly fined him $1,000 and benched him that afternoon. After the game Dick was taciturn: "I guess they don't need me" was all he would offer. Later he expounded: "I told them to get rid of me last winter. They had their chance. I don't feel sorry for them."[5]

As the media pressed Dick to explain his most recent absence, it became clear that there was more to the story than simply a jumbled itinerary. "Anyway," he said, "I wasn't going to bust my tail to get here because last year I got fined a day's pay for a bar room brawl they didn't even look into."[6] The matter of the club's fines cut both ways: perhaps he didn't have to change his behavior as a result of the fines, but the club didn't have to listen to him either simply because he preferred to pay than conform. It could just go on fining him. He was discovering that, more than he had previously thought, it mattered to him that the club listen to what he had to say. Management was, in effect, calling his bluff, collecting the fines while continuing to ignore him. More and more, this bothered him. The effects of his defiance were constrained; in the grand scheme of things, he realized, he remained powerless.

Meanwhile, in the three Philadelphia dailies, a portrait emerged of a man publicly regressing into an infantile state, finding impediments every-where in his journey to the ballpark and throwing up his hands in resigna-tion that there was nothing he could do to change things anyway. His

After finally making it to Busch Stadium in St. Louis, Dick responds to the taunts
of Cardinals' pitcher Joe Hoerner from the dugout by challenging him to settle
the score on the field, May 4, 1969.

(© 2014 Legendaryauctions.com)

helplessness seemed to run in only one direction, however. As he was
dodging an autograph request from a young Cardinals fan in St. Louis,
the boy shouted to him, "Hey Rich, you gonna catch the plane this time?"
Dick grinned and turned to the person next to him, "The kid oughta be
smart enough to know I don't miss anything going back."[7]

In so many ways, it seemed as if things in Dick's life were spiraling out
of control. This was further suggested less than two weeks later when he
was involved in yet another off-field scuffle, this time at Garden State
Park. Although the hundreds of spectators who witnessed it agreed that
Dick was not at fault, the mere incident itself seemed to fit the profile of

a man losing his grasp. Though his assailant, a sheet metal worker who earlier had been banned from a racetrack in Atlantic City for fighting, was fined $50, here was additional evidence for those looking for it of a man who seemed to have the uncanny ability to find trouble wherever he went.[8]

Nowhere was this more evident than in Dick's relationship with those in positions of authority. Although there were initial glimmers of hope that his relationship with Bob Skinner would be better than his relationship with Mauch had been, they were quickly dashed. As Skinner indicated in his February discussion of Dick's spring training expectations, he initially expressed a willingness to bend somewhat to accommodate Dick's approach to the game. "Look," said Skinner. "It's the same way in the business world. The successful business man goes places that the average business man can't. Ted Williams stayed in different hotels. He always had his own room, and this and that. It's not a question of rules for 24-and-1. It's a prestige thing. Recognition of a player of Williams' caliber."[9]

As it turned out, it was easier for Skinner to talk about giving Dick the superstar treatment than for him to actually do it. An ex-marine who led the San Diego Padres, the Phillies' top farm team, to the 1967 Pacific Coast League championship, Skinner had been conditioned to expect that rules would be followed and hierarchy adhered to. As manager, he ranked above all of the players, even the best ones. While Skinner may never have heard the term "Conveyer Belt," he was a firm believer in how that system inculcated players with certain values by the time they reached people like him in the bigs. "Attitude . . . is something that starts down low in your farm system and becomes a part of a young ballplayer as he moves up the ladder," he said.[10] Given that Dick rebelled against the Conveyer Belt with a vengeance, there was little chance that, once they got to know each other, he and Skinner would see eye to eye. The *Tribune*'s Claude Harrison summarized Skinner's approach to Dick succinctly when he wrote that the manager had "his left hand in Richie Allen's wallet and his right hand slapping the Phillies' first baseman on the back."[11] Skinner might talk a good game, but when it came to the game itself, he was someone else altogether.

It didn't take long for Skinner to rebel against Dick's rebellions. Soon he began sounding very much like his predecessor, announcing that Dick had no choice but to play "under my ground rules. And my rules are

Dick in mid-swing, June 4, 1969. Despite the turmoil, he continued to hit.
(Temple University Libraries, Special Collection Research Center, Philadelphia, PA)

pretty easy to understand, and that means reporting with everybody else two hours before game time."[12] One of Skinner's biggest backers was utility man Cookie Rojas. In June Rojas called a players-only meeting during which he berated Dick in front of his teammates. "Cookie told him we resented his coming and going as he pleased," a white player recalled. "He told him he didn't think he was hustling. Several of us said we agreed with Cookie."[13] The black players begged to differ. What ensued was a twenty-minute racially divided debate over the merits of Dick Allen. The subject of the debate sat silently at first. "It hurt me," Dick recalled. Then he rose from his chair. "To hell with you guys," he said. "You don't pay me. They pay me upstairs. If they don't like my work, let them get rid of me."[14]

The inevitable climax came a few days later when Dick missed a June 24 doubleheader against the Mets in New York. Providing support for *Los Angeles Times* columnist Jim Murray's assertion that Dick was a ballplayer "known to miss not only games, but cities," here was a direct challenge to Skinner's authority.[15] Proclaiming that "I've never been embarrassed in this game in my life," Skinner suspended Dick without pay indefinitely, adding that "I have too much pride to feel that he's made a fool of me."[16] The manager must have wondered if those on the outside assumed as much, and he was determined to disabuse them of any doubts they might have. "The worst thing a player can do is miss games," he added. "Allen is not bigger than baseball, and he'll be suspended until he convinces me he can obey the same rules as the other 24 players."[17] The Ted Williams analogies were now firmly a thing of the past. Dick's response was short and to the point: "Good. I need a vacation."[18]

*   *   *

In fact, Dick was incensed. "I was coming to the park," he said later. "But when I heard from a writer I was indefinitely suspended, I saw red. Hell, how can they suspend me until they hear my side of the story? I could have been lying dead on some highway."[19] His side of the story was a doozy: as he relayed it to the beat writers shortly thereafter, he took advantage of a Monday off-day to head up to Reading to take in little brother Ronnie's game with the Double A club. As he was out of the city, he missed the team bus trip to New York and was once again on his own to figure out how to make it from Reading to Shea Stadium in time for Tuesday's twi-night doubleheader. He had plenty of time, he figured. Enough to squeeze in an appearance at Joe Frazier's fight against Jerry Quarry on Monday night. And to meet up with Joe Namath at Bachelor III's in Manhattan after the fight (in defiance of National League president Warren Giles's memorandum issued a week earlier advising all league players to avoid it). And to watch his horse, Trick Fire, run in the third race at Monmouth Park on Tuesday afternoon (post time 3:00 P.M.). In the midst of "kibitzing on the backstretch" at Monmouth Park, as he described it to Hochman, he lost track of the time and placed a call to the Phillies' clubhouse. He reached relief pitcher Turk Farrell in the first inning of game one and asked to speak to Skinner. Skinner came in from the dugout to take the call, but when he picked up the receiver the line was dead. A few hours later, during the sixth inning of game two, another call came into the Phils' clubhouse. Skinner picked up the receiver, listened as the stadium operator informed him that Dick was calling long distance, and then waited. After a few moments of silence, Skinner hung up and returned to the dugout to watch the Mets complete their double-header sweep.[20] By this point, Skinner had decided Dick's fate; he had already suspended Dick between games of the doubleheader. While game two was still underway, Hochman called Dick, who by that point had checked into the club's Manhattan headquarters at the Commodore Hotel, to inform him of as much. Dick then promptly checked out and took off. He never made it to Shea.[21]

To Dick, Skinner's action was a betrayal. "He [Skinner] said whenever you're gonna be late just call. Well, Skinner knew I'd tried to call."[22] But he suspended him anyway. "I tried to cooperate with him," offered Skinner. "I thought we had a good thing going. I thought he was in a good frame of mind. Now he's not coming back unless he comes back under my ground rules."[23] Two days later, Dick apologized during an interview on WHAT-AM, "The Voice of the African American Community," but insisted that he was through in Philadelphia. "I'm wrong 100 percent," he said. "I'm going to face up to everything that I've done here. [But] if I'm going to exploit my talents it'll be for some other city because I've done all I can do. It's a small-minded person who's been on me ever since I've been here and it's time to make a move, brother." He reiterated that it wasn't so much the suspension itself that bothered him as much as the fact that he was suspended before he could explain himself to Skinner. When the interviewer suggested that both the club and the media blew "everything out of proportion" before he had the opportunity to speak, Dick heartily agreed. "Exactly. You took the words right out of my mouth. I hear on the radio [*sic*] that I'm suspended indefinitely—so why should I show up at the ball park?"[24]

Positions on both sides calcified almost instantaneously. Dick told Ray Kelly the day after the doubleheader that "I'm through with them. I'm not gonna do nothing until they trade me," and Skinner shot back by asserting that "It doesn't matter to me if he ever puts on a Phillies uniform again."[25] Thus began an exile unprecedented in baseball history. Not since Commissioner Landis had banished Babe Ruth for nearly half a season in 1925 for Ruth's refusal to heed the commissioner's ultimatum to discontinue his annual postseason barnstorming tours had such an action been debated so widely and feverishly within baseball circles. And even there at least it was clear who was exiling whom; in Dick's case, things weren't so cut-and-dried. The *New Pittsburgh Courier* ran a headline announcing in large type: "Allen Stages Game's First Revolt," and, despite the technical fact of Skinner's suspension, it sure felt like it.[26] For the suspension was "indefinite"—Dick was free to return whenever he chose, provided that he agreed to conform to Skinner's rules. That he steadfastly refused to buckle for weeks on end turned the suspension into something else altogether. "What he did was unprecedented in baseball history, I believe," Bill Conlin recalled. "I can't find any star-level player who missed nearly a month and who, except for a couple of racetrack sightings, virtually vanished."[27]

The writers in the mainstream dailies didn't know what to make of all this, something they'd never before witnessed. Who would willingly refuse to play baseball for money? Looking on from afar, *New York Newsday*'s Stan Isaacs was the first to question his sanity: "Has anybody with the Phillies ever suggested that he may need a doctor's help?"[28] Conlin, as well, suggested that Dick was "emotionally disturbed."[29] Sandy Grady attempted to delve deeper into Dick's psyche: "It's saddening when a man yearns to do one thing but must do another for money. Stockbrokers want to be artists, and newspapermen want to sail to Tahiti. Rich Allen plays baseball for $80,000 a year but he would rather saddle horses for hamburger money. Forget Babe Ruth, he'd rather be Hirsch Jacobs."[30]

For his part, Capozzoli claimed that none of the various sportswriters' medical diagnoses was even close to the mark: "This is a very misunderstood man. Rich is a very warm-hearted individual, who only wants to be judged for his baseball ability." He promised to smooth things over by taking Dick to a horse ranch near Monmouth Park for a few days where they could sort things out. "I have to get him out of the city," he said. "His friends keep coming in and telling him he's right, and that doesn't do anybody any good."[31] Meanwhile, Skinner stood firm, repeating over and over that Dick would be welcomed back to the club when he agreed to adhere to the same rules his teammates abided by and to conduct himself in a manner deemed acceptable to Skinner. Quinn quickly backed his manager: "Whatever Skinner did it was with the full authority of the club. The manager has the jurisdiction to do anything he deems necessary on the field."[32] All of this rattled and troubled Dick; he recalled that he "felt unloved, unappreciated, and unbelievably confused."[33]

Gene Mauch, Dick, Hank, and Ron Allen (from left to right),
March 19, 1967, in happier times.
(© 2014 Legendaryauctions.com)

Although he was debated nonstop over the next several weeks, Dick himself dropped out of sight for much of that time: "During the suspension I cut myself off from everybody, even my family. No newspapers. I began spending my time on farms in Maryland and Virginia looking for horses to buy and race. I stayed with a friend for a few weeks in a hunting lodge in Gettysburg, Pennsylvania. The sportswriters were tracking me as though I were a mass murderer, but I covered my tracks well."[34] He even spent some time in a place where nobody would think to look for him: a Jenkintown, Pennsylvania, steel mill. "[H]e spent a lot of that time with us," recalled George Heidman, president of Jenkintown Steel. "He was talking about coming to work for me. I asked him what can you do? Can you work a punch press? Can you handle a shears? Can you sell? Can you pound a typewriter? He said no, no, no. Finally, I said what can you do? He said, 'I can play baseball.' So I told him, 'Go play ball because that's where the hell you belong.'"[35]

Occasionally word either from Dick or about him would surface. In early July he was hit with yet another tax lien, this time in connection with his 1966 tax return.[36] A couple of days later, he appeared on a special edition of sportscaster Al Meltzer's *Sports Hot Spot* (Dick was the subject of three separate sports specials/documentaries that summer: one produced by Stan Hochman and narrated by Red Barber that aired in June, Meltzer's, and one hosted by Richie Ashburn that aired in August) and announced that perhaps he'd forego American baseball altogether: "I can play in Japan or Caracas, Venezuela." He reiterated his main grievance, "They suspended me without hearing my side of the story," and made it clear that he was in no hurry to return: "I haven't talked to a soul at the Phillies since I was suspended." He also explained his earlier absence in St. Louis: "I didn't plan to make the plane to St. Louis. We had a day off and I was willing to pay the $1,000 fine to have two days off in a row. It's very seldom I get two straight days off."[37]

As the days, and then weeks, passed, the question began to arise just as it did during his 1967 spring training holdout: What would happen if he never came back? This time, the issue arose under major league rule 13A, which stated that a club could suspend a player without pay for insubordination for no more than thirty days. As the thirty-day mark approached, many within the media and the league began to wonder what that might mean: Would the Phils be compelled under baseball rules to either release him or reinstate his salary against their will? Once again, Dick was sending men who claimed they had seen it all and knew it all when it came to baseball scrambling to make sense of what they were witnessing. Quinn was adamant that the club would not be pressured into doing anything: "Bob Skinner suspended him indefinitely. Allen is suspending himself each day he stays away. So each day he's away, that suspension renews itself. It lasts as long as Allen wants it to."[38] Commissioner Bowie Kuhn refused to get involved: "That is the Philadelphia club's problem and will remain its problem."[39] Mauch, on the other hand, was more than happy to weigh in: "I'm sure he could find some other means of earning a living. But if he can't abide by the rules, he ought to get out. Otherwise he's taking money under false pretenses."[40] Even President Nixon chided Dick. "You tell Richie Allen to get back on the job," he instructed Phils' pitcher Grant Jackson at the All-Star Game (albeit after Dick had already returned). "You tell him he's not going to get as good a job if he quits baseball. . . . You tell Richie it's not for the good of the

Daily News columnist Stan Hochman shakes President Nixon's hand at a banquet held in conjunction with the 1969 All-Star Game, which was played in Washington, DC (baseball commissioner Bowie Kuhn is in the background). Nixon would also find time during the festivities that surrounded the game to scold Dick Allen via his conversation with Phillies' pitcher Grant Jackson.

(Stan Hochman)

Phillies, or for the good of the fans, but for the good of Richie Allen that he get back."[41]

Finally, after twenty-six days, Dick returned. On July 20—the same day Neil Armstrong walked on the moon—the exile was over. "This must be the greatest day in history," said Cookie Rojas. "The astronauts come down on the moon and Richie Allen comes down to earth."[42] Much like his 1968 standoff, Dick did not return without Carpenter's intervention. Capozzoli served as the intermediary, bringing his client and the owner together for a meeting at the Rose Tree Inn in Media, Pennsylvania (the players later barred Capozzoli from the clubhouse for what they perceived as his constant meddling).[43] Quinn and Skinner were not invited. By that point, Dick's will was beginning to wither: the situation was wearing on his family, and he felt pressured to return. "I was perfectly set in my mind to go without playing. But I went back to ease the mind of the people close to me. And it's because of them that I'm going to finish [the season]," he said.[44] He was also shaken by the death of the wife of his close friend Pat Corrales (she died in childbirth): "That first year, when they booed me, Pat would keep my spirits up. We'd come out [to the Fairmount Park stables] and just talk. One off-day we got so drunk we didn't get home till real late. Our wives were waiting up—and mad. The next night we took them out to make up and got loaded again. His wife was such a beautiful girl."[45] Everything was closing in on him. He just wanted it all to end.

At the meeting, Dick agreed to meet with Skinner. Carpenter called Skinner afterward and said, "He's ready to come in and talk. Whether he's reinstated is up to you. He'll be in your office at nine o'clock."[46] Although Skinner was given to believe that he still maintained authority over the situation, Dick corrected that misperception the next morning when he made Skinner wait until eleven before he arrived. "I must have gotten mixed up on the time," fumbled the agitated ex-marine. "I thought Richie was coming at 9. He got here about 11. . . . But look, I'm just glad the fella came in. I'm just glad we got this thing resolved at 9 o'clock or 11 o'clock." While Skinner waited, Dick was home, in Germantown, entertaining teammate Johnny Briggs: "I buzzed over around 10," said Briggs. "I didn't know what was happening until his wife told me. I went upstairs and Richie said 'I'm going back.'"[47] The meeting between Dick and Skinner was perfunctory; there wasn't much left for the two to say to each other. Afterward, Dick reiterated that little had changed when it came to his feelings: "I can't see myself playing here another year. I'll play this out. I'll be in St. Louis with the team at the end of the season. After that they can send me all the contracts they want. It won't matter." Speaking to Sandy Padwe (the only local reporter he'd even acknowledge by this point), he once again pointed out the indignity of being judged before having the opportunity to state his case: "Did you see the story the other day about the two guys who reported late to the Green Bay Packers camp?" he asked Padwe. "A writer asked the coach if he would fine them. The coach said he wouldn't have anything to say until he heard the players' side of the story. That's the way it should be." In his opinion, "Skinner pushed the panic button in suspending me so quick. And I think I pushed it, too."[48]

Dick was also miffed that Frank Dolson put his home address in his column the previous day: "I'm tired of things like this. My address gets put in the papers and people come riding around. I have a nice home here, right? Spent a lot of money on it. I can't enjoy it. . . . We have to be careful about letting the kids out of the house."[49]

To his good fortune, the club was embarking on a road trip so he returned to the lineup away from the glare of the hometown fans. Upon arriving back in Philadelphia, weather interfered to the point where his first official postexile home game didn't take place until ten days after his reinstatement. Still, he was dreading it. He downed seven Canadian Clubs at a local pub one afternoon while watching the rain darken the skies yet again on what was supposed to be his first game back at Connie Mack. He called the ballpark. The game was still on. He then called the weather bureau. The skies were supposed to clear by game time. "He's gonna have to face it," said a friend. "Might as well get it over with." Dick called the weather bureau one more time and then headed to the ballpark. He took the field and then blew a kiss toward the smattering of fans who had gathered on the gray evening. Why? "I heard somebody cheer," he said afterward.[50] The game was rained out after three innings.

In all, Dick lost $450 per day, or $11,700 total during his absence. Quinn insisted that these fines, along with the ones imposed on Dick back in May, were final; there was no way for Dick to get any of the money back. Skinner confirmed this: "Richie understands he was suspended without pay."[51] Carpenter refused to go along. "It's too much, Bob," he told his manager. "Look, we've already hit the guy for $10,000 [*sic*]. That's enough. It would look like I'm kicking a man when he's down."[52] But to Quinn and Skinner that was precisely the point—all of the posturing of the previous several weeks would be for nothing if they didn't press their advantage now. On this Quinn and Skinner had the backing of much of the baseball establishment, which was convinced that unless Dick was brought under control—and brought under control immediately—all hell was liable to break loose.

The beat writers had been banging this drum for over a year now, ever since Allen Lewis chided Carpenter for failing to support Mauch during

Dick's 1968 sit-down strike. Now that it looked as if history was repeating itself, some of them were nearly apoplectic. Worse, Dick appeared to them to be newly emboldened, acting out in ways he never did before. He was no longer trimming his sideburns and was proud to explain exactly why not: "The contract states that this contract is solely between uniformed player and parent club for baseball services. It's not to win no beauty contest. . . . And when the day comes they don't like the way I look, then that means they don't want me as a ballplayer, they don't want my baseball services."[53] Even from within the organization, Carpenter was subjected to the wrath of the outraged. Farm Director Paul Owens found Dick's independence to be emasculating and humiliating: "He's belittled the Phils in the eyes of the country," Owens alleged. "Somewhere, the organization has to take a stand."[54] On all fronts, Carpenter was being lambasted as an enabling buffoon.

In a blistering editorial, the *Sporting News* rebuked Carpenter and his handling of the situation, admonishing that "[u]nless a firm hand is taken with Allen, he'll go through more managers than Bluebeard did wives." The only way to deal with rebellious players was harshly, so as to disabuse both them and anybody else from traveling down the same road: "Carpenter, who has an ear for Allen's wails, could take a lesson from a couple of tough owners of the past, Jake Ruppert of the Yankees and Sam Breadon of the Cardinals. When Manager Miller Huggins fined Babe Ruth $5,000 and suspended him for rules violations, Ruppert backed Huggins to the hilt. When Manager Frankie Frisch threw the book at Dizzy and Paul Dean for skipping an exhibition at Detroit, Breadon gave Frisch full support. And Ruth and the Deans were more subdued after these penalties."[55] *New York Times* columnist Leonard Koppett recalled that "when even Ruth could be brought into line, the lesson was not lost on everyone else."[56] Carpenter, the message went, needed to follow suit.

When he didn't, the *Sporting News* appealed to a higher authority: Commissioner Kuhn. "Now that Bowie Kuhn has been solidified as commissioner for seven years, let's see if he has the strength to stand up to an owner. Let's see if he will call in Bob Carpenter and tell him it's detrimental to baseball for a club owner to repeatedly undercut his manager by restoring fines and pay-dockings . . . such actions by Carpenter weaken baseball in the eyes of the public." The potential for fallout was, in the

Returning to Connie Mack for his first homestand since his twenty-six-day absence, a mutton-chopped Dick Allen greets a fan who has run onto the field seeking an autograph, July or August 1969. Dick obliges while stadium security pauses before escorting the fan off the field.

(Temple University Libraries, Special Collections Research Center, Philadelphia, PA)

paper's eyes, catastrophic: "And what of the other Phil players who have been slapped $50 and $100 for missing a curfew? Do they all get their money back?"[57]

Many in the league and the media were convinced that the game was perched on a precipice. Dick was not the only one who had pushed it there but, to many, he was exerting the most force. If he wasn't put in his place, the thinking went, baseball would be full of Dick Allens, preferring not to do whatever it was that offended them. Years later, Pirates' Hall of Famer Willie Stargell reflected on how Dick was perceived at the time: "Dick Allen played the game in the most conservative era in baseball history. It was a time of change and protest in the country, and baseball reacted against all that. They saw it as a threat to the game. The sportswriters were reactionary too. They didn't like seeing a man of such extraordinary skills doing it his way. It made them nervous. Dick Allen was ahead of his time."[58] Pat Corrales concurred, concluding that Dick "was years ahead of us [players] in seeing that it was wrong for the owners to have such complete control over our careers."[59] Dick was demonstrating a lot of things to a lot of people for the first time. More than anything else, he was demonstrating just how fragile the owners' control of the game really was—if the whole enterprise could be brought down by just one man who simply preferred not to go along with it all, what did that say about *them*?

For their part, the Phillies were determined to do whatever they could to see to it that they would never again have to contend with *another* Dick Allen. While Carpenter was now, at last, resolved to deal Dick at the end of the season, the front office as well as the organization as a whole, at several different levels, resolved to rid themselves of the independent-minded black ballplayers who were threatening management's stature—who were, in the opinion of Paul Owens, belittling the entire operation in the eyes of the country. By the late 1960s the club's evaluations of black prospects and minor league talent carried a strong whiff of something other than pure appraisals of talent. While character had always been an element of most player reports regardless of race, when it came to black players, the legacy of the organization's dealings with Dick appeared to hover over everything. Of one black prospect, a club scout wrote that while "I feel that we have a big leaguer here," the organization needed to proceed with caution: "Hope he doesn't get thrown with some bad Negros [*sic*] to lead or advise him wrong."⁶⁰ Of another, his minor league manager's year-end evaluation (of a season in which the player hit .308 and led the 1969 class-A Spartanburg Phillies in batting average, hits, RBIs, doubles, home runs, and stolen bases) pulled no punches: "This boy must be held in check and learn to take orders. I have written him a personal letter telling him very bluntly what we expect. Richie Allen, his attitude and conduct, is his idol. I'm not going to condone putting this organization through another such era with this young player." The Conveyer Belt did not appear to have had the desired effect on him, much as it hadn't with Dick; his manager fretted that "He's an individual type fellow and when some one [*sic*] crosses him, he doesn't hold back. Will fight for his rights."⁶¹ Rather than promote him, the organization assigned him to their other class-A affiliate for the 1970 season. When that season ended they released him.

* * *

Dick approached his two remaining months in Philadelphia with reticence rather than relief. Although the prevailing narrative by that point was that he had managed to become all-powerful, manipulating management to his whim, he saw himself as powerless as ever. He might engage in extended sit-down strikes as he had the previous two seasons, but in the end he was still at the mercy of Carpenter and Quinn. If they chose not to trade him, or if they wanted to punish him to set an example to other potential malcontents, there wasn't anything he could do about it. In such an environment, he repeatedly lashed out in ways that provided him with at least the illusion of control. In so many ways throughout the 1968 and 1969 seasons, he tried to assert himself such that he could at least make the argument that he controlled his destiny, that he was an active participant in a system that he believed all but rendered him a non-person once he walked off the ball field. He could prefer not to. Or at least he could try to convince himself of as much.

Although he liked to say that "I only do what my pocketbook can stand," Dick was beginning to realize that the skipped flights and late arrivals only gave him the artifice of choice. Though he did, on some level, retain a measure of control through his willingness to accept the financial consequences of his decisions, when it came to the big question of where he would be employed, he was as much at the mercy of club management as anyone else. As his tenure in Philadelphia wound down, Dick engaged in a succession of sad, futile, and even seemingly comical protests in his attempt to control what was, in the end, beyond his grasp. In none of these actions was there ever any possibility that real change would result. But to Dick, the illusion of freedom they represented was reason enough to engage in them.

The first of these occurred his initial night back at Connie Mack. Before the game he removed his uniform and other belongings from his locker and moved everything into a walk-in storage closet just outside of the clubhouse that was used for mops, push brooms, and other clubhouse cleaning implements. (Sixteen cases of beer and a season's worth of bubble gum were stored there as well.) As for why he made the move, Dick gave varying reasons—to some he said that he wanted to get away from the press, and to others he said that he was uncomfortable around his teammates. Clubhouse man Unk Russell, who ruled the roost when it came to locker assignments, made no attempt to stop him: "He just asked to dress there and I said all right. I didn't think he was serious."[62] But he was. "The Great Man's moving out on us," said teammate John Boozer. "Yeah," added Turk Farrell. "But when's he going to move Skinner's gear out here?"[63] Dick's take on his life during this period was starkly different: "I'd have to force myself out of the house. I'd get in my car and I'd drive down Wissahickon Avenue and then through the park and on down into town. Day after day of the same thing. I'd pray for a flat tire or a flash flood . . . anything so I wouldn't have to hear it all over again. Man, it was just nowhere."[64]

For a brief moment, Skinner refused to get involved. "I couldn't care less where a player's locker is as long as it's in the clubhouse. . . . I've got so many things to worry about, I'm not going to worry about where Allen dresses." But after being pressed by the media about it, the manager changed his mind and ordered clubhouse assistant Kenny Bush to return all of Dick's belongings to his old locker. While the move was taking place, Johnny Callison quipped, "I thought Skinner was moving in here and Rich was moving in there [in the manager's office]."[65] Skinner then offered his revised position on the matter to the press: "I don't care if he sits in there, but he'll dress in the room with everybody else."[66] The next day Dick returned his things to the storage closet, after which Skinner ordered Bush to return everything to his old locker once more. This battle of wills went on for a week until Skinner finally gave up—a small, yet tangible, victory for Dick. But he was still required to report to Connie Mack every day for work. The peripheral details had been altered, but the overall picture remained the same.

A few days after Skinner caved in the locker battle came the ultimate showdown. On a scheduled off-day in early August, the club organized an exhibition game between the big leaguers and the farm hands in Reading. Dick stopped by Skinner's office beforehand to inform him that he would not be attending that game. "You're coming with us," he yelled back at Dick. Not only that, the manager told him, he was riding the bus to Reading just like everybody else.[67] Dick asked him what it would cost him to miss the game, and Skinner shot back that it would cost him $1,500.[68] To Dick, it was a price he was willing to pay for an afternoon free of encumbrances. To Skinner, the $1,500 didn't represent the price tag of a day off; it was the penalty for skipping a required team function and he informed Dick of as much. Dick replied that his deal with Carpenter did not include his attendance at exhibition games and that was that. Or at least it was as far as Dick was concerned. While Dick was driving home, Skinner bolted from the clubhouse and rushed upstairs, first to Quinn's office and then Carpenter's, seeking backing for the standoff he was preparing to wage. When he didn't get it, he quit. In the interim, Capozzoli reached out to Dick and convinced him to attend the game. As Dick saw it, "I didn't feel [the exhibition game] was part of the season. But then I spoke to Clem Capozzoli. I decided to go to Reading because my brother [Ron] plays up there and my family would be going up."[69] He then received the call from Carpenter informing him that Skinner had quit.

Skinner quickly called a press conference (in which both Carpenter and Quinn were in attendance) and blasted his superiors: "I have too much pride to stay without support. There's no way a manager can be a winning manager with this lack of support. . . . It's reached the point now that [Allen's] been spoiled to the extent that no manager can handle him. . . . The manager must have complete control of Allen. There is no other way to handle it. He has to be treated like the last utility man on the club but he feels he has a lever (management)."[70] He then charged that back-room deals between Dick and Carpenter led to a remittance of the bevy of fines levied on Dick throughout the years. Through it all, Carpenter sat silently; later he returned the volley, alleging that Skinner had pressured him to renew his contract or else. At a meeting between owner and manager a few days earlier, Carpenter recounted, "[t]he first thing [Skinner] said was, 'My family comes first. Renew my contract and give me security or I'll resign and tell a lot of things you won't like.' Right then he was through as far as I was concerned."[71]

As the spat between Carpenter and Skinner played out in the local dailies and national press, one assumption went largely unchallenged: that Dick was the true power broker in the scuffle. A *Sporting News* editorial published shortly after the incident remarked that "Allen has just disposed of his second manager,"[72] and Conlin echoed as much when he lauded Skinner's "courageous" act of standing up to Carpenter, refusing to let Dick dictate club procedure. Unfortunately, wrote Conlin, "The owner wouldn't let him walk taller than his star player."[73] Dick laughed at the estimations of his influence within the organization: "They holler about me being spoiled. They say I have a lever in the front office, that I can call my own shots. How can they say that when all I want to do is get out of here? How can Bob Skinner quit on account of me? He didn't show me much. Who likes a quitter? I've been taking the rap for five years now and I'm still here. . . . All I know is that everybody is getting out of here but me and I'm the one who wants to go."[74]

In the *Tribune*, Harrison, as well, dismissed the suggestion that Dick was somehow running things within the organization: "Such a thought borders on insanity because no one tells Carpenter how to run the Phillies, a club that lingered for years after Jackie Robinson broke the color barrier before signing a black athlete. It is hard to believe that all of a sudden the Phillies are allowing a black athlete to set policy—especially on such a high level as the hiring of managers."[75] Rather than focus all the attention on Dick, wrote Harrison, why not look at Skinner's record as manager: "has anyone given thought to the fact that Skinner didn't have the stuff successful major league managers are made of?"[76] *Ebony* wondered the same thing: "most [of its readers] find it hard to believe that a black player can fire two white *baseball* managers."[77] Yet, in the eyes of so many, he was single-handedly manipulating and destroying the Philadelphia Phillies.

Carpenter appointed third base coach George Myatt interim manager and charged him with the responsibility of steering the sinking ship into October without sustaining further damage. To do so, Myatt's first order of business was to lift most of the restrictions Mauch and Skinner tried to enforce. For August and September at least, there would be no postgame curfews, no bed checks on the road, and few if any rules at the ballpark itself. Batting practice would now be optional and each player would be free to decide for himself when to arrive before game time.[78] All of these moves were made with Dick in mind, but still, the media pressed the new manager to be more specific, to address the issue that was hanging over everything. Finally, one of them just came right out with it, asking Myatt if he thought he could handle Dick Allen. "Stud," replied Myatt in his tobacco-cured rasp, "I believe God Almighty Hisself would have trouble handling Richie Allen."[79] Afterward, Dick approached him. "George," he said, "you don't 'handle' people. You treat them. Horses, you handle."[80]

For his part, Dick announced that although he wanted to play for Myatt, he did not see how things could ever improve in Philadelphia: "He's a good man. But I'm so confused. I just got to get through the season and try to start over in another city. . . . All I want to do is play ball and be left alone."[81] It was an impossible request; two weeks later Dick was the subject of the third special broadcast of the summer devoted exclusively to him. This one was hosted by Richie Ashburn, and for a half hour Dick answered questions from both Ashburn and callers. (The local television station later reported that its switchboard was flooded for the duration of the program.) In it he insisted that there was no longer any turning back—even if fans started showering him with standing ovations from here on out, he was leaving at the end of the season.[82]

By this point, the end of the road in Philadelphia, it had become obvious that none of Carpenter's patches over the preceding couple of years had done much good (the returning of the fines, firing Mauch, hiring Myatt, permitting Dick to skip the Reading exhibition game); none of them had much impact because all of them were merely temporary salves, administered solely to soothe a symptom and not cure the disease. Although to many it looked like Carpenter was bending over backward to appease Dick, in fact Carpenter was as lost as ever when it came to the deeper racial issues that had haunted professional baseball ever since Jackie Robinson broke the game's color barrier in 1947. As in the 1950s, Carpenter was still being accused of mistreatment and mismanagement by the *Tribune* when it came to black ballplayers. In 1971, a couple years after Dick's departure, the paper concluded that despite the presence of a few black players on the roster, things were hardly any better than they had been two decades earlier: "Presently, there are three Black outfielders on the Phillies roster who are subject to the same kind of 'benign neglect' suffered by their previous soul brothers. . . . It will be interesting to watch and see if they are molded into the sacrificial lamb figure and finally slaughtered by the kind of mismanagement that makes them look substandard." Just as before, its editorial board alleged that the club was hardly doing all it could to attract black fans. Given that the organization was run by the same man who in the 1950s told the paper he wasn't interested in cultivating a broader fan base, the *Tribune* didn't see much reason for hope: "The Phillies organization must awaken to the realization that if they want to attract Black fans and their dollars they are going to have to demonstrate by more than tokenism that prejudice is not the backdrop of their ownership."[83] Although prevailing wisdom in the white press at this point had it that, on racial matters, Carpenter and the Phillies had gone from one extreme to the other since the days of Tony Curry, from where the *Tribune*'s editorial board sat, little—much too little—had changed.

As Dick played out the lost season, he began expressing his artistic side to pass the time at first base. First he wrote COKE in the dirt with his foot, then NOW, followed by BOO. The next night he scratched out LEE in honor of first base umpire Lee Weyer, who returned the compliment by scrawling RICHIE ALLEN NO. 15. Two nights later he wrote OCT. 2, which everyone recognized as his putative last day in Philadelphia, followed by PETE; nobody was quite sure what to make of that one. Those with a historic bent wondered if he was paying homage to Philadelphia's baseball past, recalling the great Athletics' hurler Grover (Pete) Alexander, while the more practical minded suggested that it might be a message to Dodgers' president Peter O'Malley, indicating his desire to play for the team he rooted for as a boy.[84] Regardless, Quinn was not amused. After a few days of witnessing Dick's "Dread See Scrawls," as Conlin referred to them, the GM had had enough; he called league president Warren Giles to get permission to stop the musings.[85] Giles gave his blessing and Quinn ordered the grounds crew to immediately erase the dirt doodles.[86]

The beat writers and columnists of the three dailies pondered the meaning of these etchings for days. "One day it's all capital letters," wrote Hochman. "Another day, it's capitals and lower case with the i's nicely dotted and the t's neatly crossed. Last night it was script. 'Stop' was the word." What could this mean? Given that this last doodle took place on a muddy field, Hochman wondered, "Had Allen been beseeching the rain to 'stop'? Or did he want the booing to 'stop'? Or the world to 'stop' so he could get off?"[87] Allen Lewis saw them as proof of his assertion that Dick was little more than a scammer: "His recent word-writing in the dirt was harmless enough, but it was hardly in character for someone who claims he wants to be left alone and would like to play baseball without any fans in the park. The day after he wrote his first word in the dirt, photographs of him and the word appeared in all the papers the next day. Someone who didn't want attention would have ceased. But every night, Richie continued to write the words and next day, his picture appeared in the papers."[88] And Padwe saw righteousness in them: "There is more than a slight trace of defiance in [Dick's] wary, questioning eyes. There is contempt, too, for people and institutions—people and institutions which regulate Rich Allen's life without answering one of the questions the first baseman scrawled in the dirt at Connie Mack Stadium last week. The word is 'Why.'"[89] Like nearly everything else by this point, his earthen musings had become a Rorschach test; how anyone interpreted them invariably said more about them than Dick.

Years later, Dick provided his own explanation for his artistic endeavors at first base. "[I wasn't] allowed to say anything," he explained, "so I wrote my replies in the dirt."[90]

* * *

Even before the dwindling days of the 1969 season Dick had gallows humor when it came to his forced existence in Philadelphia. He had formed a musical group, the Ebonistics, which played in local nightclubs, and he liked to begin each performance with a request that the crowd count to three, "and then everybody boo—so I'll feel right at home."[91] In January the Ebonistics performed at halftime of a Sixers game, and the crowd lustily obliged him. (They then cheered him just as fervently once he sang the group's minor hit, "Echoes of November.")[92] He also liked to shout down from his perch in the trainer's room to fans lining up to purchase tickets at Connie Mack Stadium: "Step right up and boo Rich Allen, step right up and boo him, ladies and gentlemen."[93] Still, all of this was window dressing. He wanted out of Philadelphia in the worst way.

Although Dick and Carpenter appeared to have made an agreement in July that brought Dick back to the team in exchange for Carpenter's promise to trade him at the end of the season, nothing was formally signed, and Carpenter held the upper hand; he could change his mind at any moment and there would be little Dick could do about it. By late August, Carpenter began sending precisely these signals. As word got around that Dick was considering a movie career—he had been approached by local disc jockey Jerry Blavat to costar with him in a movie titled *Calliope*—Carpenter reminded the local scribes that he was under no obligation to do anything when it came to Dick: "If we fail to make a deal, Allen can quit and start making movies or do anything else he so desires. That will have to be his decision. However, I think he'll play."[94] The Allens counterpunched a few weeks later when Dick's wife, Barbara, appeared on *Betty Hughes and Friends*, a local talk show hosted by the wife of the New Jersey governor, and recounted what she described as the terroristic acts directed toward her family throughout Dick's tenure in Philadelphia. On the program as well were a husband and wife, both psychologists, who discussed the emotional trauma that could result from the litany of threats the Allens had endured over the years.[95]

Four days later the Phils played their last home game of the season (they were shut out by the soon-to-be world champion Mets 2–0), and although nothing had been said officially, it sure felt like the last game Dick would play in Philadelphia as a member of the Phillies. After grounding out in the eighth inning, Dick shook the startled first base umpire's hand, and in the ninth, after making the final putout at first, he "kissed his right palm and gave the ground a freedom slap."[96] On his way to the dugout, after yelling out "You'll never get a sandwich out of me again!" to anyone within earshot who might have forgotten his tussle with Frank

Thomas four years earlier, he waved to the booing crowd one last time. After the game he told the *Bulletin*'s Ray Kelly, "If they don't get rid of me I think I'll pack it in."[97] And that was that. Now it was up to Carpenter to do what by now even he conceded had to be done.

A week later it was: Dick, along with Cookie Rojas and pitcher Jerry Johnson, was dealt to the Cardinals in exchange for outfielder Curt Flood, catcher Tim McCarver, pitcher Joe Hoerner, and outfielder Byron Browne. Surprisingly, upon hearing the news one of his chief critics, former teammate (and now Baltimore Oriole) Clay Dalrymple, echoed much of what Dick had alleged for years with regard to the Phillies' management: "I played for the Phillies for nine years," he said. "It pained Bob Carpenter to have to say hello to me maybe three times during the nine years. . . . All those years I wasted in that organization. I didn't realize how bad it was, because I had nothing to compare it with." The organization was, he contended, full of "so many incompetents." As for Quinn, Dalrymple recalled that one year, "I got a $500 raise. He gave in two days before spring training started. Then he threatened me. He said, 'don't ever have a bad year.' Can you imagine? Instead of saying 'nice going, you've earned it. I hope you have a lot of good years,' he threatened me." Hochman piled on, writing that "there is something to the indictment of Quinn and his Neanderthal treatment of players."[98] Even Allen Lewis concurred, writing that perhaps the most important player acquired by the Phillies in the deal was McCarver, whom he hoped could improve a team morale that "sometimes bordered on what might be expected in a prison."[99] As for Dick, his parting shot was short and to the point: "I'm glad to get away from John Quinn and all of them. They treat you like cattle."[100]

For those who expected controversy whenever any activity involving Dick Allen was concerned, the trade's aftermath did not disappoint. Surprisingly, however, the controversy this time didn't involve Dick but Flood, who announced his retirement in the wake of the deal rather than report to the Phillies. At first, few believed Flood was serious and were convinced that, eventually, he'd report. "Chances are that Flood," wrote the old-school Lewis, "who earns in the neighborhood of $90,000 a year in baseball, will change his mind."[101] Longtime baseball (and former Cardinal) executive Frank Lane concurred, remarking that there was no way Flood, who also dabbled as an artist, would abandon baseball: "I'm sure Mr. Flood will be playing ball next season—unless he's better than Rembrandt."[102] Even Claude Harrison agreed with Quinn, who was confident that Flood would report: "After the shock wears off, Flood will see things in a different light."[103] Given the amount of money involved, Harrison couldn't fathom Flood simply walking away. Nobody, it seemed, realized that in Flood the Phils had obtained someone who shared many of the same values as Dick. To both, baseball wasn't only about the money; it was also about the pursuit of independence while plying their trade for salaries commensurate with their abilities. To Dick, money was a way to achieve these goals; to Flood, no amount of money could persuade him to abandon them. In the swap, Quinn and Carpenter had merely exchanged one individualist for another.

Initially, Flood's reluctance to accede to the trade seemed to have more to do with where he was being sent rather than the larger issues he would focus on later. "I never had any trouble in Philadelphia," he told Hochman. "But they gave Richie a heckuva time and that makes you feel bad to see that happen."[104] In his autobiography he likewise seemed to be referring to Philadelphia and its by now infamous fans whenever he spoke of the boorish behavior he wanted no part of: "I have argued in locker rooms that baseball's publicists have encouraged fans to adopt forms of behavior that would be unacceptable elsewhere in the entertainment world. When an actor blows his lines, nobody dares to boo him, much less throw bottles at him and call him names."[105] Besides referring to it as "the nation's northernmost southern city," Flood described Philadelphia as the "scene of Richie Allen's ordeals. Home of a ball club rivaled only by the Pirates as the least cheerful organization in the league . . . I did not want to succeed Richie Allen in the affections of that organization, its press and its catcalling, missile-hurling audience."[106]

Although Flood soon broadened his argument, concluding that "the problem was no particular city but was the reserve clause, which affected all players equally no matter where," it was in large part Dick's battles with the Phillies and their fans that provided clarity—Dick had already experienced everything Flood feared.[107] While Flood was, for years, shielded from the realities of the reserve clause as a result of the benevolent paternalism of Cardinals' owner Gussie Busch, who provided well for his favored players and made the team feel special, Dick was enduring life on the other end of the baseball spectrum, a fate that awaited any player at any moment and subject solely to the whim of club management. "When the proud Cardinals were riding a chartered jet," Flood wrote, "the Phils were lumbering through the air in propeller jobs, arriving on the Coast too late to get proper rest before submitting to murder by the Giants and Dodgers."[108] In an instant a player could go from the top of the baseball world to the bottom, regardless of age, experience, or ties to a particular city. In a flash he could go from living Curt Flood's privileged life to Dick Allen's tortured one and there was nothing he could do about it. Except this time, Flood was determined to.

Flood always insisted that he didn't take up his fight against baseball because he was black but acknowledged that his experiences as a black man made him more aware of larger injustices perpetrated against everyone. Indeed, when Dodgers' catcher Tom Haller asked him, "Are you doing this simply because you're black and you feel that baseball has been discriminatory?" Flood responded, "All the things you say are true and I'd be lying if I told you that as a black man in baseball I hadn't gone through worse times than my white teammates. I'll also say that, yes, I think the change in black consciousness in recent years has made me more sensitive to injustice in every area of my life. But I want you to know that what I'm doing here I'm doing as a ballplayer, a major league ballplayer, and I think it's absolutely terrible that we have stood by and watched this situation go on for so many years and never pulled together to do anything about it."[109] In his subsequent letter to Bowie Kuhn in which he requested that Kuhn declare him a free agent, Flood echoed much of what Dick had been saying for years: "After twelve years in the Major Leagues, I do not feel that I am a piece of property to be bought and sold irrespective of my wishes." When he wrote in his book, "I was not a consignment of goods. I was a man, the rightful proprietor of my own person and my own talents,"[110] he was channeling Dick as well. And when he wrote that despite the Cardinals' success on the field, to Busch "we were still livestock" he was putting down on paper the words Dick spoke upon his deliverance from the Phillies.[111] Flood may have said the words that baseball fans and historians remember as the shots across the bow that would change baseball forever, but Dick lived them.

Although Dick felt a kinship with Flood and his battle against the reserve clause, he viewed his own situation in Philadelphia as something fundamentally different: while Flood wanted the freedom to determine where he would play, all Dick wanted was to get out of Philadelphia. Others saw more similarities than differences. Even frequent critic Norman Unger of the *Chicago Defender* considered them to be "two peas in a pod . . . both are truly Black and proud." Despite their faults, Unger concluded, both were men of principle and "no amount of money in the world can buy a principle."[112] A few years later Dick told Sandy Padwe that he understood Flood's feelings of helplessness: "You ever wonder why baseball loves dumb farm boys? Dumb farm boys don't say very much. . . . What say do I have in my professional life? They tell you to go here, they send you a piece of paper and say this is your salary, accept it. . . . What choice is there?"[113] Still, he was unable to see Flood's battle as his battle so he always kept a measured distance from Flood's fight, careful to clarify that he wasn't looking to rock the system, he just wanted off of the Phillies.

As he saw things, all of his problems were rooted in Carpenter, Quinn, the sportswriters, and the fans in Philadelphia. Once he left them behind, he believed, everything would be alright. "Don't worry, Ellie," he told Yankee coach Elston Howard, "when I get out of Philadelphia, I'll be a different man."[114] While Flood quickly expanded his criticism to blanket the entirety of baseball's operations, Dick's criticisms of the game over the next couple of years were lasered toward Philadelphia and the Phillies, an organization he liked to refer to as "minor league."[115] "If a little black kid came to me for advice," he said in 1971, "I would encourage him not to play in Philadelphia."[116] Indeed, he said, it had now become his mission in life to avoid both the city and the club.

To Dick, the trade left him twice blessed: not only was he escaping the Phillies, he was heading to St. Louis, a city known for its benevolent fans and media, and to an organization with a history of treating its black players well. He was ecstatic and was eager to demonstrate his appreciation and renewed desire to play ball. When a St. Louis writer asked him if he'd consider returning to third base given that Mike Shannon, the Cardinals' third baseman in 1969, was on the sidelines, he replied, "I'll play there. I'll play first, third, left. I'll play anywhere—except Philadelphia."[117] Very quickly, though, he'd discover that the Cardinals were hardly the tonic for all that ailed him. But that was in the future. For a few months at least, he was able to bask in the glory of his perceived emancipation.

Chapter 9

❖

I Am My Own Man

1970: St. Louis .279/34/101

"BING DEVINE SITS in his office at Busch Stadium," began a July 1970 profile in *Sport* magazine. "He admits he has heard 'the word' on Rich Allen. If he hadn't heard it, he would have had to be deaf, dumb, blind and coaching volleyball." And yet he pulled the trigger on the deal that liberated Dick Allen from Philadelphia. "Yes, I'd heard all the stories. Yes, I was naturally concerned. But it wasn't what we really knew about him. It was what we'd heard about him. There's a difference."[1] To the Cardinals' general manager, what he heard was oftentimes very different from what he knew. This difference, between hearing and knowing, was what separated him from his brethren throughout baseball and what enabled him to turn the lemons that soured so many of his fellow baseball executives in other organizations into sweet lemonade in St. Louis. Roger Maris from the Yankees, Orlando Cepeda from the Giants, Lou Brock from the Cubs, Joe Torre from the Braves: all reclamation projects shuffled ignominiously to St. Louis who thrived thereafter because Bing Devine understood the difference between hearing and knowing. He was quite certain that Dick Allen would be nothing less than the next notch on his belt.

Devine had at least a few people in his corner. Jim Murray of the *Los Angeles Times* responded to the trade by announcing that "Richie Allen's not what's wrong with the Philadelphia Phillies. Philadelphia is what's wrong with the Philadelphia Phillies." As for his foibles, Murray dismissed them: " 'He drinks'—Does he now? Well, that makes him unique in baseball. Think what it might have done to Babe Ruth's career. Or General Grant's. . . . 'He forced the trade of Frank Thomas after they got in a fight.'—Frank Who? Oh, you mean the guy who's playing slow-pitch softball now? Is THAT Richie Allen's fault, too?"[2] Dick sensed a new beginning as well. "If I only hit .220, if I only hit 12 home runs, this has got to be the greatest thing that's happened to me in a long, long time. . . . Hey, man, I finally made it to the big leagues."[3] On his way out of Philadelphia he assured Padwe that things were going to be different from here on out: "Maybe, I'll go down [to the Cardinals' instructional winter league team in St. Petersburg] this winter. It's better than sitting around here. I'll work out a couple of days a week and be ready for the first day of spring training. They won't have to worry. I'll be there on time."[4]

Dick and Devine may have only seen sunshine, but when Cardinals' owner Gussie Busch surveyed the horizon he saw clouds. To Busch, the clouds began forming after the Cardinals' run to the World Series in 1968, when several key players insisted on significant raises. Busch was outraged; they didn't win the 1968 World Series after all, and, worse, many of the players seeking raises had put up inferior statistics when compared to their 1967 numbers. Curt Flood insulted him most of all, demanding $100,000. These salary demands, combined with the increasing tension between management and the Players Association, "offended [Busch's] sense of propriety," Flood alleged.[5] As the Cardinals' owner saw it, he was the benevolent dictator; the players were his obedient and faithful servants. This was the way it had always been and, to Busch, everybody— management, players, fans—benefited from the arrangement. By upsetting the apple cart, the players were threatening the entire industry. So Busch took it upon himself to put a stop to the insurgence by speaking up, he insisted, not for himself but on behalf of the fans. "The fans are going to resent this situation," he warned.[6]

Busch had successfully jettisoned Flood but in return acquired, on Devine's advice, a player who brought with him not only the biggest bat in baseball but a reputation for standing up to management like no other player before him. The resulting clash was inevitable. Anticipating the showdown that was sure to come, Busch announced, "I can't see paying Allen a salary that's the same as some of my stars. I'd have to raise their salaries out of good conscience." Since he had no intention of doing that, Dick was out of luck as far as Busch was concerned. "Instead of a sport, baseball is becoming a headache," he lamented.[7] His was about to get bigger as the coming of the 1970 season brought to the fore not only Dick's contract but pitcher Steve Carlton's, who won 17 games in 1969 and posted a sterling 2.17 ERA (the second lowest in the league) while striking out a then-record 19 batters in one game. Carlton was seeking to more than double his salary, from $24,000 to $50,000. Busch would oblige him an additional six grand but no more than that.[8] But that was chicken scratch compared to what Dick was reportedly asking: a cool $150,000—the highest salary in the history of professional baseball.[9] "I can't understand Curt Flood or the Allen case," said an exasperated Busch. To him the salary demands coupled with the increasing agitation of the Players Association signaled the end of the world as he knew and understood it: "Some of us have to take a stand for the good of baseball one way or the other. I hate to be the sucker who does it, but I am perfectly willing to do it. . . . I'm fed up and the fans are, too. The players have a great pension plan and we've been pretty fair with salaries. Now they talk strike. They must think we're a bunch of softheads. I hope to God this is not a majority view. I can't understand what's happening here or on our campuses or in our great country."[10] As for Dick's demand, Busch was clear: "We ain't going to give in. He is going to play at our figure or he's not going to play for the Cardinals."[11]

Dick had heard similar threats from Quinn, and he responded to Busch's as he had responded to Quinn's—by ignoring them. In Dick's experience, the tactic had a double benefit: it inevitably resulted in a higher salary when all was said and done and, until that point, enabled him to sit out the early weeks of spring training. "Spring training is too long," he said in March. "I don't like to make a move before my birthday on March 8 . . . I sort of had my mind set [on reporting] on March 18. It only takes me three good weeks to get ready."[12] Busch had other ideas and was unwilling to play along as Carpenter had done; when both Dick and

Carlton failed to report, Busch invoked the reserve clause and unilaterally renewed their contracts: Dick's for $90,000, Carlton's for $31,000.[13] In so doing, Dick was made to understand that, in all significant ways, it was management that held the hammer, not him. Carpenter's refusal to wield it had given Dick the illusion of the upper hand; when up against someone more willing to wield management's most powerful weapon he was helpless. Even before his first game as a Cardinal, he was schooled in the business of baseball and provided with proof that Philadelphia and the Phillies weren't the sole cause of his troubles.

If Dick failed to see the connection between his and Flood's plight earlier, by now he shouldn't have been able to miss it; Flood was rebelling against the very rule (Section 10A of the Uniform Player's Contract) that Busch had just invoked to shut Dick down and, for all practical purposes, end his holdout on the spot. Because of the reserve clause, Dick's leverage was nonexistent. He had no choice but to report to the Cardinals—and at their price, not his. A few months earlier, Flood had addressed the Players Association during its December meeting in San Juan to explain his position. In asking for the association's backing of his lawsuit against Major League Baseball, Flood recalled, "I spoke of the affronts to human dignity of a system that indentured one man to another. I pointed out that fair bargaining and real professionalism would remain distant hopes in baseball unless I fought my fight."[14] Dick now had concrete proof of what Flood was talking about.

Later, Flood would describe things more starkly: "The reserve system was the same system used in the South where the plantation owner owned all the houses that you lived in. And you worked for him and you shopped in his store and you never got over the hump." In such a system, it was obvious where everybody stood: "They're the ranchers, and we're the cattle."[15] Regardless, as Flood's case worked its way through the legal system, he found few supporters among his fellow ballplayers. Either they were too scared to align themselves against management or they refused to see the connection between Flood's argument and their own livelihoods. Dick was certainly not in the former group but he oftentimes had difficulty seeing beyond himself. Flood's situation was different, Dick still insisted even after Busch invoked the reserve clause. Flood was asking to be declared a free agent whereas all Dick sought, he believed, was asylum from Philadelphia. Though Busch's slapping the reserve clause on Dick drove him and Flood together, Dick nevertheless kept his distance from Flood and his cause. "I think the reserve clause should be modified," Dick said after Busch applied it to him. "I wish I had the intelligence to settle it. But my hat's off to Curt Flood. That 160 pounds is all man."[16] This was as close to the situation as he would get.

The system was cracking, however, and Dick was not the only one chipping away at it. In Oakland, Reggie Jackson, coming off a season where he hit 47 home runs and finished fifth in the American League MVP balloting, was holding out for more money from tight-fisted owner Charlie Finley. Although Jackson and Dick were opposites—Jackson was an extreme extrovert while Dick was an introvert, Jackson loved the media and enjoyed being the center of attention while Dick cringed at all of that—in deeper ways they shared some important similarities. Both were young, brash (in their own way), self-confident, and knowledgeable about the power of money. In 1969 Jackson made all of $20,000 for his efforts and was determined to hold out until Finley met his demand of $75,000 for 1970.[17] Finley balked and the two were quickly at a stalemate as spring training dragged on. Right after Busch invoked the reserve clause on Dick, Finley did the same to Jackson, informing him that his contract for the 1970 season would be $45,000 and ordering him to report to camp immediately. Dick followed Jackson's travails in Oakland and sympathized (unlike Flood, Jackson was, after all, doing precisely what Dick did every spring). "Baseball managers mistreat black players," he said a few months later. When Dick saw Jackson he saw a man standing up for his basic rights and being vilified and punished as a result. "A lot of people who run baseball still don't think of us, really, as human beings," he said. "I am black, see, and I am proud I am black."[18]

Later, in his autobiography, Dick would look back at this era in disbelief. "The freer you make baseball in every respect, the better the game's going to be," he argued.[19] Instead, management seemed to be tightening the screws like never before. Owners were invoking the reserve clause more willingly than they had been just a few years earlier, and, as a result of both Flood's refusal to report to Philadelphia as well as Donn Clendenon's refusal to accept a trade from Montreal to Houston (he retired in protest until he was rerouted to the Mets in time to join their 1969 title run), baseball adopted the "Clendenon Rule," which stripped a player of his de facto ability to refuse a trade.[20] Previously, and as both Flood and Clendenon demonstrated, if a player refused to report to his new club, his old club was required to make good on the deal by substituting another player in the transaction. This gave the traded player at least a modicum of leverage since his old club might hesitate to deal him to an undesired location if it knew it was on the hook if the player refused to report. Under the Clendenon Rule, that power had been taken away; now it was "buyer beware," and if a player failed to report, the burden fell on the club that dealt for him. Flood and Clendenon were the pioneers in this use of their informal veto power (which most players never knew they had). Now, barely a year later, the owners moved swiftly to close that loophole.

The owners didn't see themselves as ogres. They saw themselves as both Busch and Finley believed themselves to be: benevolent patriarchs. Busch was outraged that the perks he offered his players—chartered jets to and from all National League cities, individual hotel rooms on the road—were no longer considered to be enough for players like Dick and Carlton. Cardinals' pitcher George Culver called the organization "first-class" because, by comparison, his old club, the Cincinnati Reds, offered fewer perks.[21] In Oakland, Finley liked to charm his players by treating them to a day at his farm in La Porte, Indiana, where he would put on an apron and cook for them. "Eggs, steak, bacon, ham, sausage, pork chops, and fresh cantaloupe a la mode. It was the first time in my life I had cantaloupe a la mode," Jackson recalled.[22]

But more and more players were realizing that it wasn't the perks that mattered. It was the money. And here the Cardinals and A's were no different from anybody else. All of the cantaloupe à la mode in the world wasn't going to satisfy Reggie Jackson, and while Dick certainly appreciated the chartered flights after what he had experienced with the Phillies, they weren't going to make up for salary. "Maybe we're the suckers," Busch said of his Cardinals. "We always gave the highest salaries."[23] In one respect he was correct—his Cardinals were hardly laggards compared to most of the other clubs in baseball. But everybody's salaries were artificially depressed, and at least a few players were starting to rebel against that reality. While the sports editors of both the *St. Louis Post-Dispatch* and the *Globe Democrat* chided Dick for seeking a significant pay hike in

St. Louis,[24] Bill Nunn of the *New Pittsburgh Courier* responded that Dick "shouldn't be made a villain for trying to get the contract he thinks he's worth. Some guys are trying to make him that very thing."[25]

*   *   *

Fed up with players like Dick and Carlton, who, he was convinced, were taken care of by munificent souls such as himself, Busch began lashing out at them. He not only slapped the reserve clause on them, he sent them threatening letters, ordering them to camp or else. Dick reported the next day; Carlton continued his holdout. To those in the media who were shocked that Dick seemingly responded to an ultimatum from management, Dick quickly sought to disabuse them: "I didn't know anything about any ultimatum from Mr. Busch," he said. "I couldn't get together with the Cardinals on some fringe benefits that would take care of my mom."[26] He took pains to assure everyone that recent events had no effect on him: "I'll be happy to get down there and get started. This is the first time since '64 that I'm leaving here [Philadelphia] with a winning attitude. It's contagious."[27] Privately, though, he was irked that "they pulled that clause on me. Nobody ever did that to me before. I said, 'O.K., you'll get what you paid for—one good year.' "[28] When Dick arrived in St. Petersburg, Carlton and Busch were still hissing at each other. "I don't care if he ever pitches another ball for us. These players still think we're a bunch of tight-fisted whatevers, but I'm not going to back down," said Busch. For his part, Carlton continued to stand his ground and voice his displeasure to anyone willing to listen. "I am happy," said Dick amid all of this, "to be joining a team with such a happy atmosphere."[29]

True to form, Dick's arrival in St. Pete was not without theatrics. The Cardinals sent their publicist to the Tampa airport, along with seven reporters, to meet him when he arrived. When the passengers on the flight from Philadelphia disembarked and Dick was not among them, the publicist panicked (at that moment a media horde was assembling at the Cardinals' spring training complex for the announced press conference scheduled to take place as soon as he returned with the club's new slugger). He approached the ticket agent and asked where Dick was. The ticket agent informed him that there was no Dick Allen on the passenger list.

Dick with Bing Devine in the Cardinals' clubhouse in St. Petersburg,
Florida, March 12, 1970, after Dick reported to camp.
(© 2014 Legendaryauctions.com)

Finally Dick strolled off the plane, bedecked in a cocoa-colored, double-breasted Edwardian suit, orange shirt, and brown shoes, and the publicist exhaled.[30] Later at the press conference, Dick announced that, financially speaking, "It wasn't the best contract I ever got, but I'm satisfied 100 percent and I owe a great deal to the Cardinals for getting me out of where I was."[31] As for his drinking, he tried to downplay its significance: "I'm no angel, but I'm no troublemaker. I take a nip or two, but I don't think I drink to excess. Truthfully, I've taken a couple of belts at times before I've taken the field because I wanted to calm down. In Philadelphia, they criticized me for everything but what I was paid to do—play baseball."[32]

Afterward, Dick ambled down to the locker room to greet his new teammates. Frank Dolson followed him and reported that "Allen stood there, a cup of beer in one hand, a cup of hot soup in the other, and took alternate sips. For those who hadn't seen Richie before, it was an impressive display of two-fisted drinking." When asked if the day felt special to him, Dick responded that he was "just glad to be over here, to get a chance to show people I'm no Jesse James."[33] The St. Louis writers appeared willing to oblige with a narrative that Dick was a changed man. They were quick to mention that Dick "sounded like a man longing for acceptance" and to suggest that in a new city, Dick would have the opportunity to demonstrate that he was a new person.[34] Dick never took the bait. "No!" he exclaimed to an *Ebony* reporter who wondered whether to believe the reports coming out of St. Louis that the Dick Allen playing there was different from the Dick Allen who inhabited Philadelphia. "I haven't changed. I'm the same Richie Allen I always was and always will be. I . . . am . . . my . . . own . . . man."[35]

As for whether Dick could see himself as a role model for children, he consistently balked at the suggestion. He would continue to drink, he said, because, "look, the government sells the stuff and I'm over 21. As for setting examples for kids, forget it. The Negro race has been discriminated against for so long, how can anyone talk about that? What about all those years when they didn't even allow Negroes to play in the big leagues? What sort of example was that? Nah, I'm concerned only about my own kids, or kids I might meet and talk to, but not about somebody else's kids I've never met or seen."[36] He was nevertheless becoming a role model to some of his fellow ballplayers, none more so than his new teammate Jose Cardenal, who soon considered Dick to be his best friend in baseball. "Before I went to spring training with the Cardinals, I heard a lotta things about him," said Cardenal. "Soon I realized everything I heard about him was wrong."[37] Although Dick spoke infrequently, when he did Cardenal paid attention. "When Richie opens his mouth you listen. And you learn, too. He was really the only one who ever helped me in this game. Everything else I learned by myself."[38] Players such as Cardenal were starting to realize, through Dick's example, that they didn't need to conform to management's expectations if they didn't want to.

"I admired him because of what he went through," said Cardenal. "It was tough for the Spanish and the black athlete to play in towns like Little Rock but he was a strong man and he made it . . . it was different for black ballplayers back then because of what they went through." The overarching theme of Dick's lesson to Cardenal was that "you had to respect people for what they are." Cardenal saw a lot of himself in Dick: "I wasn't a great home run hitter but personality-wise I was like him—I didn't like to be embarrassed, I stuck to my own friends and if I didn't feel like talking, I didn't talk. I liked to mind my own business . . . [Dick] taught me to be myself, not to try to be like anybody else. Whatever it is that makes you happy, he told me, go and do it. Try to be yourself. If you want to laugh, laugh. If you want to scream, scream. If you want to cry, cry."[39]

As a symbol of black independence, Dick drew followers along with his skeptics. In the *New Pittsburgh Courier*, Bill Nunn Jr. wrote that as Dick was adjusting to his new home with the Cardinals, black fans would be well advised to learn more about him: "For those who don't know Allen, he is the kind of man most black men would like. As for the other side of the coin he couldn't care less, even though he can boast of quite a few white friends."[40] In midwestern America, this could be a problem. In St. Louis, the *Sport* magazine profile on Dick observed, "They tell stories about Grover Cleveland Alexander shuffling in from the bullpen all hung over, and whether the stories are true or not, people believe them, which is more important. They talk about the drinkers and the brawlers with love in their hearts—just so long as they have been out of baseball for 30 years. They talk about a Frisch challenging McGraw and it is all so wonderful to them. . . . Yet now they worry about Richie Allen's sideburns or ask him to shave off a mustache."[41] Which perhaps explained the St. Louis media's obsession with reassuring their readers that Dick had changed, his protestations to the contrary notwithstanding.

In some ways, Dick was becoming a modern iteration of the Negro League star Satchel Paige, a symbol of black independence from an earlier era. Paige liked to travel from town to town on his own, eschewing the team bus for his own ride. He was also a flashy dresser, and as former Negro League umpire Bob Motley recalled, "He always walked with the confident swagger of a movie star, both on and off the field. It was nothing to see him drive up to a stadium in a brand-spanking-new Cadillac every couple months." He also demanded a percentage of the box-office receipts and would often insist on being the highest-paid player on the field. But money didn't change his outlook and cause him to fall into line; he still

Baseball's newest Cardinal—Dick Allen.

(National Baseball Hall of Fame and Museum, Inc.)

preferred to arrive to the ballpark shortly before game time. "I never rush myself," he once said. "They can't start the game without me." "In all the years that I umpired him," Motley recalled, "I never once saw Satch warm up in the bullpen before a game. He'd lope out to the mound, take a few moments to look around at the crowd as if acknowledging his legions of worshippers, toss four or five easy pitches to his catcher, and then it was on." In sum, "he answered to no one," said Motley. Why not? "Because he was a superstar." Kansas City Monarchs manager Buck O'Neil once said "you don't manage Satchel Paige. You manage the team he happens to be on."[42]

Dick idolized the Negro League stars and was starstruck when he met Cool Papa Bell during an old-timers' game in 1987. He was honored when Bell told Dick that he could have played with Bell and his fellow Negro Leaguers back in the day. "It's funny," he said after speaking with Bell. "Back in their day, the Negro League players all wanted to be big leaguers. They felt deprived because they could never get in. And there I was, in my day, a big leaguer who felt like he lost out because he never got a chance to play in the Negro Leagues."[43] For this reason he always expressed ambivalence whenever the issue of his worthiness for the Hall of Fame was broached. "I ain't interested in no Cooperstown," he said in 1971. "If Cool Papa Bell and those other black stars of the past ain't there, I don't wanna be. Or deserve to be."[44]

Because of the spring training dust-up, along with the baggage he carried with him from the Phillies, Dick was booed by Cardinals' fans throughout his initial spring training appearance.[45] He quickly changed their temperament when he proceeded to hit four homers in his first four spring training games, "making a joke of spring training," according to *St. Louis Post-Dispatch* writer Neal Russo.[46] On the season's Opening Day in frigid Montreal, Dick doubled and then blasted an eighth-inning 400-foot home run—in forty-five-degree weather—to tie the game, which the Cardinals went on to win in the ninth.[47] Overall, he went 5 for 10 in the opening series. By the time the Cards returned to St. Louis for their home opener, the masses were on his side. "The cheering was deafening. And it was almost unanimous," wrote Russo.[48] "I thought Musial was making a comeback," remarked *New York Post* writer Jack Lang.[49] "That's the greatest thing that ever happened to me," Dick said after the game. "I never thought it could happen. I just wish Mom could have heard it."[50] Two days later, after hitting his first home run in front of his newfound fans—a 450-foot blast that landed in the back of the left-centerfield bullpen—he tipped his cap and blew kisses to them.[51] Still, there were limits to his affection. "I was thinking," he said a few months later, "all right, that one is for you [the fans] . . . but the others, well, the others were going to be for me."[52]

Even though Dick continued to shy away from reporters the defining narrative was that Dick was a new man. (After the season opener in Montreal he walked away when the media horde descended upon him. A few minutes later he returned and suggested that they interview second baseman Julian Javier instead: "He drove in the winning run. Give Hoolie a little ink.")[53] Cardinal teammate Cookie Rojas, who just a year earlier in Philadelphia had instigated the closed-door team meeting that led to a divisive debate over Dick's ways, now contended that there was nothing to the argument that Dick's off-field and practice habits were of any issue at all: "All I can say is I've never seen him loaf on the field. They always say blah, blah, blah and this and that about him. Every time I've ever seen him, he has given one-hundred-and-ten-percent. On the field he's a professional." As for his off-the-field demeanor, Rojas demurred: "I've never seen him off the field so I don't know." In sum, Rojas wanted everyone to know that Dick was "okay with me."[54] For a time, he seemed to be okay with everyone else as well.

*   *   *

Despite his own assertions to the contrary, Dick had changed at least a little, if only on the surface. He now took batting practice more regularly, declaring that he took those extra swings because "I'm in the big leagues now."[55] He also made it a point to show up to a workout scheduled on an early season off-day even though manager Red Schoendienst gave him permission to skip it. He praised the St. Louis fans, he praised the St. Louis writers. While he had unkind words for the Busch Stadium Astroturf ("I'll give you my feelings on playing fields. If a horse can't eat on them, I don't like it"), that was about the only thing he seemed to find disagreeable in his new home. "This is the way I thought the big leagues would be," he said in early May. "I'm only sorry I didn't come out here when I left high school. I would have avoided a lot of trouble."[56]

In mid-May the Phillies came to Busch Stadium for a series many Phillie fans had circled on their calendars. Dick did not disappoint. In the bottom of the ninth in the series opener, the teams were deadlocked in a scoreless tie. With a runner on second and nobody out, Phils' manager Frank Lucchesi ordered pitcher Jim Bunning to intentionally walk Lou Brock to get to Dick. Bunning had struck him out twice already (once with the bases loaded), and Lucchesi was betting on him doing it again. Schoendienst relayed the bunt sign to third base coach George Kissell, who flashed it to Dick; Dick just stared back at him. Kissell walked up to him, told him to bunt, and then returned to the third base coaches' box where he flashed it again. Dick squared around but took a Bunning strike anyway. Clearly, in a moment that was too delicious for a mere dribble down the third base line, his heart wasn't in a sacrifice. Schoendienst got the message; this time he allowed Dick to swing away. After taking another strike Dick connected on an 0–2 fastball and deposited it in the right-field seats. Game over. As he crossed home plate, he raised his right fist in the air.[57] After being mobbed by his teammates at home plate, he agreed to appear on Bill Campbell's postgame radio show beamed back to Philadelphia. "You can say I dedicated that homer to Paul Owens who said my brother couldn't play with a contender," Dick told Campbell.[58]

Ten days later came the homecoming itself; Dick and the Cardinals disembarked in Philadelphia and "the town's longest running morality play," as Bill Conlin described it, resumed.[59] Before the series a reporter asked Dick if he feared taking the field at Connie Mack. "I've had six years of this," he said in reply. "There's nothing to be afraid of."[60] When he took the field (before a crowd that was twice as large as usual) he heard boos but also some cheers. The bedsheet banners stringing the stadium were also mixed: "How Do You Like Your New Babysitter, Richie?" was met with "Allen MVP" and "Drexel U Digs Crash Allen."[61] As the game progressed, the boos got louder and fans threw empty beer cans and other detritus onto the field. Some in the stands had difficulty controlling themselves; a steelworker sitting in a box behind the Cardinals' dugout (Phillies cap turned sideways, one knee on the dugout roof) pelted insults at Dick whenever he emerged from the dugout. When Dick grounded into a first-inning double play the man had to be restrained by two of his seatmates from running onto the field to call Dick out at first himself. "Seeing him hit into that double play is the thrill of a lifetime for me," he told *Bulletin* reporter Jim Barniak.[62]

Once again, Dick saved his heroics for the ninth inning. With the Phillies leading 3–0 (Carlton struck out 16 but still stood to lose the game), pinch hitter Phil Gagliano's chopper hit Phils' third baseman Don Money in the eye. Money collapsed, Gagliano was on first, and a fan ran onto the field. He circled the infield, taunting the cops and security guards before finally being wrestled to the ground and handcuffed. As he was being led off the field another fan took his place, although he was rounded up more quickly. In the left-field bleachers, a fight that had been simmering for a while now raged. The natives were getting restless. Cardenal then hit a ball up the middle that forced Gagliano at second, which brought Dick to the plate. Without an opportunity to win the game outright, Dick did the best he could, launching a home run into the mayhem in the left-field bleachers. Once again he raised his right fist as he crossed home plate.[63] Later the Cards tied the game but the Phillies won it in the bottom of the ninth.

Although Phillies' broadcaster Rich Ashburn warned before the series that you pitch to Dick "the way porcupines make love . . . carefully,"[64] Phils' pitchers didn't heed his advice—he hit five home runs, knocked in a dozen, and had a 1.278 slugging percentage in his first five games against his former mates. Finally, in the sixth game, on Sunday afternoon, the Phils got to him—Dick struck out five times. But that was to be expected, Dolson wrote, because "as everybody knows, Rich Allen has always had an inordinate amount of trouble hitting baseballs out of sight—or anywhere—on Sunday afternoons, perhaps because of their close proximity to Saturday nights."[65] Still, the series did not disappoint. Fans turned out to Connie Mack as they hadn't all season to voice their opinions on Dick: an average of 12,011 showed up (despite rain on Saturday and threatening weather on Sunday) as compared with the season average of 7,327 up to that point. Dick's every appearance seemed to elicit some response, with fans eager to express themselves through their opinions of him. At one point during a rain delay before Saturday's game, Cardinals' outfielder

Leron Lee decided to have a little fun. He borrowed Dick's jersey, glasses, and batting helmet and strode onto the field. Before he left Dick told him he was on his own: "I don't know what you've got on your mind, but if you get shot don't blame me."[66] In all, the games against the Phils were harbingers of the season he would unleash against the entirety of the National League. Until going down with a hamstring injury on August 14, he was on pace to break Johnny Mize's club record of 43 home runs (he had 33 by that point) and had started all but one of the club's first 118 games of the season.

Privately, the season had taken a toll on him, although he took pains not to show it. "I had something to prove when I left Philly," he said the following year. "I wanted to show everyone that I wasn't a bad guy . . . I felt that all the eyes that watch the baseball world were watching me." The St. Louis fans and writers were likewise out to prove something, Dick believed. They were out to show the baseball world that they weren't Philadelphia. "I'm sure they were sincere," Dick said of the St. Louis fans, "but it seemed like a forced situation to me."[67] Although he went out of his way to assure everyone that he was happy in St. Louis, he later admitted that, this time at least, he was putting on a public face that contradicted his true feelings: "There are a lot of things you say because you know they will bring the fans into the stadium."[68] Neal Russo contended that, ultimately, Dick soured on the Cardinals when it became clear that, like the Phillies, they weren't going anywhere—they won only 76 games, just three more than the Phillies.[69]

He felt constrained in so many ways. Although he liked to joke that he was unable to unwind at the racetrack as he liked to do because "the racetracks there operate at night and we played at night,"[70] the truth was that he was hesitant to be seen at the track for fear that he'd be spotted there on Monday and have to answer for it on Tuesday. Instead, he just preferred to be seen at the ballpark. "I was . . . on trial in St. Louis last year," he said the following February. "Every move was suspect."[71] Add in the fact that Era refused to visit him in St. Louis for reasons he never understood ("for some reason my mother never would come to see me there. It's the only place she wouldn't visit me"),[72] and the overall experience was far from the sunny one he stressed to the beat writers throughout the season.

He was also starting to realize that it wasn't only in Philadelphia where ballplayers were manipulated and mistreated. After his holdout in Oakland (combined with his absence at the team picnic in late May), Jackson was punished by owner Charlie Finley, who insisted that manager John McNamara bench him against left-handed pitching. Finley also threatened to send Jackson to the minors and eventually insisted on benching him altogether. "I'm a prisoner," said Jackson in June as he rode the pines. "All the players are owned by the owners. . . . They're slaves to the system."[73] Dick watched the Finley-Jackson feud develop and sympathized: "They should leave a kid like Jackson alone," he said.[74] Jackson, as well, developed an admiration for the man who went through much of what he was now enduring: "He's good for the players," Jackson said of Dick in 1972. "He's good for the fans; he's good for the owners because he brings people into the park. He's one of the most valuable players to come along, to a team and to the league. People who rap him don't know anything about the game of baseball."[75]

Closer to home, he was hearing whispers within the locker room that not everything was copacetic there either. A few of his teammates were piqued that he didn't take batting practice every day and were put off when he chose to limit his time in the clubhouse and not hang around to drink beer and play cards with them.[76] Some grumbled to the media that they felt like Dick didn't have a winning attitude; they were miffed that his facial expression never seemed to change, even when he struck out.[77] During a midseason clubhouse meeting, the players all "agreed" to be at the ballpark "on time" regardless of whether they were taking batting practice, clearly a rule directed toward one man. None of these purported indiscretions was major but combined, these "small resentments," as *Sport* magazine characterized them, added up.[78] "Richie isn't really a villain," one of his former teammates from Philadelphia remarked, this time from afar, "but he breaks down a ball club in little ways. It's an accumulation of the little things he does that soon has a team upset."[79] At least a handful of his St. Louis teammates now felt the same way. "Allen, in his brief stay in St. Louis, managed to steer clear of controversy," wrote sportswriter Jerome Holtzman at the conclusion of the season. "But he was still Richie Allen and listens only to his own drummer."[80] This fomented resentment, at least from a segment of the locker room.

After the season the criticism, so muted within the St. Louis press throughout the summer, became amplified. Hitting coach Dick Sisler denigrated Dick's abilities as a winning ballplayer: "[I]n a close game Allen isn't as valuable as you believe. He would agree on the importance of making contact but he never did cut down on his swing. He had a lot of strikeouts in game-winning situations." There were also whispers that management believed that Dick was a bad influence on its younger players.[81] And there were scrapes with the media, some of which only came to the fore once the season had concluded. Some writers became frustrated with him because he refused to hold court after games. In early 1971 Doc Young wrote of a certain St. Louis writer who "took out after him in Philadelphia fashion" after Dick refused to help him fill his notebook.[82] "Easy Ed" Macauley, the former basketball star now working as a local TV sportscaster, was particularly rough on him, to the point where Dick finally called the station to complain about him, to no avail.[83] While many broadcasters, such as Cardinals' play-by-play man Jack Buck, liked to say that they found Dick to be nothing other than cooperative, to Dick these plaudits were drowned out by the chattering naysayers. For a man more attuned to hear the boos than the cheers, they would.

His mid-August hamstring injury only further complicated his relationship with his detractors. Initially he was expected to miss only a week or so, but the injury lingered and he wound up missing the rest of the season, save for a surprise appearance in mid-September that some found curious. For a short time near the end of the season he was in the hospital; only Cardenal paid him a visit.[84] Once again, rumors that he was a malingerer surfaced, exacerbated by the Cardinals' team doctor, who hinted shortly after the season ended that Dick could have played had the club been in the postseason hunt. The doctor said he saw no point in risking further injury by having him play during September.[85] He did, however, briefly return to the field, a decision that raised more questions than it answered.

On September 8 the Cardinals were set to play their final game ever in Connie Mack Stadium (the Phillies were moving to Veterans Stadium for the 1971 season). This would, as well, be Dick's last opportunity to take the field in the North Philly "shoebox," as Sandy Grady called it. Although he had not played in the three weeks since his injury (and wasn't penciled into manager Red Schoendienst's lineup this evening either), he called Schoendienst that afternoon to inform him that he would indeed be taking the field this one last time. He arrived at the ballpark at 7 P.M. for the 7:35 start and took the Phillies by surprise. "We were under the impression he was too hurt to play," said Phils' manager Frank Lucchesi after the game. "I even had the batboy sneak past their dugout [last night] to make sure he wasn't down in the corridor to pinch hit."[86] He wasn't, but that was because he didn't have his eye on the Cards' penultimate game at Connie Mack; he was focused on the finale itself. Because nobody expected Dick to play, only 3,995 fans bothered to show up. Dick gave them their money's worth and more.

He was clearly hobbled, running stiff-legged, but managed to work a walk in the second and a single in the third. All the while he was serenaded by the locals. After striking out in the sixth he stepped up in the eighth for what was surely going to be his final Connie Mack Stadium at-bat. With the Cardinals nursing a 3–2 lead, Dick lined a Rick Wise pitch into the left-centerfield bleachers. "That ball was never more than ten feet high the whole 400 feet," remarked Phils' catcher Doc Edwards, who watched it clear the fence from his spot in the bullpen.[87] The ball was hit so hard that it hit a young fan square in the chest, causing him to collapse; he had to be carried out of the stadium. Dick rounded the bases, blowing kisses to the faithful, and then disappeared into the dugout. He never stepped onto the Connie Mack Stadium turf again; he was replaced at first the next inning and was likewise gone from the stadium itself by game's end, not bothering to stick around to chat it up with the Philadelphia beat writers who had descended into the Cardinals' clubhouse mainly for that purpose.[88]

In the aftermath of the blast Conlin questioned Dick's dedication: "If Rich was well enough to swing a bat four times last night, lashing a single and his 34th homer, where was he during the crucial late innings of Monday night's 13-inning barn burner?" Lucchesi chimed in as well: "Let's face it. I hate to see him in there against us. I have a lot of respect for his bat—I emphasize it's his bat I respect."[89] With that at-bat Dick's season was all but finished (he made one more start after that game and then appeared once more as a pinch hitter). He wound up hitting .279 with 34 home runs and 101 RBIs in only 122 games. Although he essentially missed the last six weeks of the season, he still led the team with a dozen game-winning RBIs. In the end, however, the list of his detractors seemed to be growing. As Schoendienst said to Devine one day: "You wanted him—I didn't."[90]

Chapter 10

Public Relations Men, Not Ballplayers

1971: Los Angeles .295/23/90

"AUGIE BUSCH NEITHER forgets nor forgives," wrote former Cardinal pitcher Jim Brosnan in his reflection on Dick's time in St. Louis.[1] Despite the 34 home runs and the 101 RBIs, Dick's spring training holdout irked the Cardinals' owner, and he peddled Dick to the Los Angeles Dodgers shortly after the season ended. (Steve Carlton's holdout lingered with Busch as well; the pitcher was exiled to Philadelphia at the conclusion of the following season, after he won 20 games.) Absent free agency, there was little Dick, or any player, could do about his employment situation; he could be "booted about like a football," as journalist Doc Young wrote in an article about Tommy Davis's travails with multiple clubs in 1970. Davis was painted as a malcontent and peddled three times within the space of a year. "The word 'demoralized' fits me to a T," Davis said after the season. "I've been built up and let down, built up and let down, built up and let down."[2] So it was with Dick. "Think of Richie Allen," wrote Jerome Holtzman after the 1970 season, "and it sounds like . . . trouble."[3] Busch had had enough of what he considered "trouble." So he sent Dick packing.

For his part, Dick would have preferred to play another season in St. Louis, irrespective of the pressures he felt there. A couple of years later he said, "I wanted to stay there the rest of my career," and while that might have been overstating things a bit, he certainly was not looking forward to packing up and shipping out so quickly after he had just arrived.[4]

To Doc Young, Dick's tenure with both the Phillies and the Cardinals demonstrated the need for free agency in baseball: "Baseball needs to—it should—revamp its reserve clause; a player should have an option, too. When Richie Allen wanted to get out of Philadelphia, he was locked in. When he wanted to stay in St. Louis, he was locked out. It's a rather ridiculous scene, wouldn't you say?"[5] Busch's treatment of Dick appeared to have softened Young's stance toward him, at least somewhat. He would continue to criticize Dick from time to time but was beginning to realize that Dick was hardly the madman he was oftentimes portrayed to be (sometimes by Young himself). Upon his trade to the Dodgers Young wrote: "Los Angeles has begun to weave a welcome mat for Richie Allen, the baseball star. That's good. Abused in Philadelphia, unceremoniously traded out of St. Louis, Richie deserves the goodwill of a major league city."[6]

The trade itself was puzzling in multiple ways. That Dick was sent to the Dodgers, of all clubs, was surprising given the public statements about Dick that had emanated from the organization. Less than a year earlier Dodger vice president Al Campanis remarked, "When the Phillies made him available [after the '69 season] we thought twice. We wanted his bat, but not his personality. We would have been making a travesty of everything that Dodger spirit represents."[7] Manager Walter Alston reportedly concurred, adding, "The day Allen walks in the clubhouse, that's the day I pack." Yet here Dick was, a Dodger. As soon as he arrived Alston backpedaled. When confronted with his earlier quote, he denied it. "I don't know how these things get started," the manager said. "I wouldn't say anything like that about anybody."[8]

Beyond that, the trade—essentially Dick was swapped for second baseman Ted Sizemore—simply didn't make sense, baseball-wise. Sizemore was a handy player (he was even the National League's Rookie of the Year in 1969) but was hardly a player of Dick's caliber. Ray Shore, a Reds super scout, couldn't believe the trade when he heard the specifics: "Boy, they like to have given him away, didn't they?" he said. Even Dick's harshest critics in Philadelphia were stunned: "Why the giveaway?" asked Frank Dolson.[9] In the *Sporting News*, Melvin Durslag wondered aloud what was going on: "Outwardly he was no problem in St. Louis, which leads people in the sport to wonder why the Cards would trade a batsman of this quality for two lesser players [the Dodgers also threw backup catcher Bob Stinson into the deal]."[10] According to the St. Louis beat writers, although the Cardinals were largely biting their tongues, they moved Dick because, as some of his teammates had whispered, "The Cardinals lost games *and* team unity." One writer confronted Cardinals' GM Bing Devine directly: "In other words, Bing, you got rid of Richie because you feel everybody has to arrive at the park at the same time. You feel there should be no special treatment for one player. No double standard."[11] Devine refused to confirm this, but to many within the press, he didn't have to: the trade spoke for him. A story in the *St. Louis Globe-Democrat* alleged as much. In an article framed by an eight-column headline blaring "Cards Peddle Allen to Help Team Morale," beat writer Jack Herman made his case that Dick was a disruptive influence on the club, and as such, it was more important to the Cards to rid themselves of him than to acquire equal value in return.[12] Dick responded the next day: "These were grown men I was playing with. How could I hurt their morale? If I couldn't have helped the club I'd have just packed up and left."[13] Dick's friend Jose Cardenal was miffed at the deal and even decades later had trouble making sense of it: "They traded him for nothing. I have nothing against Ted Sizemore, but how do you trade a power hitter like [Dick], a superstar, for a singles hitter? I think they just wanted to get rid of him."[14]

In many ways it seemed as if Dick was headed into a hornet's nest in Los Angeles. Although Alston walked back his earlier remarks about cohabitating with Dick in the Dodger dugout, he stopped short of rolling out the red carpet for him. "I kind of felt we needed pitching more than hitting myself, to be honest with you," he said the day after the trade. Regardless, like the Cardinals before them, the Dodgers seemed to go out of their way to preach to their fans that the Dick Allen they were acquiring was hardly the Dick Allen they had heard so much about when he was in Philadelphia. "As far as we know," said Alston, "his behavior has changed considerably . . . he seemed like a different fellow [in St. Louis]."[15] For his part, Dick was resigned to the reality of the nomadic baseball life to which he seemed destined. "I guess I won't last long in Los Angeles either," he said morosely in the wake of the trade, adding shortly thereafter, "Once you're traded the first time, you're a marked man."[16] Several months later he admitted that the trade hurt him deeply: "I don't care how you say it, but when you're traded, somebody didn't want you."[17] Alston's lukewarm welcome didn't make things any easier for him.

Doc Young saw the trouble brewing almost immediately: "I wonder about the deal now because Allen is being brought, probably against his will, into a potentially nasty situation. And, if the deal goes bad, regardless of how innocent Allen may be, he'll probably be made the scapegoat for it." Young saw three potential areas of trouble as they related to Dick and the Dodgers: (1) his salary negotiations; (2) the Dodgers' affinity for their current first baseman, Wes Parker (a Gold Glover with a mediocre bat who, Young feared, might displace Dick at first and therefore cause Dick to be exposed defensively at third or in the outfield, where he'd be subjected to abuse); and (3) Walter Alston. Although he wished Dick well, Young wrote that the Dodgers were hardly the ideal situation for him: "If Richie Allen could have 'played out his option' in Philadelphia, most probably he wouldn't be carrying that 'bad boy' tag today."[18] He would also be somewhere other than with the Dodgers, Young believed.

Just as he had in St. Louis, Dick put on a good face in front of the Los Angeles media: "Coming to Los Angeles is like coming to the major leagues. Everyone wants to play for Walter Alston, and I like Dodger Stadium, too."[19] The trade was "a dream come true," he stressed. "I guess about every little Black kid in America who ever picked up a baseball bat—his favorite team was the Dodgers. I know it was mine when I was coming up as a kid. The Dodgers were the first team to have Blacks—to allow Blacks to play in the majors. This is where I really wanted to be when I first signed up in baseball. I finally made it."[20]

Still, Dick hadn't signed his contract yet, and regardless of his public statements he wasn't planning on joining his new team until he was satisfied financially. Los Angeles sportswriter Melvin Durslag predicted fireworks in the upcoming negotiations: "As general manager of the Dodgers, charged with bringing Allen to gaff, Al Campanis suspects that Richie may not like spring training, which isn't entirely the truth. He may like it for

$155,000 but not for eighty-five."[21] Campanis offered Dick a contract calling for the same salary he had with St. Louis. Dick was seeking considerably more. As for whether he planned to show up on time for spring training, Dick remarked, "That's something Mr. Campanis can arrange very easily."[22]

Journalists' predictions notwithstanding, the negotiations were surprisingly quick and amiable; in late November Dick signed for $105,000. He beamed when the agreement was announced: "This is the earliest I've signed. It's also the best contract I've ever been offered and I couldn't be happier. I've always wanted to be a member of the Dodgers."[23] He seemed to be itching to get his Dodger career off the ground: "Now that I'm out here, I see that color doesn't mean a thing. It's how well you play."[24] And he went out of his way to defuse the Wes Parker situation by stating that "if the man (Alston) wants me to catch, then that's what I'll do. Left field is fine with me. Anyplace is fine with me."[25] Parker, as well, was working on defusing any tensions. "Every time I look at Richie I see a World Series check," he said. Dick refused to second Parker's boast: "No predictions, my man. I leave predictions to Muhammad."[26]

Dick was determined to get off on the right foot. He announced that he would be moving his family to Los Angeles and agreed to participate in the club's optional winter workouts in late January. A few weeks later he even played in an exhibition game the Dodgers scheduled against the University of Southern California. Thirty-one thousand fans showed up to Dodger Stadium in mid-February to watch Dick take batting practice—a record for the event. They gave Dick repeated ovations when he stepped on the field, took his swings in the cage, and knocked one out of the park off Claude Osteen. In the five-inning game that followed, he grounded out. Regardless, the crowd left satisfied.[27]

The next week there Dick was, in front of his locker, dressing for the season's first spring training workout. "For the first time in a long time," he said, "I know I don't have to run and hide every time the door opens. I have this beautiful feeling that the players and people of Los Angeles are anxious to accept Rich Allen, ballplayer."[28] In an about-face, he extolled the value of spring training: "Spring training is a serious thing. This is your job and you have to tear yourself away from the rest of the world for six weeks. If you care anything about what you're doing, it's worth it."[29]

A few weeks later he begged off a bit: "I've probably overdone it. I mean all the extra hitting is what I wanted to do, but when people took such delight in it, I probably did more than what was good for me."[30] He went to Alston and asked for a few days off. Alston acquiesced. A few days later, while shagging balls in the outfield, Dick crashed into a palm tree while going full-out and was knocked unconscious. He was unable to get up and was rushed to a hospital where he was diagnosed with a mild concussion.[31] Although there was speculation that this would cause him to miss Opening Day, he was determined to return in time to make his debut with his new teammates.

Although the organization had reservations about signing Dick, the club desperately needed his bat. In 1970 the Dodgers hit only 87 home runs, the fewest in all of baseball, and had rarely shown much power since moving into Dodger Stadium in 1962. In their nine seasons there they had out-homered their opponents only three times. "Our club needs two or three hits to accomplish what the opposition accomplishes with one swing," Campanis said. So, despite his misgivings, the GM pulled the trigger on the deal. While he was concerned about the club's image within a public relations context, its image among its baseball brethren, as well as with baseball fans overall, was that of a Punch-and-Judy ball club. "Perhaps," wrote Bob Hunter of the *Los Angeles Herald Examiner*, "it will be . . . Rich Allen who, at long last, changes the image of the Dodgers."[32] So it was that Dick was greeted with thunderous applause whenever he stepped up to the plate at Dodger Stadium in the early going. When he hit his first home run of the season—a monstrous blast well over the center-field fence—everyone wanted to show their appreciation for the man they believed was going to single-handedly turn the Dodgers around: "They greeted him enthusiastically in the dugout," Ross Newhan of the *Los Angeles Times* wrote the following morning, "but that reception paled in comparison to the standing ovation tendered by the fans."[33]

On the whole, the media's reception of Dick in Los Angeles was far more benevolent than anything he had received in Philadelphia, and even more generous than what he experienced in St. Louis. While the St. Louis media trumpeted the "Richie has changed" theme throughout 1970, the Los Angeles media, although striking the same tune to a degree, also challenged the notion that Dick was ever as bad as he had been made out to be. "The one thing I want to get across," Dick told a *Los Angeles Times* writer a few years later, "is that I never try to make people like me. I just want people to appreciate what I've done, that's all." "He was the type of player," added Alston, "who couldn't be told, 'You be at the park three hours early or I'll fine you $1,000.' But if you asked him to come early in a decent way, he'd show up 10 minutes before everybody else."[34] If approached with respect he'd respond respectfully.

More folks in Dick's world were now keen to this reality, and his relationship with the media and management appeared to thaw somewhat. "[His teammates] all felt he was a terrific guy . . . they liked him, I think the reporters liked him, he got along with the press as I recall," remembered the *Los Angeles Times*' Ross Newhan.[35] In the *Los Angeles Sentinel*, Doc Young's skepticism soon gave way to outright support; now exposed to him up close for the first time, Young embraced Dick as never before: "With the trade to Los Angeles, he has been emancipated. More precisely, he has emancipated himself—just being himself: a naturally friendly man, a highly-intelligent, articulate man, a hard-worker, a man who loves baseball, a man who has come close to busting his bones for the ball club. His reward, despite an early-season slump, is tremendous fan-love. And great press notices. Richard Anthony Allen—great, gawd a'mighty—is free at last."[36]

Not all was as it seemed, however. Though Campanis agreed to pay Dick $105,000, the *Sentinel* alleged that he had no intention of raising the club's payroll to do so; instead he asked the club's unofficial captain, Maury Wills, to take a pay cut to offset Dick's salary.[37] And despite the club's growing understanding of the importance of giving Dick his space, higher-ups were nevertheless irked at his refusal to engage in the club's myriad public relations activities. "The Dodgers expected [Dick] to make an occasional appearance on behalf of their charitable wing, or they'd have autograph days at the ballpark and expect him to be part of them," said Newhan. "Those kinds of things are bigger now than they were then," he added, but still, to the Dodgers of the early 1970s, they were important.[38] "We wanted to be an active, involved, concerned, caring member of the community," recalled former Dodger president Peter O'Malley of that era. "That philosophy was explained to our management team, to the manager, the coaches, the major league ball club, the farm teams, [and to

Dick in action against the Atlanta Braves, May 12, 1971.
(© 2014 Legendaryauctions.com)

those at] the training site at Vero Beach. It was a policy, a philosophy, of the organization. . . . Whenever we found that we explained to the players what we wanted to do and why we wanted to do it, the pushback was at a minimum. . . . Ninety percent, 99 percent of the players, when they were told [or were] asked about an occasion coming up, they were all in."[39]

But not Dick. "My main interest was just playing baseball," he said a few years later. "But they wanted me to run here and appear there when we weren't playing. I knew I wasn't ready to project that kind of personality yet. . . . The trouble is, I'm not comfortable in all the situations that baseball presents. I have to be my own man—I can't perform as well when I have to be like somebody else." For an organization that cherished its reputation as "baseball's most image-conscious team," that could be a problem.[40] In 1972 Dick reflected on the pressures inherent in being a Dodger: "I couldn't have taken it out there for another minute. The manager and the guys on the team were great, but it's such a different scene out there. There are so many public relations demands, so many people to meet, so many distractions."[41] Contrary to the aims of the Dodgers' public relations campaigns, he continued to bristle at the notion that ballplayers should be, or even could be, role models for children. "People buy a ticket to see you play; that should be all," he said a few years later. "People idolize ballplayers. I don't want to be idolized. There are too many things you got to get through before you get to the field. Let a kid idolize his father; maybe there would be less drug problems. . . . Even bubble gum is bad for a kid's teeth."[42] As for the Dodgers, Dick became convinced that they believed that the off-field activities trumped the ones that took place on the diamond: "The Dodgers wanted public relations men, not ballplayers."[43]

Bristle as they might, the Dodger brass understood, as the Cardinals did before them, to back off. Consequently, Dick's refusal to follow the club's promotional mandates didn't result in the same eruptions in Los Angeles as they had in Philadelphia. At last Dick was starting to gain some traction in having his employer deal with him on his terms. In Philadelphia, he suffered the repercussions of his independent streak, but in Los Angeles things were somewhat different. Although the Dodger brass might have wished he participated more fully in the club's off-field functions, they didn't publicly malign him for refusing to follow along, nor did the fans or the writers find anything sinister in his determination to do things his own way. Slowly but surely, the winds in the conservative baseball universe appeared to be shifting.

By the early 1970s Dick began to have some followers along his independent path, most notably Reggie Jackson in Oakland. Jackson refused to attend certain team functions as well (such as the club's midseason picnic at owner Charlie Finley's ranch), and though Finley ordered him benched for a time, he eventually gave in. Allen and Jackson both refused to be subservient to club management's idea of how they "should" act. Both demanded that their opinions be heard and heeded. While the overwhelming majority of players still acceded to management's wishes, a growing minority felt emboldened to go their own way. With each passing year, these players found incrementally more support among the public and working press, who increasingly came to realize that a player's off-field habits and on-field performance could be two distinct things with one having little effect on the other. No two players demonstrated this changing sentiment more than Dick and Jackson.

Of course, both players were talented enough to compel management to deal with them on their own terms. Finley might be offended that Jackson refused to visit him at his farm, but there was no replacing his bat in the middle of the A's lineup; once Finley recovered from his pique he had Jackson reinstated in the starting lineup where he would be the key element in the club's three consecutive World Series championships in the early 1970s. Same with Dick—regardless of the level of O'Malley's agitation with him there was nobody else on the roster who could supply the offensive firepower he could. Lesser talent would not command the same level of tolerance. Nevertheless, more players were stepping out than ever before, although they often paid a price for doing so: Lou Johnson, Oscar Gamble, Jose Cardenal, Dock Ellis, Mike Marshall, Vida Blue, Ted Simmons, and then, finally, Andy Messersmith and Dave McNally, who, in 1975, challenged the game's reserve clause and brought the players free agency at last.

Ultimately, however, irrespective of a player's talent, management still pulled the strings in the game's pre–free agency era. The Dodgers might tolerate Dick now, but that didn't mean they would tolerate him forever. Indeed, even before the season ended there were whispers that Dick's time in Los Angeles was going to be brief despite the solid season he was having. And, true to Doc Young's preseason fears, the club continued to stick by Wes Parker, who wound up playing 148 games at first, hitting .274 with 6 home runs. This was to Dick's detriment, as he wound up splitting the majority of his time between third base and the outfield, where he struggled defensively but hit .295 with 23 home runs and 90 RBIs. As the season progressed, Young sensed that the Dodgers were trumpeting Parker much as the Phillies had trumpeted Callison a few years earlier: "Richie started the season in left field. His best position was first base. But the Dodgers had Wes Parker playing first base and Wes Parker is highly touted as 'Mr. Golden Glove' and the publicity department was trying to sell him as baseball's newest super star. Which he isn't. Which is one reason why the Dodgers are lagging and sagging."[44]

Parker was the polar opposite of Dick in many ways. In fact, he was such a management shill that the following season, when the players voted

to strike, Parker (the Dodgers' player representative) was the lone absten-
tion. (The vote was 47–0–1 in favor of a walkout.) As Marvin Miller
recalled, "Parker had been quoted several times as being opposed to players receiving 'ridiculously high' salaries (such as $150,000 a year); not long
after the meeting he was removed from office by his teammates, who
described their action as 'impeachment.'"[45] The Dodgers' preference for
company men was obvious: a couple of years later Steve Garvey would be
the apple of their eye; they touted him as the "flawless Dodger" and were
thrilled when he announced that he planned to spend his off-season
studying that which Dick despised—public relations.[46]

By season's end, and despite the absence of overt turmoil, both sides
realized that Dick Allen and the Los Angeles Dodgers were hardly a match.
The problem with the Dodgers, as Dick saw it, "was all that Dodger Blue
jive. Not Dick Allen style. The organization tries to get you to believe that
being a Dodger is all you've ever needed in this world. They want you to
feel blessed. It's one way they keep their players in tow. A lot of guys fall
for it."[47] Dick didn't, and as a result, his year there fell far short of his
preseason expectations. "Dick was never happy in Los Angeles," his wife,
Barbara, remarked the following year. As for why he wasn't, she believed
that, irrespective of everything that went right, it was the initial slights
that trumped all else: "How can you be happy when the manager says he
doesn't want you?"[48]

* * *

When things got tough for him in Los Angeles, when he felt pressured
and stressed, Dick retreated to the stables where, for as long as he could
remember, he had found comfort and solace. Indeed, it was the lure of
the horses that convinced Alston that, despite his reservations, Dick might
eventually take not only to Los Angeles and the Dodgers but to Alston, a
horse owner, as well. "I'm afraid that Rich may go Hollywood on me," he
told a gaggle of writers at a preseason banquet. "I don't mean the movies,
I mean the racetrack."[49] The proximity of Hollywood Park to Dodger
Stadium offered Dick the opportunity for respite that Alston hoped would
calm him through the storm of a frenetic season. While Dick hesitated to

go to the track in St. Louis, Alston made it clear that it was not off limits with the Dodgers.

People often misinterpreted Dick's affection for thoroughbreds. "It's ridiculous the fuss they make about horses," he said in May. "So many guys stand around the clubhouse talking about golf and reading golf literature in the clubhouse. I've never read horse racing literature in the clubhouse. So they knock my love of horses."[50] A few weeks earlier he had remarked, "When I go to a track, I'm combining relaxation with business. I don't like to see a baseball player on a golf course. To me it reflects contentment. I get the same feeling when I see a player smoking a pipe." Whenever he was spotted at the track, an issue would be made of it and an impression formed that fit the longstanding narrative of Dick as a troublemaker: "People who say they see Rich Allen at the $100 window aren't telling the truth. I go to the track because I like the form, the breeding and the racing. I'm basically a $2 bettor. Maybe I'll take a horse across the board. If I think I've got it figured out pretty good, I may go as high as $10. That's it. During my baseball career I've simply been involved in too many hassles and lost too much money because of them to be able to afford throwing it away at the track."[51]

As a child he loved his family's horse and was heartbroken when his father sold it. "All he could think about was having another horse," recalled his brother Hank. "He got a paper route and saved about $100 and he went off and found some old broken-down nag that he could get for $75. Well, naturally, mother wouldn't let him do it—he was only a little kid—so he stomped around and finally said, 'well, someday I'll get me a horse.'" When he joined the Phillies he got that horse and had a few on and off from that point forward. "My big interest," he said in 1973, "really is to see how big a heart a horse has. They're just like athletes, even baseball players. You see a guy who's maybe got a pulled muscle and he don't want to play today. Well, there are horses, too, who won't run with any little discomfort. Then there's the one horse whose heart is as big as this room, who by the time he gets to the gate has forgotten all about any tender sore spot, whose mind is only on racing. He's the one I watch."[52]

By the time he had settled into his life in Los Angeles, Dick owned four horses and announced his intention to "have the biggest Black-owned stable in America." "I'm going to breed thoroughbreds like the brothers, you know. I want to do this for my son. Horse racing is just about the oldest sport out and the Black man doesn't get the credit for his efforts around horses. From my reading, I see that the Kentucky Derby has been won by a black jockey named Isaac Murphy [he won it three times—1884, 1890, and 1891]. You never hear anything about it."[53] In 1989 brother Hank became the first African American trainer of a Kentucky Derby entrant since 1911, and for years Dick would haunt the local racetracks.[54] After his retirement he could sometimes be seen walking the grounds at Santa Anita, shaded by a Sherlock Holmes cap. "An old horse trainer from England got me to wearing these," he said in 1983. "He told me that with the double bill, you'll know where you've been and you'll know where you're goin'."[55]

For years Dick spoke of his thwarted desire to become a jockey himself: "I wish I could weigh 115 pounds for a couple of hours in the afternoon and then go back to my own size at 5 o'clock. That way I could be a jockey and still play baseball."[56] Regardless, whenever there was trouble in his world he'd withdraw to his horses and could usually be found riding one. In Philadelphia he would deal with the swirl of issues that surrounded him by heading out to the Monmouth or Garden State racetrack or by riding his horse through Fairmount Park. In a world he felt to be spiraling out of control, horses provided him with a measure of calm and order: "[T]here's a lot of phoniness in baseball and I can find relaxation around horses."[57] A little while later he added that "sometimes I feel like going back to the country to raise horses and do little thinking and no worrying."[58]

Throughout his career Dick was repeatedly asked by a curious and oftentimes perplexed media to explain his fascination with horses and gave varying responses. At times he defined his interest in practical terms—they were his path toward establishing a business to sustain him and his family after his baseball days were finished—but at other times he'd speak more metaphorically. A horse is like a ballplayer, he sometimes said. "You put your money on the line to buy him and after that it's all up to him. Either he's worth what you paid or he isn't."[59] After he retired he expanded on this point: "Racehorses and ballplayers—they're bought, they're sold, they're traded. Today in this barn; tomorrow in somebody else's."[60] They reminded him of some people he knew: "they've got very little brains, but a whole lot of sense."[61]

Dick atop Blaze, July 21, 1968. He liked to ride Blaze through Fairmount Park.
(Temple University Libraries, Special Collections Research Center, Philadelphia, PA)

Clem Capozzoli, like Coy before him, had Dick on a budget (by 1969 it was up to $35 per week), leaving Dick with little pocket money despite his large salary.[62] As such, he was compelled to seek Capozzoli's permission for any large purchases, such as horses to add to his stable. It was only after receiving Capozzoli's blessing that he was permitted to purchase

Trick Fire and three other horses in the spring of 1969, and he often let off steam by working with them or by simply watching them run. (Indeed, it was because he took time out on his way to Shea Stadium a few months later to watch Trick Fire race that he missed the double-header with the Mets that precipitated his indefinite suspension.) Heading into the 1970 season he sold two of his horses and transferred the title of a third to Barbara so as to quell the media's speculation over his equinal interests. "I had to do it," he explained shortly after doing so. "They [the Philadelphia writers] made it appear that I was more interested in racing than I was in baseball."[63] On this one occasion at least, he heeded the optics of the situation. Lesson quickly learned, however, as putting on this false face contributed to his unhappiness in St. Louis. When he arrived in Los Angeles, he reestablished his stable. He kept a pair of horses at Santa Anita and more on his farm, Sweetbriar Acres, in Perkasie, Pennsylvania. When asked why he chose to establish a stable in Pennsylvania and not Kentucky like most thoroughbred breeders he replied, "That's the way I am. Everybody runs to Kentucky, I've got to go the other way. The trend-setter."[64]

*   *   *

"Loners don't fit easily into the Dodger family," wrote Jim Brosnan in 1972. "The Dodgers have the most tightly-knit, clannish organization in baseball."[65] An introverted, shy individualist like Dick never really had much hope of succeeding there in the long term. Here again he harked back to an earlier age in baseball: "A proud free spirit in a game that has grown increasingly uptight—a colorful throwback to giants such as Babe Ruth and Grover Cleveland Alexander, the hard-drinking, swashbuckling individualists of baseball's golden age," read a *Newsweek* portrait of him a few months earlier.[66] But that sort of thing wasn't going to fly with the Dodgers. As for why not, perhaps Maury Wills put it best: "The Dodgers are like a woman . . . to be loved . . . not understood."[67]

Besides begging off on public relations requests, Dick reverted to his tradition of routinely skipping batting practice. He was not the only Dodger to do so, but the way he did it proved irksome. "Occasionally he would watch batting practice from the club level at Dodger Stadium," recalled Newhan, "with a cup of something in his hand."[68] In early June he was benched for a game by Alston when he didn't see Dick on the bench shortly before game time. Dick contended that he was in fact in the ballpark and in uniform but was chatting with a friend in a corridor between the clubhouse and dugout when Alston peered down the bench. Just prior to the game's first pitch Dick arrived on the bench only to be informed that Bill Russell was taking his place in the lineup that afternoon. Alston covered for Dick after the game, reminding the beat writers that the game was unusual in that it was scheduled to start only fifteen minutes after the completion of an old-timers' game and that "almost everyone was caught short." "This whole thing will probably look worse than it really was. It was very unintentional on Allen's part," he said. When the reporters gathered around Dick's locker, he expressed bewilderment over the issue: "I can't see why this is being made into such a big deal. I actually appreciated the rest. Wes Parker ASKED for the night off yesterday and nothing was said about it."[69] A few months later he told the *Los Angeles Times*' Jim Murray, "This is a job. Only, you can't call in and say 'I think I'll take the day off.'"[70] If you did, particularly if your name was Dick Allen, you'd be expected to answer for it.

In so many ways Dick wasn't the prototypical Dodger; at some point the decision was made to see how far he could take them in 1971 and then move on. "Late in the season, Alston had a meeting with several of his veteran players, asking them what they would do with Richie Allen," Newhan recalled. "The consensus was that 'he can help us. We'll deal with it. Let him alone and it will play itself out.' . . . The veterans told [Alston], 'We can win with him,' and they almost did."[71] (The Dodgers finished at 89–73, one game behind the San Francisco Giants in the Western Division.) There was also suspicion that Alston laid off when it came to Dick because he was good friends (and roommates) with centerfielder Willie Davis, who finished the season with a .309 average, an All-Star Game appearance, and a Gold Glove. In other words, Davis was in the midst of a fine season that Alston didn't want to see come apart in the stretch run as a result of any dust-up between Dick and management.[72]

Late in the season there were a couple of other incidents—both involving his former teams—that further sealed Dick's fate in Los Angeles. In the first, Dick arrived late to the ballpark for an August game against the

Cardinals in St. Louis and was benched.[73] Less than two weeks later he hit a mammoth home run in the Phillies' new home, Veterans Stadium, that nearly hit the stadium's replica Liberty Bell in dead centerfield. After being removed for a pinch runner in the eighth, Dick—perhaps dreading the inevitable horde of Philadelphia writers who would no doubt descend upon him once more, asking for his take on the blast among other topics—took off toward the clubhouse and was gone from the stadium before the game was over. "That made him even for the day," ran the story in the next day's *Los Angeles Times*, "as he had shown up at the stadium 15 minutes before game time, a fact that did not escape some of his teammates."[74] As the 1971 season began to weigh heavily on him, the prospect of returning to St. Louis and then Philadelphia, with all of the freighted media obligations that came along with those games, was perhaps too much for him. So he stayed away from the ballparks beforehand and then, in Philadelphia, took off as quickly as he could once he believed he had discharged his professional obligations on the field.

By the end of the season, Dick and the Dodgers had irreparably soured on each other. As for his teammates, he had few nice things to say about them: "The old Dodgers were my team, but these guys were a bunch of crybabies, always arguing with umpires and throwing their helmets. Maury Wills was hard to play with. Walt Alston treated me like a man, but he'd been quoted as saying he'd quit if they got me. Maybe he was misquoted, but he never said anything different to me."[75] As for the allegedly laid-back Southern California fans, Dick saw that, in the end, they were not all that different from the ones he had had to deal with in Philadelphia. "The fans [in Los Angeles] have the same problem as those in Philadelphia and other cities where the team isn't winning," he said shortly after the conclusion of the season. "Well, during these losing years, fans develop hostilities. They come to the park angry and frustrated. And they drink to forget about their team."[76]

Reflecting upon the season in its final days, Dick concluded that as far as he was concerned, it was "money well-earned." As for the specifics of his production as a Dodger, he demurred: "There's too much attention put on batting averages and personal achievements. Why? Why should it be? If I go out and just try to bat .300 I could bunt and scratch around and protect my figures and forget about putting the ball in the air when

Phillie fans welcome Dick to Veterans Stadium in August 1971 by reminding him that even though he no longer played for their team, they followed his comings and goings.

(Temple University Libraries, Special Collections Research Center, Philadelphia, PA)

it might mean a run or concentrate on hitting a home run when it doesn't help anything but myself." But how would management know who was producing and who wasn't if the statistics could be deceiving? "They know," he said. And when asked if he hoped to return to the club in 1972, he was nonchalant about it all: "We go where they tell us to go. We don't have any say about it. If they want me, I'll stay. If they don't, I'll go."[77] To the *Philadelphia Tribune* he was more forthcoming. When asked if he was happy with the Dodgers, he shot back, "How in the world can a black man be happy when the manager and all the official representatives of the team are white?"[78]

In December he was traded yet again, this time to the Chicago White Sox in a three-team deal that brought the Dodgers Frank Robinson from the Orioles and Tommy John from the White Sox. According to the official Dodger line at the time of the trade, Dick was traded because first base was his best position, which made him expendable given the presence of Wes Parker (who would follow up his 1971 six-home-run campaign with four in 1972 and then retire).[79] But the real reason he was moved—because of what the Dodgers thought he represented—emerged later. "After a lot of thought we reached the conclusion that our success through the years stemmed from a team spirit that ran right down to the clubhouse people," said Campanis the following year. "We didn't feel it was worth compromising our standards. From a long-range view we felt we could win more often with players who conformed to the rules."[80] Employing a player who seemed to signal that the Dodger Way wasn't the only way was a bridge too far for them.

This wasn't the first time that Dick's nonconformist ways caused him to be shuffled out of town, but this time the reactions in both the white and black press were, on the whole, more critical of management than of Dick. In the *Sentinel*, Doc Young blasted the organization, writing that "it now seems true that, based on his past 'reputation,' the Dodgers decided to rid themselves of Allen long before he began to play his best ball for the team." With regard to the Dodger higher-up who told Young, "You can't have one rule for 24 players and another for a single player," Young countered, "The question, or problem, of rules can be solved in one of several ways, all having to do with human understanding or leadership. With a player like Allen, you start with his desire to be a winner—and go from there. . . . Are the Dodgers so hung up on acquiring players who 'won't cause any trouble' that they are handicapping themselves? I think that is a question Dodger executives should ask themselves. Not all great ballplayers are great gentlemen. Jackie Robinson was the most controversial player in the game; Duke Snider sometimes had problems as, admittedly, did Don Newcombe; Carl Furillo spent lots of time in his own peculiar bag and so it went. But the Dodgers won."[81] In a later column he was even more blunt: "The organization places too much emphasis on the so-called 'nice guy' image . . . [Walter] Alston, a decent human being personally, has lasted all these years as a Dodger manager not because he actually is as great as he is rated, but because he doesn't give the front office any trouble."[82] Young's tone was a significant shift from how critical he had been of Dick earlier. Seeing the interaction between Dick and his employer firsthand, Young was coming to the realization that Dick wasn't the villain he had been made out to be. Instead, he was an individualist who was largely being punished for being himself. Perhaps, Young was finally starting to realize, the organizations played a larger role in Dick's troubles than he had assumed.

The *Los Angeles Times* agreed. In 1972, after Dick won the American League's Most Valuable Player award with the White Sox, the paper ran an editorial that eviscerated both the Dodgers and the venerated "Dodger Way": "The selection of Dick Allen as the American League's most valuable player should give the Dodgers second thoughts. They traded the 30-year-old first baseman to the Chicago White Sox on the grounds he was a nonconformist whose ways hurt team discipline. In Chicago, manager Chuck Tanner used all the arts of persuasion—tact, friendliness, guile—to make Allen feel at home so he could play his best. It worked. The Dodgers . . . didn't try hard enough or adroitly enough. Under Dodger-style reasoning, the Lakers should have traded Wilt Chamberlain and the New York Jets should have unloaded Joe Namath. They're nonconformists, too."[83] Individualism, it was beginning to seem, was no longer a crime. Even the mainstream press was beginning to acknowledge that at last. As both Young and the *Los Angeles Times*' editorial board signaled, it was now up to organizations, staid as they may be, to come to grips with this shifting reality and to learn how to acknowledge it in their dealings with their employees. Failure to do so, as the Dodgers' on-field results over the previous few seasons seemed to indicate, would be to their ultimate detriment.

That the *Los Angeles Times*' coverage of Dick throughout the 1971 season was markedly different from how the Philadelphia papers covered him just a few years earlier was evident in its handling of what, in previous years, might have been an explosive piece of information. In a December article detailing the trade, Newhan wrote of an earlier discussion he had had with club president Peter O'Malley: "On a warm night at Dodger Stadium last July, with the Dodgers a discouraging 10 games behind the Giants, president Peter O'Malley confided: 'I've made up my mind that Allen will have to be traded. He's been an unsettling influence on the club.'"[84] In Philadelphia during the 1960s, this quote would have undoubtedly been front-page news the following morning. Newhan, though, decided to sit on it. Later, he explained his rationale: "When Peter O'Malley said Allen was a problem player and would be traded, the team was ten games behind the Giants. I felt to say anything about Allen then would have been unfair to him and would have given the appearance he was the reason the Dodgers were not doing well." This, Newhan decided, would have been inaccurate: "Alston did not make a fuss about Allen, and the other players did not complain about Allen's behavior off the field."[85] As Newhan understood the situation, Dick's habits and the team's struggles represented merely a correlation, not causation. To conflate the two, as those in Philadelphia had done, was to present Dick as the scapegoat. Newhan concluded that it wasn't Dick's arriving shortly before game time or not taking batting practice that caused the club to fall so far behind the Giants; myriad other, on-field and front-office, decisions and moves were the problem.

Two years earlier Dick told Sandy Padwe, "As far as I'm concerned, there's too much emphasis on this Joe College approach [to baseball]. This is a professional sport, not a college sport. These guys . . . come in here and do the job they have to do. When the game starts, you pull together as a team; when the game ends, you go your own way as an individual."[86] As he had understood for years, there was something different about being a professional athlete. Although the fans and the media treated professional sports as games, the athletes themselves didn't. They understood what it took to perform at their best and very little of it called for being the prototypical "team player." One could be a productive member of a professional ball club and still retain one's individuality. "Individuality is what you own; it's who you are," said Larry Christenson, a teammate of two staunch individualists—Dick and Steve Carlton. "Lefty did his thing. Dick did his. I was fine with it. It didn't affect the locker room." Professional athletes understood that being an individualist and a good teammate were not mutually exclusive. "Dick was one of my greatest teammates," he recalled. "He was always rooting for you." Whenever Christenson was going through a rough patch or suffering a crisis of confidence, he knew that Dick would be there to calm the waters. "I was just a kid," Christenson continued. "He'd put his arm around me and say, 'Hey kid, I'll get you some runs.'" That was all the young pitcher needed to hear to collect himself and focus on the task at hand. After the last out, it was no sin if a teammate decided to go his own way. "You didn't see him out to dinner," Christenson recalled. "He had his own friends."[87] From one professional athlete to another, this was not a problem. As Jackson's A's were about to demonstrate, a successful club could be comprised of a whole locker room full of individualists who were also superior teammates. Dick had always known this. Finally, everybody else seemed to be catching up.

Chapter 11

Dick, Not Richie

1972: Chicago .308/37/113

WHEN HE LEARNED that Dick was on the market yet again, White Sox president Roland Hemond didn't hesitate. "There was a great [basketball] coach, John 'Honey' Russell, who had a great coaching career at Seton Hall and even coached the Boston Celtics for a time, who was also a scout for the Milwaukee Braves when I was in that organization [in the '50s], who had talked to me about Dick Allen [way back]," Hemond recalled. Russell told him, "Had [Allen] gone into basketball instead of baseball, he could have been another Bob Cousy." Russell impressed upon Hemond that Dick was a once-in-a-generation athlete. "[Russell] scouted Allen as a high school player and was tremendously impressed with his all-around basketball ability—his dribbling, rebounding, speed, passing, the whole bit." Russell was equally impressed with Dick as a baseball player and succeeded in placing him on Hemond's radar even before Dick signed with the Phillies. Now that he finally had a chance to get him, Hemond jumped. "In the [1971] winter meetings, I went to our manager, Chuck Tanner, and I said, 'Chuck, how would you like to have Dick Allen?' He said, 'Oh, I'd love to have him on our ball club. I know him well.' Chuck lived in New Castle, Pennsylvania, about eight miles from Wampum. He said, 'I know his brothers, I know his mother well. I think he could be a real good asset to our ball club.' So we decided to make the trade."[1]

This time around, Dick wouldn't come cheap, but to Hemond, whatever it took to get him would be worth it: "Campanis was asking for [pitchers] Tommy John and Terry Forster, a young left-handed pitcher. . . . we [eventually] gave up a utility infielder, Steve Huntz, in the trade instead of Forster, along with Tommy John. Tommy had pitched well for us but we weren't blessed with a tremendous infield and he was a groundball pitcher so this wasn't helping him much. I figured that we could part with Tommy John and Dick Allen would add some punch to our lineup."[2] Tanner, who had tried to convince the Sox front office to swing a deal for Dick after the 1970 season, was ecstatic: "We've got a bomber!" he exclaimed to the Chicago media upon hearing the news. Combined with young slugger Bill Melton (who had hit 33 home runs each of the previous two seasons), Tanner believed that he might have the best one-two punch in the club's history. Like Bing Devine before him, Tanner said all of the right things when asked about acquiring Dick's reputation along with his bat. "I know when he goes on the field he gives you 100 percent," he said. "He gives you a good day's work. I judge a player strictly on what he does for me."[3] Unlike Devine, however, Tanner had, in Hemond, institutional support. Perhaps things could work out better here than they had in St. Louis and Los Angeles.

Indeed, one of the club's first official acts in welcoming Dick was small but significant: they would refer to him by his preferred name. "When we got Allen from the Dodgers last month," a member of the Sox front office told the *New York Times*, "we offered him two things—to raise his pay five percent from the $105,000 he got last year and to change his name to Dick. He took us up on one of the offers." Immediately the Sox announced that they had acquired "Dick" and not "Richie" Allen and that henceforth he would be referred to as such in all of the club's publications. Club president Stu Holcomb was still a bit confused: "I wrote him a letter as 'Dear Dick,' . . . because Al Campanis of the Dodgers had told me that Allen wanted to be called Dick after all the confusion. I don't know how he signs his contract because I haven't gotten it back yet."[4]

As willing as the Sox seemed to be to work with him, Dick was hesitant about moving to yet another club, another city. "He was disappointed that things hadn't worked out well in Philadelphia," Hemond recalled, "and then it was just one season with the Cardinals and then one season with the Dodgers—he was disenchanted and wondering whether he should continue with his baseball career."[5] "The Dodgers only wanted me for a quick fix," Dick wrote in his autobiography. "After the '71 season, they told me I was traded to the White Sox for Tommy John. I couldn't get myself to even care. The fix was in. Dick Allen was a guy to use for one year and then trade off. I was getting the quick shuffle . . . a fast shuffle to oblivion."[6] A few months after the trade he expanded a bit: "Look, I'd just been traded the fourth time in four years [sic]. Baseball doesn't want me, I tell myself. I'm a bad actor, right?"[7]

By February 1972 Dick had gone MIA. Holcomb admitted that he had been unable to reach his new player in the months since the trade. "Perhaps we won't hear from him until it's time to report to spring camp February 21," he said. "But with the money he's getting, I'm sure he wants to play baseball. And when the time comes, we won't have any problems signing him." Holcomb reached out to Dick's wife, Barbara, who told him that Dick hadn't even looked at the contract Holcomb sent to his Germantown home. Instead, the envelope remained on his kitchen counter, unopened. "We know he received it because the signed receipt was returned to us," he said.[8] But that was about all he could say. As for his whereabouts, even Barbara claimed ignorance, offering that she thought he was somewhere in California but didn't have a number at which he could be reached. All anybody knew for sure was that if and when Dick signed, it would invariably be for the highest salary ever paid by the White Sox organization, dwarfing Luis Aparicio's $90,000 contract two years earlier.

Tanner was convinced that his personal connection would make a difference with Dick and eventually lure him into the fold. Not only did he know Dick and Era, he played basketball against Coy growing up and, like Dick many years later, Tanner had once been named Lawrence County's outstanding athlete of the year. Beyond that, he employed Dick's close friend and mentor Joe Lonnett as his third base coach. "I saw Richie grow up," Tanner said. "I always liked and respected him."[9] The atmosphere on the Sox was going to be warm and welcoming, he insisted. Dick would feel wanted there, he believed. But Dick wasn't so sure. He was concerned about how yet another move would affect his family: "another move, sell the house . . . and my kids' grades are going down."[10] This led him to "a period of deep thought," as he later described it, over the very idea of plowing on in what had become an increasingly nomadic life. There were multiple factors to consider, multiple lives affected, and everything only got more complicated as everyone got older. It wasn't as simple as just packing up and moving on. There was significant baggage—metaphorical as well as literal—involved in each move. "I feel deflated," he told Sandy Padwe. "I'm tired of bouncing around. It's hard on a family, on kids. People who own horses try to find a nice home for a horse when it comes time to retire the horse from racing. I'd do at least that for a horse. Face it, ballplayers are horses. But when an owner is through with a ballplayer, he doesn't care about that ballplayer's future. Baseball doesn't teach you anything . . . that's why I'm thinking about the future."[11] Maybe, he thought, the future was now. Maybe it was time to move on from baseball.

In mid-February he reluctantly entered into half-hearted negotiations with Holcomb, demanding $120,000 mainly because he assumed that Holcomb would reject it out of hand. When, to his stunned amazement, Holcomb accepted it Dick rejected it even though he was, in effect, spurning his own demand.[12] The next day Holcomb spoke to Alfred Morris, whom Dick had anointed his financial advisor in the negotiations, and the two hammered out what appeared to be an agreement. "We reached an agreement to terms to the point that when Allen comes down here we can sit down and sign," said Holcomb. "I think we've got the number [the same $120,000 Dick rejected the day before], now it's a matter of getting him down here." As for when that would be, Holcomb was as much in the dark as ever: "Morris did not name a definite date. All he said was Dick will be here as soon as he clears up a few things. I've been hearing that statement for six weeks."[13]

Weeks passed without a word from Dick. While Chicago's baseball writers, now ensconced in Sarasota, Florida (the spring training base for the Sox), buzzed over where he might be, for a day at least Dick was right there among them. He arrived, incognito, for the start of spring training and hid out, evaluating the club for himself to see if it was worth going through it all once more, this time in Chicago. He knew very little about the Sox, having played his entire career up to that point in the National

League. "I called [Sox infielder and Philadelphia native] Pat Kelly. I asked him what kind of team it was. He said, 'Man, we got a good team, we got this and we got that.'" But Dick wasn't convinced. "Hey, I didn't even know Kelly hit left-handed," Dick recalled; it would be difficult to trust his judgment given how little he knew firsthand. "So I flew down there. Nobody knew. I swear. Got there at 4:30 in the morning. Went out to the ballpark and hid behind a tree in centerfield. Beard and all. Nobody saw me. I took a look at what they had." He was not impressed. "Caught an 8:30 plane out of there that night. Didn't stay a day."[14]

A few weeks later, in mid-March, Dick flew down to Sarasota once more, this time openly. He checked into the Sarasota Sheraton Sandcastle (the spring training headquarters for the Sox), took a nap, strolled over to Holcomb's office to discuss the contract Holcomb had assumed he'd already agreed to, and fifteen minutes later announced that he wanted to be traded. He then checked out of the hotel and took off. Holcomb was dumbfounded. "I don't see how anyone in his right mind could turn down such a contract," he said. "We're not even close," Dick countered, adding, "I'm going home to mamma." As for the alleged contract negotiated by Morris, Dick clarified things by informing Holcomb that "my financial advisor doesn't speak for me."[15]

Given his avowed distaste for spring training, some within the Chicago media as well as the Sox front office believed that this was simply another ploy by Dick to delay his arrival until its waning days, but Hemond wasn't convinced. This time, he sensed, the situation was different—there was a real possibility that Dick might never report. "We'll just have to figure out something else," he said, when pressed on the matter.[16] Waiting Dick out might leave the club without a first baseman come Opening Day and Hemond, the director of player personnel and the point man for trades (Holcomb dealt with contracts), wasn't comfortable with that prospect. For his part, Tanner was resigned to let the situation play itself out. There simply was no other option but to sit tight and profess optimism: "I still want him but there is no point in having him until he is mentally satisfied about the arrangement . . . I don't know what he's thinking but it doesn't bother me. I am not disappointed at all."[17] Although he repeated his refrain, "he'll be here when he gets here," to reporters all spring, Tanner was sensitive to the portrait this was painting of his relationship with his

AWOL first baseman. "Sometimes I say Richie, sometimes Dick, and once I even called him 'Sleepy,' he told an inquiring reporter, "[but] one thing for sure I don't call him is sir." Broadcaster Harry Caray backed him up: "Chuck Tanner will never call anybody sir. He'll always run this ball club and everybody will know it."[18]

As the days passed, the articles coming out of Sarasota, painting Dick as a malignant force, multiplied and intensified. "Feel like telling the boss to go to hell?" screamed the front page of the *Chicago Tribune*'s sports section one morning. "Do you have the urge to chuck the rat race for a few days? Go ahead, do it! Just take off, don't even phone. You may be severed, but your exceptional talent assures you of another position at a higher salary." The article contended that Chicago fans wouldn't stand for such behavior: "The *Tribune*'s 'Sound Off' column has been averaging 40 letters a day, 99 percent of which prescribe that the White Sox tell Richie (Dick) Allen to go to hell; they don't need him and don't want him."[19] Another writer bemoaned that "He's ruined my spring training. I have to get up in the morning and go out to the park in case he comes." And a pack of writers, piqued that the team's main attraction was not available to help them fill their notebooks, took to organizing a sarcasm-laden tour of Dick's spring training to that point for curious out-of-town scribes. "Here's his locker," the tour guide said. "It has Bill Melton's clothes in it and Ed Hermann's golf clubs. Here is his mail. I'd say it's a stack about three inches thick."[20] He then led the group to the Sheraton Sandcastle, stopping at room 407, where Dick had spent the evening a few weeks earlier.

Dick wasn't the only player not in camp that spring. Oakland pitcher Vida Blue, fresh off a season where he went 24–8 with a league-leading 1.82 ERA—good enough to garner him *both* the AL Cy Young and Most Valuable Player awards—was a holdout as well. Blue believed that A's owner Charlie Finley was exploiting him. He noticed that he was often held back in the rotation so that he could pitch at home on Monday evenings, typically the most difficult day of the week to sell tickets.[21] Dick had expounded on this very point in his discussions with Holcomb. "One of his complaints," Holcomb said, "was that over the last few years in St. Louis and Los Angeles, he was just being 'used' to sell tickets. He felt that this was the way it would be in Chicago and he didn't want that."[22]

Neither did Blue. He and his lawyer explained to Finley that, using Finley's own numbers, Blue was responsible for increasing the A's revenue by $500,000 in 1971 and the overall worth of the franchise by about $2 million.[23] If Finley was going to pressure his manager into juggling his rotation just to put some extra coins in Finley's wallet, Blue was going to demand his share or he wasn't going to play at all. Blue earned all of $14,750 in 1971 (along with some fringe benefits, such as a Cadillac and the use of a couple of Finley's credit cards to purchase a few thousand dollars' worth of items) while enriching Finley enormously. For 1972 Finley was offering Blue $50,000. Blue and his lawyer considered $115,000 to be a bargain for Finley given that Blue was an asset worth well over a million dollars. Soon they reduced their demand to $75,000 but were determined to stick there or walk away. "He'll sign," said his lawyer, "when Charlie Finley is convinced he's not able to force Vida Blue into what he wants, as soon as Charlie is convinced that Vida is for real as a man as well as a pitcher."[24]

Blue and his lawyer borrowed directly from Dick's playbook in rationalizing their demand. "What we're trying to do," explained Blue's lawyer, "is get rid of the fallacy that a salary should be based on number of years in the game. Blue is already one of baseball's top ten pitchers. He should be paid accordingly."[25] Anything short of that was the equivalent of Finley keeping "a ball and chain on Blue."[26] The resulting negotiations were certainly about money but they were also about something else: respect. To Blue, these notions were implicit in his dealings with Finley. "[T]he Vida Blue case proves," opined *Ebony*, "that there will always be doubt about the real worth of a major league baseball player, from the standpoint of money, and also from the standpoint of manhood."[27]

Blue was adamant that he would not budge. The most he would do, he offered, would be to sign for Finley's offer of $50,000 provided that Finley also agreed to allow him to become a free agent at season's end. "Absurd," replied Finley, who also reacted by invoking the reserve clause on Blue, renewing his contract for that $50,000. Still, Blue refused to report. By the end of March, headlines blared that Vida Blue and Dick Allen were the game's only unsigned stars as the new season approached.[28] As spring training's days dwindled to a precious few, Blue, again like Dick before him, turned to Hollywood for financial support, signing a contract to star with Richard Roundtree in a *Shaft* sequel. He also accepted a position as vice president in public relations for the Dura Steel Products Company, a Los Angeles manufacturer of plumbing fixtures.[29]

Once the games began for real, though, Blue's resolve began to wither, and in May he finally accepted Finley's revised offer of $63,000 and returned to the club. Although most recognized that he was badly underpaid, there was little he could do about it if he wanted to remain in the game. During an earlier visit to the White House, Blue had had the undivided attention of President Nixon, who joked that given his talent, Blue unquestionably held the upper hand when it came to dealing with Finley ("I've read that you're the most underpaid player in baseball. I wouldn't like to be the lawyer negotiating your next contract"),[30] but this was hardly the case, as Blue's holdout demonstrated—a million-dollar asset was left with no choice but to settle for $63,000.[31] It was, as Blue alleged, exploitation, but ultimately he had no choice other than to submit to it. He wanted to play ball, so he swallowed his pride and signed.

Dick, as well, was finding that he still had the itch. He returned once more to Sarasota and convinced Lonnett to throw him early morning batting practice; the two would take the field before the newsmen arrived and be gone well before the rest of the squad showed up. Hardly anyone realized he was back in town.[32] Meanwhile, Holcomb was growing impatient. He asked for waivers on Dick and when only the Cleveland Indians put in a claim for him, withdrew them. If this was any indication, he believed, the trade market for his wayward slugger was virtually nonexistent. He then informed the press that he had set April 1 as the deadline for Dick to report. "If he's not here by the day we play our first exhibition game against the Cubs then we have to take some sort of action," he said.[33] With the pressure mounting, Dick turned to his two most trusted confidants for advice. "Listen son," said Era when Dick called her seeking counsel, "go help Chuck out."[34] He also called John Ogden. "When things are going bad for me, Ogden always has stuck by me," Dick said after the season. "He has been like a father to me. And that has been tremendously important to me, since I was raised without a father. Ogden told me 'Go on and play ball. Play it the way you want to play it.' "[35] And so he decided that despite everything else, he would.

He wouldn't rush back to sign his contract, however; a few days later, despite his decision, he remained unsigned. Finally, on March 31, Dick's contract situation moved to the back burner at last—the Players Association announced that every player on every club would be walking out of training camp, en masse, to commence the first players' strike in modern baseball history. With the camps emptying, everything else player-related became of secondary importance. As Holcomb contemplated the prospect of a player-free spring training, he received the most unexpected news of all: while everybody else was leaving, Dick was coming in. An hour after the players walked out, Dick, along with Morris, arrived, and sat down with Holcomb to iron things out. "I think we reached a little better understanding," Holcomb announced to the assembled media from his hotel room. "Morris was a help. He helped me understand Allen a little better."[36] The irony of the situation did not escape him. "Wouldn't you know it," he said. "All the players are on strike and now Richie might start working out."[37]

The next day, April Fool's Day, he ended his forty-one-day holdout by signing a one-year deal for $135,000—the highest salary ever paid a professional baseball player in the city of Chicago. "For the first time in my career," he said at the accompanying press conference, "I really feel wanted." Holcomb explained that the chief stumbling block in Dick's return was the prospect that he would be traded yet again; he wanted assurances that he would at last have the opportunity to root himself in one place. "It was a mental situation with Dick," said Holcomb. "He was bothered about being traded so often. We spent an hour assuring him that the White Sox wanted him very much and we reached a verbal agreement that this is where we wanted him to play for many years to come." Although Dick pronounced himself ready to begin working out at the team's spring training faculty, he was informed that it was impossible given that the players were now locked out of the camps because of the strike. "That's O.K.," he replied. "I'm from the country. I learned to work on a hillside. I'll find a place around here somewhere. I'll be ready."[38]

Less than an hour later Dick was true to his word: he found an empty baseball field, recruited a college pitcher to throw to him, and proceeded to take batting practice.[39] He soon became involved in player-organized workouts in Florida and, borrowing from coach Hennon at Wampum

In a White Sox uniform at last.
(© Chicago White Sox Archives)

High, took to wearing a fifteen-pound weight around his waist for hours at a time.[40] Looking back on his activities during the strike, Dick considered it to have been his favorite spring training.[41] He was in charge of his workout routine and was free to prepare himself for the season as he saw fit. By the time the season finally got underway on April 15 he was in better shape than most of his teammates. Shortly thereafter, readers thumbing through their copy of the *Chicago Defender* and wondering what to make of the mysterious man who had grudgingly arrived in their hometown came across Doc Young's "Prayer for Richie":

> Dear God, if you will permit such a mundane request, I want to ask a favor for Richie Allen, my favorite baseball player.
> Richie seems happy with the Chicago White Sox. He says he feels wanted. He says he wants to play out his career with the White Sox. Dear God, let it be. Let it be.
> Let it be, Dear God, because Richie Allen needs a baseball home. He needs a spot to call his own. He's been booted around and kicked around and traveled around much too often and much too long.
> Let it be, Dear God, because Richie Allen, down deep, is a really nice man. He is a good guy who loves his mother and family and baseball. He isn't raucous. He is rarely, if ever, ungentlemanly. . . .
> I know, Dear God, that Richie Allen isn't an angel. You know it too, of course. But who on earth is an angel? Not many, as you know, Dear God. . . .
> Dear God, if it isn't too much trouble, keep an eye on Richie Allen this year. Keep him happy. Just keep him happy and contented. You don't have to worry about his hitting, Dear God. You know he can handle that all by himself.[42]

*   *   *

That Chuck Tanner would be profoundly different from any of Dick's previous managers was immediately obvious. For starters, the lens through which Tanner viewed Dick was wider than that of his predecessors. "He has a magnetism," Tanner once remarked, "like Clark Gable, say, or Marilyn Monroe. He's above the ordinary."[43] From the outset Tanner made it clear that he would protect Dick like no previous manager had. Early in the season, when Dick was late for the team bus to the airport, Tanner held it for seventeen minutes and, in doing so, set the tone for the entire year. "Let's go right now," moaned one of Dick's teammates. "Why don't *you* take a cab to the airport?" Tanner shot back.[44] When the accusations began to fly that Tanner was doing little more than capitulating to the double standard Dick had insisted on for years, Tanner upped the ante on his accusers: "I don't have one rule for 25 players. I have 25 rules. I think communication is more important than regimentation."[45] On another occasion he expanded on his philosophy: "People say baseball is tough because you have 25 ballplayers and then they say, 'What are your rules for all of them?' In other words, they say people are different but you have to have rules for all of them. You can't do that. I have rules for my 20 and 21 and 22-year-olds and other rules for the older guys. If there are young kids who are in the bright lights for the first time, I'll tell them, 'Hey, you'd better get in because it's for your own good.' But if the older guys are used to eating late, staying up a little later, that's OK. I handle each player as an individual."[46]

Although Tanner himself was gregarious and outgoing, he recognized that his locker room was comprised of men with disparate personalities. And so he embarked, in the words of sportswriter Melvin Durslag, on a "Dr. Spock approach" with his players. "Do you want a pretty living room, or a well-adjusted child?" Durslag asked.[47] In Los Angeles, the condition of the living room was the highest concern. In Chicago, Tanner ignored the disordered space and focused on the individuals inhabiting it instead. Mauch would never have stood for the mess; Skinner, Schoendienst, and Alston claimed to not be bothered by it but ultimately couldn't coexist with the disorder regardless of how beneficial the results on the scoreboard. "Chuck was a players' manager long before the term became popular," recalled Bill Melton. "He handled every player separately, he allowed the players to do what they wanted to do. He demanded that they respect him and that was about it."[48] The game of baseball was difficult enough, Tanner realized; there was little to be gained in making a tough situation tougher by calling out a player for something unrelated to his play on the field. "As the manager, he would absorb all the pressure," said White Sox outfielder Ken Henderson. "He wouldn't put the pressure on the players. He would take the pressure from the press, he would take whatever he needed to take to insulate the players so they could go out and just play. He wanted the players to play and not worry about anything else."[49]

When it came to Dick, Tanner relieved a cauldron of pressure before the season even began. "[Chuck] told Dick, 'Give me 140 games,'" said

Hemond. "He said, 'I'll rest you here and there.' It was the first time [Dick] ever heard that somebody would look out for him."[50] "Dick needed an atmosphere where he enjoyed the people around him," said Melton.[51] Tanner was intent on doing all he could to make that happen, at least as far as the manager's office was concerned. As for his teammates, they quickly learned to adapt to and ultimately accept Dick as well. "Whether we like it or not," added Henderson, "superstars are always treated differently than other players, and that's just the way it is. And that's the way it should be. They can carry a team, they're the guys you want to make sure you get as much production from as you can . . . you want to treat a superstar like you do your other athletes, but everybody on the team knows that when you've got a special player, you're going to have to rest him, you're going to have to maybe attend to some special needs that he has, maybe give him a little more attention, and I think that is accepted by all players in baseball. At least I know that it was for me. I knew that if Richie didn't want to take batting practice, Richie didn't take batting practice. If Richie didn't want to play a particular game or was tired, Chuck wouldn't put his name in the lineup. Other players wouldn't think of telling the manager, 'I'm tired, I think I need a rest today,' but a superstar has the right to say, 'Today I need a day off.' . . . But not once did I see Richie bow out of a big game. That wasn't his style. If there was a game on the line, a game that meant something, Richie would play."[52] Dick relished the freedom that Tanner granted him. "I had an agreement with Tanner," Dick said a few years later, "that I had to play in only 120 games or so, and if we weren't going anywhere, that would be it for me. After that I would be free to do what I wanted."[53]

Obviously Tanner's promise to Dick, whether it was to limit his commitment to 120 or 140 games, wasn't something that could be pledged to his teammates—the Sox would have been unable to complete their schedule if he had. But for one player with the ability to carry the club as none of his teammates could, Tanner concluded that it was worth it. "He knew how to get the most out of Richie," said Henderson. "Even on those days when Richie would get down on himself or those days where he did not want to play a game, Chuck had the ability to go to Richie and talk to him and be a friend to him. . . . Richie wasn't an easy guy to manage. He was very much his own person, aloof at times . . . he was a private person.

Richie was very shy and very much a loner. That was just him—that was the way he was. [But] it wasn't malicious in any way. He was a kind man—very gentle." Tanner understood this. Hemond did as well. "Roland and Chuck both had a special relationship with Richie in the sense that I think they could communicate with him, they understood what kind of person he was and how to handle him and manage him and everything else," Henderson added.[54]

Tanner made sure to project his feelings toward Dick publicly in an effort to counteract the negative press Dick was getting as a result of his holdout. He called Dick "my untouchable" and added that when it came to his spring training absence, it was as it should have been: "I don't even want him down there," he responded when a reporter prodded him.[55] "In fact, I'm going to have Lonnett guarding the gate to the field with instructions not to even let Allen in the door. I don't want to see him until the season begins."[56] A couple of years later he doubled down on this point: "I can't be concerned with how they conducted spring training 20 years ago. I'm doing it the way I think is best for each individual player. Everyone says Allen, Allen, Allen, no matter what he does. Well, Dick Allen is a human being. He's a sensitive, shy person who just wants to be left alone to get ready in his own way for the season. And his program has no effect on the other players . . . I treat every player differently, according to what I think is best for them. This is what I think is best for Dick and I don't care what anybody else thinks."[57]

Regardless of his childhood connection to Tanner, Dick was initially hesitant to embrace his new home. "The press thinks I like it here," he said a few months into the season. "But I like it any place I can make money. I'll play in Alaska if the snow stops long enough, as long as they pay me."[58] Soon he softened as he realized that Tanner understood him as nobody in baseball had before. "Nobody can say anything against him to me," Tanner said a couple of years later. "I've known the problems he had to overcome. He was an introvert and the more money he made the more pressure there was on him . . . I didn't blame him for coming in at 6 or 6:30 for night games. If he came any earlier, there'd be 15 guys wanting interviews and tapes. By game time he'd be a wreck. I understood that."[59] Tanner recognized that as an introvert, Dick was physically incapable of performing at his best if he was required to do all of the ancillary activities his extroverted teammates took for granted. Because he was wired differently, Tanner realized that if he expected peak performance from him, he had no choice but to treat him differently.

Dick knew himself better than any of his superiors in baseball did, but he was perpetually ignored or ridiculed until Tanner came along. "There's too many distractions around the batting cage," Dick once said. "I can be ready to play, in fine spirits, and somebody can hit me with what you call a sensitive question and that makes me mad. Then, some guy is throwing the ball 900 miles an hour at me, and I'm thinking about the question the guy asked."[60] While being hounded by the Chicago press corps about his refusal to take batting practice with his teammates, Dick shot back: "I know in my heart that I can play better without that. Why do I have to do that when I know it's going to hurt my performance rather than help it? . . . Today when I come to the park early and just sit around it seems something usually happens that gets me teed off, then I'm no good for the game. . . . That's why I come to the park late. I want to avoid that bull." When one reporter asked him whether it was too much for him to "swallow[] your pride or stubbornness or whatever" and just show up for regular batting practice regardless of his nature, Dick's response was not simply a rebuke but also a subtle attempt to reorient the writer's perceptions: "It would kill me. I'm just not made that way."[61]

Tanner as well often tried to educate the press, attempting to quash the long-held notion that there was an inevitable causal link between one's participation in batting practice and his subsequent performance when it counted. "I was a great hitter at 6:30 and then a lousy one at 8," he once lectured the assembled masses. "Dick's game begins at 8."[62] Hemond also chimed in on occasion: "I've sat with him in the dugout during batting practice and he's sitting there with a bat in his hand getting himself keyed up mentally. I've never seen a guy so ready to hit the ball early in the game. He might be like Caruso—I don't know if Caruso rehearsed a lot."[63]

Despite Dick's introverted nature, Tanner and Hemond recognized that he could nevertheless be a team leader. Although Dick would often slough off the suggestion that he could lead his teammates, Tanner disagreed: "He's the leader," he said two months into the season. "Last year at this time we were 15 and 23; this year we're 22 and 16, and I think he's the guy who's made the difference."[64] Tanner believed that it wasn't simply Dick's production on the field that led to the club's turnaround, it was the way he took younger players such as second baseman Jorge Orta and pitcher Goose Gossage under his wing and mentored several of their young teammates privately, away from the spotlight. "He taught me how to pitch," Gossage would proclaim whenever asked about the teammate he considered something of a pitching tutor, which he reiterated in his 2008 Hall of Fame induction speech: "He taught me how to pitch from a hitter's perspective. He took me under his wing and we would talk for hours on end about pitching. It was amazing."[65] Veterans as well recognized his expanded role within the clubhouse: "He was the ultimate team guy," remembered pitcher Stan Bahnsen.[66] "He had a deep sense of family," Henderson recalled.[67] Once he felt comfortable with the Sox he began to see his teammates as family; soon he looked out for them as he would Hank and Ron. By season's end, Tanner formalized Dick's role on the club by bestowing upon him the honor that had been dangled in front of him but was snatched away by Mauch five years earlier: the designation of team captain.[68]

Irrespective of his new role, Dick continued to be himself—at times mentoring, at times keeping to himself, but always making sure that he prepared for the games the way he knew best, regardless of the flak he received for doing so. "This year," Dick announced early on, "I plan to take batting practice every day in the early months and the last month . . . twice a week in the hot months. Your body is like a bar of soap . . . it gradually wears down from repeated use."[69] This didn't sit well with the beat writers who were required to show up several hours before game time just like the players. "The pressures are tough," Tanner observed. "When other guys miss buses or are late, nobody says anything about it because they're not the superstar. If Dick Allen eats left-handed in a restaurant, they're gonna write about it and wonder what happened to his right hand. He's magnetic. When he walks, people look at him. Whatever he does, they watch."[70]

They may have watched, but many of them still couldn't see. While the Chicago beat writers, closer in temperament to their Philadelphia brethren than those in St. Louis or Los Angeles, filed hyperbolic early season stories focusing on Dick's absences from one team activity or another, they often missed the real story—that Dick was more often than not working as hard, if not harder, than his teammates, preparing for the games and the season right under their noses. "People are always saying I don't like spring training or I don't like batting practice but that just isn't so. When I go out to the ball park, before I even pull off my pants somebody wants me for something. Then I get dressed and the minute I hit the field, a million people want my autograph. Man, if I talked to everybody and signed everything, the day would be gone." To avoid the disruptions he devised his own schedule, one that would allow him to get his work in without the distractions he knew hampered his performance. He liked to arrive early in the morning, "when there's nobody to break my concentration. I work; I work hard. I put in as many or more hours than anybody out there."[71]

Dick's early morning workouts with Joe Lonnett in 1972 were hardly the first ones: a surprised Ross Newhan had bumped into him early one morning in Vero Beach the previous spring: "I got up real early—I couldn't sleep—at 6 A.M. or so, and decided to get dressed and go over to the clubhouse to get a cup of coffee in the press room. On my way to the press room—it was a real foggy morning, real cold—I heard this bat-against-ball sound coming from the batting cages. I couldn't make out if somebody was in the cage or not because of the fog but it sounded like it so I wandered over and here was Richie Allen taking batting practice. I asked him, 'Have you been up all night or are you just getting in or what?'"[72] Dick then confided to Newhan that he'd been taking the early morning BP three or four days a week. "I get a lot more done when nobody's around," he liked to say.[73] He would get his running in, build up the calluses on his hands, and work on situational baseball. Sometimes he'd hit off a machine, sometimes he'd recruit a college pitcher to throw to him, offering him $15 for an hour's worth of pitches, all thrown with the specific purpose of enabling Dick to work on a particular facet of his game at the plate.[74] By the time his teammates would arrive at the park, where they'd shag balls in the outfield and take perfunctory batting practice, Dick was gone. Around this time he also began videotaping his at-bats and studying them throughout the season. While his teammates and the beat writers were mingling in the clubhouse before the games, Dick was off by himself, becoming one of the first players in the game to incorporate video technology in his game preparation routine. Pitcher Wilbur Wood took notice: "Dick Allen borrowed a videotape machine recently," he said in 1974, "and he's been taping all the home games and he tapes on the road occasionally. I looked at it several times and I think it really helped me and it will help the ball club, too. If you have a couple of bad outings and a couple of good outings you can see the difference and study it."[75]

With Tanner's blessing to prepare as he wished, Dick thrived in Chicago. He started off hot (hitting .373 in April) and then got hotter. He displayed not only power but speed as well as his extraordinary base-running ability: on July 31 he hit not one but two inside-the-park home runs off of Twins pitcher Bert Blyleven, becoming the first player to do so since, of all people, Yankee outfielder and former Phillies' manager Ben Chapman. Those two capped off a month where he hit 13 homers in all—a club record. On August 23 he hit a 470-foot blast into the center-field bleachers, a feat previously performed only by Jimmie Foxx, Hank Greenberg, and Alex Johnson. Harry Caray was broadcasting from out there that afternoon and couldn't believe his eyes as the ball headed right toward him. "He sat around ten rows from the top [of the stadium]," Hemond recalled. "He had a table out there, and everybody laughed because Harry took his fishing net with him. He used to try to catch foul balls when he announced from behind home plate and they laughed because obviously nobody could hit a ball that far [into the bleachers]. But lo and behold, Allen hit a ball off of Lindy McDaniel of the Yankees that went over the centerfield wall and into the far reaches of Comiskey Park. Harry almost caught it. He was leaning over and almost got it. . . . Today, with Sports Center and all of that stuff, that would have been shown forever."[76] Former teammate Bill White was in the Yankee broadcast booth that afternoon and, unlike Caray, was hardly surprised by the home run. "Listen," he said after the game. "When Rich wants to be hot with the bat, he'll get hot. If he really wants to he'll go . . . not just two for four . . . he'll go four for four. Hell, he might go *five* for four!"[77] Although no video of the blast exists, audio of Caray's call has survived. In the clip one can hear both Caray's awe as well as his pique that a fan jumped in front of his net and snagged the ball before Caray could capture it. He then brought the fan on the air to confirm that the ball would indeed have landed in his net had the fan not jumped in front of it at the last moment.

Within months, the city of Chicago embraced him like no place else he had ever played. At one point Tanner chirped, "I know I've got the best hitter in baseball on my side. He'll finish his career with the Sox and go right to the Hall of Fame."[78] After only a couple of months into the season, few would disagree. He had won over the fans: those "99 percent" who had told the *Tribune* in March that Dick could go to hell were nowhere to be found, replaced by hundreds of thousands who flocked to the South Side for the first time in years to cheer Dick and the Sox on. Bill Veeck estimated that, in all, Dick was worth $750,000 to the Sox and that might have been a significant understatement.[79] For his part, Dick proclaimed, "I'm enjoying myself more than I ever did in my life."[80] He said he relished the sensation of finally feeling wanted. "And that's what life's all about, isn't it?"[81] A month into the season he had decided that he had at last found a home: "I like it here in Chicago and I made up my mind that no matter what happens, this is the last club I'm going to play baseball with. I'm just too tired of moving around."[82]

Of all of the highlights of the 1972 season, perhaps the one that resonated with him most deeply was a moment that led to a seat on the bench rather than a spot on the field. On Sunday, June 4, Tanner walked over to him and informed him that he could take the second game of that day's doubleheader off. "He had played every inning of every game for one-fourth of the season," Tanner explained after the game. "He goes hard in every game, doesn't pace himself. He came off the [road] trip on which we did a lot of traveling and he was tired. In fact, I was tired and I knew if I was tired he had to be tired, too. I plan on giving him more rest this season. These players are human. It takes a lot out of them. It's a grind."[83] That game would soon go down in Sox lore as the one in which Dick slammed his "chili dog homer," as Dick would wind up appearing in the game nevertheless, and with dramatic results. With the Sox trailing the Yankees 4–2 in the ninth inning, Tanner called for Dick to pinch-hit with two men on base against lefty Sparky Lyle. Years later Dick recounted the game thus: "I was eating a chili dog when I heard Chuck wanted me to hit. I had chili all over my shirt so I put on a new one and a pair of pants

Anticipation mounts as hope (along with fans) returns to Comiskey Park.
(© Chicago White Sox Archives)

with no underclothes." He then smacked a game-winning, three-run home run into Comiskey Park's left-field upper deck.[84] "Sparky Lyle threw me a slider and it wound up in the seats."[85]

Outfielder Jay Johnstone remembered that game fondly as well, although his recollection was somewhat different:

Dick played the full game at first base in the first game and then Tanner gave him the second game off. Dick knew he wasn't going to play
so he went into the locker room, took his clothes off, and got into the
whirlpool. He was relaxing in there, having a good time, singing, all
that stuff. Little did I know, because it was where I couldn't see it,
there was a bottle of J&B back there with him. And he's singing away
like crazy. And I'm thinking, "He's really happy. I wonder what's making him so happy." Well, I later found out. He's sitting in the whirlpool, buck naked, drinking J&B right out of the bottle, and we're
going into the seventh inning and Chuck says, "If [Yankee manager
Ralph Houk] decides to bring in a left-hander, go tell Dick I'm gonna
need him to pinch-hit." So Ed Hermann and I go, "Holy crap. He's
in the whirlpool and he's half shit-faced. We've gotta go in there and
get him ready." So we go, "Dick, Dick, you gotta get dressed, Chuck
wants you to hit," and he says, "What? What? I'm not hitting, Chuck
gave me the game off." Cut to the ninth inning and we're getting him
dressed and Dick has no idea where he is. We get him down to the
end of the dugout and Chuck goes, "Where's Dick?" And we say,
"He's down here, Skip. He's okay." He says, "Well, tell him to get
ready. I may need him to pinch-hit." So [Houk] goes out and takes
out the right-hander [Mike Kekich] and he brings in Sparky Lyle, who
was their closer at the time. And [Tanner] says, "Okay, now tell Dick
I'm gonna put him in." So I go to Dick and say, "Are you okay?" And
he says, "Yeah, just point me toward home plate." . . . So we push
him up the steps and I say, "Dick, can you see the umpire?" He says,
"Yeah." "Just walk toward the umpire," [I tell him]. "That's where
home plate is." So Dick gets up there and [Ed and I] are going "Omi-
god, he's got to hit and he can't even see; he's half in the bag." Sparky
Lyle was known for throwing first-pitch breaking balls, and he threw
him a great curveball and Dick swung and hit it into the upper deck.
Now Dick runs to first base and he stops. And [the first base coach]
says, "No, no! Dick, go to second!" So he runs to second base. He
stops. And [the third base coach] says, "No, Dick. You've gotta come
to third!" So Dick trots over to third and he goes to stop and the
coach says, "No, Dick! No, Dick! You gotta go home! You gotta go
home!" He had no idea he hit a home run. No clue whatsoever. He

ran to every base and stopped. And Tanner's going, "What the hell's going on out there?" And I say, "He's okay, Skip. He's just tired." Only a couple of us knew that he'd been in there with the J&B and drank half the bottle.[86]

To nobody's surprise, Dick was named to the American League's All-Star team, an honor that left him with mixed emotions in that attending the game would force him to miss the annual yearling sale in Kentucky that was scheduled for the same day: "I've never been to one of those sales but I know enough about horses that I think I could buy as well as the next man. It looks like I'm not going to make it because that's the day of the All-Star game. It doesn't seem as if I'm going to be able to avoid that one."[87] While there wasn't anything Tanner or Hemond could do about that, Hemond did make one more move that season with Dick in mind. On September 1, when the rosters expanded, Hemond signed Hank Allen to a major league contract and told him to report to Chicago where he'd spend the final month of the season with his brother. At the time, Hank needed 117 more days on a major league roster in order to qualify for the pension and Hemond helped him lop 34 days off of that. Clearly this wasn't a baseball move—Hank was thirty-one years old and had been out of baseball completely for over a full season before Hemond signed him to a big-league contract. "It is indeed unusual," wrote Doc Young, "if Dick Allen 'had nothing to do with' brother Hank Allen's pension-plan break with the Chicago White Sox. Dick Allen always has been concerned about his brothers' welfare and has gone to bat for them repeatedly."[88]

"We decided that we'd sign his brother Hank so that maybe it would help Dick to be more comfortable in his surroundings," Hemond recalled.[89] Although Hank had been out of the game for some time, his new teammates were onboard with the move. "There was nothing wrong with bringing his brother in," said Melton. "It didn't make any difference to us as players."[90] "It was perfectly okay," with Henderson as well. "Those kinds of things, we have no control over them anyway and I never heard from any of my teammates, nor did I have any feelings of my own, that he was taking a roster spot that somebody else should have had . . . we were okay with it."[91] Dick embraced the move immediately; soon he employed Hank as a shield to help him escape the press. "See my agent," he'd say to snooping reporters who were begging for his time, directing them to his brother, who would then shoo them away for good.[92] Eventually he and Hank became roommates, sharing a two-bedroom apartment in the city.[93]

All of this resulted in Dick putting together what Tanner claimed was the best single season he'd ever witnessed in baseball. "And I've watched a lot of good ones," he said in mid-September. "I got a good look at guys like Ernie Banks, Hank Aaron, Eddie Mathews, Joe Adcock, and Rocky Colavito. Don't take anything away from these players. They were all great. But Dick Allen is doing more for the White Sox this year than any player I have ever seen did for his. He's doing it all—at the bat, in the field, and on the bases."[94] Ultimately it wasn't enough. After battling the A's all season, the Sox fell off the pace in September, eventually finishing second, 5.5 games behind the eventual world champs. (In 1971 they finished 22.5 games behind the A's.) Once the season was no longer in doubt, Tanner made good on his preseason promise to Dick by informing him that his obligations to the club were over. After hitting .308 with 37 home runs and 113 RBIs, Dick had the final six games of the year off (he was the only Sox player to appear in all 148 games up to that point in the strike-shortened season). "I don't plan on using him anyway," Tanner said. "He's been playing with a bad knee and he's done such a great job for us, he deserves the rest of the season off."[95] At the time Dick was leading the league in home runs and RBIs (he'd finish the season atop the league in those categories) and was within shouting distance of Rod Carew for the batting title (Carew would eventually win it with a .318 average), so by sitting out the final six games Dick was forfeiting a shot at the Triple Crown. Regardless, he was grateful for the time to himself. Both the *Chicago Defender* and *Black Sports* applauded Tanner's move.[96] "To top off the rousing season sported by Allen, the brass gave him the last week to go hunting, fishing, or take care of his horse business—or whatever," read the "Locker Room Chatter" column in the November 1972 issue of *Black Sports*. "This only goes to show that you can't treat all men alike in any phase of life, especially sports."[97]

In their attempts to reconcile the Dick Allen they girded themselves for with the Dick Allen who captivated the city with his bat, if not his personality, all summer, the mainstream press fell back upon the old rationale that, once again, just as he allegedly had in St. Louis and Los Angeles, Dick had changed: "[Y]ou'll not convince veteran Allen watchers that he isn't a different Allen this year. He's still not Mr. Sunshine, but all the evidence is that he likes being liked and has mellowed." Brother Hank vehemently disagreed: "He hasn't changed since he was a kid," he protested to a *Los Angeles Times* reporter who was ardently claiming otherwise near the end of the season. "[A]nd he's no happier than he was. . . . I don't think there's any particular reason to change. When you put on that false face, you get kind of tired of living with yourself, wouldn't you say?" Dick concurred: "I just like to play and be left alone. I can play for anybody; it doesn't make a difference. I liked Philadelphia, they just didn't give me a chance. In St. Louis, I had to prove a point. It was personal. And I didn't know what I was doing in L.A.; they didn't want me." Still, the narrative persisted—it was Dick who had changed, not those around him. For evidence, writers pointed to small gestures by Dick throughout the season such as the time he doffed his cap to the Sox faithful—it was the first time in his career he had ever so acknowledged the fans, they alleged.[98] It wasn't, and in fact these surface gestures signified very little. Dick was just being Dick—just as he had been in Philadelphia, St. Louis, and Los Angeles beforehand.

What *had* changed was his employers' understanding of him—Tanner and Hemond's recognition that Dick was a human being first and a ballplayer second and that if they had any hope of ever reaching the athlete they had to reach the individual residing within. Although the hard-boiled Chicago beat writers still harbored their resentments, they were a bit more malleable as well; slowly, gradually, the tone of their coverage softened as at least some writers were willing to concede that perhaps there was something to the idea that ballplayers weren't interchangeable, disposable widgets. While perhaps still piqued at Dick's stonewalling when it came to their attempts to know him better, they couldn't argue with the results on the field: Dick was far and away the best all-around hitter in baseball in 1972, a season dominated by pitching. In November the writers made it official, overwhelmingly voting him the American League's Most Valuable Player. (He received 21 out of a possible 24 first-place votes.) Dick, given to hyperbole in emotional moments, responded accordingly: "The fans of Chicago have done a lot for me. I don't say I've been fair to the people in baseball, but sometimes they haven't been fair to me. Coming to Chicago made a human being out of me."[99] After his initial hesitation he admitted that "coming to the White Sox has proved a blessing in disguise." He also announced that "I'd like to take this opportunity of thanking each one of you [the print, radio, and television reporters] personally."[100] Ultimately, though, it was his teammates he appreciated the most: "We became tighter than pantyhose two sizes too small," he said later.[101] Finally, once again Dick reiterated his desire to put an end to his nomadic existence for good. "You may trade me," he told Hemond, "but I'm coming back here. I'm going to play out my career right here in Chicago."[102]

In light of the significance of his role, the *Chicago Defender* called for Tanner to be recognized as well: "Tanner realized that the only thing that really counted was what Allen did on the field. He didn't care if he showed up only a half hour before the game as long as Allen produced. And Allen produced. Tanner even made a point of calling him 'Dick' instead of 'Richie,' the nickname Allen dislikes. In this kind of environment, Allen thrived."[103] A week later Tanner received his due, winning the Associated Press's 1972 Manager of the Year award.

Chapter 12

The System

1973: Chicago .316/16/41
1974: Chicago .301/32/88

IT DIDN'T TAKE long for things to start unraveling once again. In the wake of the announcement of his 1972 MVP award, a reporter asked Dick what it would take for him to sign for the 1973 season. "I don't know," he replied. "How much do you have?"[1] Given past precedent, Holcomb was convinced that negotiating with the league's reigning Most Valuable Player would be torturous. So he devised an end-around, one that the Dodgers' Al Campanis was accused of attempting before the 1971 season: taking from the lesser players to satisfy his star. From where Holcomb sat there was no apparent downside to the approach. Dick would be satisfied, and as for the lesser players, who cared—they had no leverage anyway. The problems with this tactic would become apparent very quickly, both in the front office and within the clubhouse, ripping the organization apart before the spring thaw.

First to fracture was the already uneasy relationship between Holcomb and Hemond. Holcomb had hired Hemond in September 1970 as part of owner John Allyn's attempt to resuscitate the moribund franchise. From the start it was a rocky relationship. "He [Holcomb] was the president of the club and he told me, 'We won't have a general manager, what title would you want?' I said, 'Al Campanis of the Dodgers has the title of director of player personnel—that's satisfactory with me.' But people saw me as the general manager because I was the baseball guy . . . that didn't sit too well with Stu Holcomb."[2] Holcomb also had his difficulties with manager Chuck Tanner. They battled continuously over the makeup of the roster, with Tanner pleading for veteran bats off the bench and Holcomb offering instead the cheaper talent residing in their minor league system. Holcomb was particularly irked with Hemond and Tanner's request that he reach out to Hank at the end of the 1972 season. "Hank is on the roster because Chuck Tanner wants him there," he said with disgust at one point. Although he had hired both men, Holcomb grew to resent that both Hemond and Tanner soon had more influence with John Allyn than he did. "Hemond and Tanner were my choices originally," Holcomb grumbled to the press one day. "I could have hired 'name' people instead, and protected myself. Then, if they'd failed I'd be off the spot because I'd gone with proven baseball men."[3] He gave them an opportunity, he claimed, and now they had marginalized him. What resulted was a power struggle with Dick in the middle.

The fireworks started with Holcomb's stunning announcement that the Sox had signed Dick to a three-year, $675,000 contract—the first three-year contract in the franchise's history and one that made Dick, with an average annual salary of $225,000, not merely the highest-paid player in baseball at the moment (Hank Aaron, on the verge of breaking Babe Ruth's all-time home run mark, was set to make $200,000 with the Braves) but the highest-paid player in baseball history. For Holcomb, the commitment removed the annual off-season drama with Dick for the next three seasons at least; for Dick, who liked to profess that "I try to do the least bit of worrying that I can," it put his mind at ease. When asked about the specifics of the deal, Dick replied, "All I know is I can't count that high."[4]

The contract was an impressive statement that nobody in Chicago missed. "Baseball writers called him 'Dick' last year," one fan wrote in the *Tribune*'s "Sound Off" column. "This year, just call him 'Rich.'"[5] Doc Young saw validation within the terms of the deal. "As much as I am impressed by Dick Allen's athletic ability," he wrote, "I am impressed even more by his manly qualities, his family loyalty, his love for his mother. On the basis of past problems, communications media people have tried their best to give Dick Allen a bad name. . . . Even now, when he is doing so much to prove that he is one of the nicest, most positive thinking men in the game, there are baseball people who are waiting for him to fall on his behind. Well, they have a futile wait ahead of them. Dick Allen never was as bad as some people said he was. He always was a better man than they gave him credit for being."[6] A man like that, Young believed, deserved to be the highest-paid player in the game. Once a pariah, Dick was now bigger than the teams he played on. "Giving Dick Allen [$675,000]," remarked Melton, said something huge. "That's more than the ball club was worth."[7]

That's what Holcomb believed as well; he had no intention of breaking the bank to pay Dick. Rather, he intended to balance the club's ledger by reducing the salaries of several of Dick's teammates. Chicago sportswriter Jerome Holtzman saw what was coming and cautioned Holcomb to rethink his strategy. In Allyn and Holcomb, the Sox front office was, Holtzman wrote in the *Sporting News*, "heavy at the top with amateurs," and disaster was looming.[8] In the aftermath of Dick's signing, Holcomb warned several of his unsigned teammates that they should prepare for salary cuts as a consequence. When the players received their 1973 contracts in the mail, several saw smaller numbers than they had the previous year despite the club's success and increased attendance. By the end of the first week of March, Holcomb had cut outfielder Jay Johnstone and reserve infielder Ed Spiezio, who had refused to report to spring training because they were dissatisfied with Holcomb's offers.[9] While they may have been waiting Holcomb out in the hopes that he'd counter with a better deal, Holcomb was instead looking for reasons to expunge their contracts from his payroll altogether—he released them without warning.[10]

Three other players, infielder Mike Andrews, outfielder Rick Reichardt, and pitcher Stan Bahnsen (who won 21 games for the Sox in 1972), remained holdouts. Eventually all three reported to camp after Holcomb triggered the reserve clauses in their contracts and automatically renewed them—Andrews's and Reichardt's with significant salary reductions, Bahnsen's with a small increase but for significantly less than he was willing to sign for. "It is the wise general manager," Holtzman wrote, "who is aware that it is important not to take unfair advantage of utility men, and particularly when they have major league tenure. It is surprising, during the course of the long season, how many games are won by players coming off the bench." Taking money from these players to pay Dick could only result in dissension, warned Holtzman, who was also surprised that the young All-Star left fielder Carlos May (who hit .308 in 1972) didn't hold out for more money given what Dick received. (May quickly signed for $75,000.) "If I were Carlos," Holtzman wrote, "I would have held out for at least $100,000."[11]

With the turmoil surrounding them, many of the White Sox bench players felt pressured and uneasy. Richard Dozer of the *Tribune* described the atmosphere as one of "sign or walk the plank."[12] Finally, in late June, Reichardt had had enough—he walked out on Holcomb and the Sox. While some of his teammates were dismayed that he walked out on them midseason, they were more upset with Holcomb, who seemed intent on dismantling a club that appeared to be on the verge of winning the division. Even Holcomb's method of releasing Reichardt seemed particularly cruel and short-sighted. Rather than simply requesting regular waivers, which would have brought the Sox $20,000 when another club claimed Reichardt, Holcomb chose to unconditionally release him instead just to make the statement that, to him at least, Reichardt was worth nothing more than the single dollar a club would have to spend to claim him.[13]

Bahnsen's and Andrews's situations eventually broke the camel's back. In early June Bahnsen's father suffered a stroke, obliging Bahnsen to leave the club for a short while to be with him before he eventually passed away. Upon his return, Holcomb, seemingly out of the blue, offered to reopen contract negotiations. "I meet with him and he offers me the same five thousand dollar raise that he did over the winter," Bahnsen recalled. "I think the timing was deliberate, that Stu was trying to take advantage of the difficult time I had just been through. I didn't sign it and walked out." Bahnsen was livid. He approached Tanner and Hemond and told them he was quitting. As Bahnsen was heading home, Tanner and Hemond met with owner John Allyn. Although Holcomb wanted to release Bahnsen as he had several of his teammates, Tanner and Hemond objected, threatening to quit themselves if Holcomb was permitted to summarily release players on a whim. Allyn sided with Tanner and Hemond and approved Bahnsen's raise. The next day Bahnsen was informed that his demand was accepted, and he signed at last. The incident further soured the players on Holcomb. "Nobody on the team respected Stu Holcomb," said Bahnsen. "He wasn't a baseball guy."[14]

That left Mike Andrews, a second baseman who had developed "the yips," an inability to accurately make the throw to first (a problem he'd carry with him to Oakland where he'd commit a throwing error in game two of the 1973 World Series and then become the center of controversy when Finley attempted to release him mid-Series and replace him on the roster). While Andrews was battling the problem, Holcomb denigrated him publicly. "I don't have to talk about Andrews," he said. "A blind man could tell how he's doing."[15] A few days later Andrews requested, and Holcomb granted, his unconditional release. The Sox bench now depleted, Tanner looked to Holcomb to replace Johnstone, Reichardt, and Andrews. Holcomb refused, insisting instead that Tanner's replacements were waiting in the wings down on the farm. No trades were possible, Holcomb insisted. Moreover, if the club's prospects weren't major league ready, that was Tanner and Hemond's fault, not his. "Hemond and Tanner didn't think the kids were ready," Holcomb said a few weeks later. "If we had brought them up, though, they'd have been ready by now." At this point Tanner had had enough. He went to Holcomb and said that if he wasn't willing to pick up some veterans for the bench, he was quitting. Instead, it was Holcomb who "resigned." On his way out he blasted Tanner, whom he accused of being underhanded and manipulative. "The reason I'm leaving is Chuck Tanner," insisted Holcomb. "That's all. It's not so much what Tanner says about our operation, but what he doesn't say."[16]

The clubhouse responded to the news with relief. Several players smiled broadly for seemingly the first time in months.[17] From afar, Reichardt was pleased as well. "When I left I told Chuck Tanner and Roland Hemond that I wasn't just leaving because of the salary dispute. I felt my leaving would also crystallize the whole thing in the eyes of the public. Somebody had to have the 'chutzpah' to do it. . . . It was obvious the people who made this club from the start were Chuck and Roland. I thought Roland should have had the job from the start. Hemond has much more ability than most any other front office man in the business.

I don't think Stu ever was comfortable in the job. He knew nothing about baseball and I really believe he did more to start the team on the downgrade than anyone else."[18] Knowing nothing about baseball could be a problem in any situation; knowing nothing when it came to Dick would only lead to disaster. Earlier, on his own, and without checking with either Dick or Tanner, Holcomb announced shortly after the American League approved the use of the designated hitter for the 1973 season that Dick would be ideal in that role. Both Dick and Tanner immediately rebuked him. "The designated pinch hitter?" smirked Dick. "I don't want to be that fellow. I always wanted to be known as the complete ball player."[19] "No way, absolutely not," concurred Tanner. "Dick will be playing first base, just as he did last season."[20] With Holcomb finally gone it seemed as if disconnects such as this one would be a thing of the past and the Sox could finally get back to the business of winning games on the field. But that was not to be; Holcomb's departure was too little, too late to halt the club's descent back into the nether regions of the American League West. And here again, Dick would be the focal point.

In this swirl of turmoil, it was perhaps inevitable that attention would turn to Dick. Now that the club was beginning to struggle (the Sox started hot but collapsed in June when the dissension spilled out into the open), fingers began to point in Dick's direction even though he was one of the few players still performing at the same high level as the year before. He still avoided the press whenever possible just as he had in 1972, but now, with the team on the skids, it became an issue. The *Chicago Defender* later surmised that Dick "met a lot of jealous criticism from sports writers who thought that Allen didn't act so jolly at their presence," and though he encountered some of that criticism upon his arrival in Chicago, most of it came at the confluence of his large contract signing and the club's collapse.[21] From Los Angeles, Jim Murray wondered loudly and often why Dick should be earning more than Babe Ruth: "Richard Anthony Allen now makes more than Carl Yastrzemski, Willie Mays, Henry Aaron or the late Roberto Clemente. In fact—get this—he makes more in three years than Babe Ruth did in his career! I wonder if Richard ponders the historic injustice of all this?"[22]

Regardless, Dick continued to perform on the field, playing through a series of injuries—a broken thumb, a sty that forced him to play with one eye shut for a portion of the season—and hitting over .300 with 16 home runs through late June. Then, on June 28, while leaping to corral a wild throw by Bill Melton, he collided with Mike Epstein of the Angels and suffered a hairline fracture of his left fibula. Initially the injury wasn't thought to be serious, and though it looked like Dick would be out for one to four weeks, he claimed that he'd be back in the lineup "in a couple of days." For that reason, Tanner decided not to place him on the disabled list. The examining physician also indicated that the injury did not appear to be as serious as it might have been: "There is no displacement at all. It's just that he probably won't be able to get up on his toes for a while. . . . The injury is not to a bone that supports any weight. Rather, it is to a muscle-attaching bone."[23] Sox physician Gerald Loftus concurred, noting that although such an injury might cause pain (which he suggested should subside within three weeks), it wouldn't require a cast.

Three weeks came and went, however, and Dick still felt pain. Nevertheless he approached Tanner and suggested he could play in the team's game in Kansas City after the All-Star break, but Tanner refused to put him in the lineup. When pressed, Dick admitted that the pain was, at least for a hitter, disabling: "When I swing and pivot on my left foot there's still a twinge of pain."[24] He dismissed a suggestion by a beat writer that he might return as the club's designated hitter. "I want to come back fully," Dick said, "ready to play." Toward that end he returned to Chicago to begin working out. All the while, and as they had earlier in Philadelphia, the media speculated as to why he was seemingly unable to play. After all, he didn't appear to be injured—he wore no cast and seemed to be able to amble about pretty well. Yet he contended that he was in pain. Hemond recognized that here again, the optics were terrible: "What may have thrown people is that the doctor felt that a cast wasn't necessary, that he could simply stay off the leg while it healed. So Dick was on crutches, but then at the All-Star game [he was selected for the AL squad despite his injury], he was there in the seats with his son, and when the team was announced, he climbed over the rail—leaving his crutches behind—and walked out there to stand on the line with the other players in his civilian clothes."[25]

Dick was cognizant of just how much the past informed the present, at least as far as sportswriters were concerned, so he was reluctant to accept Tanner's advice to take the time needed to allow his leg to heal. Fearful of being labeled a malingerer once again, he instead worked out and kept insisting that he would indeed return, and return shortly. All of this only increased speculation as to what was really going on when his return kept getting delayed. He eventually took the field again on July 31 and went 3 for 4. He pinch-hit the next night and grounded out, and then that was that. By now the Sox were reeling—they followed up an 11–18 June with a 14–20 July—and Tanner didn't see the point of prolonging Dick's agony. "He tried to take batting practice Friday night," Tanner said in early August, "and couldn't even follow through with his swing and he almost had tears in his eyes. He can't hit or play on his leg now and I told him to just stay off it until it is better, no matter how long it takes. There is no use in jeopardizing his career by trying to rush him back into the lineup. It might even be best for him to sit out the rest of the season, we just don't know."[26] While Tanner hoped that his statement would reduce the media's glare on Dick, it only heightened it. After finally taking Tanner's advice to go home, Dick was chastised by the beat writers for no longer accompanying the club on road trips. "Anybody see Dick lately?" wondered George Langford in the *Tribune*.[27]

Finally in late August Tanner put an end to the speculation for good— Dick was finished for the season, he announced. Dick was relieved to finally be done with it all. "It was a drag, before, being around here," he said after Tanner's announcement. "Everybody asks first thing: 'When you gonna play?' I didn't know. The doctor said I couldn't hurt my leg anymore so I should try to play. But it got swollen. I thought I had broken it again. Well, at least now it's settled. I won't play anymore this year. I probably should have forgotten about it from the beginning."[28] With Dick now at home collecting his major league–leading paycheck, the sensibilities of some of the writers were rubbed raw: "He played in 72 games which amounts to about $3,125 per game," readers of the *Los Angeles Times* were informed the day after Dick's season officially ended. "[S]lightly less than $1,000 per time at bat."[29] In Chicago, Bears coach Abe Gibron chimed in as well: "Allen has ruined that team," he contended.[30] While sportswriters in Chicago and across the nation took delight in dividing Dick's salary by his at-bats, one *Tribune* writer, Bob Markus, stood up for him: "They write as if there is something shameful in Allen's taking the money while sidelined with the aftereffects of a broken leg. Some of these same writers who would knock a man who got hurt while doing his job have been known to miss a deadline or two because they were too hung-over to work. None of them have ever been known to return their salary for days they've been sick and unable to turn out their copy." As for Gibron, Markus highlighted the hypocrisy of his comment: "Nor was it ever suggested that the Bears' Gale Sayers give back his salary the year his knee—and ultimately his career—was shattered midway thru [sic] the season. Nobody ever accused Sayers of 'ruining the team.' "[31]

The light shone on Dick in the aftermath of his injury was considerably darker than it had been when he was on his way to his MVP season. In September, a *Sports Illustrated* article pointed out that the apartment Dick was sharing with Hank was conveniently located near a liquor store and the track. And Hank's presence on the club was rehashed as well. He hit only .143 in 1972 yet was invited to spring training the following year. While there he hit well and made the club again. But he struggled in limited action once the season began, hitting only .103 with four hits all year. Now that Dick was on the shelf, some of the writers wondered why Hank was still around.[32]

The following spring Hank was gone, but Dick was still with the club, and a new controversy enveloped him almost immediately. In February, Gerald Loftus, the team physician who was let go after the 1973 season, charged that Dick could have played in the second half of the season and was, in fact, a malingerer. "Richie Allen was healed well enough to finish the season last year," he said. "But so far as I know, the true story never had come out. I don't want to be the bomb thrower, but the image of Richie Allen wanting to play, and standing with tears in the locker room, isn't true."[33] Loftus also alleged that Dick was noncooperative: "He was really hard to catch. We'd have to track him down, usually thru [sic] his brother, Hank. In fact, that's my understanding of why Hank was on the club. You hear a lot of theories, but Hank was the only one who could find Richie. And that seemed to be Hank's principal function."[34]

All of this weighed on Dick as he contemplated his third season with the Sox. He arrived to spring training early, smoking a pipe. Reporters who recalled his earlier theory on ballplayers and pipe smoking pressed him as to whether this signified anything. Dick shooed away the suggestion. "The pipe? It's a concession to old age. Naw, I've always smoked it, just not at the ball park. It's a sign of contentment."[35] At the time, he made it clear that he didn't plan on joining the club until sometime around the middle of March and would be preparing on his own before that. When the middle of March arrived, however, Dick disappeared. He took off for eight days and when he returned, he was in no mood to talk about it. "Get away . . . get away . . . nothing today," he said as the beat writers descended upon him. A few minutes later a reporter asked him about his leg. "My leg is fine," he replied. Five minutes later another reporter asked him the same question. "It hurts like hell," he said. When pressed about his absence, he responded, "Who said I've been away?" When informed that the club said it, he replied, "That shows how they lie—they lie like everybody else."[36] A few days later he left camp again and returned to his farm in Perkasie. Upon his highly anticipated return in early April, he missed his plane to Sarasota and didn't arrive to the ballpark until the third inning.[37] In all, he stepped to the plate only six times all spring—a fact duly noted by the beat writers filing their stories for the fans back in Chicago. On Opening Day the fans responded accordingly, booing him as he went 0 for 4 and hit into a double play.[38] When both Dick and the Sox started the season slowly, the floodgates opened. The Sox lost six of their first seven games, during which Dick hit .129. "And [he] has not taken batting practice the last three days," pointed out a typical *Tribune* article.[39]

After a rough start, Dick found his groove: he hit .309 in May with 5 home runs and .330 in June with 9 more. Still, with the Sox scraping to stay over .500, he became the focal point of the critics. Jerome Holtzman alleged in the *Sporting News* that he was "just going through the motions." For evidence, Holtzman remarked that, despite his production on the field, "Allen hasn't been prancing out of the dugout and marching to the plate with the old gusto." As for why this might be the case, Holtzman suggested, "Allen is one of the few major league players with a no-cut contract." Noting that Dick would be paid regardless of whether he was "at the race track, or at the beach in Malibu, or wherever his drummer would lead him," Holtzman surmised that perhaps Dick just didn't have the drive to compete anymore.[40] By now it was clear that some writers just could not see beyond Dick's contract. No matter what he did on the field, to them Dick could never play to the level of his salary.

Although the Chicago dailies implied that Dick was not worth the money he was being paid, the Sox knew better. For a franchise that had struggled for years to draw fans, Dick's arrival provided the shot of adrenaline that ensured its continued existence on the South Side—the club finally drew over a million fans in 1972 and was north of that number all three years he played for the team. (In 1975, after his departure, attendance at Comiskey plummeted to 750,802—second worst in the league.) "He brought such excitement to the South Side of Chicago," Hemond recalled, "and revitalized the franchise. Chuck Tanner and I both felt that Allen helped save the franchise."[41]

Dick's presence was felt by everyone in the clubhouse as well as by those who went out to the ballpark. "Dick Allen had a mystique whenever he'd walk into a room," said White Sox slugger Bill Melton. "He was one of the few players in baseball, like Willie Mays or Willie McCovey or, of today's players, Albert Pujols, where, if you were losing a game by ten runs or ahead by ten runs, those players were such that, as a fan, you still wouldn't leave your seat. You just wanted to see them hit one more time. That's mystique. You wondered, 'Was he going to hit one 550 feet? Was he going to swing that big bat and strike out?' Dick was like Reggie Jackson—he had a beautiful swing even when he struck out. He just had an aura about him."[42]

Regardless, by the middle of the 1974 season Dick was being rapped repeatedly in the dailies. In June he arrived late for a regular season game for the first time during his tenure with the Sox, and afterward everybody wanted to know why. "It was something he had no control over," said Tanner, attempting to stanch the bleeding. "He can't help it if the plane doesn't leave on time."[43] (Dick and four of his veteran teammates had been permitted to fly from Chicago to Baltimore on their own rather than take the club's late-night flight the day before. The four teammates traveled together and made it to the park on time. Dick took a separate flight and didn't.) Tanner insisted that he wouldn't fine him for his late arrival. "Hell, no, there's no fine," said Tanner. "I wouldn't fine anyone in that situation." Holtzman, though, pointed out that while the plane may indeed have been delayed, it was Dick who chose the latest possible flight out of Chicago that afternoon.[44]

With the club mired in mediocrity, Dick continued to take a pounding, and his lucrative salary became intertwined with the club's performance on the field. He was mystified as to why it had become such a focal point for the writers: "I play baseball because I like it. It's fun. But if you were doing something you liked, but you saw a dollar bill on the ground, what would you do? Wouldn't you stop and pick it up? It's the same way with me. I'm not going to turn down money for doing what I like to do."[45] Finally, confused as to why he had once again become a target for derision, he looked a reporter in the eye and asked, "What have I done wrong? If I've done something wrong I want to apologize and straighten it out."[46]

Doc Young called for a cease-fire from the daily press. "Today, fans, I'm writing to suggest that it is time to end the persecution of Dick Allen, to quit nit-picking with him and to give him more credit, which he deserves, for being the kind of athlete and person he actually is—above average in each category."[47] But it was too late. By this point Dick and his supporters within the organization were all being singled out for ridicule. "Why don't you kiss him now, Tanner!" yelled a fan during spring training after Tanner removed Dick from a game.[48] By season's end, broadcaster Harry Caray piled on, telling reporters that Tanner "did a horrible job" managing his players in 1974. If Holcomb was still around, Caray believed, things would have been different. "Tanner and Hemond," Caray said in astonishment. "What a deal those two have."[49] He later called Tanner "a horseshit manager."[50] Caray had no love for Dick either: "I used to be friends with Richie. The thing that turned me off, I'll never forget it, was when we were down in Sarasota [during spring training 1974] and this little old couple from Philadelphia plunked down $7, maybe from their Social Security check, just to see Richie Allen play. And the sonofabitch was off at some race track 300 miles away. Jesus, when I think of Stan Musial and Pete Rose and Ernie Banks—those kind of people and their attitude toward baseball—and this guy, with all the God-given talent he has, is rippin' people off."[51] Just as before, everybody in Dick's orbit was receiving shrapnel; nobody in baseball, no matter what the circumstance, it seemed, was able to emerge from a relationship with

Dick unscathed. Years had passed, the specifics had changed, and then changed again, and then again once more. Still, the story was a familiar one. The more curious among those who followed Dick's career could only scratch their heads. What, they wondered, was going on here?

*　*　*

To go in search of the villains in Dick's story is to encounter an inordinate number of red herrings. Clearly Tanner and Hemond didn't fit the mold, disposed as they were to compassion, but the Phils' Carpenter, Quinn, Mauch, and Skinner didn't either, and most fans would agree that they were men of ordinary abilities confronting extraordinary circumstances. What to do with the franchise's first black superstar who needed an additional year of seasoning back in 1963? Call him up to the big club and watch him struggle, or send him to the symbolic epicenter of the segregationist South, which also happened to be home to your only Triple A affiliate? What to do to quell the potentially disastrous effects of an interracial dustup among teammates on the heels of a bloody race riot in the neighborhood that housed the ball club's stadium? What to do when your superstar third baseman refused to conform to the game's established hierarchy and traditions when the nation itself was being torn apart by the civil rights revolution?

As most fans watched these dramas unfold, they no doubt were more likely to see themselves reflected in Carpenter and Quinn et al. than in the seemingly strange and mysterious Dick Allen. On the surface, Tanner and Hemond were a break from anyone Dick had previously encountered: they demonstrated kindness rather than pique; they worked to understand Dick rather than demonize him; their attempts to accommodate him were tangible and hardly superficial. And for a short time their efforts seemed to be successful. But ultimately they were doomed to fail. Because ultimately, the true villain in Dick's story was bigger and more all-encompassing than any individual, even a powerful general manager. And there was nothing anyone, no matter how kind-hearted, could do to neutralize it on his own.

In the end, what made Dick's situation so difficult for all involved—players as well as managers and fans—was the system of Organized Baseball, a system that had been established a century earlier to protect the power and interests of the owners. It was this system that Dick entered when he signed on with the Phils in 1960, one that he rubbed up against repeatedly in the fifteen seasons afterward, first through the guise of the Phillies, then the Cardinals, then the Dodgers, and now the White Sox. It was a system that treated all players poorly and black players even worse. Dick could not abide this system and slowly, owing to the resistance of players such as Dick and, later, Reggie Jackson, Vida Blue, Curt Flood, and then ultimately Dave McNally and Andy Messersmith, it began to crack. However, Dick rarely viewed his situation through such a wide lens; he mistakenly believed that his adversaries were within arm's length—in the front-office men who dickered with him over his contracts and in the managers who chided him for not doing things precisely how his teammates did them. Tanner and Hemond were good men; Carpenter, Quinn, Mauch, and Skinner might not have been nearly as enlightened but they were hardly evil. Rather, they were merely playing by and enforcing the rules of the system. And the rules were what caused Dick to act out, often in self-destructive ways.

To a far greater degree than most of his fellow players, Dick was aware that no matter how highly he was compensated, he nevertheless did not own his own labor. Whatever he earned, his employer would earn more; whatever value he received, it was but a fraction of what his employer received as a result of his toil. Under the system as it existed, there was no cure for this disparity. He would be exploited no matter what; there was no measure of kindness or compassion from management that could alter that reality. Which was why he repeatedly said that he resented being used, as he saw it, by club owners "to boost their earnings at my expense." He took notice that as soon as he finally signed with the Sox after his holdout in 1972, the club saw a surge in ticket sales—a benefit they reaped throughout his tenure in Chicago. He saw that even when he acted out management stood to gain. "It wasn't that I was a troublemaker or hard to get along with," he said shortly after arriving in Chicago, "it was a case of my being used. The Phillies were always out of contention. . . . Management needed me for a gate attraction so they let that crap go on," he alleged. "Had they really been interested in me they would have called a press conference and tried to clear the air. But they didn't and I turned out to be the 'Controversial Richie Allen.'"[52] Controversy, he understood, sold tickets, brought attention to a product that otherwise would have been ignored. The Phils never won anything while he was there, but they were always in the local and national conversation. That was because of him. That, he believed, was exploitation.

Consequently, Dick decided early on that he would refuse to engage in any sort of publicity for his employers—he was exploited enough as it was. Part of his reticence to step out in this regard was due to his introverted nature, but part was his attempt to keep the exploitation of him to a minimum. Beyond the more formal publicity events he bristled at while with the Dodgers, he even saw the act of signing autographs as exploitative: "I don't like to sign autographs," he said in early 1974. "What I like to do is play baseball. Sure, some little kid might come up for my autograph. I still don't want to sign it. What does it mean? People want my autograph so they can show it to someone else and say, 'See, I got Dick Allen.' Autographs don't mean anything to black people. I can walk in the ghetto and out of 500 people five might ask for my autograph. A lot of people will want to shake my hand, though, and I'm happy to do that. That means something."[53] As he saw it, an autograph could be monetized and subsequently bartered; a handshake could not.

In a system geared toward exploitation, nobody who laid it bare could hope to escape undamaged. Whether they were defending it or fighting it, there was going to be blood. As Dick made it a point, unwittingly or otherwise, to expose not merely the exploitation of players but especially the exploitation of black players in Organized Baseball, everyone in his orbit was going to get hurt. The battlefield would be bloody until the battle itself was over. There was simply no way around it. The controversy that surrounded what would turn out to be Dick's final All-Star Game appearance, in 1974, was indicative of all this.

The game was to be played in Pittsburgh, only a short drive from Wampum—as close to a home game as he could get. Amid hype that the game could turn out to be a celebration of the life and career of Dick Allen, what with hundreds of friends and family expected to make the trip (he purchased a block of tickets for them), a much different narrative quickly emerged. On the Monday before the game Dick skipped out on the Chamber of Commerce luncheon and was absent the entire day. On game day he missed the traditional commissioner's luncheon as well as the pregame workout, which was designed more to provide the press with the opportunity to interact with the All Stars than anything else.[54] As the hours, and then the minutes, before the game's first pitch dwindled, Dick was nowhere to be found. Writers milling about the American League's clubhouse stared into his empty locker. Finally, about an hour before game time, Frank Robinson announced, "He's here!" and then quickly attempted to pass himself off as Dick once the writers turned in his direction. "We all look alike to you guys anyway," he said. Finally, at 7:48 P.M.—forty-two minutes before game time—Dick arrived. "I told you he'd make it," pitcher Gaylord Perry shouted. "I told you he'd make it. He's early." A's manager Dick Williams joined in: "He must've thought it was an eight o'clock game." As the assembled masses gathered around Dick, he started with a joke: "Sorry to hold you guys up," he said with a laugh. Then he turned serious. "It's an 8:30 game," he said. "That's what time I should be here. On time is game time, right?" Frank Dolson, for one, was not amused. "It must be nice to make $250,000 a year and be bigger than the game that pays you," he wrote the following morning.[55]

The hullabaloo didn't end there. Although the custom at the time was for the starters to play a minimum of three innings, American League president Lee McPhail ordered manager Dick Williams to do more and keep his starters in the game as long as necessary to ensure an AL victory (the AL had lost 10 of the previous 11 games). Dick made it through two and a half. After fouling a ball off his foot, he took himself out of the game after lining a two-out RBI single in the top of the third. He was gone from the premises by the time the fourth inning started. Again, Tanner defended him. "I don't blame him at all," he said the next day. "He did a job. He hit a rope for them. What more do they want?" He also pointed out that Dick wasn't the only one to skip out on batting practice or the ceremonial lunches. "I didn't read anything about that being bad for the game," he added.[56] The game was a study in contrasts as across the way in the victorious NL locker room, the PR-savvy Steve Garvey was lauded and celebrated after being named the game's Most Valuable Player. "I can't express in words my thanks to all the people in the country who helped me get here," he said of the hundreds of thousands who participated in a campaign to have him added to the squad as a write-in candidate. "This isn't my trophy; it's theirs."[57] Garvey also won the National

League's MVP award for the season and celebrated by making nearly seventy appearances at various ceremonial lunches and dinners during the off-season. "I missed being with my family," he said afterward, "but on the whole it was a very satisfying experience. It was a real opportunity for me to be a good-will ambassador for baseball and for the club."[58]

As for where Dick was on the Monday before the game, numerous theories were bandied about, none of them flattering. In reality, he had made the short jaunt to Kentucky to finally take part in the annual yearling auction at last. He had his eye on one colt in particular but was outbid when the colt went for $625,000. "That was out of my league!" he told *Baltimore Afro-American* columnist Sam Lacy.[59] "He liked his horses," explained Jose Cardenal. "When you have a day off, you're entitled to do what you like."[60] To Dick, the day before the All-Star Game, as well as the hours that preceded it on game day, was his. To those ingrained in the expectations of Organized Baseball, that time belonged instead to the amorphous concept known as "the Game," and it was the responsibility of the players, particularly superstars such as Dick, to do whatever they could to promote it. Dick couldn't see it that way, particularly when the monetary benefits of his time would go primarily to the owners and not to him.

By this point there was no going back. Even Tanner and Hemond's gentle hands couldn't dissuade him from the conclusions he had reached regarding the men who ran the game, conclusions formed at the time he was a youngster in the Phillies organization. As Dick understood it, Organized Baseball was a machine greased by an imbalance of power, one operated by callous men who didn't care a whit about the players they employed beyond their ability to pad their pockets. When it came right down to it, Dick believed, the Sox were no different from any other organization he had played for. "Basically, I was like a mule to them," he said the following summer. "I had to pull the plow. All the people knew about was the money I was supposed to be making. But there was a lot more to it than that." He saw just how much the Sox benefited from his presence—the increases in attendance, skyrocketing revenue from the concession stands and parking. Whatever he was making was a pittance by comparison. Eventually he had had enough. "[A]ll the Sox wanted to do was play .500 baseball and go over a million at the gate," he concluded.

If they did that, they could maximize their revenue, largely on the sweat of his brow. "My idea of playing baseball is to win every game, not just half of them."[61] When you're the star, he believed, you were exploited more than anyone else—you brought in the fans but the ball club kept most of the money.

Just as he had done in his waning days in Philadelphia, Dick looked across the baseball universe and figured that if he could just get out of Chicago and into a situation that better suited him, everything would be fine. He saw the talent-rich Oakland A's and New York Yankees (who were beginning to stockpile talent on their way toward dominating the league just two years hence) as places where he might thrive. In those places, he'd be simply one of the guys; he'd blend in, he believed. It would be much more difficult to exploit him in such an environment. "If I had to do it all over again," he said, "I'd like to be a utility man. Just play the game, work hard, and then be left alone."[62] To those charged with covering him in the press, Dick's worldview was baffling. "He repeated to me a number of times along the way," Larry Merchant recalled, "that he didn't like being considered a slugger. He wanted to be considered [just] a ballplayer. . . . The very thing that helped make him famous, as a player and as a potential heir to Mays and Aaron and [Frank] Robinson and Banks was the thing that he didn't want to be known as. I sometimes wondered whether he was undermining himself."[63]

The final straw came on September 13. Dick, frustrated and unhappy, went to see owner John Allyn and told him that he was thinking of ditching it all and walking away from the game. He was looking for guidance. He was looking for reassurance. What he got instead was confirmation of everything he had come to believe with regard to the game's hierarchy. "By no means is this slavery," Allyn lectured him. "You can go any time you want to."[64]

And so he did.

*　*　*

What Dick interpreted as evidence of villainy was in fact little more than an owner telling it like it was. Baseball surely wasn't slavery; one had to look no further than Dick's record-breaking contract for confirmation.

But that didn't mean it wasn't oppressive, and to a player who acutely felt that oppression for years Allyn's response was a punch in the gut. That Dick looked to places such as Oakland, run by the tight-fisted Charlie Finley of all people, as possible sanctuaries showed just how myopic his worldview could be when it came to the problems inherent within the system of Organized Baseball. At every stop along his journey he had his eye on someplace else, someplace he believed contained the cure for what perpetually ailed him. But it would never get any better than it was in Chicago. Indeed, Organized Baseball was structured to ensure that it *never* got any better than it was in Chicago. Although by now the Players Association was at last broaching many of the issues Dick had spoken out on for years, he preferred to decamp to the next club in hopes of better times ahead to tackling the issues on a systemic level. He was never particularly active in the union, never saw himself in Flood's battle against the reserve clause. The remedy for his ills lay in Marvin Miller's office, in the united voices of his fellow players, not in the likes of owners like Charlie Finley and his cohorts. For all that he saw when it came to the evils of the game, he never saw this.[65]

With no better option that he could discern, Dick did the one thing he was still empowered to do: walk away. With the Sox fading from the pennant chase, although still mathematically with a fighting chance to catch the A's, Dick "retired" from professional baseball. Although many of his teammates appeared to be stunned by his announcement—"My jaw dropped a foot," said Terry Forster—they should have seen it coming, since he had been talking about it all year long.[66] "Look buddy," he told Dave Nightingale of the *Chicago Daily News* in April, "you gotta understand, I just don't care anymore. I've had it."[67] He told a *Tribune* beat writer in spring training that he only returned to camp after walking out once Tanner pleaded with him in a lengthy phone call to stick it out for one more year, and he confided in Bob Markus of the *Tribune*, who by this point had become the Chicago equivalent of Sandy Padwe, that even after he returned he had his doubts. "I thought very seriously of calling a press conference in the morning [before the season's opening game] and announcing that it was all over," he told Markus. "I began to think that maybe this town was going to be like all the others after all. I didn't really even want to come here after bouncing around from town to town," he added. "But the team here was down, just getting started, and I knew Chuck Tanner. . . . So I came here and I gave it everything I had. It cost me 17 pounds and who knows how much off my life." After their conversation, Markus wrote in April that "I left Dick Allen feeling that I had been talking to a ticking time bomb. I know that the last thing Chuck Tanner wants to see is Dick Allen walking off into the sunset. But I'm convinced that Allen would do it . . . I hope nothing happens to trigger the explosion."[68] To Markus's surprise, the bomb remained intact for six months. But it was going to detonate at some point no matter what.

Dick's decision to walk away from the game after receiving his contract infuriated many of the writers and no shortage of fans. "I've accomplished everything I wanted to accomplish in baseball, and I think it's time for me to go on to something else," he said shortly after his announcement. "There's a lot more to life than hitting a ball with a bat."[69] Added Cardenal: "You know, some may say they can't see how any ballplayer can give up a $225,000 contract the way Richie is doing. I don't make that kind of money, but I can see him doing it. The more you make, the more people demand. They're never satisfied. They want more, more, more."[70] Several months later Dick expanded on his rationale for walking away. "When I left," he explained, "it was because there were a lot of things pressing in on me. I did all that I could do for the Sox in my three years [there]." Regardless, he became convinced that "the Sox were going to trade me anyway. They didn't come right out and say so, but I felt it coming. Except for the fans which I was bringing into the ballpark each day, I had practically outlived my usefulness."[71] Consequently, he felt like a "potential slave awaiting his turn in the 'meat market.'"[72] As he read the tea leaves in his increasingly agitated state, beating management to the punch was the only way he could grab at least a sliver of control over his future, his only opportunity to gain some small measure of power. So he jumped when he had the chance.

There were other factors as well. "I know he was hurting physically," Tanner recalled years later.[73] He injured his shoulder at some point in August and soon the pain had settled in his lower back. His production suffered: by the time of his announcement he had gone nearly a month without a home run (he would finish the season leading the league—with

32—nevertheless). At one point he admitted, "I just can't hack it any-more."[74] Joe Lonnett sympathized: "He's really hurtin'. His back is killing him."[75] Yet he played on until he decided that, along with everything else that was building up inside of him, it was no longer worth it. "With the injuries and everything in '74, given that he had played at such a high level, it was hard for him [to continue]," said Henderson.[76]

Dick was also frustrated about the narrative that had been developing over the previous few seasons, one that suggested his success in Chicago was largely attributable to Tanner and Hemond, who had somehow fig-ured out how to handle him. Dick bristled whenever anyone suggested this. In April he lashed out at the suggestion: "You know, everybody says that Chuck Tanner knows how to handle me, that he's able to get more out of me than anybody else could. That's not true. Any time I have ever pulled these [uniform pants] on I've given everything I've got."[77] Even at the height of his MVP season Dick took time out to correct the supposi-tion that he was achieving so much because of Tanner's ability to manipu-late him: "To be a manager, all you have to know is how to write your players' names. Somebody's got to put up a line-up card. There ain't no such thing as a good manager. Take Walt Alston of the Dodgers. What gives him the authority to tell me if I'm doing something wrong? He couldn't do it himself. . . . Take Mauch or Chuck Tanner of the Sox. My evaluation of them: helluva guy. But they couldn't play worth a damn, not even a little bit. So now they're getting some of the glory and publicity they wanted when they played. To me, a manager is nothing but a big flunky."[78] The overwhelming response to that comment was shock and disdain. "It appears to be a strange comment coming from a man so well defended by Chuck Tanner," wrote *Ebony* two months later.[79] After Dick had been awarded his MVP trophy, Sam Lacy sat down with him and offered him the opportunity to retract or amend his "big flunky" state-ment. Didn't he feel differently now, Lacy asked him, after the wonderful season he just completed, having been managed by the empathetic Tanner and embraced by the city of Chicago? "Let's set the record straight," Dick replied, reiterating his newest favorite refrain: "Dick Allen likes any place he can make money."[80]

After things went downhill in Chicago, he lashed out at both Tanner and Hemond. He alleged that he and Tanner weren't all that close after all and that there was dissension in the Sox clubhouse that was, at least in part, caused by resentment resulting from Tanner's relationship with him.[81] He accused Tanner of showing him up at one point by putting him in the starting lineup when he was injured and then pulling him after he committed an error.[82] He also expressed misdirected anger toward Hemond. "Before he went to California, and then came to the White Sox," he said in 1975, "Hemond used to be with the Phillies. We didn't exactly have a love affair going then. In fact, I'm almost sure he was the one who started a lot of my problems there with the press about spring training and so on."[83] In fact, Hemond never worked for the Phillies. His wife, Margo, though, was the daughter of Dick's prime adversary in Philadelphia, John Quinn. Dick apparently conflated the various relationships and, in the process, connected Hemond himself to the Phils and all of the ugliness he had experienced there for so many years. By the end of his tenure in Chicago he was no longer able to separate Hemond from any of the management types he'd encountered throughout his career. "There's nothing but lying and drinking in a lot of front offices, you know," he'd say later.[84] "[W]hether from past scars or not," wrote Dave Nightingale of the *Chicago Daily News*, "he eventually turned on everyone who was his friend: the Chicago press, players and fans. And, eventually, his manager. He became the greatest enigma I have ever known."[85] Dave Wolf, the former *Life* magazine reporter who was by this point struggling to pen Dick's biography, was alarmed by what he was witnessing: "He was convinced that Chuck Tanner was plotting against him. He had wild thoughts about his wife, fears about his kids. I felt he was losing touch with reality."[86] Soon Wolf would walk away from both Dick and the project.

Even before Dick walked into Allyn's office on the thirteenth he was leaning toward chucking it all; he cleaned out his locker at the conclusion of the club's homestand on September 1 and paid off the clubhouse boys. The day of his official announcement, the fourteenth, Dick dressed and, of all things, took batting practice. He then went out to shortstop and joked with his teammates. For a man who had been nothing but morose the previous several weeks it seemed as if something had suddenly lifted. After fooling around in the infield for a spell he called his teammates together and gave them the news. "This is hard for me to say," he began.

"I've never been happier anywhere than here. You're still going to be a good ball club without me." With his hands at his waist, he continued, "It's tough to walk away from the game I've been playing since I was this high." His eyes welling, he stopped and then walked away.[87] He was gone from the clubhouse before word had filtered down to the media, who by now were scrambling to catch up with the mysterious man who had just made his career disappear.

*   *   *

Dick never did file his official retirement papers with the league. "I never did believe in messing with unnecessary paperwork," he would say.[88] He preferred not to play; he preferred not to retire. While baseball waited for Dick to act, he was content with the status quo. Meanwhile, everyone around him took a pounding, none worse than Tanner. "It was Richie Allen who managed Tanner and not Tanner who managed Allen," wrote Holtzman. "Regardless of what any bleeding hearts might say, it is team discipline that helps win pennants. Discipline is considerably more important than 10 extra Richie Allen home runs." Because of this lack of discipline, Holtzman alleged, "The Sox players . . . don't respect [Tanner]."[89] It was Tanner, Holtzman and others argued, along with a generous assist from Hemond, who permitted a situation to fester where Dick managed to avoid not only spring training, batting practice, and other team rituals but the conclusion of each of the three seasons he played in Chicago. Rather than bring the Sox close to the top, the emerging narrative went, Dick succeeded only in tearing the organization apart.

The criticism stung. With Dick's status uncertain and the rumors growing that despite the seeming finality of his exit Dick might want to play ball again in 1975 after all, Tanner insisted that he would not be returning to the Sox no matter what. "It would be awfully hard to backtrack on this," he said in early December. "Tony Muser is my first baseman. If Allen came back, how could we be certain for how long before he might quit again?"[90] Hemond as well was clear that Dick's tenure in Chicago was over: "Once he left our ball club last September, and subsequently didn't file for retirement status, that meant he just left the club. . . . That created a problem."[91] John Allyn agreed. "When you've cut the string, you've cut the string. When you walk in and say goodbye to 25 ballplayers, you've said you don't want to play with them. Under those circumstances, I don't think you can welcome him back."[92]

From afar, Stan Hochman, who had followed Dick for so many years in Philadelphia, mused as to what might have been: "Maybe someday baseball will trudge into the 20th century and recognize psychology. Maybe professional guidance would have enabled Allen to use his fantastic skills to their full potential." Maybe, he wondered, some professional guidance would have enabled Dick to achieve even more than he had and would have helped him to have done so with a smile on his face. But maybe not. "I have this vivid memory of a long conversation with Hank Allen," Hochman wrote shortly after Dick left the Sox. "I suggested that Dick was hitting .311 every year, scorning the rules, sneering at conformity. 'Maybe he'd hit .411 if he conformed,' I suggested. 'Maybe he'd hit .211,' Hank Allen countered, ending the discussion."[93]

Dick's unsettled status resulted in a self-fulfilling prophecy: unsure of what else to do with him, the Sox dealt his rights to the Atlanta Braves in early December. To Dick, this was the final betrayal. "You may remember," he told Markus the following summer, "that when I came to Chicago there was some doubt on my part as to whether I wanted to come. But I decided to come as a favor to Tanner. The guys [Tanner and his coaches] were from my hometown so I wanted to help them out. When I came, Tanner said I'd always have a job with the Sox. Then they traded me."[94]

Chapter 13

— ❖ —

The Return

1975: Philadelphia .233/12/62

FOR A LONG time Dick had talked about getting away from it all and becoming a simple stable hand. "My mother has five acres [in Wampum]," he said. "Get a few horses. That would be nice. I don't want to be a headline all of my life."[1] In the late fall of 1974, after walking away from the White Sox, he studied for and then passed the difficult exam for a trainer's license at Keystone Race Track, where he also kept six horses. "There's an oral test and a written test," a Keystone steward explained. "Takes about an hour and a half. . . . It starts with questions about the difference between a colt and a horse, a filly and a mare, and some of them get tricky. How do you treat a bowed tendon? An osselet? Where is the sesamoid?" The steward was impressed by Dick's performance. "Allen is an athlete," he observed, "he knows how to condition himself and it's the same with horses. I always say horses are like people. Every one's got a different personality and you have to handle each one a little different."[2]

By not filing his retirement papers with the league, Dick was keeping his options open. Had he filed them he would have been ineligible to return to the field for sixty playing days; by not filing them he was placed

275

on the "disqualified list," which sounded ominous but was little more than baseball purgatory—he could be removed from it immediately should he ever desire to return to the game. As he puttered about on his Perkasie farm, rumors abounded that he had little choice but to return if only to support his passion for horses. "He almost has to play," said a Keystone publicist, remarking on the costs involved with keeping six horses at the track. "I'd say it costs between $15,000 and $20,000 a year to keep a horse." Moreover, Dick's horses had little success initially—only two of them had even gone to the post and both finished out of the money. "It will be some time before his horses begin paying for themselves," the publicist said.[3] Complicating things was Dick's nature: "Rich is a gentle, compassionate man. He won't push his horses into anything too quickly." A jockey concurred: "He loves horses. He won't abuse them. Least thing wrong, he don't run 'em."[4]

By mid-November, Dick, too, was talking of returning: "Everybody says I'm retired except me. I'm only retired if they don't want me back. I'm going to play somewhere next year—even if it's Jenkintown, Pa."[5] He added, "There's some pitchers I've still got to get. And I can't hit 'em with a rolled-up trainer's license."[6] Confronting life without baseball—for real this time—left him with a new appreciation of the game he had struggled with for so long and in so many ways: "Asking me if I want to play is like asking somebody else if he wants to eat."[7] Once he resolved that he wanted back in baseball, Dick resolved just as firmly that it would be once more with the White Sox.

But it was too late. The Sox weren't taking him back. Given that Dick wasn't amenable to playing elsewhere, both sides seemed to be stuck. White Sox management—John Allyn, Roland Hemond, and Chuck Tanner—were determined to move him, but how and where? One October day a solution presented itself in, of all places, Philadelphia. Ruly Carpenter, who had taken over ownership of the ball club from his father, called together Phillies' director of player personnel Paul Owens, vice president Bill Giles, farm director Dallas Green, and manager Danny Ozark and sounded them out: What would they think if he took a stab at luring Dick back to the club? After agreeing that it was at least worth exploring, Carpenter phoned Hemond and requested permission to contact Dick. Hemond not only gladly gave it but quickly worked out a deal with Carpenter: Dick to Philadelphia in exchange for Phillies' outfielder Bill Robinson and cash.[8] There was one catch: before Carpenter would agree to the deal, Dick had to assent, in writing, to return to Philadelphia. With that, Carpenter headed off to Dick's farm to sound him out. (Newspaper accounts had it that Carpenter spoke to Dick via the telephone at his farm, but Dick's farm was not equipped with a phone at the time.) The conversation was pleasant, but Dick insisted that he had no interest in returning to the Phillies; the press buried him once, he said, and there was no reason why they wouldn't do it again.[9] After the meeting Dick did indeed make his intentions clear in writing, but it was through a telegram to Hemond in which he stated that there was no way he would ever return to Philadelphia.[10]

Wandering the halls of baseball's winter meetings in New Orleans that December, Hemond was flummoxed. "I'll have to admit," he said, "I'm not making much progress on this. We want equal value for the guy, but nobody wants to risk a top player for him. But we've got to do something. We can't let it stay in limbo."[11] Everyone the White Sox GM approached recoiled at the mere mention of his name. "I don't want to say we're not interested," said Yankee general manager Gabe Paul, "That's not good to say." But then he had to say it: "Everybody's scared of him." While appreciative of his talent ("I stand in awe of Richie's accomplishments," gushed Orioles' general manager Frank Cashen), nobody was willing to take him on.[12] No matter how much they needed a power-hitting first baseman, nobody was willing to take a flier on the game's reigning AL home run champion. At last, after everybody else passed, the Atlanta Braves bit; vice president in charge of operations Eddie Robinson parted with all of $5,000 for the rights to one of the game's premier power hitters. Paul Owens, for one, breathed a sigh of relief. "We are not interested in him in any way," he now said. "There are just too many complications involved."[13]

Ironically, the morning after he was traded (and before he was made aware of it) Dick finally reached out personally to Hemond to indicate his desire to remain with the Sox. "He said to me, 'I don't want to be traded,'" Hemond recounted the day after the deal was completed. "It kind of knocked me for a loop. 'The deal had been made,' I said. 'I'm afraid you have been. If that's how you feel, I wish you'd have called me a few days ago and maybe you wouldn't have been.'" "But none of you people contacted me," Dick replied. "Since you told us you had retired, I didn't feel it was up to us to contact you," Hemond responded. Dick could only reply once more: "I don't want to be traded." A few hours later, after Robinson tried without success to contact Dick via telephone to welcome him to Atlanta, he informed him via telegram. Dick responded in kind a few hours later: "Received your message. However, at this time, I must decline. Thank you for your interest taken in me. I wish you continued success."[14]

There were several reasons why Dick recoiled at the idea of playing for Atlanta. For one, there was Braves' manager Clyde King, who, commenting on the trade, appeared to draw a racial line when it came to his players. "I managed Hank Aaron and Willie Mays—both players with gifted abilities," he said. "And I don't anticipate any trouble with Allen."[15] King had managed scores of white players as well but they didn't make their way into his statement. Moreover, both Aaron and Mays were black players from the first wave of integration—players who acceded to, if not with open arms, the game's racial double standard. While unquestionably outstanding players on the field, their approach to the politics of baseball represented everything Dick found distasteful—he wouldn't put on a public face. That King "managed" Aaron and Mays told Dick everything he needed to know: King certainly wasn't going to "manage" him like he did them.

Dick also took umbrage at the Braves' treatment of his brother Hank, who briefly played in the organization in 1971: "He only needed a few more months on the big league roster for his pension," Dick said. But rather than promote him to the big league club, "they . . . cut him loose."[16] He also harbored concerns that the sorry franchise simply wanted him more to sell tickets than to win games. In order to improve, it would all be on his shoulders, he believed: "In Chicago, it got to the point where they expected too much. It would be the same way in Atlanta."[17]

And then there was Atlanta itself. As Dick told one white reporter, he wouldn't have been as dead set against playing in the city "if you would let me borrow your skin."[18] This ruffled the feathers of all those, black and white, who, by the early 1970s, were heralding "the New South," with Atlanta as its de facto capital. "The attitude shown by Dick Allen in his refusal to come out of self-imposed retirement to play with the Atlanta

Braves is something out of the past," wrote Charles Price, field secretary of the Georgia NAACP in the *Atlanta Daily World*. "The fear that northern bred blacks had for the land of cotton, I thought, had been forgotten. This attitude that race relations were so terribly different in the South than that of the North is gone with the wind." Still, Dick wasn't swayed. That he didn't believe things could possibly have changed in the dozen years since his time in Little Rock angered Price: "Allen apparently has not taken the refresher course on the South and Atlanta in particular. His mind must still be tied to a past that the South is fastly forgetting."[19]

Regardless, Dick wasn't budging. Which left him with little else to do but claim his own "Curt Flood moment": he simply refused the trade even though he, like Flood before him, had no right to do so under baseball's reserve clause as it then existed—unchanged from October 1969 when Flood challenged it in court. Since he still wanted to play ball, Dick would have cherished the opportunity to become a free agent and select his next employer; but Flood had lost his case in the Supreme Court two years earlier, and the reserve clause remained as it was. Dick, like Flood, was stuck. The Braves, like the Phillies in 1969, held all the cards. Dick had a choice, but it was a stark one: play for Atlanta or retire from the game.

Braves' vice president Eddie Robinson wanted him to decide, and decide quickly, so the club could plan for the 1975 season. Once it became obvious that there was no way Dick was going to ever suit up for him, Robinson pressured him to simply retire and move on with his life.[20] Dick, taking his cue from Flood's case, thought he could respond as Flood did—by suing baseball under the reserve clause. Robinson responded by pointing out the obvious stumbling block that would prevent such a suit from seeing the light of day: "He's signed a contract for 1975, pure and simple," Robinson observed. "I don't even know how he'd go about challenging the reserve clause." The cold reality of Major League Baseball was this, he added: "He's our player and if he plays he'll play for us."[21] Dick pressed on regardless, claiming that, by trading his rights to an organization he didn't want to play for, the White Sox were illegally preventing him from earning a living in his chosen profession. White Sox manager Chuck Tanner scoffed at the very idea: "I'm sure Dick knows the White Sox ball club did not deprive him of making a living."[22]

Behind the bluster of his talk about taking the game to court, what Dick really wanted was simply to return to the White Sox. This was an impossibility for two reasons. First, even if the Sox wanted him back, now that his rights were owned by the Braves, a National League club, they were forbidden from trading them to an American League club until the next interleague trading period, which was still several months away, well into the 1975 season. And second, regardless of the league rules, it was obvious by this point that the Sox were finished with him anyway. Although some Sox players said that they'd welcome him back if he apologized for walking out on them in September and promised to play out the season with them, Tanner and Hemond's position was less benevolent.[23] After Dick reached out once more, during spring training, in the hopes of convincing them to take him back, interleague trading rules be damned, they shut the door on him when he scheduled a meeting with Tanner and Hemond and then failed to show. "A meeting was set up, but we waited and Dick never showed up," said Tanner. "So we went to the ballpark."[24] Apparently Dick backed off when word of the Sarasota rendezvous spread among the Chicago beat writers. Dick feared a media circus, and even though he had driven all the way to Florida for the sole purpose of meeting with Tanner and Hemond, he turned right around and headed home once he became aware that he was driving into a media hailstorm.[25]

That was the end as far as Tanner and Hemond were concerned. Tanner said that the Sox would not be making any claims for him in the future even if they could, nor were they interested in dealing for him down the road.[26] On top of this, even Marvin Miller of the Players Association refused to support Dick's cause despite the fact that Miller was currently working overtime to eliminate the unilaterally imposed reserve clause from the game (he would succeed after the 1975 season). Finding himself compelled to comment on Dick's threatened litigation, Miller had no choice but to state the obvious—that Dick didn't have a case. "I don't really know what's happening here, but there can be no doubt that a club has the right to assign a player's contract," he said. "If there's anything in the contract that denies the White Sox the right to trade him, that's a different story," he added.[27] But Dick's contract didn't contain a no-trade clause; he was out of luck.

Each spring training day seemingly saw yet another potential suitor pass on the prospect of obtaining him. "He just isn't in our plans," said Mets' general manager Joe McDonald, and Mets' manager Yogi Berra added that he wouldn't be interested even if Dick could be had without the Mets surrendering any players. Though Reds' manager Sparky Anderson praised Dick as "one of the top hitters in the league," Cincinnati wasn't biting either.[28] Later Reds' All-Star catcher Johnny Bench explained why: "Our team would never have taken him. They worry about what has happened in someone's past."[29] The Cardinals, as well, passed on rekindling their relationship with him. "He didn't fit into the Cardinals' type of operation," offered former Cardinal Joe Torre. "They try to run it like a family and Richie didn't do a lot of the stuff off the field that Mr. Busch likes you to do—interviews and dinners and luncheons, a lot of public relations."[30] Meanwhile, Dick was insistent that he was going to return. "I'm available and I want to play baseball," he told a gathering of reporters at Keystone Race Track in late March. "I'm in good shape. I could be ready to play in five days to a week." However, despite his enthusiasm he had his limits: "I'd love to play, but at the same time, I'm not going to beg for a job."[31] Increasingly, it was looking like he was going to have to.

With his options dwindling Dick turned once more to John Ogden, who, at seventy-eight, had settled comfortably into his role as a special assignment scout for the Phillies. Though the days of beating the bushes were long behind him and he now spent his days traveling the 130 miles round-trip between his home in Oxford, Pennsylvania, and Baltimore's Memorial Stadium to scout American League talent for the Phils, Ogden never lost contact with his most prized find, even after Dick had officially severed his ties to the Phillies. Indeed, he maintained contact with Dick throughout the winter and early spring of 1975, visiting his farm on several occasions. Finally, the two began talking about Philadelphia and the Phillies. "I've never forced any opinions on Dick or on any man," Ogden said a few months later. "I don't tell him what he should or shouldn't do or give him any of that church business from the pulpit. If Dick asks me a question, I'll give him a straight answer, that's all."[32] Dick wanted to know: Was Philadelphia different? Were the Phillies different? "John Ogden is the finest man I've ever met in baseball. He's never lied to me yet. He told me that the organization was different than the last time I was here."[33] So Dick began to reconsider what he had summarily dismissed only a few months earlier.

Ogden wasn't the only one who had his ear. Former Phillies great and current broadcaster Richie Ashburn likewise put on no small amount of miles traveling to and from Dick's farm during this period. Once the Braves were out of the picture, Ashburn began to talk up the young and exciting Phillies on his weekly visits to Perkasie. As word spread throughout the Delaware Valley that Dick just might return, the reaction was, to Dick at least, surprising: a February *Daily News* poll found that fans wanted him back by a 2–1 margin.[34] The club's front office likewise was increasingly enthusiastic about the possibility despite Dick's previous demurral. Still, Dick preferred Chicago.

Not to be deterred, Ashburn organized, in early February, a clandestine visit (to avoid tampering charges given that Dick's contract was still owned by the Braves) of representatives from the Phillies to Dick's farm to see if they could convince him to change his mind. Tagging along with Ashburn were Dave Cash, the second baseman and leader of the young "Yes We Can" Phillies, and Mike Schmidt, the rising superstar third baseman.[35] The trip wasn't secret for long: Allen Lewis broke the story of the visit almost immediately after Ruly Carpenter, with his foot firmly placed in his mouth, spilled the beans to Lewis: "I understand," Carpenter told Lewis, "Ashburn and a couple of our players talked to Richie and played cards with him out there and talked to him about this [agreeing to play in Philadelphia]."[36] Carpenter continued by telling the newsman that the club needed to be careful about things in order to avoid tampering charges. Lewis reacted by printing his scoop on page one of the *Inquirer*'s sports section. Robinson responded by reiterating that Dick was "under contract to the Atlanta Braves. He is already signed and on the third year of a three-year contract. I'm not going to negotiate with any other team."[37] If there was any doubt as to Robinson's intentions when it came to Dick, he reiterated: "I assume if he intends to play, it will be for the Braves unless he intends to retire." He then asked Commissioner Bowie Kuhn to investigate the nature of the visit by the Phils' contingent.[38]

Seemingly just like old times, the Phillies as well as a Philadelphia sportswriter found themselves in a rapidly expanding mess with Dick Allen planted firmly in the center. Hoping to stanch the bleeding, Lewis then backtracked from his story by denying much of what he had just written. Cash supported Lewis's revised take on the visit by arguing that the contingent was "invited out by Allen for a social evening. There is no way anybody could send me out there. You can't do that. That's against the rules." He insisted that, contrary to Lewis's initial story, the true intent of their visit was culinary, not professional: "Dick's wife is a great cook," he said, noting that Barbara "makes great ribs."[39] A week later Kuhn cleared the Phils of tampering and at least that crisis was averted. Still, Dick was not budging—he wanted to play but in Chicago, which didn't want him, and not in either Atlanta or Philadelphia, which did. Weeks passed; no movement on any side could be detected. Meanwhile, other clubs continued to pass on him.

The man who would be in charge of dealing with Dick on the field— manager Danny Ozark—was unsure as to how he should feel about the club's pursuit of the player still blamed for the departures of Mauch and Skinner less than a decade earlier. To be sure, Ozark was not cut out of the Chuck Tanner mold. He would not willingly bend to the will of any one player, no matter how talented. He came up through the Dodger organization and was schooled in the "Dodger Way" of playing the game, both on and off the field. He had been a member of that organization since signing as a player in 1942, transitioning from a career minor league first baseman to minor league manager, and then finally becoming a coach with the big-league club in Los Angeles. Ozark brought with him to the Phillies three decades of observations and experience with regard to how a successful organization was run. With the Dodgers it was the "Dodger Way" or the highway, something Dick experienced firsthand in his lone season there, and Ozark expected to run the Phils much the same way. "I'd have to talk to him," Ozark said when queried about Dick in February. "Would he really fit into our plans? If we talked, we'd talk about being at the ballpark, abiding by the rules. There would be one set of rules for 25 players."[40] Two weeks later he softened a bit. "Hell, Dave Cash didn't take BP the final month [of the '74 season]," Ozark offered as the Phils' pursuit of Dick heated up. "Allen could use his discretion there."[41]

With the Phillies increasingly relentless in their pursuit of Dick, Eddie Robinson sensed an advantage. Irrespective of the fact that general managers across both leagues turned their noses up at him during the winter meetings, and that it cost Robinson all of $5,000 to obtain his rights, he submitted his compensatory demands to the Phils in late February: if the Phils wanted Dick so badly, they'd have to send him either former Cy Young Award winner Steve Carlton, young slugger Greg Luzinski, or former first-round draft pick (sixth overall in 1969) and top prospect Mike Anderson.[42] (If those weren't acceptable to the Phils, Robinson indicated that he'd also accept the top overall pick in the 1973 amateur draft, Alan Bannister.)[43] Although players such as Schmidt were pushing the club to make the move ("I'd love to have him," Schmidt said in early March), Robinson's asking price essentially shut everything down on the Phillies' side.[44] Two weeks later Owens publicly walked away from the negotiations. "It was a case of our not wanting to give up more and a case of them not wanting to back down either," he said from Clearwater.[45] Ozark, for one, was relieved. "If I were in Danny Ozark's position," said Dick's former teammate and the Phillies' current Triple A manager, Jim Bunning, "I wouldn't want him." Neither did Ozark. "Last summer," wrote Frank Dolson in the *Inquirer*, "the Phillies gave [Ozark] a new two-year contract. Now, by not saddling him with Dick Allen, they have appreciatively improved his chances of completing it."[46]

There things stood for several weeks. The 1975 season opened, and for the first time since 1963, Dick was not on a major league diamond. At the conclusion of the season's first month the Braves tried to sneak him through waivers, but the Phils claimed him. The Braves then withdrew waivers on him, which meant that they now had forty-eight hours to either work out a trade with the Phils or lose him to Carpenter and Owens for nothing. While both clubs were now clearly motivated to work something out, the man in the middle remained cool toward both Atlanta and Philadelphia. Dick still held out hope for a return to Chicago and, assuming the Sox could be persuaded to change their mind about having him back, clearing waivers was the only way he could get there. Paul Owens was not going to let that happen. "He won't get back to the American League," Owens said defiantly. "The hell with it. I wanted him as a talent. I still like him as a talent if I don't have to break up my ball club to get him."[47]

Shortly thereafter, Carpenter trekked to Perkasie—alone—to make his case to Dick. As for why he traveled unaccompanied, he suggested that because he knew Dick better than anyone else in the organization, he was unquestionably the man for the job: "I had a good relationship with Richie—uh—Dick . . . I just felt I was the best man to go out there."[48] He returned successful if not triumphant; the sunniest spin Carpenter could put on things was that Dick finally agreed that he "could live with the situation" in Philadelphia.[49] Norman Unger of the *Chicago Defender* put it more bluntly: "So Dick Allen, the Patrick Henry of baseball ('Give me liberty or give me death'), has decided that it's worth $225,000 a year to be aggravated for six months."[50] "It's a calculated risk," Carpenter added. "I just think it will work."[51]

The deal was finalized a few days later—the Phils obtained Dick along with catcher Johnny Oates in exchange for minor leaguers Jim Essian and Barry Bonnell and $150,000—and a chain reaction was set in motion to prepare the club for Dick's arrival. The day before the deal was officially announced, the Phils shipped their current first baseman, Willie Montanez, to the San Francisco Giants in exchange for centerfielder Garry Maddox. Alan Bannister, the club's prized prospect, remained with the club but lost both his centerfield position to Maddox and his uniform number, 15, to Dick. "Great for the team," Bannister remarked when the dust settled, "lousy for me."[52]

At the news conference held to announce his return to the ball club, Dick wanted to make one thing clear: "From the very beginning I didn't want to leave here. But I was kind of like pushed."[53] He also promised to be an important member of the city's black community: "I never got the chance to relate to the kids in North Philly the last time I was here. But I'm going to become involved this time."[54] Looking on from afar, Doc Young called his return "the biggest, most interesting, story about-a-player in the 1975 baseball season. . . . It's a story which reads, and sounds, like fiction. It's a story no one would have believed in 1969; nor, for that matter, this time last year."[55] Young, along with most of baseball, was instantly fascinated by it. What would happen this time around? Seemingly everybody had an opinion. Depending upon where one stood on the matter of Dick Allen, the question was either "Why would he ever agree to go back *there*?" or "Why would they ever agree to take *him* back?" Would the Phillies, the Philadelphia media, and the Philadelphia fans bury him before the heat of summer kicked in? Or would he mope around, refuse to conform, and then take off before season's end just as he did each year in Chicago? Would things work? Could things *possibly* work? Why would either side even want to try to make things work? The Dick Allen game was already underway and he hadn't even taken the field yet.

*   *   *

Actually, it was obvious why Dick would agree to return to Philadelphia: he wanted to play ball and the Phillies were one of only two clubs still willing to employ him. Given a choice between the Deep South and Philadelphia, Dick chose Philadelphia, albeit reluctantly. For him, that was the extent of his deliberations. He had nothing further to prove by returning, no unfinished business. For so many others in Philadelphia, though, it was a different story. As became evident very quickly, Ruly Carpenter, the great swath of the Philadelphia sports media, and the overwhelming majority of the city's fan base *needed* him to return. Not for him, but for them. Dick might be able to "live with the situation" in Philadelphia but Carpenter, the media, and the fans were out to right what, in the six years since Dick's departure in 1969, had plainly established themselves as wrongs. The culture had shifted dramatically during that interval, to the extent that when it came to the city's history with Dick Allen, ever more folks were starting to realize that they might be on the wrong side of it. Here was their chance to cleanse their collective consciences. Here was their chance if not to rewrite history to at least script the final chapter so as to better conform to their newly enlightened ways. Dick Allen was coming back, allegedly to salvage what was left of his career but really it was they who were in search of salvation.

Initially many within the black press were convinced that there was no way the white fans and media in Philadelphia would give Dick a chance to succeed this time around. Doc Young wrote about a Philadelphia radio commentator who, Young relayed, "was reminding listeners of all the bad-boy tales baseball and media people had told on Allen over the years. . . . He sounded as though he never had heard the story about the Phillie players who, prior to the season, had 'campaigned' to have Allen brought back to the team."[56] In the *Philadelphia Tribune*, the concerns were similar: "Will Richie Allen, the most feared and respected slugger in major league baseball, be given a second chance by the fans who booed him out of Philadelphia and the press who stood around like a pack of vultures six years ago to pick his controversial carcass?"[57]

Their fears were well-founded and, to a degree at first, somewhat borne out. Dolson, Conlin, and even Hochman dripped a bit of sarcasm over Dick's return.[58] Before the prospect of such a return was even broached, Bill Lyon, who had joined the *Inquirer*'s sports department in 1972, jumped into the fray as well, seemingly itching to demonstrate to his journalistic elders that he could dish it out as well as they had in the 1960s. In a September 1974 column written in the wake of Dick's departure from the White Sox, the young journalist wrote a blistering screed that concluded that Dick was little more than a petulant child who was never forced to grow up.[59] In the hands of a master wordsmith like Lyon (who would go on to receive six Pulitzer nominations), Dick was eviscerated.

Regardless, the venom and scorn proved to be short-lived and were replaced with, of all things, respect and admiration. Leading the charge was not a media member but the leader himself, Ruly Carpenter, who seemed determined to demonstrate that he was not his father. Although he insisted that "I'm not trying to make up for things," he stressed his firm belief that as far as Dick's first go-around with the club was concerned, "I do feel that if I had more to say at that time, some things would have been different."[60] During Dick's welcoming press conference, Carpenter expanded: "Chuck Tanner and Joe Lonnett felt they could handle Dick in Chicago. I'm convinced I can. I feel I have a better chance than they did." To him, it was important that he, "millionaire's son, prep schooler, Yale man," as Hochman noted, and Dick connect. It would make a statement, it would say something on a larger scale. "Maybe," he said, "it will help the world go round. Maybe people with different backgrounds . . . can work together." Hochman was skeptical. Perhaps Carpenter was onto something here, he suggested. "But [he] couldn't be conned into quoting odds on a peaceful, productive season. How does one-in-ten sound? It sounds terrific. The Derby was over in 2:02. This horse race lasts all summer long. Do not destroy your pari-mutuel tickets until the result is official."[61]

Carpenter appeared driven to erase the stain left by his father's troubled approach to integrated baseball in Philadelphia. The Carpenters were an Old World family with Old World values—Ruly's grandfather, a DuPont executive, married into the DuPont clan in 1906, and with that came the trappings of privilege that were first passed on to Ruly's father, Bob, and then on to him. Ruly watched from the sidelines as his father struggled with the black press to justify the absence of black players in his declining clubs in the 1950s and then as he struggled again throughout the 1960s to deal with the organization's first black superstar. He by no means repudiated many of the old ways of his progenitors, but he was resolute in his conviction that his Phillies would not be like his father's. His Phillies would be progressive when it came to race. And there was no better way to demonstrate this than through Dick's return.

Carpenter's mission filtered down through the organization. Once Dick was onboard, Ozark, at least publicly, changed his tune in all things Dick Allen. "I would be foolish not to want the guy," he now said upon Dick's signing. "I believe in his ability . . . I'd have to be an idiot not to accept that. When we started negotiations with Dick, I wasn't concerned with anything he did in the past. I don't hold a grudge against anybody."[62] He also indicated that he'd be there for Dick no matter what: "When I feel that Dick's being bothered in any way, I'll try to help out. I understand most of his problems, on and off the field." He had a history with Dick, he now stressed, and it was a good one: "Dick and I got along very well when I coached at Los Angeles." Now that they were together again, this time in Philadelphia, things could only be better. Still, there were limits, and Ozark was prepared to enforce them. "But no one will take advantage of me, either," he added. Even the scoreboard operator got the message: upon his return to the field, the big board in right-center blared: "Welcome Home, Dick."[63] "Richie" Allen was gone forever.

Following Carpenter's lead (along with Dick's biggest cheerleader, Dave Cash, who pleaded with the beat writers to "give him a chance"), the media fell into line. "Okay," Dolson responded, "let's give him a chance."[64] Conlin, it turned out, was more willing than perhaps even he realized to do the same. In a column discussing the "subtle change in Dick Allen," another subtle change was evident: Conlin had consigned "Richie" Allen to the dustbin as well.[65] Beyond the nomenclature, Conlin's articles were now overwhelmingly sympathetic whenever he turned his gaze toward Dick; he no longer seemed as conflicted as before. Hochman like-wise was determined not to let history repeat itself: this time around he went out of his way to compliment Dick's attire upon his arrival in Phila-delphia. "Allen appears at a mass press conference in handsome civilian clothes, a brown leisure suit with leather inserts," he wrote.[66] His days of mocking Dick's "way-out taste in clothes" were over. Even Dick's chief nemesis, Allen Lewis, called a truce. "'Good luck, Rich,' I said, mindful that at one point in his stay here he refused to speak to me. 'Thanks a lot,' Richie replied, smiling as we shook hands."[67]

In Lewis's case, his respect for Dick was begrudging. In Hochman's, the admiration ran deeper. To him, Dick had grown into something of a countercultural icon, someone who bucked the system and took his lumps (at times deservedly) but stood above for his willingness to stand apart—to take on what so many others meekly shied away from. Which was why Hochman came away from Dick's introductory press conference disheartened when he saw on display not the defiant Dick Allen he had come to know but a conciliatory one he didn't recognize. "I'm not antici-pating any trouble," Dick said at a conference the disappointed Hochman termed "mawkish." "I've learned a lot through my journeys. There's a lot of difference between man and boy. I'd like to think I've grown up." Hochman couldn't believe his ears. "It was one thing to be humble," he wrote the following day. "One thing to be polite. One thing to be contrite. One thing to be charming. But he didn't have to grovel. He didn't have to crawl around on his knees and plead forgiveness because he was too young the first time around."[68]

The media might have been fawning but that didn't mean the Philadel-phia fans would be likewise. Dick braced himself for whatever might hap-pen. "I'm prepared," he said of the crowd reaction to his return to Philadelphia, "however it goes."[69] He needn't have worried. As soon as word leaked out that Dick would take the field for the first time in his second go-around in Phillies pinstripes in the Wednesday, May 14, game against Cincinnati, ticket sales exploded. The advance sale for that game had been a meager 7,000 (only 11,634 bothered to show up to see the Phils beat the Reds the night before); after the leak the lines at the Vet's ticket gates formed rapidly—30,908 would eventually buy a ticket to wel-come Dick back.[70] While an increase in attendance didn't necessarily mean that the throng was anxious to cheer rather than boo, the crowd's intent became clear even before the game's first pitch was thrown. In announcing the starting lineups, public address announcer Dan Baker made it only as far as "Batting fifth, number 15." At that, the crowd erupted—cheering, clapping, stomping their feet. Baker waited for them to quiet down. They didn't. He tried to talk over them but it was futile. Eventually he gave up.[71]

During the game the crowd continued to shower Dick with love; every time he touched the ball at first base (he made the game's first putout on a Pete Rose grounder, made the second by catching a Johnny Bench foul pop, and then made the third by tagging Joe Morgan, who was picked off first by pitcher Steve Carlton) the crowd rose in appreciation. When he came to bat in the bottom of the first the crowd rose again. Dick responded by singling to center with a bat he had given clubhouse man Kenny Bush nine years earlier. The Phils had forgotten to order Dick's 40-plus-ouncers from the Louisville Slugger Company until it was too late; Bush ran home at the last minute, removed the bat from his trophy case, and presented it to Dick before game time.[72] In all, they showered him with three extended standing ovations and several shorter ones.[73] When Tommy Hutton took the field in the seventh to replace him for defensive purposes (the Phils were up 2–0 at that time, on their way to a 4–0 victory), they greeted Hutton with boos. At last, Conlin wrote after the game, the Philadelphia faithful had decided to "[cheer] a Christian instead of the Lions."[74]

In Presbyterian Hospital, Officer Joe Hand listened to it all on his portable radio. Two weeks earlier he had suffered a massive heart attack that almost killed him. Now he very badly wanted to make it to the Vet somehow, some way, to cheer Dick on. His doctor wouldn't allow it. So he contented himself with cheering from his hospital bed. "I'd like to be one more pair of hands clapping for the guy," Officer Hand said. Six years earlier, cops, firemen, and white-skinned blue-collar workers across the Delaware Valley were jumping out of their skin to jeer him; now they couldn't wait to shower him with applause. "Peace. Love. Happiness," wrote Hochman.[75]

Dick was less enthralled by his return than were those around him. He had spent the early part of the day mowing his lawn back in Perkasie. Once he arrived at the Vet he didn't take the field with his teammates but instead spent forty minutes in solitary practice, taking 70 to 80 swings against the club's batting practice pitcher, Hank King.[76] After the game, while some fans remained, chanting for him to pop his head out of the dugout one more time, Dick met with the assembled media—nearly a hundred in all—in the press room. He spoke appreciatively of his welcoming: "This is just plain terrific. You don't know what it means to me. This is an entirely different atmosphere," but he had obviously had enough of the day's festivities. He was already dressed even though the game had just ended and his car keys dangled from his hand the entire time. As soon as the postgame conference ended he was on his way back to Perkasie.[77]

All summer long the club, the media, and the fans embraced him no matter what he did, or did not do, on the field. The *Los Angeles Times* termed it "The Summer of Dick Allen's Content," and it was that and then some. [78] Between the lines he struggled—by late August he was hitting a meager .220 and had yet to reach double digits in home runs. Still, the media was kind, the fans cheered, and the front office did not point fingers at him as the Phils futilely chased the Pirates in the NL East. Conlin had dubbed the 1975 Phils "Superteam" after Dick's signing and predicted a cakewalk to the division title. Schmidt concurred: "This might sound like popping off," he said in May, "but when I start hitting the ball, it's over."[79] Dick believed a division title to be inevitable as well: "[B]y mid-August we'll all but have this thing wrapped up."[80] When the team faded in the final six weeks of the season it was Ozark, not Dick, who took the heat. Instead, as Dick's struggles persisted, his teammates protected him. Luzinski credited him with teaching him how to be a cleanup hitter, predicting that soon Dick would start producing on the field as well and at that point there would be no stopping the Phillies.[81] Schmidt likewise found Dick to be invaluable: "I like to talk to him. He knows a lot about hitting, but he also has the ideal outlook. He has helped me with the mental part of hitting. He accepts things as they are. He acts the same whether he does well or strikes out. You never see Dick Allen break a bat or crack helmets in anger. He knows how to handle himself and it's helped watching him."[82]

He would not emerge from his offensive funk all season. He finished up hitting .233 with only 12 home runs. In only 416 official at-bats, he struck out a staggering 109 times. Defensively his range was limited and he not only committed 18 errors but failed to scoop out many throws that his predecessor, Willie Montanez, did with both ease and flair. Still, he was pleased to have returned. "There are plenty of other sluggers here, like Mike Schmidt and Greg Luzinski, so I don't have to carry the load all the time," he said. "I wear a uniform and I have to make a contribution like everyone else. But that doesn't mean I have to carry the whole team."[83] More important, this time around there seemed to be more flexibility and less rigidity when it came to the club's rules. "I'm happy," he said, that the new Phillies "are the kind of club who will let me do my own thing."[84] Sometimes he took batting practice, sometimes he didn't. Sometimes he arrived early, sometimes he didn't. This time, at last, it didn't seem to matter. "[I]f you're a bricklayer, businessman or what-have-you," he told the *Philadelphia Tribune* a month into his return, "say your reporting time is 9:00 A.M. and you're good at your trade. Do you go to work and do abc's at 6:00?"[85]

A new script was being written in Philadelphia and the ones penning it were those circling Dick's orbit, not Dick himself, who had no interest in rewriting history. Although Ozark liked to proclaim, as did so many in St. Louis, Los Angeles, and Chicago before him, that Dick had "turned a new leaf," in reality, the opposite was true.[86] "There are new faces, new management, a new park, new fans," Dick said shortly after his return. "But me, I'm the same man, the same ballplayer. I have the same feelings."[87] Irrespective of the deluge of articles and front-office declarations proclaiming that somehow Dick had finally "reformed," the numerous standing ovations, the gentler press, and the tender touch of management from 1970 onward were testament to the fact that it was they who had changed, not Dick. In Philadelphia, all of this was taken to new heights, as now it was the same fans, the same club, the same press who had previously pilloried him who were now tripping over one another to praise him. The contrast between then and now was startling, and at some point the enthusiasm generated by Dick's return began to say something more about those in praise of Dick than about Dick himself. So many folks in Philadelphia desperately wanted a mulligan for what went on between them and Dick between 1963 and 1969, and here at last was their chance. But erasing the past would not be as simple as standing and cheering every time he came to bat, or lauding him in print despite his declining numbers, or forgiving and forgetting his refusal to engage in pregame activities. True, the past was past. But it also informed the present. And nobody could erase that.

Chapter 14

No Apologies

1976: Philadelphia .268/15/49

EVEN DECADES AFTERWARD, Dick's minor league year in Little Rock remained indelibly burned into his character. "He was an instructor [with the Phils during spring training] in the '80s," recalled former Veterans Stadium groundskeeper Mark "Frog" Carfagno, "and I'm up in his room with him. We're sitting there watching TV and he gets his sandwich and he puts it on top of a lamp and then turns the lamp on. I said, 'What the hell are you doing?' and he said, 'I'm heating my sandwich up. I learned how to do this when I wasn't allowed to go into the restaurants. Somebody would buy me a sandwich and I had to go to the hotel room and heat the sandwich.'"[1] No matter how much everybody in Philadelphia wished it were otherwise, the past could not simply be forgotten.

As he entered his second go-around with the Phillies, Dick tried to accommodate those around him: he spoke more freely with the media, he tried to arrive earlier to the ballpark, he suffered through pregame batting and infield practice more often than before. But eventually he grew tired of all the genuflecting toward conformity, and as he continued to struggle through the 1975 season, he pointed a finger at those efforts. "Right now," he said, "it's more important for me to be there on time. Time seems more important than production. The thing is, I've never played this way. I'm not loose at all. So much TV, so much press."[2] Hochman couldn't help but recall his conversation with brother Hank the previous September: "Maybe he'd hit .211" if he conformed, Hank offered at that time. Dick was very nearly there. "Maybe," Dick suggested near the end of the season, "this means I'm washed up." He quickly disabused himself of that notion, however. "No, I don't believe that. Yeah, I'm 33. But I want one more year to show these guys what I can do. I want to show them I can play the game better than any of them. Any of them."[3] He very badly wanted that one more year. And if he got it, he was going to do things his own way once again.

Ruly Carpenter wasn't so sure. To the Phillies' owner, though Dick's on-field results weren't what he had hoped for, everything else worked out splendidly—Dick was embraced by the city, the season was devoid of off-field controversy, everybody could now part ways feeling better about things. Carpenter had achieved what he had set out to do: prove that he could succeed where his father had failed. Wasn't that enough?

Dick's answer was just as surely "no." He had returned to Philadelphia solely for the opportunity to play ball and to play it better than anybody else on the field. He hadn't done that, so there was no question in his mind that he needed to return to accomplish what *he* had set out to do. "I have a purpose," he exclaimed after the 1975 season, and it had nothing to do with making a point to management.[4] His fealty to the Carpenters or the Phillies was of such little matter to him that he intimated it was fine if Carpenter wasn't willing to sign him to a new contract; he'd just as well play without one and then take advantage of the newly instituted free agency rule at the conclusion of the 1976 season. Carpenter wouldn't have that; after some dithering he agreed to engage in negotiations with Dick but wanted him to take a 20 percent pay cut—the maximum permitted under the Collective Bargaining Agreement.[5] Dick swallowed hard, said that he'd be at least open to negotiations, and set off to make *his* point to the baseball world, and in his way.

There was one snag: following independent arbitrator Peter Seitz's December ruling abolishing the perpetual reserve clause and granting pitchers Andy Messersmith and Dave McNally free agency, the owners locked the players out of spring training in what would become a futile attempt to pressure them to make what were now, from the players' standpoint, unnecessary concessions in the 1976 Collective Bargaining Agreement. "Here I am and baseball is not ready," Dick said with a smile from Clearwater in March. "If baseball wants to join me, that's okay."[6] Until that time, he contented himself with preparing for the season with his oldest and best friend in baseball, Tony Taylor. They, along with most of their teammates, took over rickety Grant Field in nearby Dunedin and conducted spring training their way: "No rules. No games. So we got a lot more hitting in," said Dick. "We just did our work and went home."[7] He loved it. Everything was perfect except that the power alley in left-center was only 320 feet and right behind it stood an elementary school playground. After Dick and some of the other Phils bombarded the playground, causing the schoolchildren to duck for cover (amazingly, no one was ever hit by a ball), the school's principal complained and an agreement was reached: Dick and his pals could use the field for batting practice only when the playground was not in use.[8]

After a nineteen-day lockout the camps finally opened. Upon hearing the news, Dick quickly took off for Clearwater and arrived at the Jack Tar Hotel, which he assumed was still the Phillies' headquarters. Times had changed. He arrived at the hotel around 9 P.M. and, with Era in tow, ascended the hotel's marble staircase to the lobby to check in. He was stopped by a guard armed with a shotgun who informed him that he was trespassing and that it would be in his best interest to retreat as quickly as possible; unbeknownst to him, the Jack Tar Hotel had been sold during his absence and was now the Eastern Headquarters of the Church of Scientology.[9]

Once his lodging situation was clarified, Dick became an active participant in the club's formal spring training activities. Manager Danny Ozark even gave Dick and Taylor, who were now (along with pitcher Jim Kaat) the club's elder statesmen, leadership roles. "Ozark put Dick Allen and Tony Taylor in charge of me," recalled Jay Johnstone, who had joined the Phillies in 1974. "He said, 'These guys are gonna get you in shape.'" They demonstrated how they were going to do that immediately. "I'll never forget the first time they told me to go out and run wind sprints. I said, 'How many am I going to run? Six? Eight? Ten?' Taylor responded, 'Ten?

[Dick and I] are running forty.' And that's what we did, every day during spring training: forty wind sprints from the foul line to centerfield and then back."[10] Dick led more by example than through words. "He was always laughing with you, rooting for you," recalled pitcher Larry Christenson. "Dick and [later] Pete Rose were both leaders but were completely different, with different perspectives. Rose said a lot but Dick only needed to say a few words—'Let's play ball.' It could be a rocky road in that locker room," Christenson remembered, but he knew that Dick would always have his back.[11] In his own quiet way, Dick began to exert himself as a mentor just as he had in Chicago.

Dick relished not only the opportunity to mentor but the chance to spend more time with his old friend Taylor. They were the lone survivors of the 1964 club, the only active links to the old days, and though Dick had many bad memories of that era, his time spent with Taylor was not one of them. Dick and Taylor had first bonded in Clearwater, back in the days of segregated spring training, when Taylor not only cooked for Dick and the other black players but found them housing in the North Greenwood section of the city, near Jack Russell Stadium.[12] They had been close ever since. In Dick's eyes, Taylor deserved all of the accolades that now came his way. Nearing the end of his playing days, Taylor had become a de facto coach who occasionally pinch-hit; the Veterans Stadium crowd would rise and applaud every time he did so. If ever the opportunity arose for Dick to stick his neck out for Taylor (for a change), he would seize it.

As the shortened spring training waned, the issue of Dick's contract remained unresolved. Without much leverage, there was little Dick could do this time around, and he was determined not to let it distract him as he prepared for the season. "I'm letting Clem [Capozzoli] ride that horse," he told Ray Kelly in late March.[13] A little more than a week later Capozzoli was dead of a heart attack. "He was so close to Clem," said Ozark. "I'm more worried about what this will do to Dick than Greg Luzinski's injury, the flu or anything else that's setting us back. Losing somebody that close—like Dick's father—could have a big effect on him."[14] Dick immediately returned to Philadelphia to help organize the little baker's funeral. He then instructed the equipment crew to affix the black armband to his uniform that he would wear in Capozzoli's honor the entire season.

Tony Taylor (right) and Dick embrace upon Dick's return to Philadelphia, May 13, 1975.
(Temple University Libraries, Special Collections Research Center, Philadelphia, PA)

Capozzoli's death instantly changed Dick's demeanor. Beforehand, Capozzoli predicted a return to greatness for his friend and client: "Dick's in a good frame of mind, getting himself in terrific shape."[15] Afterward, everything was different. When he returned from the funeral, he was withdrawn and morose.[16] The gloom wouldn't lift all season. While he still engaged with his teammates (he and Johnstone would sometimes talk at the hotel bar after games), he was reluctant to fully express himself. "Dick kept to himself," Johnstone recalled. "A lot of stuff he kept inside. That's what built up some of that rage. . . . You could ask him, 'Hey, Dick, is there a problem?' and he'd say, 'No.' He just wasn't going to divulge any information to anybody."[17]

Capozzoli's death also brought an immediate halt to Dick's contract negotiations. So he entered the season unsigned (Carpenter then exercised his right to unilaterally cut his salary 20 percent as he had indicated he wanted to do). Things then went from bad to worse in a hurry. Dick looked sluggish in the field, his spark was gone. "There are . . . people who contend that Allen is 34-years-old going on 50," Conlin wrote in May. "[T]hat his reflexes have slowed, that, to use boxing parlance, he is a shot fighter."[18] Ozark noticed this as well; a few weeks into the season the manager began platooning him at first base with Bobby Tolan. This upset Dick, and a few days later Ozark intensified the issue when he pulled him from the lineup before the club's April 25 game against the Braves after initially penciling him in in the starting lineup. During the game, a puzzled media was informed that Dick had injured his shoulder sliding into second base two days earlier and was unable to play even though he played the day after his alleged injury and singled. The press then swarmed around club publicist Larry Shenk for an explanation; Shenk insisted that he had no knowledge of any such injury.[19]

After the game, which the Phils lost 3–2 (and during which, according to Dolson, Dick, still smarting from the benching, ignored Ozark's command to pinch-hit in the ninth), the horde descended upon Ozark, demanding to know what was going on.[20] Ozark attempted to change the subject, but the writers wouldn't let him. Finally Ozark exploded in a cursing, stomping rage. He vacated his office, now packed with reporters, slamming the door behind him, and headed toward Dick's locker, where another six writers were perched, and ordered them and everyone else with a media credential out of the locker room.[21] AP reporter Ralph Bernstein refused, at which point Ozark threatened to punch him. Clubhouse man Kenny Bush held Ozark back from Bernstein, who continued to egg Ozark on, daring him to make good on his threat. The situation then devolved even further, with Ozark and Bernstein cursing at each other and Bernstein loudly maintaining that he had the right, as a reporter, to remain in the locker room. "You can take it to the fucking commissioner or anybody else," Ozark yelled back.[22] He did. Accompanied by his colleagues, Bernstein first marched into Giles's office, then Owens's, before finally catching up with Carpenter, who was in his private elevator on the way to his office. "Danny's sick and tired of the bull, the second-guessing, and so am I," Carpenter told them.[23] Then, as the elevator doors closed, Carpenter left them with one final thought: "You're all a bunch of fucking cocksuckers!"[24]

A few days later, the Phils put Dick on the fifteen-day disabled list. Dick was incredulous. It was likewise news to him when he came off the list two weeks later. "Am I off?" he asked. "Nobody has said nothing to me. Nobody said nothing when I went on, while I was on or to tell me that I was off. The whole thing's a big mystery to me." When he returned, the platoon arrangement became official—something else Ozark didn't inform Dick of before word leaked to the beat writers. "I'm finding out all kinds of things," he said. "Platoon me, huh? Well, I shouldn't be surprised at age 34 and the way Bobby's been playing [Tolan was batting .299 at the time, to Dick's .231]. But I don't like the way it's been handled. . . . What's next for me, a release? That's okay, too. I don't have much cash but I got a little land. I could get by."[25] What in fact followed hurt almost as much: for the first time in his career, Dick would bat seventh in the lineup. While his shoulder might be fine, his pride was clearly hurt. "If I'm gonna slow 'em up that much," he said, "I'd rather not be in there at all."[26]

His official return to the lineup was preceded by an unpleasant trip down memory lane when he refused to participate in the club's exhibition game against its Triple A affiliate two days earlier. This time, he made the trip (to Oklahoma City) but begged off after Ozark penciled him in at first base and batting sixth. "I just didn't care to play under the circumstances," Dick explained during the eighth inning of the game, standing behind the clubhouse, eschewing a seat on the bench. "The man wants me to get the work . . . [b]ut why didn't he play me a couple of innings in that 12–2 game Sunday in Houston? He don't play me then when I had a chance to see some big league pitching. Instead, he asks me to hit sixth against a lefthander in an exhibition. I don't need that stuff anymore." The past became present once more when Ozark approached Dick after he finally learned that he was going to be platooned from then on out and instructed him not to speak to reporters. This time, Dick refused to acquiesce. "I'm as smart as he is," he told Conlin. "I can answer questions for myself."[27]

If 1975 offered up a rose-colored image of Dick Allen, 1976 showed clearly that he was as he always had been—stubborn, prideful, and determined to go his own way. He was also still, through all the controversy and criticism, the loyal friend and teammate. Johnstone credits him with jump-starting his career. "He helped me immensely, hitting-wise," he said. "I used to use a lightweight bat and he kind of got on me one day and said, 'Big, strong guy like you, what are you, a wimp? I've got a two-year-old who can swing that. Let me order you some bats.' He ordered me a 36-inch, 36-ounce P89 and that's when I really started to become a hitter."[28] He befriended the young, introverted slugger Mike Schmidt, who reminded him of himself in his younger days, and mentored the third baseman through the club's late-season slump when all the pressure seemed to fall on Schmidt's shoulders. "The damn guy's always telling me how good I am," Schmidt said in September. "At a time like this, that's what you like to hear. At a time when you might be losing your confidence, that means a lot to you."[29] He took it upon himself during the season's final game, after the division title had been wrapped up, to make sure that Steve Carlton, shooting for his twentieth win of the season, got it. In the fifth inning of a 1–1 game that was meaningless for everyone other than Carlton, Dick walked, stole second, took third on an errant throw, and then scored what would become the deciding run that gave Carlton his milestone victory.[30] He resuscitated a sobbing Rick Bosetti after the September call-up cost the club a crucial game when he was picked off first base in the ninth inning after being inserted as a pinch runner. Dick grabbed the inconsolable Bosetti in the locker room and took him to the maintenance room where he locked the door, put Bosetti in a recliner, and sat with him for over three hours until Bosetti had calmed down and regained his composure and perspective.[31] As for why he assumed such a role, Dick said it was only right: "What I'm trying to do to this ball club and the youngsters around me is what Tony Taylor did for me my first time around with the Phillies. Tony Taylor was my first roommate, he taught me the little things that are necessary to play this game. After Tony came Bill White who did the same thing. He always inspired me. I'm trying to do the same thing on my second trip around."[32]

As always, he paid little attention to established hierarchies: some of his closest friends during both of his stays with the Phillies were the club-house guys and members of the grounds crew. "The first time I met him," remembered Carfagno, "was in 1971 [Veterans Stadium's inaugural year]. We [the grounds crew] were eating our dinner. It must have been about 4 o'clock. In walks a guy with a vanilla leisure suit, big fedora hat, cream-colored shoes, yelling, 'Where's Vic?' Vic was the old groundskeeper from Connie Mack Stadium and [Dick] wanted to make sure that he was still around. He then sat down at our table, had a sandwich, and bullshitted with us for three and a half hours. Fast forward to 1975. Right after his [welcoming] press conference, he came downstairs off the elevator and he comes walking by our room and I hear him yelling, 'Where's Pete?' Pete [Cera] was the trainer in Williamsport and some of the other minor league teams [he played on]. He knew Pete had gotten promoted to the majors and was working as Kenny Bush's assistant. He bypassed everyone else and ran right in to see Pete Cera."[33] He didn't bypass Carfagno, though; the two quickly became reacquainted and soon grew close. By September, after the premiere of *Welcome Back Kotter*, Dick was referring to Carfagno as "Kotter" (Carfagno bore a passing resemblance to Gabe Kaplan, the show's star) and to the grounds crew as the "Kotter Gang." Often he would sidestep the waiting media horde upon entering the stadium, saying, "Sorry, gotta go see the Kotter Gang"; he would then sit with them until game time. "Before the games," recalled Carfagno, "he'd hang out not in the clubhouse but in the grounds crew room. We had a room behind home plate where we could cook food and stuff like that. He'd come in and have a sandwich with us."[34] Larry Christenson took notice: "The grounds crew, the ushers, the people who worked around the stadium—he was always nice to them. I never saw him mistreat anybody."[35]

In many ways, the 1976 season was a mirror image of the one that preceded it: the club ran away from the pack at last but everything surrounding Dick began to unravel. For the first few months of the season the fans and the writers remained solidly behind him; the team's sparkling play overshadowed his diminishing skills. His average was a bit higher than it was in 1975 (he was still hitting a respectable .289 in September until a late-season slump caused it to plummet), but his power was gone. The whispers grew louder. By late June he had only 7 home runs and folks were starting to openly wonder if it was gone for good. "[Dick] would drive from his farm in Perkasie to [groundskeeper Gary Tinneny's] home in Manayunk," Carfagno recalled. "Gary lived on one side of the street and his mom had a trailer on the other. Before he would go to the ballpark, he would stop in and Mrs. Tinneny would make him a meatball sandwich, which he would take with him [to the ballpark]. 'You gotta eat. You gotta eat,' she would say to him. Finally, she said to him, 'C'mon,

Dick and the Kotter Gang, 1976.
(Mark Carfagno)

Dick. I've given you all these sandwiches and you haven't hit any home runs. How about hitting a home run for me tonight?' She was a stern old woman who could be stubborn at times and Dick looked at her and said, 'Boy, you're serious, aren't you, Mrs. T.?' And she said, 'Yeah I'm serious. C'mon! Get your ass moving!' "[36]

That night, he hit two. After rounding the bases to a roaring standing ovation following the first one, he winked at the grounds crew huddled in the tunnel behind home plate. After the second one he just shrugged his shoulders as the crowd roared once more. This time, the 38,474 in attendance would not let the game continue until he took a curtain call. Home plate umpire Nick Colosi finally had to walk over to the Phillies' dugout and plead with him to acknowledge them. Taylor, along with Tommy Hutton, urged him on as well until, finally, he stepped out, doffed his cap, and bowed.[37] No one knew it at the time but it would be the last sustained cheer Dick would receive as an active player in Philadelphia.

One month later, in late July, Dick was involved a nasty collision with Pirates' pitcher John Candelaria on the base paths that led to a succession of events that ultimately released all the tension that had been building up. The day after the collision Dick phoned Ozark (from where it was not clear) complaining of dizziness and soreness around his face and chest. Ozark excused him from the game and told him to stay home. The day after that he failed to show as well, but nothing much was made of it even though he hadn't called beforehand. The next day he arrived at the stadium, hung around for three innings, then left without telling anyone. When he failed to show for the following day's game, temperatures began to rise although much effort was made to keep things in check. Carpenter and Owens pulled Ozark aside and chided him for being too lenient with Dick; he had to make some sort of show of authority or risk losing the entire clubhouse, they suggested. Ozark responded by calling a closed-door team meeting and, with Carpenter and Owens standing behind him, announced that Dick was AWOL, that he would be docked two days' pay, and that he would be fined on top of that.[38] The club then took off for New York, where, to everyone's surprise, they found Dick waiting for them at Shea Stadium. Dick met with Ozark and explained that he still didn't feel right but that he had been unable to call Ozark the previous few days because he was recuperating at his Perkasie farm, which didn't have a phone. He then went out to take batting practice. Ozark huddled with Owens while Dick hit and decided that even though Dick had yet to be examined by a doctor, the best thing to do would be to place him once more on the disabled list. He also rescinded the previously announced fines. "Dick is a proud man," said Ozark. "He'll play hurt but I don't think he ever wants to embarrass himself on a ball field." The conciliatory words and gesture didn't change things as far as Dick was concerned. "They said I left town," he told a reporter. "That I was missing . . . same old crap in Philly."[39]

He was scheduled to come off the disabled list on August 10. On that day he took batting practice, reported significant pain in his right shoulder, and told the club that notwithstanding his aversion to doctors (Hochman noted that he even resisted aspirin), he would be seeing an orthopedic specialist the following day.[40] Despite the parallels between what was now developing and what had occurred as his first tenure in Philadelphia wound down, both the club and the media remained determined to approach him differently now. "I'll listen to what the man has to say, when and if I see him," Ozark insisted whenever he was asked about his approach to Dick's absence, until Carpenter and Owens finally intervened.[41] "The man is seriously injured," Ozark added after he and Dick finally talked in New York. "That's why he didn't come to the park Thursday. He didn't feel he could play. He felt he couldn't help the club."[42] When Dick reported pain on the tenth, Ozark didn't question him. "I don't want him to have to go out and embarrass himself on the field. I want him to come back when he's physically ready and able to play."[43] Bruce Keidan, who had taken over the Phillies' beat at the *Inquirer* from Allen Lewis, likewise expressed faith in Dick's assessment of his condition. "That Allen was placed on the disabled list without the advice or consent of a doctor seems particularly revealing," he wrote. It was an indication not that Dick was faking it but, rather, that "the Phillies organization had enough faith in Allen, even after three days of trauma over his absence, to take him at his word." Keidan continued: "Such respect was not a gift that the Phillies bestowed upon Allen. It was something he had earned. He had earned it by playing the game of baseball, hurt and healthy, the way few men in the game's history have played it. He had earned it by clawing his way back from a disastrous 1975 season to become once more one of the game's most feared hitters. He had earned it with great base running, with hustle, with leadership by example."[44]

Finally, on September 4, Dick returned to the lineup. The Phils were skidding badly at the time, in the middle of an eight-game losing streak (and a 6–17 stretch that would whittle their seemingly insurmountable 15.5-game, late August lead to 3 games by September 17). Schmidt and Luzinski were slumping as well. Hoping to prime Dick to carry the club through the tough stretch, Carpenter reached out to him before his return and signed him to a formal contract, one that returned to Dick the 20 percent that Carpenter skimmed before the season opened.[45] On top of that, the contract granted Dick his longstanding wish to become, at the conclusion of the season, a free agent at last. "I'm happy and he's happy," said Carpenter of the signing. "We felt it would be a good idea to get him signed. We thought it would help him and help us." Carpenter believed that reaching out to Dick would send an important message to him. "We think he felt he wasn't a Phillie," he said.[46] Now, with a generous contract in hand, he would feel wanted at last, and victories would inevitably follow. It wouldn't be that simple.

Dick struggled in the season's final month, at one point going 3 for 40 as the club continued its slide. As the pressure mounted and the whispers of 1964 turned to roars, patience and compassion fell by the wayside. When Dick arrived only thirty minutes before a crucial game against the second-place Pirates, Hochman called him out for it. "People are looking for Allen to hit the ball every so often," he wrote as Dick was mired in his slump. "People are even looking for him to show up, horrors of horrors, at the ballpark on time." Dave Cash quickly shot back in Dick's defense: "What did he miss?" Cash wanted to know. "I got here around 4:30, played cards for two and a half hours, never touched a bat or a ball. The last half-hour, I do what I have to do to get mentally ready to play."[47] After Dick went 0 for 3 in the game, Ozark had had enough. He benched Dick for the following series in Chicago—he never left the dugout, even to pinch-hit. Ozark and Owens seemed to be on the verge of panicking. They held another closed-door meeting during a rain delay in Chicago in an attempt to turn things around. Dolson laid much of the blame for the team's collapse at Dick's feet: "They got him for a September pennant push, and here it is, September . . . a four-game lead . . . and they are not using him. If ever there was an admission that the Great Dick Allen Rehabilitation Program, Philadelphia Chapter, has failed, this is it." Dick was the calm in the middle of the storm. "He told me," Owens relayed after the closed-door meeting, " 'All we need is 95 wins.' He said, 'You tell me where the pressure is. We don't even have to play .500 [the rest of the way] to win.' "[48] The following night, when the club returned to Philadelphia to play the Cardinals, Ozark put him back in the lineup. He went 3 for 4, with two doubles and a homer in the Phils' victory over St. Louis. After the game he offered up all of six words to the throng that had encamped at his locker: "Excuse me, fellas, I've gotta go," and left them standing there in a slowly settling cloud of hair spray.[49]

Everything came to a head on the day the Phillies finally erased the ghost of 1964 and won the National League's Eastern Division title, sending them to the postseason for the first time since the days of the Whiz Kids. On a frigid afternoon in Montreal's Jarry Park, where the tensions of the previous few weeks ought to have given way at last to relief, controversy reigned once again. To be sure, there was celebration. But amid the spilled champagne were vitriol and finger-pointing. In later years, Ozark would claim that much of what happened never actually occurred and that the little that did was of such minor consequence that he had long since forgotten it. But all of it did in fact happen. And it was unlikely that he had forgotten any of it. And it brought Dick's second tour in Philadelphia to a close that echoed the tumultuous end of his first.

The seeds of what would become the final showdown between Dick and the Phillies were sown two months earlier, in July, when Dick sat down with *Philadelphia Tribune* reporter John Rhodes and presented him with a startling scoop. Still smarting from the pay cut Carpenter had subjected him to, Dick began by making it clear to Rhodes that all was not well between him and the club, at least as far as he was concerned. "The Phillies are the only club that I have been associated with that has given me problems about my money. They don't want to pay you what you're worth," he alleged, the 20 percent cut being only the most recent example of that. He then moved on to what would become the heart of the September controversy: "Tony [Taylor] is an unselfish person and a guy who puts team in front of himself. I remember when I was playing with the Phillies before and having a fantastic season. It was Tony who made it possible. He always encouraged me and suggested things that would help me. He used to get on second base and flash me the sign of what the pitcher was going to throw," Dick said with a laugh. "If we get to the playoffs, and I know we will . . . I think it's only right that a guy like Tony that gave so much should be there."[50] At last, here was the opportunity Dick was waiting for—the chance to do something nice for the person who had done so much for him and who asked almost nothing in return. Whatever leverage he had, he was determined to use it now to give his good friend a chance to play in a World Series before he retired.

Dick was aware of the explosiveness of his plan; he told Rhodes to sit on his scoop until things played out.[51] Rhodes did, and for the next two months only he and Dick were aware of what was awaiting Phillies' management the moment the club officially clinched the division. Two days before that happened, after the club had stopped its slide and regained enough of its lead to make the title all but inevitable, Dick sought Conlin out between games of a doubleheader. "You know," he told Conlin, "I never ask anything of myself. But I think you've got some good in you, even though you've ripped me pretty good over the years. I only ask one favor: Write something nice about Tony Taylor in the next week. I think it will mean a lot to him." He and Conlin then engaged in a discussion about Taylor wherein Dick dropped his bomb: "That man deserves the chance to be in the playoffs in a Phillies uniform after what he's contributed to this club over the years. . . . If Tony Taylor is made ineligible after we win the division I won't play in the playoffs or World Series. As sure as God made me and guides my hand I won't play if they take him off for the playoffs. Let them take me off it if it comes down to a choice."[52]

Upon hearing the news, Owens called Dick's bluff: "[N]obody will make any decisions for us. Hell, we just might keep Tony and the pitcher [either Wayne Twitchell or Ron Schueler] and take him off." As a baseball move, activating Taylor made little sense—he spent two-thirds of the season on the inactive list, played in only 26 games during the season (all as a pinch hitter with the exception of two innings at third base), and was essentially an extra coach on the bench. But to Dick, this had nothing to do with baseball. Owens could only shake his head at the development. "One minute Dick Allen can be the most likeable person around and the kind of guy you'd want on your ball club, rather, love to have on your ball club. And a minute later, well . . ."[53]

On the day the club officially clinched, word filtered down to Dick that Taylor would not, after all, be added to the postseason roster. The Phils were scheduled to play the Expos in a Sunday doubleheader and needed to win only one of the two games that afternoon to wrap things up. They took care of that in the first game and celebrated their championship in the cramped Jarry Park locker room. Dick declined to join them, choosing instead to remain on the frosty bench accompanied only by his thoughts.[54] As the celebration wound down and the bench players and September call-ups prepared to take the field for what was now the meaningless second game, Dick finally entered the locker room. He, Cash,

Bobby Tolan, Garry Maddox, and Mike Schmidt then repaired to a small broom closet where they held a private celebration.[55] Maddox later claimed that it was a prayer session wherein they thanked God for the division title they had just won; Dick insisted that they privately toasted the season and their good fortune with champagne; some within the media gossiped among themselves that there were stronger substances involved (although there was no hard evidence and those allegations never made their way into print).[56] Regardless, once again, the optics were bad: other than September call-up Freddie Andrews (who was on the field during the second game), Ollie Brown (who had assumed that he was starting game two as well), and Taylor, every black player on the squad, along with Schmidt, was in the broom closet. Ozark, his denials in later years notwithstanding, was livid. "I don't even know if I should make this public," he said a couple of days after the clincher, "but the only guy on the bench for the second game was Freddie Andrews and he was playing. I don't know if it's some kind of black thing developing or what."[57]

Immediately after the game, two flights left Montreal's Dorval Airport with members of the Phillies' contingent aboard: one on its way to St. Louis, where the club was scheduled to play the Cardinals, and another back to Philadelphia, where some front-office personnel were dispatched to begin preparations for the postseason. "Bill Giles was still vice president in charge of fun and games," Conlin recalled. "He had to hurry back to Philly to get the Vet ready for the playoffs. He was on a Delta flight from Dorval to Philly. [Giles] settled into his first-class seat, looked across the aisle, and there was Dick Allen. 'They didn't need me the second game, so I decided to go back to Philly and celebrate with my family. I'll fly to St. Louis in the morning.' He had not informed Danny Ozark or Owens, of course."[58] Both men were made aware that Dick was not on their plane headed to St. Louis only once they themselves were on it. In an attempt to stave off yet another face-off with his first baseman, Ozark thought quickly and granted Dick leave from the club in absentia.[59]

Back in Philadelphia, Dick busied himself by taking batting practice while the rest of the club took on the Cardinals. When asked, he said that he returned to Philadelphia so that he could celebrate the division title back home in Perkasie with his family. He also claimed that he had not slipped out of Montreal without notice as he told Carpenter's younger brother, Keith, that his shoulder was bothering him and that he was headed home.[60] Relief pitcher Tug McGraw was beside himself when Dick's words were relayed to him. "He makes $250,000 a year," McGraw said. "If he was so hot to celebrate the championship with his family, he should have flown them to St. Louis."[61] Broadcaster Rich Ashburn tried to make sense of it all, without much luck. "Allen did communicate with one club official in the middle of the season," he wrote in his *Evening Bulletin* column, "that 'When we win 95 games, my job is over.' Allen has been saying right along that 95 wins would win the title and ironically the title game was the 95th win. Allen became a prophet without honor, though, when he came back to Philadelphia."[62]

In the days leading up to the club's League Championship Series against Pete Rose and the Cincinnati Reds, infighting among the players and management dominated the local dailies. During a contentious team meeting in St. Louis, presided over by Ozark, several black players challenged Ozark's managerial moves, particularly the one he made in the second game of the Montreal doubleheader when he sat black outfielder Ollie Brown in favor of white rookie Jerry Martin. Dick had come to the conclusion that the Phillies "were working a quota" when it came to their black players and now others were wondering if in fact he was on to something.[63] "Ollie knows why he wasn't in the lineup," a frustrated Ozark replied, a nod to the fact that Brown had been struggling with the bat for the previous month.[64] The answer did little to satisfy the doubters. Some of the white players voiced their displeasure with how things were going as well, aiming most of their ire toward Dick and his decision to return to Perkasie after the clincher rather than accompany the rest of the team to St. Louis. The Broom Closet Incident was also rehashed, with McGraw remarking that "some of us white guys looked around Sunday and wondered where the black guys were."[65] Maddox was incensed by what he thought the comment implied. "That's when my head turned," Maddox said after the meeting. "He said that and I turned and looked at him. . . . The black guys on the team, none of them have come out and said anything racial. But then to have something said like that. 'Some of the white guys were wondering.' A couple of years ago, everyone was pulling for everyone." He continued: "Either we had great unity on this team all year or it's been a great acting job by the players keeping their feelings inside. You may think a guy's thinking something about you, you may think he's prejudiced, you may think he doesn't like you, but you never know until he tells you. Now when all the racial stuff starts coming out, when guys start to say how they actually feel, then you know how it is . . . I signed a five-year contract with this team. Five years. I'll tell you, I hope I didn't make a mistake."[66] The quarreling did not escape the national media; on the eve of the series against the Reds, *Sports Illustrated* cited the dissension as a primary factor in its prediction: "An angry team can be a winning team, as the A's have proved. Or it can come apart, as hundreds of other angry teams have in the past. Chances are the Phillies are not as resilient as the roustabout A's. . . . In the battle of Big Red Machines, pick Cincinnati to win in four."[67]

Carpenter realized as much himself; he understood that if the Phils were to have any chance in the series, he'd have to calm the waters beforehand. He also needed a fully engaged Dick Allen. "Hank Aaron has been more consistent and used his talent better," opined David Condon in the *Chicago Tribune*, whose writers were taking in the drama from afar. "The late Roberto Clemente certainly was greater all-around. Bush leaguers have had more class. Yet since the heydays of Ted Williams and Mickey Mantle, baseball has not seen the electric voltage that Dick Allen can generate merely by going to bat. He is master of the trick of rising to the occasion."[68] All of this explained why, once again, Carpenter took off for Perkasie to sit down with Dick one last time. Finally he was able to come away with an agreement—"The Perkasie Compromise"—wherein the Phils agreed to designate Taylor a coach in uniform for the series and Dick agreed to return to the club to finish out the season and participate in the playoffs. Dick acceded to this, stating that so long as Taylor was in uniform for the postseason that was fine with him. Not satisfied with what he had achieved, Carpenter then muddied things by releasing a statement announcing that not only had détente been reached but Dick had essentially acknowledged that most of the blame for the club's recent problems resided with him: "Phillies President Ruly Carpenter met with Dick Allen on his farm this afternoon and announced that everything has been straightened out. Allen apologized for any problems which he may have created."[69] Dick followed up by correcting the record. "I didn't apologize to anyone," he said, "and there was no need for [an apology]. I think Ruly was being a little unfair in his statement."[70] Regardless, he took the field the following night for the season's final series against the Mets. The Veterans Stadium crowd booed him as soon as he stepped out of the dugout.[71]

Although he was once again back in the fold, the chatter did not dissipate—the papers were jam-packed with articles focused on Dick as well as the racial divide that was seemingly tearing the ball club apart. Until this moment the Phils appeared to have come so far from the era of suspicion that dominated the franchise for decades and that underlay the Tony Curry incident. They had escaped Connie Mack Stadium and the racial tensions that enveloped that neighborhood; they had transitioned from Bob to Ruly Carpenter and, in so doing, had seemingly severed ties with the era that saw the franchise hold out until the last moment in signing black talent and the confusion that reigned once it finally had; they had an exciting, young ball club on the field that was led by the swaggering Dave Cash and his "Yes We Can" mantra, which very quickly permeated what had been for so long a skeptical city. They had done all this and had won a divisional title to boot. And now things suddenly seemed to be as they had always been.

Maddox, a Vietnam War veteran, painted the issue with a broader brush during the season's final days: "I've seen race trouble happen. In Vietnam, of all places, we had racial trouble . . . I'm telling you, you have to watch what you say around people . . . I guess people were looking for it all along," he added, "because it had been there in the past."[72] The past was past. But there was no way to prevent it from providing the context for the present. Whether there was, in fact, a racial problem on the club was, in many ways, beside the point. Context was everything and, given all that had taken place before, that context couldn't be changed simply by moving to a new ballpark or by transferring the reins of ownership from father to son. If it wasn't impossible to wipe the slate clean, the turmoil of the season's final days illustrated the reality that doing so was at least going to take far longer than the six years that separated Dick's departure from his return.

The League Championship Series, much anticipated throughout the city all summer long, became an aborted, desultory affair. Before the first game, Dick told Ray Kelly that Era would not be attending the series. "She's too upset," he explained. "She doesn't want to sit in the stands and

Dick flies out against the Reds on October 12, 1976 in game three
of the 1976 League Championship Series—his last as a Phillie.
(National Baseball Hall of Fame and Museum, Inc.)

listen to the things the fans say or watch them throw things at me—or the
obscenities."[73] After the Phils dropped the first game, Dick dressed down
the crowd of reporters surrounding his locker: "I don't think enough of the
truth is told here. The city itself doesn't know how to tell the truth about
things. When I say the city I mean the press because they control it. . . .
There's a difference between what is said and what is so."[74] The series ended
in a three-game sweep that was not without its own drama—Cash and
Schmidt refused to take pregame infield practice throughout the series in
their attempt to divert the media's attention from Dick.[75] No matter, the
media horde descended upon him nevertheless. The inevitable contrast
between Dick and Pete Rose was made more than once as well, with Dolson
writing that Rose was "thoroughly professional" and remarking that Dick
could learn a few things from him. "The champions," he wrote, "are doing

it Pete Rose's way. The challengers, sadly, seem to be doing it Dick Allen's way."[76]

The final out of the series would mark the end of Dick's second tour of Philadelphia. After being replaced defensively in the bottom of the eighth in the final game, Dick took off down the tunnel, showered, changed, and was gone before the Reds had even begun their on-field celebration.[77] After the game, Owens made it all but official. "I'm out to improve the ball club," he told reporters. "And one of the areas I'd like to improve is first base."[78]

"Pax vobiscum," wrote Conlin the following morning to the man who was once more on the move.[79] Peace be with you.

Chapter 15

Free Agent

1977: Oakland .240/5/31

THE PROSPECT OF free agency thrilled Dick. At last, after a career spent seeking ways to gain a modicum of leverage in a system designed to prevent even a sliver of it from trickling down to the players, now came true clout: the ability to walk away from an unfavorable situation at the completion of a contract and negotiate freely for more favorable terms in a new location. With the advent of free agency came a new way to measure a player's value: Dick's way. Under the terms of the 1976 Collective Bargaining Agreement, once a player completed six years in the majors, his level of productivity would determine the value of his next contract rather than his years of service. Free agency also normalized the presence of player agents in the negotiating process. Agents had been slowly infiltrating the game in Clem Capozzoli's wake over the previous several seasons but now, with complex multiyear, multiteam negotiations taking place, few players would risk entering into them without a representative. So much that seemed blasphemous in baseball only a decade earlier had by now come to pass. Dick's view of the business of baseball, previously marginalized and criticized as outrageous and dangerous, was the new reality. In so many ways, Dick was born to be a free agent.

Still, even as a free agent, Dick was determined to do it his own way. Rather than declare by the November 1 deadline, as all of the other players with expired contracts had done, Dick chose instead to orally petition the Players Association for his freedom, which was his right under the new Basic Agreement, provided he did so within three days of the deadline.[1] By so doing, he opted out of the game's first free agent draft, held in November, and instead became the main (and only) attraction of a special one-man draft to be held at the general managers' annual meeting in December—a solitary draft for a solitary man.[2]

Under the free agency rules in place at the time, Dick would be compelled to negotiate with only the clubs that "drafted" him; however, if fewer than two clubs put in a claim, he'd be free to negotiate with any club he desired. On the day of his draft, one club after another passed on the opportunity to claim him. "Aren't there any receptions?" a frustrated Paul Owens wanted to know. (The Phils would receive compensation for Dick if two or more clubs drafted him; none if fewer than two did.)[3] Finally Charlie Finley of the Oakland A's (who was present at the meeting because he was also the club's GM) put in a claim. While it might have seemed odd that Finley, who detested free agency more than anyone, would draft him, Finley had few viable options other than Dick when it came to replacing the boatload of talent that, now with the opportunity to be free of the tyrannical owner/GM, had just departed. Finley drafted twenty-four free agents in the November draft, but most of them had no interest in even speaking with him.[4] Dick, who appeared to have no other alternatives, could be had and had cheaply.

Now free to negotiate with anyone he desired for the first time since he signed with the Phils in 1960, Dick felt around for other offers, hoping to increase his leverage with Finley. He found no takers. "I don't want a Dick Allen on our club," said the Angels' owner, Gene Autry. "Allen would hurt us more than he would help us. I think he hurt the White Sox. And he probably hurt the Phillies in the playoff."[5] Peter Bavasi, general manager of the expansion Toronto Blue Jays, concurred: "At this time I think we would have little interest in Richie Allen for our club next year. From what we know about Dick Allen's contributions to the clubs he's played for, we're not interested in going in that direction with our club." The expansion Seattle Mariners also demurred.[6]

Dave Cash, who exercised his free agency rights after the season and signed with the Montreal Expos a few weeks later, tried to drum up interest by encouraging his new club to pursue Dick: "This man is an asset to any club. I know because I played with him."[7] Still, the Expos begged off. "I've always liked the guy," said Herman Franks, the former Giants' manager who provided refuge to Dick in the Giants' locker room during his 1968 sit-down strike and who grew fond of him in the process. Franks had just been hired to manage the Cubs for the 1977 season and encouraged Cubs' management to at least talk to him. He met a wall of resistance. "I brought up Allen's name at the club meetings last month," he said in late December, "but got pretty much a negative reaction. Everybody wants to know what made me think I could handle Allen when nobody else could."[8] Perhaps, suggested *Chicago Tribune* reporter Rick Talley, "the Cubs and Sox should work out a deal. Maybe Allen could be hired by both clubs to play only home games. Then he wouldn't have to travel [and thus couldn't miss any buses], and when he wasn't playing baseball, he could be within short distance of a racetrack—now that Chicago has year-round thoroughbred racing."[9] By the arrival of the new year, it was apparent that there would not be a competitive market for Dick Allen's services in 1977. He had tumbled so hard that his only option was someone who was as much of an outcast as he had now become.

Even before he was officially on the market, and as he had said on more than one occasion, Dick made it clear to anyone listening where he wanted his next home to be: "I would like to play on the West Coast next year," he told John Rhodes of the *Philadelphia Tribune* back in July.[10] And though the A's, run by the notoriously penny-pinching Charlie Finley (and whose run-ins with Reggie Jackson and Vida Blue were well-known to Dick), seemed like a dubious destination, Dick had a few reasons for being attracted to the club. First was the aura the A's of the early and mid-1970s exuded. Dick had long fantasized of hitting in a lineup the likes of the one the 1972–74 World Series champions put together, with stars such as Sal Bando, Jackson, and Joe Rudi batting back-to-back-to-back, one that would allow him at last to become simply another man in the batting order rather than the focal point. Now the birth of free agency gave him his chance. True, Jackson had been traded to Baltimore by the 1976 season but Rudi and Bando were still on the club's roster, along with Blue, Rollie Fingers, and enough complementary talent to enable the A's to win 87 games and finish second to the Royals, only 2.5 games short of their sixth consecutive Western Division title.

The club's seemingly more permissive atmosphere was attractive to Dick as well. In 1972 Reggie Jackson refused to shave his mustache, and rather than fight Jackson, Finley embraced his defiance as an opportunity for publicity, offering bonuses to any of his players who wanted to grow mustaches themselves.[11] (By doing so, Jackson is often given credit for becoming the first ballplayer to sport facial hair during the regular season in the modern era, but in fact Dick wore a mustache during a portion of the 1970 season with the Cardinals.) The result was facial hair of all varieties on the great A's clubs, lending them a panache that the rest of the staid baseball establishment sorely lacked. Combined with their colorful, mix-and-match uniforms and white shoes, the A's radiated a style that spoke to Dick's sense of fashion. And then there was Finley himself. Perhaps embracing the theory that the enemy of his enemies had to be his friend, Dick believed that he could relate to the rebellious Finley, who fought with other owners and who had been a thorn in Commissioner Bowie Kuhn's side for years. Everyone said that Finley was cheap, but to Dick this was of little matter; he considered every owner he had ever played for to have been cheap. How much worse could Finley really be?

A lot, as it turned out. A control freak to an extreme Dick had yet to experience, an autocrat whose diminishing influence only increased his thirst for power, Finley had become, particularly since a heart attack in 1974, a player's worst nightmare. Sal Bando recalled a man who liked to demonstrate just how ruthlessly he could treat his employees. "What he liked to do, and I know he did it with people like me," Bando remembered, was to "call me into his office [in Chicago], and then he would call someone and put them on the speakerphone, and then he would just crucify them. And you had to sit there and listen to him demean [them]."[12] For years he mixed his nasty side with one that could be exceedingly generous, but he was becoming more spiteful to those within his orbit with increasing frequency. Even his fellow owners, spendthrifts as they were, considered Finley to be a problem, said MLB's attorney Lou

A mustachioed Dick Allen with teammate and future Phillies' and Cardinals'
executive Lee Thomas in St. Petersburg, Florida, March 13, 1970. Dick would
keep the mustache and muttonchops for much of the season.
(The Cardinals would not keep Thomas beyond spring training.)

(© 2014 Legendaryauctions.com)

Hoynes, because of how he "squeezed the players unmercifully."[13] Not all of his players hated him, but his supporters in the clubhouse dwindled as the great A's dynasty was dismantled in the mid-1970s. "My relationship was great with him. I liked him a lot," said Johnstone, who played for Finley after Stu Holcomb released him during spring training 1973 and before Finley's heart attack. "He was innovative. Look at the different things he tried to bring to baseball: colored shoes, different colored uniforms, an orange ball for night games. He did a lot of crazy things. But a lot of them stuck." When it came to financial matters, however, Finley was a different person. "He was stingy with his money," Johnstone recalled. "What he'd tell you was, 'I'm not gonna give you a raise but if you give me five grand I'll make twenty-five for you in the stock market.' He made Dick Green [a lot of money] over a three-year period that way. But he wouldn't give you a raise."[14]

By 1976 Finley was in an all-out war with seemingly everyone in baseball. He despised his fellow owners, complaining that "the stupidity of the owners" was ruining the game: "In the end, the rich clubs will end up controlling baseball. . . . Some owners ask me where we are headed. I say to them, 'To the crapper.'"[15] He sued Bowie Kuhn for voiding his sale of Blue, Fingers, and Rudi for $3.5 million cash during the 1976 season (but succeeded in selling off his manager, Chuck Tanner, to the Pirates in exchange for catcher Manny Sanguillen and $100,000 in November). And he was becoming more embittered seemingly by the hour. Free agency threw the A's into chaos. Those players who could (and who were not sold off first) were determined to jump ship at the first opportunity and Finley was racing to beat them to it, hoping to at least get a little cash back in the process. Everybody wanted out of Oakland. Except Dick, who couldn't wait to get there.

In the aftermath of the November draft, Finley's pettiness and vindictiveness were on full display when he put in a claim for rarely used free agent Paul Dade and then refused to negotiate with him. As Dade had also been selected by the Cleveland Indians, Finley's claim became the second (and only other), thereby stripping Dade of his ability to negotiate with all twenty-six clubs. In the process, Dade's bargaining leverage became nonexistent and threatened his ability to catch on with a club for the 1977 season. "I'm running out of money," Dade said as he watched his fellow free agents shop bids while he sat on the sidelines. "I didn't play winter ball because I didn't want to take a chance on getting hurt. . . . It's a sorry Christmas for my wife and two kids." Finley's claim was clearly bogus and Marvin Miller tried to pressure American League president Lee McPhail to convince Finley to withdraw his phony bid, to no avail.[16] Lacking options, Dade eventually signed with the Indians.

Now Finley set his sights on Dick—another player without any leverage—and few could imagine the relationship lasting long or ending well. "I find Dick Allen to be very charming," Finley said in February 1977. As Dick continued to sniff out competitors for his services (for a short time, new White Sox owner Bill Veeck expressed mild interest but only if Dick would agree to be a designated hitter), Finley waited him out. "I'm hopeful and optimistic that we'll sign him," he added. "We spent three-and-a-half hours together last Saturday in my apartment. He loved my homemade chili." He insisted that "I won't have two sets of rules" for him but then backed off, allowing that he wouldn't mind if Dick chose to forego batting practice. "My only rule is that you arrive at the ballpark on time."[17]

Once the calendar turned to March, Finley grew impatient. "There's an old song, sittin' all alone by the telephone waitin' for it to ring," he told reporters from the A's spring training base in Mesa, Arizona. "Well, I'm sure as hell not waiting any longer. I couldn't care less where he is."[18] A week later Dick arrived in Mesa and pronounced himself fit to grind out one more season. Without any competing offers, Dick had no choice but to submit to Finley's bargain basement salary offer—$150,000 for one year.[19] This time, there was almost no chance that he'd see that supplemented later on. He tried to look on the bright side: "I thank God I have a job in baseball," he said the day after his arrival. "At my age (35), I have only one goal—to love Jesus Christ in my heart and to have fun. When the fun goes, I go."[20] As for whether there'd be fireworks between him and Finley, Dick demurred. "I anticipate no trouble whatsoever with the A's, certainly not on my part."[21]

While the balance of power had now clearly tilted against him, he took pains to insist otherwise. "I didn't go hunting for this job," he declared. "There were several other offers but I decided this is where I wanted to be."[22] This was a big moment in his life, something he'd dreamed about for years, and he refused to let the realities of the situation get in the way. "[T]his was the first time since I was 17 that I was able to go somewhere as a free man," he told Talley of the *Tribune*. "This was my choice." That he had to take a substantial pay cut was something he refused to let blemish the occasion. "I'm not all that excited over money," he said. Still, the diminished market for his talents stung him and he indicated that he wasn't looking forward to enduring another humiliating off-season: "Once I thought I'd like to stay in the game until I was 40. But this may be it. I don't have the same enthusiasm for baseball I once did."[23]

Things started off well enough. Dick arrived early for spring training workouts and expressed excitement over the prospect of helping the A's return to prominence. It would be a tough haul: so many players had now departed that the 15 home runs Dick hit in 1976 (in only 85 games) nearly matched the 18 the current entire A's roster hit that season. Finley pronounced himself capable of working with him. "Dick Allen just wants to be treated like a man," he said in late March. "Treat him with respect and he'll treat you with respect." At least one Oakland writer snickered at Finley's mention of the word "respect": "[A]t times [Finley] has been accused of doing exactly the opposite by Reggie Jackson and Vida Blue."[24] Very quickly, things deteriorated as turmoil reigned. Nearly every day during spring training it seemed as if a horde of players had departed and was replaced by a new group of anonymous faces. The turnover was so great that Dick considered walking away from it all before the season's first game but decided to stick it out to see if things would settle down.[25] They wouldn't. By the time the squad lined up for the team photo, only six players from the 1976 club remained. Dick was one of the multitude of new faces. But not for long.

*　*　*

When negotiating his contract with Finley, Dick was able to wrangle at least one concession: he would never have to DH. Finley hesitated before agreeing to the stipulation but eventually granted the request; after all, it wasn't something that was going to cost him any money.[26] Finley neglected to inform manager Jack McKeon of the agreement, however,

Oakland, 1977—the end of the road.

(Oakland Athletics)

which brought on the season's first showdown between Dick and his manager. That Finley left McKeon out of the loop was not unusual; McKeon wasn't informed that pitcher Mike Torrez had been dealt to the Orioles until Torrez himself informed him. It took only three games into the regular season for Dick and McKeon to clash. Before the second game of a doubleheader, McKeon penciled Dick in at the DH spot. He then brought the lineup card out to the umpires to make it official. Once Dick found out he set McKeon straight. "No way," he said to him. "I'm not a DH. I play first base or I don't play."[27] He didn't play. Jerry Tabb pinch-hit for him in the bottom of the first and Dick spent the game on the bench. "I didn't know he didn't like it," McKeon said afterward. "Now I know."[28]

By early May the A's, and Dick, were surprising the doubters. The club was above .500 and Dick was hitting .303 with 4 homers and 23 RBIs. Yet things were unraveling. Players continued to come and go—on the roster and, apparently, during the games as well. McKeon ran a loose ship, perhaps out of necessity: at times he was penciling as many as six rookies into his starting lineup and it was all he could do to simply corral the players on the field. In the clubhouse and in the dugout, the players policed themselves and quickly proved incapable of doing so. One umpire filed a report with the league after working an A's game, complaining that the bench players were traipsing around the vast foul territory at the Oakland Alameda Coliseum and conversing with fans while the game was taking place; other players retreated into the clubhouse during the games to listen to the radio and drink beer.[29]

McKeon's fate was sealed during a late May game in Toronto when he pulled Dick off the field for defensive purposes in the tenth inning. After the A's took the lead in the top of the inning, McKeon told Earl Williams to replace Dick at first in the bottom of the frame. He neglected to tell Dick, though. When Dick ran on the field and found Williams there, he exploded. He found the act of publicly slinking off the field after having taken it embarrassing and yelled at McKeon to "find someone else to play there the rest of the year" as he exited. At that point, Finley became convinced that McKeon had to go; though the A's were still flirting with the .500 mark, Finley began searching for his replacement. Two weeks later he found him in Giants' third base coach Bobby Winkles. He then fired

Safe at home, 1977. At least for the moment.
(Oakland Athletics)

McKeon and installed Winkles at the helm. As his first official act as the new A's skipper, Winkles sat down to hash things out with Dick.[30]

Ten days later, the explosion everyone had expected finally came. The A's struggled after the managerial change, losing seven of their first nine games under Winkles's command. When the club landed in Chicago to take on the White Sox, Finley (who still operated out of Chicago even though his A's played half a continent away) decided to check in on them. After the club lost the first three games of the four-game series, Finley edged a little closer so he could see for himself what was going on. During the sixth inning of the fourth game, he went into the clubhouse to use the bathroom and found Dick inside, taking a shower. Finley was enraged. He ran out to the dugout, called Winkles back to witness what he had just seen, and then, after the game, suspended Dick for a week. "I've been going along with Allen and trying to show the world I can work with him," he said in a fury to reporters after the game. "But I found out I'm just like the rest of the suckers. I don't care if he never shows up again." Dick was not on hand for the announcement—he left the park after his shower (and without ever speaking to Finley), in the eighth inning.[31]

Dick couldn't understand what all the fuss was about. He had approached Winkles before the game and asked to be platooned from there on out—his shoulder was still bothering him and he had recently completed a three-day resting period where he was not required to be with the club.[32] He had played a few times since then but was under the impression that when he wasn't playing he was free to come and go as he pleased. Later he provided his take on the incident: "In the seventh inning [sic] Winkles said 'Do you want to hit?' I said, 'No, I don't *want* to hit but I will.' He said, 'We'll save you for later.' We had a big lead [6–1] and in the eighth inning the lead was bigger [7–1] so I took a shower. Charlie came through the clubhouse and saw me and waved and gave me the power sign. The next morning I was talking to my brother on the phone and as we were talking he heard on the radio that I'm suspended."[33]

The following day Finley met with Dick in Milwaukee and asked him to remain with the club during his suspension so he could work out with his teammates.[34] Dick returned to Perkasie instead. A week later, when his suspension was up, Dick stayed away. Finley tried to contact him through a telegram, through Era and Hank, to no avail. "I told him in the telegram if he didn't report, he would remain on the disqualified list and would not receive any pay until he was ready to play," Finley said.[35] Dick never responded to the telegram, and both Era and Hank insisted that they hadn't seen him since he had been suspended.[36] For a time Dick considered rejoining the club but "well . . . I just couldn't come back. A lot of things had been happening. They'd just fired the manager, Jack McKeon, and Bobby Winkles had been on the job only a few days. Some guy called me a bastard by the dugout that night in Chicago. Maybe I took it too personal."[37] Things were closing in on him again—the insults, the pressure, the persistent pain in his shoulder. His average had dipped to .240 and his power disappeared after his hot start—he hit only one home run after early May. So he walked away.

After two weeks of silence, Dick finally called Finley and asked that his lost pay be reinstated. Finley refused.[38] In the interim, Herman Franks reached out once more and expressed interest in obtaining him from

Finley. "I don't care what other people say about this guy," Franks said. "I think he'll play for me and I think he'd be a good man on our club."[39] Nothing came of it so Dick finally sent Finley a letter announcing that he was "retiring from baseball for the rest of 1977."[40] He also stated that he might want to play in Japan in 1978 and asked Finley how that could be arranged. From Philadelphia, a bemused Conlin pondered the spectacle of Dick Allen in Japan: "Wouldn't you give a case of saki [sic] to watch No. 15 go through a Japanese spring training[?] Dave Johnson [current Phil and former second baseman for the Yomiuri Giants] says the daily workout over there makes Marine boot camp look like a finishing school for debutantes. . . . Long mandatory workouts are held on open dates. And the press? One Tokyo daily recently did a 30-part series on Sadaharu Oh, the legendary slugger who will soon surpass Hank Aaron's world record for career home runs."[41] Dick decided not to pursue the possibility.

*　*　*

Dick enjoyed his time away from baseball, choosing to spend it with his family. "I hadn't been around in 12 years," he said the following spring. "I gave my brother a hand, put up some hay, stayed fit, visited my mother."[42] The A's, meanwhile, tanked, finishing last, behind even the expansion Seattle Mariners. At the box office things were, if anything, worse—the club drew a league-worst 495,578 fans. After the season Finley attempted to trade his last remaining star, Vida Blue, to the Reds for minor league first baseman Dave Revering and $1.75 million.[43] Everything was now closing in on Finley as well—his heart problems persisted, his marriage was falling apart, and his insurance business was crumbling.[44] On top of all this, Kuhn voided this sale as he had several of Finley's earlier ones. Needing the money to keep the A's afloat, Finley insisted that Revering was not irrelevant to the deal, that it was *not* merely a sale of Vida Blue for $1.75 million. He insisted that Revering was going to be his first baseman in 1978. After Kuhn voided the sale, Finley and the Reds restructured the deal, replacing Blue with relief pitcher Doug Bair and reducing the cash payment to just under the $400,000 limit Kuhn had set with regard to deals involving players and cash (in March Finley finally succeeded in trading Blue, this time to the Giants). Revering was now the property of the A's and Finley was going to make sure that Bobby Winkles wouldn't make a liar out of him—Revering, who had yet to make his major league debut, was going to play first base for the A's in 1978.[45]

Heading into the 1978 season the A's seemed intent on making the 1977 squad look downright professional by comparison. Finley dropped the club's longtime radio outlet and opted instead to have the team's games broadcast on KALX, a ten-watt college station operated out of Cal-Berkeley. The signal was so weak that most fans were unable to pick it up at night. He released all of the club's full-time scouts as well as its minor league hitting and pitching instructors. He reduced the major league squad's coaching staff to four (other teams employed five or six). He instructed his front-office staff to make no long-distance calls unless the charges could be reversed. And he hired a teenager, Stanley Burrell, to do odd jobs for him in the front office, eventually giving him the (honorary) title of vice president and insisting that he join the broadcast team in the booth.[46] (Burrell later gained fame as MC Hammer—Finley provided him with his nickname by pointing out to him that he resembled a young "Hammerin' Hank" Aaron.)

Meanwhile, Dick was once more starting to get the itch to play. He just didn't want to endure another season in the chaos that was Finley's A's. "There's no place I'd rather end my career than in Chicago," he said in March. "Who've they got over there?" On the Cubs, Bill Buckner, Larry Biittner, and Dave Kingman were three first base alternatives that rendered their pursuit of him pointless. On the Sox, Lamar Johnson, Ron Blomberg, and Mike Squires likewise quashed any further deliberations concerning his return. Still, he held out hope: "Would it be tampering if I talked to them?" In the *Tribune*, Richard Dozer stated the obvious: "Allen was starting to sound like a man grasping at the last threads of a shredded career—trying somehow to turn something from his past into his future."[47] If his options were limited heading into the 1977 season, they were virtually nonexistent as he pondered the prospect of playing in 1978.

Finding no other takers, Dick turned up without advance notice in Mesa once again. "I come here to play ball," he explained to the astonished media assemblage who thought they had seen it all, having covered Finley's A's for the previous several years. "I didn't retire. You don't retire until you're 65." As for his status with the A's, Dick confirmed that it was, to put it mildly, up in the air. "I haven't seen a contract," he admitted. Still, he decided to show up anyway. "It never really was a thing of decision, the spring training dates are there, if you want to play ball, you either show up or you don't. I showed up." He was adamant about where he thought he fit in with the 1978 club: "I want to be the first baseman."[48] With Revering in camp, that was not going to happen.

The A's did not exactly welcome him back with open arms. His old locker was empty, and when Dick asked the equipment man "if an old-timer can get a pair of pants," he was issued hand-me-downs. "[S]econd-hand pants, second-hand shirt, no glove, no shoes," he remarked. "[S]ee, they're hinting." The equipment man made things a bit more comfortable for Dick by sewing "Wampum" onto the back of his jersey and issuing him number 60 (as he had in 1977) to commemorate his hometown and year of graduation from high school, but that was about as far as anyone within the organization was willing to go. Dick was not put off by the less than royal treatment, convinced, as always, that his talent and experience would win out in the end. Revering, he believed, didn't know what he was up against. "A price is paid to get to the top," he said. "Sometimes a young rookie don't know what it is to pay that price."[49]

As for whether he and Finley could coexist after what had happened the previous summer, Dick professed confidence that they could. "I like [Finley] a lot," he insisted. "I have the same respect for him I had before." It was an open question as to what he meant by that. Regardless, he said that he was in a mood to forgive Finley for his transgressions. "He's a baseball man. Flesh is weak. Everybody's going to make some mistakes. You look at the baseball man and the businessman and you have to separate the two." He also maintained that he didn't believe anyone should have been surprised at his return: "Why would they be surprised? That old fella never had any intention of leaving. Really, there's been no reaction here. . . . They could care less about Dick Allen or anybody else, they just want to get into shape." Then he turned the tables on the reporters gathered around him (he still enjoyed playing games with the press and would only talk to those who followed his ground rules for the day—on some days they could take notes but not record him, on others they could record him but not take notes): "I'd like to ask you guys a question.

From 1970 to now, what has it been that Dick Allen has done to cause controversy?"[50]

He pressed on: "They're talking DH for me, but I want to play. These legs are good. I want to use them."[51] After being informed that Winkles was committed to Revering at first base, he softened a bit. "I guess I'm 36, gee whiz, he's (Revering) capable of playing first base and the good Lord has let me have some fun. Maybe it's time to move aside and let another guy have fun." As he talked about fun they continued to press him on his contractual situation. He sighed. "God put me here to play ball, and I'd like to do so. Everything's a legality." Finally he left them with this: "I'm not trying to explain anything because bygones are bygones. The truth is in the end, not the beginning."[52]

Two weeks later, and without ever making it into a spring training game, the A's released him.[53]

The long journey was finally over. Dick Allen, "[a] marvelous physical specimen," lamented the *New Pittsburgh Courier*, "who possessed the strength of Paul Bunyan, the quickness and grace of a panther, and the demeanor of a king," was finished.[54] A king with a court no more.

Epilogue

His Way

"BASEBALL QUIT ON me, I didn't quit on baseball," Dick wrote in his autobiography, *Crash*.[1] Regardless, it was over. He would continue to make headlines now and then throughout his retirement, a significant portion of the baseball public still fascinated by one of the game's most enduring enigmas. In 1979 his home on the Perkasie farm burned to the ground. Although Dick, Barbara, and their three children were sleeping in it at the time, all escaped unharmed. There was no insurance and the house had been reduced to smoking rubble (there was a delay in notifying the fire company as Barbara had to run to a neighboring barn to make the call; there still hadn't been a phone installed at the house), but Dick considered 1979 to have been a good year nonetheless.[2] "[M]y kids walked out, I walked out—nothing was lost. It was a very good year."[3]

In 1982, after divorcing Barbara the previous year, Dick returned to baseball, this time as a spring training hitting instructor with the Texas Rangers. He was hired by Eddie Robinson, who had moved on from the Braves and was finally able to convince Dick to work for him. Asked what advice he'd give to the Rangers' hitters, Dick replied, "nothin'." He added, "Hey, I'm new around here. I'm not going to crowd anybody. I'm not taking up anybody's space. They want to talk, I'll talk. But I ain't rushing into anything."[4] In his new role he offered up the kind of wisdom he would have appreciated in his playing days: "Whack on that son of a gun," he instructed a hitter in the batting cage. "I'll give you a high-five when you come around. Buy you a beer, too." He let the hitter know what to look for at the plate: "They're going to run the ball away from you. They'll try and make you chase the bad one. Don't do it. Be patient. Three-twenty, baby, .320, a high-five and a beer."[5]

Even Dick was surprised that he was now a coach. His old friend Pat Corrales, who managed the Rangers through 1980, helped facilitate the arrangement (there were whispers that he needed the money after the fire and his divorce), something Dick was never quite comfortable with.[6] "Hitting coach," he laughed scornfully. "First thing I got to do is learn how to chew tobacco and get the belly out. Got to have a big belly." Although he was on the coaching staff, he refused to align himself with management. "I'm a ballplayer," he insisted.[7] And as a ballplayer he chose not to socialize with the coaching staff or manager Don Zimmer (as always, he preferred the company of the clubhouse staff). On occasion they invited him to the racetrack but he usually begged off. He had little in common with the other coaches, he told a friend; they were only interested in betting on the races, he was interested in the horses themselves. While they socialized as a pack, Dick stayed apart, choosing to take his meals at an ordinary diner rather than partake of the more lavish ones the coaching staff was indulging in at the team's upscale hotel on Pompano Beach. And while he liked to fish, he spurned the charter boats that were sometimes arranged, choosing to drop a line off a bridge instead.[8]

In all matters, on and off the field, Dick did things his way. If he was going to become a full-time coach once the season started, there would be parameters the Rangers would have to adhere to. "I don't know if they want me around," he said. But if they did, "I won't go on the road. I don't want to travel. I had enough of that. I got a broken marriage from this game as it is."[9] As for the suggestion that getting back into the game now might help soften his image, might help convince some of the writers he'd alienated that he wasn't a bad guy after all, that he was someone worth voting into the Hall of Fame, he bristled: "The Hall of Fame? I ain't interested in the Hall of Fame. Heaven. That's what I'm aiming for. You don't need any votes to get into Heaven."[10]

As the spring progressed, some writers wondered if his coaching position wasn't more of a ruse, mere cover for an attempted comeback.[11] Although he'd been out of the game for four seasons by that point, he was only forty; there were older men in the game then who didn't appear to be in anywhere near the shape he was. Pete Rose, one year Dick's senior, was still grinding out hits in Philadelphia: he hit .325 in 1981 and hadn't lost the ability to reach base even though "Charlie Hustle" had clearly let himself go physically over the previous few years. When confronted, Dick dismissed the idea, realizing that the only way he could come back now was as a DH: "No way. The DH is nowhere. That's no way to play baseball. If you're the shortstop, you should play shortstop."[12] That didn't stop him from stepping into the cage on occasion just to see what he had left. One time he dug in with a bunch of reporters in tow. He ripped a succession of line drives but the crowd wanted to see him go long. Try as he did to put more air under the ball, he was unable to send one over the fence. "It ain't going to happen," he told the disappointed onlookers, who now knew for certain that a comeback was out of the question.[13]

Robinson and the Rangers were impressed with the wisdom Dick imparted to the club's hitters and expressed interest in keeping him on the staff; they'd even agree to his condition that he not travel with the club. Robinson also figured out a way to ensure that any payments made to Dick would end up in his pocket and not in those of his creditors: Dick would receive the bulk of his salary through means the creditors could not touch—per diems and reimbursement of expenses. (If Dick stayed on Robinson suggested that he not establish a residence in Arlington. This would allow Robinson to funnel money to Dick through the guise of living expenses during the season as well.) It was a tempting offer but Dick rejected it. There were several reasons why he found the offer ultimately unappealing, but one of the biggest was that he concluded that he just wouldn't be happy working for Zimmer. Zimmer, he believed, and as he confided to a friend, was something less than a straight shooter and he'd had enough of that.[14] More to the point, he'd simply had enough of managers.

As with most of Dick's decisions, once he made it, he acted. He decided to leave the Rangers one day and was prepared to take off the next morning. There was one problem: he'd promised Stan Reynolds, one of the clubhouse guys, an autographed ball and he hadn't delivered it as of yet. At around 6 A.M. on the morning of his departure, while the clubhouse crew was getting things ready for the day's activities, Dick walked in to keep his promise. Because the gates to the ballpark were still locked at that hour of the morning, he scaled the tall chain-link fence that surrounded the park in order to gain entry. He then signed the ball, gave it to Reynolds, and disappeared into the early morning haze.[15]

A year later, in 1983, Dick became eligible for induction into the Hall of Fame. Here at last, the writers took their revenge: he received only 14 votes—267 shy of the mark. Despite his 351 home runs, .292 lifetime average, .378 lifetime on-base percentage, .534 slugging average, .912 OPS (and 156 OPS+)—his on-base percentage, slugging percentage, OPS, and OPS+ numbers were better than those of all of the eligible candidates that year—only 3.7 percent of the writers included him on their ballot. Brooks Robinson, in many ways Dick's mirror image as a third baseman—spectacular fielder, pedestrian hitter, and always a compliant interview subject—received 92 percent of the vote. Juan Marichal, notorious in his own right for clubbing John Roseboro with a bat six weeks after Frank Thomas similarly struck Dick, also gained admission that year after being bypassed on his first two attempts and after he publicly apologized for his transgression. Meanwhile, Dick focused on his diminishing stable. After the fire he took his horses west and eventually sold all but one—Briar Bend, the son of Never Bend.[16]

He spent much of his time in California, haunting the Santa Anita track and hanging out with the trainers, jockeys, and other folks associated with the horse-racing business. He claimed to have given up baseball for good. "I never liked to watch baseball," he said in 1984. "Since I got out, I was with the Rangers one spring but otherwise I haven't been to one game. I got to Dodger Stadium twice, but that was just to see Chuck (Tanner) when he was with the Pirates. I didn't stay for the games."[17] Still, baseball tugged at him. He briefly resurfaced in Chicago as a minor league spring training instructor for the White Sox in 1986, but he came and went so quietly that many of the players never realized he was there. One day, he was shagging flies hit by rookie-leaguers. When one of them was asked if he realized who was shagging for him, he replied, innocently enough, "No. I'm still having trouble getting the names down."[18] Shortly thereafter, Dick agreed to work with a Philadelphia journalist, of all people, on his autobiography. In 1989, *Crash* was released and even his detractors found it fascinating. "One of the best baseball books in recent years," crowed Bill James, who nevertheless held firm in his conviction that he was a clubhouse cancer. "If that's a Hall of Famer," James concluded, "I'm a lug nut."[19] But *Crash* failed to clarify much. "That the biography that was supposed to define Dick Allen only puzzles, whatever its intent, should be no surprise," wrote the *Wall Street Journal* in its review. "He always raised more questions than he answered." Dick raised even more while out promoting the book, remarking that he didn't like the book's cover photo (of him smoking a cigarette in uniform) or the title. "I didn't crash, I'm here. I'm working and I'm OK."[20]

In 1991 his twenty-eight-year-old daughter, Terri, was murdered in suburban Washington, DC.[21] Once again, in the wake of tragedy, Dick turned to baseball. "It knocked me down," Dick said a few years later of his daughter's death. "I have my days it's still hard for me. But we have to keep going. God gives us these children but they're only on loan."[22] Baseball couldn't make him forget his loss, but at least it might provide him with a diversion for part of the day. "She was born while I was playing ball [shortly after he completed his season in Little Rock] and that's what fed her. I thought maybe I should get back into the game if only to get my mind on something solid." He looked around and, for a time, found no takers. "They told me to send a resume," he said of the clubs he contacted. "A resume? All they had to do was look on the back of one of my bubble gum cards." He grew frustrated. His earlier protestations to the contrary, he admitted: "I still love baseball, I do." But now he saw just how right he had been all those years ago in his contract squabbles with Quinn: "[O]nce you're done with the game," he lamented, "the game is done with you."[23]

* * *

In 1994 Dick returned at last to both baseball and the Phillies, agreeing to work as a minor league instructor and in their community relations department. He soon was given a title with the club that dripped with irony: fan development representative.[24] Yet it was not ironic in the least;

in the decades since his initial departure in 1969, he had developed into a genuine folk hero. People lined up to see him; interest in any club event was always heightened whenever there was a rumor that Dick might, just might, show up (no one could ever be sure that he would in fact appear until the very last moment). He was a legend, a myth, a madman, or a manipulator—his admirers, along with his detractors, were free to take their pick. Some chose all of the above. Whatever they chose, they rarely missed an opportunity to see him in the flesh. Dick was stunned by his reception: "You know, it's been a surprise to me to get out in public again like I do now. I never realized I was this well-liked."[25] Still, he was as he always had been—himself. When the nation piled on the bad boy of the 1990s, Cleveland outfielder Albert Belle, Dick defended him. "He's actually walking around right now like Dick Allen," he said before Belle's appearance at the 1996 All-Star Game in Philadelphia. "I'm completely sure. He's misunderstood." Belle, he believed, was good for the game. "The people love the guy that they love to hate. See what they are going to draw if Cleveland goes into Kansas City. But as long as they hate him, they'll draw people. Turnstile now, of course, is actually production. And the man produces."[26]

By the 1990s the sports world had been turned on its head and the "bad boy," Albert Belle notwithstanding, was now in vogue. Charles Barkley, Dennis Rodman, Allen Iverson, Michael Irvin, the entire roster of the late 1980s Detroit Pistons—the list only seemed to be getting longer as the years passed. Occasionally they'd be compared to Dick, but the analogy was always a hollow one: Barkley was a corporate spokesman for McDonald's, Irvin was a network studio host, Rodman never hurt for endorsements. Dick Allen was never a friend of Madison Avenue; it had no use for him and he surely had no use for it. Perhaps he could have bent a bit, been a bit more cuddly like Barkley or cartoonish like Rodman, done something to reassure the suits on the top floor that he was, underneath it all, harmless. But as everyone who ever encountered him eventually was made to understand, Dick could not be "handled." He was who he was, take him or leave him. Most left him. By all accounts, he was fine with that.

The tragedy of Dick Allen is that if he had played in the 1980s or 1990s, he most likely would have been embraced rather than caricatured, in the sports world at least, as public enemy number one. And then who knows what his final numbers would have been. But the 1980s and 1990s would have been easier for him only if another Dick Allen had come before to pave the way. Of course, there are many reasons why the "rebel pitchmen" exist today and in such great abundance. But one of them is, without question, Dick Allen. Professional sports, and the men (and, at last, the women) who write about them, finally evolved and caught up with what he'd been preaching all along, to the point where what was radical then had become generally accepted. In the 2000s, Tampa Bay Rays' manager Joe Maddon pronounced himself a disciple of everything Dick fought for nearly a half century earlier. "I truly believe that the more freedom the players feel out there, the greater discipline and respect you're going to get in return," Madden said in 2013. "If your employees have to come in and be concerned about a bunch of tedious nonsense, it's going to prevent them from performing as well as they possibly can. God, if I added to the tediousness of the day to any of these guys, I'd feel awful."[27] Gene Mauch's worst nightmare had come true, and the low-budget Rays were frequent postseason contenders at least partly because of it.

The looking glass through which the world at large now viewed Dick Allen revealed itself in toto during the run-up to the announcement of the Hall of Fame's class of 2015. Eligible once more for inclusion on the Hall's "Golden Era" ballot (reserved for players whose careers primarily spanned the era between 1947 and 1972), he at first appeared to be little more than a long shot just to earn a spot on the ballot (he failed to make it in 2012 and the Golden Era committee only convened once every three years). Not content for history to repeat itself, "Kotter" Carfagno orchestrated a campaign to right the wrong he believed the Hall's voters had perpetrated upon his friend ever since he first became eligible for induction. The campaign gained steam and supporters quickly—writers, stat geeks, a filmmaker, family members. So many people wanted nothing more than to see Dick Allen inducted into the Hall of Fame. Except Dick Allen himself, who refused to have anything to do with the crusade. "This whole campaign has been amazing," remarked Hochman, who wrote supportive articles in the *Daily News*. "A diverse collection of friends and fans and analytics guys all bonding in support of Allen, who is chuckling somewhere in Florida."[28]

The movement intensified and expanded after he was indeed named to the ballot. Although there were ten finalists printed on the ballot, most of the nationwide chatter centered around the life and times of Dick Allen. Supporters identified themselves from outlets such as *USA Today*, ESPN, and the *New York Times*. Commentators took to the baseball airwaves across the nation to express their conviction that he should be rightly voted in without hesitation. Still Dick refused to enter the fray. The most he would say, when pressed, was "I'm humbled and I'm embarrassed. Baseball is a team sport, and for me to go out in the forefront is a little embarrassing. Where are the other guys, and what do they get? It takes all nine of us to be successful. It's all of us or none of us." Given a chance to make a last-minute plea to the committee members, one final opportunity to soften the edge so many were now, at last, buffing down on his behalf, he demurred: "I could have handled things a little better but I wouldn't have changed a thing" was all he would offer. "I said what I said, did what I did, meant what I meant—and I'll stand behind every word of it."[29] Needing the votes of twelve of the committee's sixteen members, he fell a single vote shy. His supporters were crushed; Dick would only say that given the opportunity to campaign for himself in 2018, to lobby for that one additional vote, he'd refuse once again.[30]

Today many black athletes are largely revered and embraced by the public—white and black—despite (if not *because of*) their status as rebellious outsiders. Individuality, on the field and off, is now accepted without a second thought. The athlete who goes his own way can no longer expect to be disparaged; he might even be worshiped for his steadfastness and resolve. Although many wouldn't know him if he passed them on the street, all of these athletes owe a debt to Dick Allen for making their lives easier and more prosperous, for going through everything he went through simply because he believed that if he wasn't himself he wasn't anybody. For making the sports establishment realize that it didn't matter so much after all what one did before or after the game provided he could perform at a peak level when it counted. They have reaped the benefits; Dick has paid the price. Scores of athletes in his wake have held out, battled management, struggled with alcohol, and missed games for one reason or another. Nearly all of them have asked for and received forgiveness. A true rebel, and not merely one simply playing the part, Dick has always refused to ask and so therefore has never received. Consequently, although his overall popularity has only grown with the passage of time, he is still largely shunned by much of the baseball establishment; his transgressions remain as they were, as if perpetually suspended in amber. And so Dick Allen himself remains, encased within the prism of history, the angle of refraction dependent as much upon the position of the viewer as that of Dick Allen himself.

Notes

PROLOGUE

1   Lacy J. Banks, "'I'm My Own Man,'" *Ebony* (July 1970), 88, 93.

2   Ibid., 93; Linda Du Breuil, *The Greengage Affair* (New York: Tower Publications, 1969).

3   Banks, "'I'm My Own Man,'" 93.

4   Du Breuil, *The Greengage Affair*, 28.

5   Banks, "'I'm My Own Man,'" 93.

6   Ibid., 92.

7   Du Breuil, *The Greengage Affair*, 139.

8   William Leggett, "A Bird in Hand and a Burning Busch," *Sports Illustrated*, March 23, 1970.

9   Bill James, *The Politics of Glory: How Baseball's Hall of Fame Really Works* (New York: Macmillan, 1994), 322–25.

10   Bill Conlin, "Players, Fans Say, 'Welcome Back, Rich,'" *Philadelphia Daily News*, June 19, 1968, 55.

11   Roy Blount Jr., "Swinging in His Own Groove," *Sports Illustrated*, September 10, 1973.

12   Jerry Izenberg, "Richie Allen in St. Louis: Can the Love Affair Last?" *Sport* (July 1970), 44, 48.

13   Ronald E. Kisner, "Dick Allen: Baseball's Big Drawing Card," *Jet* 42 (August 3, 1972), 55.

14   "Richie Allen Says: Managers Can Be Brutal," *Cleveland Call and Post*, July 4, 1970, 12B.

CHAPTER 1

1   Denez Jones, "George Anthony Curry Is Laid to Rest," *Nassau Guardian*, October 23, 2006, C1.

2   Claude Harrison Jr., "Phils Expect Player Development Program to Pay Dividends in '61," *Philadelphia Tribune*, June 11, 1960, 13.

3   Claude Harrison Jr., "Phils Decide Not to Bring Curry Up," *Philadelphia Tribune*, June 27, 1961, 1.

4   Dallas Green, interview with author, May 11, 2013.

5   Harrison, "Phils Decide Not to Bring Curry Up."

6   Claude Harrison Jr., "Allen and the Phils," *Philadelphia Tribune*, March 16, 1968, 18.

7   Ray Robinson, "A Barrier Unbroken," *New York Times*, May 19, 2013, Sports 8.

8   John Drebinger, "Yankees and Senators Battle with Fists," *Milwaukee Journal*, April 26, 1933, 7.

9   Robinson, "A Barrier Unbroken."

10   Mitchell Nathanson, *The Fall of the 1977 Phillies: How a Baseball Team's Collapse Sank a City's Spirit* (Jefferson, NC: McFarland, 2008), 123. Recently, some baseball historians have questioned the veracity of this alleged incident. See Frank Fitzpatrick, "Racism Claim Still Clouds Hall of Famer Pennock's Reputation," *Philadelphia Inquirer,* November 10, 2014.

11   Arnold Rampersad, *Jackie Robinson* (New York: Alfred A. Knopf, 1997), 172–73.

12   See Chris Lamb, *Conspiracy of Silence: Sportswriters and the Long Campaign to Desegregate Baseball* (Lincoln: University of Nebraska Press, 2012), 14.

13   Ibid., 24.

14   See Nathanson, *The Fall of the 1977 Phillies*, 87; Larry Merchant, interview with author, July 5, 2015 (regarding Carpenter's perpetual suntan).

15   Eustace Gay, "Phils' Boss 'Seeks' Negro Super-Player," *Philadelphia Tribune*, October 27, 1951, 1.

16   "All But the Phillies," *Philadelphia Tribune*, May 22, 1956, 8.

17   "Phillies Called 'Most Prejudiced,' " *Philadelphia Tribune*, June 26, 1956, 1.

18   "8 Negroes on Roster of Phils Farm Teams," *Philadelphia Tribune*, July 3, 1956, 1; "43 Negroes Are Holding 'Odd Jobs' at Connie Mack Stadium," *Philadelphia Tribune*, July 24, 1956, 2.

19   Claude Harrison Jr., "Phillies Looking for More than Just Average Negro Player," *Philadelphia Tribune*, July 31, 1956, 10.

20   Claude Harrison Jr., "Fans from All Walks of Life Expressing Opinion About Phils," *Philadelphia Tribune*, July 24, 1956, 11.

21   Claude Harrison Jr., "Phillies Say They Are Interested in a Good Negro Player," *Philadelphia Tribune*, July 28, 1956, 7.

22   Harrison, "Phillies Looking for More than Just Average Negro Player."

23   "Phillies Fall in Line," *Philadelphia Tribune*, April 9, 1957, 10.

24   Claude Harrison Jr., "Large Crowd Expected to Watch Phillies 'Unveil' John Kennedy," *Philadelphia Tribune*, April 16, 1957, 12.

25   Allen Lewis, "Roberts Seeks Fourth Inaugural Victory over Brooks in Phils' 1st Game," *Philadelphia Inquirer*, April 16, 1957, 28.

26   "Phils' 11 Negroes Being 'Taken Care Of' by Bell Capt.," *Philadelphia Tribune*, February 28, 1961, 10.

27   "NAACP Threatens Phillies Ball Club with Season-Long Pickets," *Philadelphia Tribune*, March 10, 1962, 1.

28   Randy Dixon, "Phillies Give in to NAACP Boycott," *Philadelphia Tribune*, March 13, 1962, 1.

29   See Dick Allen and Tim Whitaker, *Crash: The Life and Times of Dick Allen* (New York: Ticknor and Fields, 1989), 46; Willie King, interview with author, August 19, 2013; Guy Demaio, interview with author, July 1, 2013.

30   Blount, "Swinging in His Own Groove."

31   Demaio, interview with author.

32   Louie Robinson, "The Importance of Being Dick Allen," *Ebony* 27 (October 1972), 194–95.

33   Demaio, interview with author.

34   Ron Galbreath, interview with author, July 3, 2013.

35   Allen and Whitaker, *Crash*, 36; Blount, "Swinging in His Own Groove."

36   Blount, "Swinging in His Own Groove."

37 Jeff Prugh, "The Summer of Dick Allen's Content," *Los Angeles Times*, June 13, 1975, C1.

38 Norman O. Unger, "Allen's 'Aura' Is a Relic of the Past," *Chicago Defender*, August 10, 1974, 25.

39 Galbreath, interview with author.

40 Bill Conlin, "Allen's 'Father' Dies," *Philadelphia Daily News*, March 30, 1976, 35.

41 Bill Bryson, "How Screen Door Nearly Kept Allen from Phils," *Baseball Digest* (December 1964), 65.

42 Dave Nightingale, "The Human Side of Richie Allen," *Baseball Digest* (July 1972), 18.

43 Allen and Whitaker, *Crash*, 37.

44 Ron Hughes, interview with author, April 29, 2013.

45 Ibid.

46 Ron Mazzano, interview with author, April 25, 2013.

47 Demaio, interview with author.

48 King, interview with author.

49 Allen and Whitaker, *Crash*, 41–42.

50 Demaio, interview with author.

51 "Training Tricks Help Wampum Swamp 'Em," *Life* 44, no. 1 (January 6, 1958), 47.

52 See "Wampum High Gymnasium—Wampum PA," in *Lawrence County Memoirs*, www.lawrencecountymemoirs.com.

53 Stan Hochman, "Dick Allen Might Not Be His Own Best Historian," *Philadelphia Daily News*, May 8, 1975, 83.

54 David Wolf, "Let's Everybody Boo Rich Allen!" *Life* 67, no. 8 (August 22, 1969), 50, 51.

55 Hochman, "Dick Allen Might Not Be His Own Best Historian."

56 Galbreath, interview with author.

57 Bill Conlin, "Ex-Coach: Allen Easily Led," *Philadelphia Daily News*, July 2, 1969, 57.

58 Wolf, "Let's Everybody Boo Rich Allen!"

59 Mazzano, interview with author.

60 Demaio, interview with author.

61 Sandy Grady, "Rich Praise Flows from Ron Allen," *Philadelphia Evening Bulletin*, August 23, 1966, 61.

62 Green, interview with author.

63 Bill Conlin, email interview with author, May 3–July 6, 2013.

64 Mazzano, interview with author.

65 Demaio, interview with author.

66 Galbreath, interview with author.

67 Bill Conlin, "Meeting the 'Reel' Rich Allen!" *Philadelphia Daily News*, June 6, 1969, 73.

68 Demaio, interview with author.

69 Galbreath, interview with author.

70 Demaio, interview with author.

71 Larry Merchant, "Allen, Ogden and Banks," *Philadelphia Daily News*, April 16, 1964, 74.

72 See Claude Harrison Jr., "Death of Negro Loops Meant Birth of Bonuses for Negro Players," *Philadelphia Tribune*, August 19, 1961, 9.

73 See Nathanson, *The Fall of the 1977 Phillies*, 123–24.

74 Allen Lewis, "Allen's TV Profile 'Factual,'" *Philadelphia Inquirer*, June 6, 1969, 37.

75 "If Phils Win Flag Credit Allen with Solid, Major 'Lift,'" *Philadelphia Tribune*, May 5, 1964, 22.

76 Ron Smith, "Allen Bound to Blaze Long Hitting Trail," *Philadelphia Inquirer*, June 23, 1964, 40.

77 Unger, "Allen's 'Aura' Is a Relic of the Past."

78 Leonard Shecter, "Richie Allen and the Use of Power," *Sport* (July 1967), 67, 72.

79 Hochman, "Dick Allen Might Not Be His Own Best Historian."

80   Blount, "Swinging in His Own Groove."

81   Claude Harrison Jr., "Phillies' Bonus Baby Growing into Giant-Sized Star," *Philadelphia Tribune*, June 26, 1962, 12.

82   Allen and Whitaker, *Crash*, 107–8.

83   Stan Hochman, "Ruly Learns Allen Doesn't Forget," *Philadelphia Daily News*, October 4, 1976, B5.

84   Hochman, "Dick Allen Might Not Be His Own Best Historian."

85   Bill Conlin, interview with author.

86   Bill Conlin, "A Forum for Sportswriters . . . That's Rich," *Philadelphia Daily News*, August 23, 1968, 66.

87   Stan Hochman, "The Book Closes on Dick Allen," *Philadelphia Daily News*, April 10, 1975, 60.

88   Stan Hochman, "Phillies Training Suspense Ends with Allen at Third," *Philadelphia Daily News*, February 27, 1964, 62.

89   Allen and Whitaker, *Crash*, 14–15.

90   William C. Rhoden, *Forty Million Dollar Slaves: The Rise, Fall, and Redemption of the Black Athlete* (New York: Three Rivers Press, 2006), 177–78.

91   Ibid., 194.

92   Ibid., 120.

93   Blount, "Swinging in His Own Groove."

CHAPTER 2

1   "Richie Allen: Pride of the Phillies," *Sepia* 13 (September 1964), 54.

2   Matthew Frye Jacobson, " 'Richie' Allen, Whitey's Ways, and Me: A Political Education in the 1960s," *In the Game: Race, Identity and Sports in the Twentieth Century*, ed. Amy Bass (New York: Palgrave Macmillan, 2005), 20, 23.

3   Ibid., 25.

4   Frank Dolson, "Phillies Album: Dick Allen," *Philadelphia Inquirer*, September 12, 1976, D10.

5   Nightingale, "The Human Side of Richie Allen," 20.

6   Jim Bailey, interview with author, April 30, 2013.

7   Ibid.

8   Stan Hochman, "Rocky Little Rock Sharpens Allen for Big Time Shot with Phillies," *Philadelphia Daily News*, September 6, 1963.

9   Bailey, interview with author.

10   "Dick Allen: 'Still My Own Man,' " *Newsweek*, August 21, 1972, 83.

11   Bob Razer, "The Black Traveler: Dick Allen and Little Rock Baseball, 1963," *Pulaski County Historical Review* 61 (2013), 2.

12   Ibid.

13   Allen and Whitaker, *Crash*, 11–12.

14   Ibid.

15   Nightingale, "The Human Side of Richie Allen," 20.

16   Bob Razer, Archie F. House Fellow for Arkansas Bibliography in the Butler Center for Arkansas Studies, Central Arkansas Library System, interview with author, April 2, 2013.

17   Razer, "The Black Traveler."

18   Ibid.

19   Sarah Riva, "Desegregating Downtown Little Rock: The Field Reports of SNCC's Bill Hansen, October 23 to December 3, 1962," *Arkansas Historical Quarterly* 71, no. 3 (Autumn 2012), 264.

20   Ibid., 270.

21   Bob Razer, interview with author, April 3, 2013.

22   Bailey, interview with author.

23   Quoted in Razer, "The Black Traveler."

24   "Integration in Little Rock," *Sporting News*, May 4, 1964, 12.

25   "Richie Allen Breaks Baseball Color Barrier in Little Rock, Ark.," *Philadelphia Tribune*, May 21, 1963, 10.

26   Razer, interview with author, April 2, 2013.

27   "Richie Allen Breaks Baseball Color Barrier."

28   Bailey, interview with author.

29   Razer, "The Black Traveler."

30   "Phillies' Allen Prefers 'Dick' as First Name," *Philadelphia Tribune*, August 8, 1964, 9.

31   Galbreath, interview with author.

32   Myron Cope, "The Cheerful World of Richie Allen," *Sport* (September 1964), 82.

33   Ibid.

34   Curt Flood and Richard Carter, *The Way It Is* (New York: Trident Press, 1971), 35.

35   Jack Olsen, "The Cruel Deception," *Sports Illustrated*, July 1, 1968.

36   Bill Christine, "Dick Allen Puts Baseball in the Past," *Sporting News*, January 16, 1984, 55.

37   Shecter, "Richie Allen and the Use of Power," 72.

38   See "Amis Robert Guthridge (1908–1977)," in *The Encyclopedia of Arkansas History and Culture*, www.encyclopediaofarkansas.net.

39   Ibid.

40   Bailey, interview with author.

41   Wolf, "Let's Everybody Boo Rich Allen!" 51.

42   Allen and Whitaker, *Crash*, 14–15.

43   Dolson, "Views on the Life and Times of Richie Allen," *Philadelphia Inquirer,* June 12, 1969, 28.

44   Izenberg, "Richie Allen in St. Louis: Can the Love Affair Last?" 45, 47.

45   William Leggett, "The Rookie from Wampum, Pa.," *Sports Illustrated*, April 20, 1964.

46   Bailey, interview with author.

47   Bruce Keidan, "Today's the BIG Day That Allen Comes Back," *Philadelphia Inquirer*, August 10, 1976, 2-C.

48   Blount, "Swinging in His Own Groove."

49   Bill Conlin, "For One Great Ballplayer, Philadelphia Was a Traffic Jam," *Jock* (January 1970).

50   Frank Lucchesi, interview with author, April 29, 2013.

51   "Richie Allen: Pride of the Phillies," 54.

52   Allen Lewis, "A Con Man with Muscles," *Philadelphia Inquirer*, August 11, 1969, 18.

53   Ibid.

54   "Integration in Little Rock."

55   Sam Lacy, "Thanks to Gov. Faubus and Little Rock," *Baltimore Afro-American*, November 25, 1972, 7.

56   "Reporter Finds Allen, Phil Star Placing Orchids on Little Rock," *Chicago Defender*, April 20, 1964, 22.

57   Allen and Whitaker, *Crash*, 15.

CHAPTER 3

1   Stan Hochman, "'Write' or Wrong, Allen Had Stormy Era with Phils," *Philadelphia Daily News*, May 9, 1975, 87.

2   Claude Harrison Jr., "Outfielder Richie Allen: Phillies' Hottest Prospect for Next Season," *Philadelphia Tribune*, November 19, 1963, 15.

3   Green, interview with author.

4   Arthur Daley, "The Sleeper," *New York Times*, March 10, 1964.

5   Leggett, "The Rookie from Wampum, Pa."

6   "Rookie Allen Has Tools to End Third Base 'Drought,'" *Pittsburgh Courier*, May 2, 1964, 23.

7   Larry Merchant, "Hoak's Vow: I'm Going to Play," *Philadelphia Daily News*, March 26, 1964, 58.

8   Stan Hochman, "Hoak's Eyes Pinned on Allen," *Philadelphia Daily News*, March 9, 1964, 48.

9   Merchant, "Hoak's Vow: I'm Going to Play."

10 Ibid.

11 Larry Merchant, "Allen Knows He's Better than Good," *Philadelphia Daily News*, April 6, 1964, 52.

12 Brad Pye Jr., "A Note on Richie Allen," *Los Angeles Sentinel*, May 28, 1964, B1.

13 Wolf, "Let's Everybody Boo Rich Allen!" 50.

14 Cal Fussman, *After Jackie: Pride, Prejudice and Baseball's Forgotten Heroes: An Oral History* (New York: ESPN Books, 2007).

15 Merchant, "Allen Knows He's Better than Good."

16 Arthur Daley, "A Quick Getaway," *New York Times*, April 21, 1964.

17 Eric Primm, Summer DuBois, and Robert Regoli, "Every Picture Tells a Story: Racial Representation on *Sports Illustrated* Covers," *Journal of American Culture* 30, no. 2 (June 2007), 222, 228.

18 Claude Harrison Jr., "Phils Have Pride and Richie Allen," *Philadelphia Tribune*, May 19, 1964, 16.

19 Richard Dozer, "Phils' Richie Allen in a Class by Himself," *Chicago Tribune*, April 19, 1964, C1.

20 Allen Lewis, "Phils' Allen Called Winning Player; Getting Better, Too," *Philadelphia Inquirer*, July 9, 1964, 33.

21 Larry Merchant, "Something Special," *Philadelphia Daily News*, July 13, 1964, 50; Cope, "The Cheerful World of Richie Allen."

22 Stan Hochman, "Richie Allen: Way-Out Clothes, Way-Out Bat," *Philadelphia Daily News*, March 17, 1964, 74.

23 "Phillies' Allen Prefers 'Dick' as First Name."

24 Hochman, "Richie Allen: Way-Out Clothes, Way-Out Bat."

25 Cope, "The Cheerful World of Richie Allen," 81.

26 Ibid., 82.

27 Allen Lewis, "Allen Sorry About Fight," *Philadelphia Inquirer*, July 8, 1965, 35.

28 Sandy Padwe, "Rich Wanted to Sit Out Year," *Philadelphia Inquirer*, August 9, 1969, 22.

29 Stan Hochman, "Momma Allen's Sure That Her Son Hasn't Set," *Philadelphia Daily News*, July 30, 1975, 71.

30 Rhoden, *Forty Million Dollar Slaves*, 233.

31 See generally, Flood, *The Way It Is*; Rhoden, *Forty Million Dollar Slaves*.

32 Cope, "The Cheerful World of Richie Allen," 82.

33 Red Smith, "Will Rich Allen Dress with Other Cards?" *Philadelphia Inquirer*, October 10, 1969, 37.

34 Sandy Padwe, "Owner: 'If Deal Fails, Allen Can Try Movies,'" *Philadelphia Inquirer*, August 25, 1969, 19.

35 Merchant, "Something Special."

36 "Allen: I'm Not Hard to Get Along With," *Los Angeles Times*, March 29, 1974, B10.

37 John Dell, "Allen Plays for Phils, Family, Not for Rookie of Year Halo," *Philadelphia Inquirer*, August 24, 1964, 26.

38 Larry Merchant, "Richie Allen: First at Third," *Philadelphia Daily News*, June 29, 1965, 54.

39 "Allen Walks off Interview Show," *New York Times*, June 15, 1969.

40 "Insouciance," *Sports Illustrated*, September 7, 1964, 20.

41 Stan Hochman, "Boo Birds of Unhappiness Find Nest in Allen's Glove," *Philadelphia Daily News*, September 4, 1964, 49.

42 Ray Kelly, "Larsen Cooks Phils as Fans Roast Allen," *Philadelphia Evening Bulletin*, September 4, 1964, 23.

43 Frank Bilovsky, "Allen Rips Cubs," *Philadelphia Evening Bulletin*, August 18, 1967, 27.

44 Bruce Kuklick, *To Every Thing a Season: Shibe Park and Urban Philadelphia, 1909–1976* (Princeton, NJ: Princeton University Press, 1991), 28.

45 Ibid., 22–24.

46 Ibid, 67–70.

47 Lee Vilensky, "Ode to Dick Allen," *Elysian Fields Quarterly* 20, no. 3 (2003).

48 Ibid.

49 Kuklick, *To Every Thing a Season*, 139.

50 Stan Hochman, "Dick Allen: I'm No Messiah," *Philadelphia Daily News*, May 8, 1975, 84.

51 Robert Gregg, "Personal Cavalries: Sports in Philadelphia's African-American Communities, 1920–60," in *Ethnicity, Sport, Identity: Struggles for Status*, ed. J. A. Mangan and Andrew Ritchie (London: Routledge, 2004), 71.

52 "Rioters, Hoodlums Are What They Are Because America Made Them That Way," *Philadelphia Tribune*, September 1, 1964, 5.

53 Mark Bricklin, "Social Agencies See Recent Violence as Product of 'Centuries of Injustice,'" *Philadelphia Tribune*, September 5, 1964, 4.

54 "Most Tan Philadelphians Have a Heart," *Philadelphia Tribune*, September 5, 1964, 5; Jacobson, "'Richie' Allen, Whitey's Ways, and Me," 26.

55 Arnold Hano, interview with author, August 11, 2014.

56 Arnold Hano, "A Week with the Phillies," *Sport* (December 1964), 33, 34.

57 Ibid., 82.

58 Shecter, "Richie Allen and the Use of Power," 71; Jim Murray, "Richie Allen—Now There's a Case for You," *Sporting News*, October 11, 1969, 21.

59 Rhoden, *Forty Million Dollar Slaves*, 162.

60 John Hoberman, *Darwin's Athletes: How Sport Has Damaged Black America and Preserved the Myth of Race* (New York: Houghton Mifflin, 1997), 35.

61 Wolf, "Let's Everybody Boo Rich Allen!" 53.

62 Hano, interview with author.

63 Stan Hochman, "Sleepy-Time Super-Star," *Philadelphia Daily News*, July 10, 1967, 42.

64 Jim Murray, "It's a Game of Love," *Los Angeles Times*, March 20, 1973, E1.

65 Claude Harrison Jr., "Vic Power Can Help Phillies to Win the Pennant," *Philadelphia Tribune*, September 12, 1964, 1, 4.

66 Banks, "'I'm My Own Man,'" 94.

67 Art Spander, "Allen Marches to Own Drummer," *Sporting News*, October 5, 1974, 22 (quoting Murray).

68 Kelly, "Larsen Cooks Phils."

69 Ibid.

70 Frank Dolson, "Fans Didn't Give a Hoot for Richie," *Philadelphia Inquirer*, September 8, 1964, 32.

71 Frank Dolson, "Phils Grateful There's No Place Like Home," *Philadelphia Inquirer*, September 29, 1964, 36.

72   Edward Tyburski, "Backer Claims Loss of Pennant on Phils' 'Fair Weather (Boo) Fans,'" *Philadelphia Evening Bulletin*, October 5, 1964, 1.

CHAPTER 4

1   Flood, *The Way It Is*, 50.

2   Marvin Miller, *A Whole Different Ball Game: The Inside Story of the Baseball Revolution* (1991; reprint, Chicago: Ivan R. Dee, 2004), 39.

3   Ibid., 46.

4   Ibid., 47.

5   Flood, *The Way It Is*, 51.

6   Ibid., 52.

7   Claude Harrison Jr., "Figures Back Up Richie Allen's Demand for Big Pay Boost," *Philadelphia Tribune*, February 13, 1965, 12. Allen's rookie contract called for a salary of $7,500 but he received a $2,500 raise during the season.

8   Stan Hochman, "Allen Warns Phils: Big Raise or I'll Quit," *Philadelphia Daily News*, January 11, 1965, 49.

9   Allen Lewis, "Allen and Phillies Not Close to Terms," *Philadelphia Inquirer*, March 5, 1965, 30.

10   Lewis, "Allen and Phillies Not Close to Terms"; Sandy Grady, "Phillies Payroll Goes into $800,000 Orbit," *Philadelphia Evening Bulletin*, January 16, 1966, 3.

11   Stan Hochman, "'Unhappy' Allen Arrives in Camp," *Philadelphia Daily News*, March 15, 1965, 47.

12   Hochman, "Allen Warns Phils: Big Raise or I'll Quit."

13   Stan Hochman, "Allen, Quinn Draw Battle Line$," *Philadelphia Daily News*, March 3, 1965, 45–46.

14   Allen Lewis, "Holdout Is Costing Allen Needed Drills on Fielding," *Philadelphia Inquirer*, March 13, 1965, 19, 20.

15   Ibid.

16   Sandy Grady, "Mom Keeps Richie Home," *Philadelphia Evening Bulletin*, March 12, 1965.

17   Claude Harrison Jr., "Wes Is Man Who Stands Up for His Rights," *Philadelphia Tribune*, September 18, 1965, 16.

18   Ibid.; Allen Lewis, "Allen, Covington Now Phil Holdouts," *Philadelphia Inquirer*, March 4, 1965, 31; Grady, "Mom Keeps Richie Home."

19   Harrison, "Wes Is a Man Who Stands Up for His Rights."

20   Ibid.; Grady, "Mom Keeps Richie Home."

21   "Have No Fear," *Sporting Life*, March 23, 1912, 2.

22   "How Much Is a Player Worth?" *Ebony* 27, no. 8 (June 1972), 152.

23   Flood, *The Way It Is*, 18.

24   Jim Murray, "The Hard-Hat Blues," *Los Angeles Times*, September 30, 1971, D1.

25   Flood, *The Way It Is*, 18.

26   "Late Arrivals Allen and Covington Are Early Phillies' Pace Setters," *Philadelphia Tribune*, May 4, 1965, 12.

27   Grady, "Mom Keeps Richie Home."

28   Sandy Grady, "Bitter Allen Gave in Because of a Friend," *Philadelphia Evening Bulletin*, March 15, 1965, 25.

29   Hochman, "'Unhappy' Allen Arrives in Camp."

30   Ibid.

31   Ray Kelly, "Allen: That's Over With," *Philadelphia Evening Bulletin*, March 16, 1965, 63.

32 Allen Lewis, "Reluctant Allen Signs Pact: On 'Mom's Terms,' Not His," *Philadelphia Inquirer*, March 16, 1965, 31.

33 Hochman, "'Unhappy' Allen Arrives in Camp."

34 Ibid.

35 Grady, "Bitter Allen Gave in Because of a Friend."

36 Conlin, interview with author.

37 Sandy Grady, "Three 'Wrongs' Do Not Make a Pinch-Hitter," *Philadelphia Evening Bulletin*, July 6, 1965.

38 Sid Ziff, "The Fight Figured," *Los Angeles Times*, July 8, 1965, B3.

39 Craig Wright, "Another View of Dick Allen," *Baseball Research Journal* 24 (1995), 2, 4; Allen Lewis, "Thomas Regrets Fight, Calls Waiver Unfair," *Philadelphia Inquirer*, July 5, 1965, 20.

40 Merchant, interview with author.

41 Allen and Whitaker, *Crash*, 4.

42 Wright, "Another View of Dick Allen," 4.

43 "Richie Allen Says: Frank Thomas Had Been Told to 'Lay Off,'" *Philadelphia Tribune*, July 20, 1965, 9.

44 Melvin Durslag, "A Non-Love Affair," *Sporting News*, May 8, 1971, 12.

45 Allen and Whitaker, *Crash*, 6.

46 Lewis, "Thomas Regrets Fight."

47 Allen and Whitaker, *Crash*, 6.

48 Conlin, interview with author.

49 Kisner, "Dick Allen: Baseball's Big Drawing Card," 52.

50 Ric Roberts, "Thomas Used Racial Insult . . . Allen," *Pittsburgh Courier*, July 10, 1965, 1.

51 Lewis, "Thomas Regrets Fight."

52 Durslag, "A Non-Love Affair"; "Thomas Claims He Got Unfair Rap," *Philadelphia Tribune*, July 15, 1965, B4.

53 John Husar, "Dick Allen Is 'Funny Dude,' Soul of Sox," *Chicago Tribune*, April 1, 1973, B1, 4.

54 Durslag, "A Non-Love Affair."

55 Claude Harrison Jr., "Third Sacker Clouts Thomas, Ruben Amaro," *Philadelphia Tribune*, July 6, 1965, 1.

56 Lewis, "Thomas Regrets Fight."

57 Frederick Klein, "A Slugger's Story," *Wall Street Journal*, April 14, 1989, A12.

58 Conlin, interview with author.

59 John Brogan, "Thomas Put on Waivers After Fight with Allen," *Philadelphia Evening Bulletin,* July 4, 1965, Sports 1.

60 Lewis, "Thomas Regrets Fight."

61 Bill Koenig, "Dick Allen Reflects on Career with No Regrets," *USA Today Baseball Weekly*, July 26–August 1, 1995, 37; "Richie Allen Says: Frank Thomas Had Been Told to 'Lay Off.'"

62 Brogan, "Thomas Put on Waivers."

63 Grady, "Three 'Wrongs' Do Not Make a Pinch-Hitter"; Allen and Whitaker, *Crash*, 8.

64 Ibid.

65 Lewis, "Thomas Regrets Fight."

66 "Frank Thomas Regrets Richie Allen Incident," *Philadelphia Tribune*, July 17, 1965, 13.

67 Lewis, "Thomas Regrets Fight."

68 Scott Baillie, "Thomas Calls Ouster 'Unfair,'" *Philadelphia Tribune*, July 19, 1965; "Frank Thomas Regrets Richie Allen Incident."

69 Grady, "Three 'Wrongs' Do Not Make a Pinch-Hitter."

70 Sandy Grady, "Allen Asked Mauch to Give Him Release," *Philadelphia Evening Bulletin*, July 9, 1965, 25.

71   Bonventre, "Dick Allen: 'Still My Own Man,'" 84; Wolf, "Let's Everybody Boo Rich Allen!" 52.

72   Bonventre, "Dick Allen: 'Still My Own Man,'" 84.

73   George Kiseda, "Allen Ignores Fans' Catcalls," *Philadelphia Evening Bulletin*, July 8, 1965, 33.

74   Grady, "Allen Asked Mauch to Give Him Release."

75   Ibid; Larry Merchant, "Two Games and an Apology at Richie Allen Dell," *Philadelphia Daily News*, July 8, 1965, 52; Grady, "Three 'Wrongs' Do Not Make a Pinch-Hitter."

76   Grady, "Allen Asked Mauch to Give Him Release."

77   Allen and Whitaker, *Crash*, 59–60.

78   Ibid., 71.

79   Bilovsky, "Rich Disturbed by Booing."

80   Roberts, "Thomas Used Racial Insult . . . Allen."

81   Merchant, "Two Games and an Apology."

82   "What's Behind Booing of Richie Allen?" *Philadelphia Tribune*, July 10, 1965, 7.

83   Claude Harrison Jr., "Phila. Is Where Roy Was Barred; Rich Allen Booed," *Philadelphia Tribune*, July 13, 1965, 12.

84   Barnett Wright, "Dick Allen Reflects on His Controversial Career," *Philadelphia Tribune*, August 26, 1988, 6C.

85   Dick Young, "Behind Baseball's Fights and Fines," *Sport* (November 1965), 52.

86   "Richie Allen Tells His Version of the Thomas Scuffle on TV," *Philadelphia Tribune*, June 10, 1969, 17.

87   Merchant, interview with author.

88   Larry Merchant, "Fighting Phil Waived Goodbye," *Philadelphia Daily News*, July 6, 1965, 62.

89   Ibid.

90   Merchant, "Two Games and an Apology."

91   Larry Merchant, "Allen vs. Thomas: Round Ten," *Philadelphia Daily News*, July 12, 1965, 53.

92   Merchant, interview with author.

93   Conlin, interview with author.

94   Merchant, interview with author.

95   Ibid.

96   Ibid.

97   A. S. Doc Young, "Let's Have a Brawl," *Chicago Defender*, July 13, 1965, 25.

98   Michael Sisak, "Rich Allen Admits He's '100 Percent Wrong,'" *Philadelphia Evening Bulletin*, June 27, 1969, 27.

99   Bonventre, "Dick Allen: 'Still My Own Man,'" 84.

100 Jim Barniak, "Allen 'Super' in First Show as '75 Phil," *Philadelphia Evening Bulletin*, May 8, 1975, 29, 31.

CHAPTER 5

1   See Bill Jenkinson, *Baseball's Ultimate Power: Ranking the All-Time Greatest Distance Home Run Hitters* (Guilford, CT: Lyons Press, 2010). Jenkinson ranked Allen as the game's fifth-best "tape measure home run" hitter.

2   "Allen Misses First Game as a Phillie," *Philadelphia Tribune*, October 5, 1965, 12.

3   Stan Hochman, "Allen's Tummy All Upset—So Is Bunning After 1–0 Loss," *Philadelphia Daily News*, September 28, 1965, 67.

4   "Police Tag Richie Allen," *Philadelphia Tribune*, November 9, 1965, 1.

5   Chet Coleman, "2 Eyewitnesses Say Phillies Richie Allen Beaten by Cops," *Philadelphia Tribune*, November 9, 1965, 1.

6   Fred Bonaparte, "Richie Allen Mum on Police Beating Report," *Philadelphia Tribune*, November 13, 1965, 1.

7   "Silence Prevails in Richie Allen Brutality Case," *Philadelphia Tribune*, November 20, 1965, 2.

8   "Sees Allen Probe," *Philadelphia Tribune*, December 11, 1965, 7C.

9   Ray Kelly, "Bunning and Allen Draw Fast Pens," *Philadelphia Evening Bulletin*, January 14, 1966, 27.

10   "Allen Signs Contract for Substantial Increase," *Philadelphia Inquirer*, January 14, 1966, 23.

11   Stan Hochman, "Allen Reports Late and Overweight," *Philadelphia Daily News*, March 3, 1966, 58.

12   Stan Hochman, "Richie Bats .555 But Already Weary," *Philadelphia Daily News*, March 14, 1966, 51.

13   Ken Henderson, interview with author, June 4, 2013.

14   Claude Harrison Jr., "Richie Allen Set to Open at Third," *Philadelphia Tribune*, April 12, 1966, 13.

15   Stan Hochman, "How About Taylor on Third, Allen in Left? Richie Isn't Sold on Idea," *Philadelphia Daily News*, March 23, 1966, 49.

16   Allen Lewis, "Richie Allen May Wind Up in Outfield," *Philadelphia Inquirer*, March 26, 1966, 20.

17   Stan Hochman, "Allen 'Scared' in Outfield," *Philadelphia Daily News*, March 26, 1966, 27.

18   Hochman, "How About Taylor on Third."

19   Hochman, "Allen 'Scared' in Outfield."

20   Ray Kelly, "Mauch, Not Allen, Serious About Shift to Outfield," *Philadelphia Evening Bulletin*, March 26, 1966, 13.

21   Conlin, interview with author.

22   Stan Hochman, "Rich Allen Works Out—Good Hit . . . No Throw," *Philadelphia Daily News*, May 7, 1966, 31.

23   Bill Conlin, "Mauch Wants Allen . . . Healthy," *Philadelphia Daily News*, May 13, 1966, 67.

24   Bill Conlin, "Rich in a Pinch Is Premature Promise: A Long Wait Before He's Back in Lineup," *Philadelphia Daily News*, May 20, 1966, 63.

25   Frank Dolson, "A 1966 Injury Heals 1965 Wounds," *Philadelphia Inquirer*, May 21, 1966, 26.

26   Ibid.

27   Stan Hochman, "Momma's Out, Allen Is In," *Philadelphia Daily News*, May 31, 1966, 72.

28   Ibid.

29   Bill Conlin, "Rich Allen May Roam Phils Outfield Tonight," *Philadelphia Daily News*, May 27, 1966, 58.

30   Stan Hochman, "Horses Gentle on Allen's Mind," *Philadelphia Daily News*, November 12, 1974, 58.

31   Ray Kelly, "Mauch Hints Allen Violated Curfew," *Philadelphia Evening Bulletin*, July 24, 1966, Section 3, p. 1.

32   Bill Conlin, "'It Makes a Guy Want to Give Up,'" *Philadelphia Daily News*, July 27, 1966, 45.

33   Bill White, interview with author, April 20, 2013.

34   Hughes, interview with author.

35 Frank Dolson, "Too Many Pro Stars Take But Don't Give," *Philadelphia Inquirer*, July 25, 1974, C1, 2.

36 Flood, *The Way It Is*, 83–84.

37 Henderson, interview with author.

38 Bill Conlin, "Allen: A Real Swinger's Swinger," *Philadelphia Daily News*, June 24, 1966, 56.

39 Ibid.

40 Miller, *A Whole Different Ball Game*, 133.

41 Donald Hall with Dock Ellis, *Dock Ellis in the Country of Baseball* (New York: Simon and Schuster, 1976), 177.

42 Frank Dolson, "Is Allen Case Really Resolved?" *Philadelphia Inquirer*, June 11, 1968, 33, 34.

43 Henderson, interview with author.

44 Jerome Holtzman, "Chisox Crowing Over Allen-Melton Power Duo," *Sporting News*, December 18, 1971, 51; Robert Markus, "Allen's Departure Not a Complete Surprise," *Chicago Tribune*, September 16, 1974, C4.

45 Flood, *The Way It Is*, 75.

46 Robert M. Jiobu, "Racial Inequality in a Public Arena: The Case of Professional Baseball," *Social Forces* 67, no. 2 (December 1988), 524, 532–33.

47 Harrison, "Allen and the Phils."

48 Carl Nesfield, "New Team. New Town. New Richie?" *Black Sports* (July 1971), 70.

49 Kisner, "Dick Allen: Baseball's Big Drawing Card," 56.

50 Banks, "'I'm My Own Man,'" 93–94.

51 Klein, "A Slugger's Story."

52 Claude Harrison Jr., "Does Baseball Consider Black Athletes All Brawn and No Brains?" *Philadelphia Tribune*, May 27, 1969, 15.

53 Klein, "A Slugger's Story."

54 Shecter, "Richie Allen and the Use of Power," 69.

55 Ibid.

CHAPTER 6

1 "People," *Sports Illustrated*, January 2, 1967, 41.

2 Claude Harrison Jr., "How Many Phillies' $$$ Will Richie Allen Demand in 1967," *Philadelphia Tribune*, September 20, 1966, 12.

3 "Phillies Tell Richie Allen His Asking Price for '67 $100,000 Is Too High," *Philadelphia Tribune*, February 21, 1967, 12.

4 Ray Kelly, "Allen Says He Won't Negotiate," *Philadelphia Evening Bulletin*, February 1, 1967, 49.

5 Bill Conlin, "Allen Demands 100G Salary," *Philadelphia Daily News*, February 1, 1967, 51.

6 Stan Hochman, "Arm Injury Made Allen Reach for $100,000," *Philadelphia Daily News*, February 23, 1967, 49.

7 Sandy Grady, "Will Richie Sell Cars Full-Time?" *Philadelphia Evening Bulletin*, February 28, 1967, 53.

8 Stan Hochman, "AWOL Allen: 'I'd Be Different on Another Club,'" *Philadelphia Daily News*, March 9, 1968, 26, 28.

9 Hochman, "Arm Injury Made Allen Reach for $100,000."

10 Frank Dolson, "Did You Think Rich Would Sell Cars All Summer?" *Philadelphia Inquirer*, March 17, 1967, 40; Sandy Grady, "Looking Through a Rear-View Mirror," *Philadelphia Evening Bulletin*, February 24, 1967, 27.

11 Hochman, "Arm Injury Made Allen Reach for $100,000."

12 Bill Conlin, "Allen May Put Owner on the $pot," *Philadelphia Daily News*, March 3, 1967, 63.

13 Bill Conlin, "Rich Agrees to Let Some Air Out of $100,000 Balloon," *Philadelphia Daily News*, March 4, 1967, 32.

14 Ibid.

15 Stan Hochman, "Economics and Richie," *Philadelphia Daily News*, March 13, 1967, 57.

16 Sandy Grady, "Allen Takes Salary Demands to Boss," *Philadelphia Evening Bulletin*, March 3, 1967, 35.

17 "Phillies Sign Allen; Salary Is Reported Around $75,000," *Philadelphia Evening Bulletin*, March 16, 1967, 1.

18 Ray Kelly, "Allen Gets Record $85,000," *Philadelphia Evening Bulletin*, March 17, 1967, 46.

19 "Phillies Sign Allen; Salary Is Reported Around $75,000."

20 Frank Dolson, "Mustache Off, Allen Is Ready," *Philadelphia Inquirer*, March 20, 1967, 22.

21 Frank Dolson, "Mauch to Allen: Something Better," *Philadelphia Inquirer*, July 6, 1969, section 3, p. 1; Wolf, "Let's Everybody Boo Rich Allen!" 53.

22 "Dick Allen: 'Still My Own Man.'"

23 Allen Lewis, "'I'll Say It Again,' Says Richie, 'I'm Riding Out,'" *Sporting News*, September 6, 1969, 15.

24 Frank Dolson, "Richie Arrives Early, Stays Late," *Philadelphia Inquirer*, July 10, 1967, 23, 28.

25 Ibid.; Ray Kelly, "Allen Admits Being Late Saturday; Homers over Centerfield Fence," *Philadelphia Evening Bulletin*, July 10, 1967, 21.

26 Arthur Daley, "Into the Basket," *New York Times*, June 25, 1968.

27 A. S. Doc Young, "Still More: Richie Allen," *Chicago Defender*, September 9, 1969, 24.

28 George Kiseda, "Allen Knocks Some Writers . . . And They Talk Back," *Philadelphia Evening Bulletin*, August 23, 1968, 29.

29 Conlin, "For One Great Ballplayer, Philadelphia Was a Perpetual Traffic Jam."

30 Joe Falls, "Heaven Can Wait on Richie Allen," *Sporting News*, April 3, 1982, 9.

31 "Ellsworth Raps Richie Allen," *Los Angeles Sentinel*, January 25, 1968, B3.

32 White, interview with author.

33 Larry Christenson, interview with author, February 20, 2015.

34 Green, interview with author.

35 Merchant, interview with author.

36 Henderson, interview with author.

37 Allen and Whitaker, *Crash*, 116.

38 Conlin, interview with author.

39 Ron Fimrite, "Big Fish in Turbulent Waters," *Sports Illustrated*, April 29, 1974, 18.

40 James Smith, "A Man Concerned," *Philadelphia Tribune*, March 20, 1973, 8.

41 Conlin, interview with author.

42 Allen Lewis, "Richie Allen Falls Something Short of Super-Star," *Philadelphia Inquirer*, July 7, 1967, 29.

43 Sandy Grady, "Advice for '68: 'Shut Out Boos,'" *Philadelphia Evening Bulletin*, August 25, 1967, 27.

44 George Vass, "Baseball's Five Most Over-rated Players," *Baseball Digest* (February 1970), 16.

45 Bill Conlin, "With Fame's Headaches, Rich Ought to Sell Used Cars," *Philadelphia Daily News*, November 1, 1967, 52.

46 Dolson, "Richie Arrives Early, Stays Late."

47 "Gene May Be Grooming Rich for Post of Captain," *Sporting News*, April 29, 1967, 16.

48 Frank Dolson, "What's in a Title for Rich Allen?" *Philadelphia Inquirer*, April 14, 1967, 33, 36.

49 Lewis, "Richie Allen Falls Something Short of Super-Star."

50 Durslag, "A Non-Love Affair."

51 Conlin, "'It Makes a Guy Want to Give Up.'"

52 Stan Hochman, "A Bark Up the Wrong Three," *Philadelphia Daily News*, August 9, 1966, 51.

53 Murray, "The Hard-Hat Blues."

54 Shecter, "Richie Allen and the Use of Power," 71.

55 Dolson, "Richie Arrives Early, Stays Late."

56 Allen Lewis, "Tardy Allen Denies 2 Sets of Rules, One for Him, One for Other Phils," *Sporting News*, July 22, 1967, 22.

57 "What Ever Happened to . . . Dick Allen," *Sports Illustrated*, July 19, 1993, 84.

58 Hochman, "Sleepy-Time Super-Star."

59 Gary Cartwright, "Mauch Tells Allen to Cool It," *Philadelphia Inquirer*, July 15, 1967, 22.

60 Stan Hochman, "Must Allen Pay the Price?" *Philadelphia Daily News*, May 24, 1967, 61.

61 Ibid.

62 Bill Conlin, "Rockin' Richie Still Wrecking Records. Booooo . . . ," *Philadelphia Daily News*, August 8, 1967, 54.

63 Quoted in "Fans Called 'Slobs,'" *Philadelphia Inquirer*, July 26, 1967, 27.

64 Frank Bilovsky, "Phillies Lose as Fans Still Heckle Allen," *Philadelphia Evening Bulletin*, August 19, 1967, 11.

65 Bill Conlin, "Allen's Answer to Boos: 'I Think I Might Like Being Traded,'" *Philadelphia Daily News*, August 18, 1967, 55

66 Allen and Whitaker, *Crash*, 72.

67 Merchant, interview with author.

68 "Dick Allen: 'Still My Own Man.'"

69 Conlin, interview with author.

70 Wolf, "Let's Everybody Boo Rich Allen!"

71 Bill Conlin, "Phillies Lose Allen for Season with Slashed Hand," *Philadelphia Daily News*, August 25, 1967, 59.

72 Conlin, interview with author.

73 "Young Friend Helped Allen Push the Car," *Philadelphia Evening Bulletin*, August 25, 1967, 27.

74 Ibid. Dick's mother, Era, had recently flown in from Wampum to help Barbara and Dick manage the last few weeks of Barbara's pregnancy.

75 Conlin, "Phillies Lose Allen for Season."

76 Bill Conlin, "Medical Verdict on Rich Allen Must Wait Six Weeks," *Philadelphia Daily News*, August 26, 1967, 26.

77 Conlin, "Phillies Lose Allen for Season."

78 Conlin, interview with author.

79 Ross Newhan, "Richie Allen Arises Early for Hitting Practice," *Los Angeles Times*, March 8, 1971, E1.

80 "Allen Leaves Hospital, Avoids News Session," *Philadelphia Inquirer*, August 31, 1967, 30.

81 Conlin, interview with author.

82 Bill Conlin, "Johnson's Memories in a League of Their Own," *Philadelphia Daily News*, July 30, 1987, 91.

83 Allen Lewis, "Phils Cross Fingers as Allen Recovers from Wrist Injury," *Sporting News*, September 23, 1967, 13.

84   Bill Conlin, "Rich Allen Pays a Visit to the Phillies," *Philadelphia Daily News,* September 7, 1967, 56.

85   Conlin, interview with author.

86   Claude Harrison Jr., "Richie Allen Gets Good News from Doctors," *Philadelphia Tribune*, December 12, 1967, 14.

87   Ibid.

88   Claude Harrison Jr., "Florida-Bound Allen Says He Will Play This Season," *Philadelphia Tribune*, February 3, 1968, 18.

89   "Phillies Sign Richie Allen," *Chicago Defender*, February 3, 1968, 17.

90   Sandy Grady, "Allen-Quinn Feud Simmers in Florida," *Philadelphia Evening Bulletin*, March 1, 1968, 29.

91   Stan Hochman, "Even Rich Allen's 'Manager' Wishes He'd Grow Up," *Philadelphia Daily News*, March 12, 1968, 55.

92   Conlin, "A Forum for Sportswriters . . . That's Rich."

93   Kiseda, "Allen Knocks Some Writers."

94   Ray Kelly, "Allen Finds Gold on Two-Bit Range," *Sporting News*, March 9, 1968, 19.

95   Grady, "Allen-Quinn Feud Simmers in Florida."

96   Wolf, "Let's Everybody Boo Rich Allen!" 51.

97   John Hall, "A Happy Ending?" *Los Angeles Times*, June 9, 1970, D3.

98   "Richie Allen: An Unhappy Phillie," *Philadelphia Tribune*, March 12, 1968, 15.

99   "Richie Allen Quits Phillies' Camp," *Philadelphia Evening Bulletin*, March 8, 1968, 1, 41

100 Allen Lewis, "Allen's Walkout Triggers Phils' 'Get Tough' Policy," *Philadelphia Inquirer*, March 9, 1968, 20, 22.

101 "Allen May Wear Heated Glove on Injured Hand," *Sporting News*, April 13, 1968, 21.

102 Bill Conlin, "Is Richie Crossing Fingers? He Can't . . . ," *Philadelphia Daily News*, March 26, 1968, 71.

CHAPTER 7

1   Allen and Whitaker, *Crash*, 71–72.

2   Frank Dolson, "Missing Allen Miffs Mauch," *Philadelphia Inquirer*, May 1, 1968, 41; Ray Kelly, "Allen Is Back in Doghouse for Being Late," *Philadelphia Evening Bulletin*, May 1, 1968, 69.

3   Dolson, "Missing Allen Miffs Mauch."

4   Kelly, "Allen Is Back in Doghouse."

5   George Langford, "Allen: 'What Have I Done Wrong?'" *Chicago Tribune*, June 27, 1974, C1.

6   Stan Hochman, "Yakyak—and Work," *Philadelphia Daily News*, October 12, 1976, 62.

7   Hochman, "Ruly Learns Allen Doesn't Forget."

8   Green, interview with author.

9   Padwe, "Rich Wanted to Sit Out Year."

10   "Afternoon Workouts Get Richie to Park on Time," *Sporting News*, May 25, 1968, 10.

11   Wright, "Another View of Dick Allen," 3.

12   Allen Lewis, "Carpenter's Answers Merely Raise More Questions," *Philadelphia Inquirer*, August 26, 1969, 26.

13   Padwe, "Owner: 'If Deal Fails, Allen Can Try Movies.'"

14   Sandy Grady, "Rich Waits for a Hand," *Philadelphia Evening Bulletin*, May 20, 1968, 17.

15   Ibid.

16   Stan Hochman, "Unless Mauch Gets Allen in Line, He Himself May Go," *Philadelphia Daily News*, May 16, 1968, 57.

17 Bill Conlin, "Carpenter 'Cures' Allen . . . But Is Mauch Sick Now?" *Philadelphia Daily News*, June 11, 1968, 56.

18 Ray Kelly, "Someone's Gotta Go: Mauch or Allen?" *Philadelphia Evening Bulletin*, June 10, 1968, 27.

19 Allen Lewis, "Allen Tries to Get Phils to Trade Him Before Sunday," *Philadelphia Inquirer*, June 10, 1968, 30; Kelly, "Someone's Gotta Go."

20 Conlin, "Carpenter 'Cures' Allen."

21 Allen Lewis, "Allen's Bat Sings, But Glove Strikes Philly Sour Note," *Sporting News*, June 15, 1968, 10.

22 Stan Hochman, "As Long as Both Wear Same Uniform: Bitterness," *Philadelphia Daily News*, June 12, 1968, 63.

23 Bill Conlin, "Phils' Spring Thing: Refusing, Abusing—Resolved, Absolved," *Philadelphia Daily News*, June 13, 1968, 55.

24 Bill Conlin, "Phillies Ask: Who'll Trade for Allen?" *Philadelphia Daily News*, June 10, 1968, 51.

25 Wolf, "Let's Everybody Boo Rich Allen!"

26 Kelly, "Someone's Gotta Go."

27 Bill Conlin, "Skinner 'Poor Loser' But . . . ," *Philadelphia Daily News*, June 17, 1968, 53.

28 Sandy Grady, "Phils Face More Changes," *Philadelphia Evening Bulletin*, June 23, 1968, Section 3, p. 1.

29 Conlin, "Phils' Spring Thing."

30 Conlin, interview with author.

31 Rick Talley, "Sox, Cubs Interested in Signing Allen," *Chicago Tribune*, December 31, 1976, B1.

32 Conlin, "Phillies Ask: Who'll Trade for Allen?"

33 Ibid.

34 Lewis, "Allen Tries to Get Phils to Trade Him Before Sunday."

35 Hochman, "As Long as Both Wear Same Uniform: Bitterness."

36 Conlin, interview with author.

37 Allen Lewis, "Allen Set to Play After Talk with Owner," *Philadelphia Inquirer*, June 11, 1968, 33.

38 Conlin, "Carpenter 'Cures' Allen."

39 Lewis, "Allen Set to Play After Talk with Owner."

40 Dolson, "Is Allen Case Really Resolved?"

41 Frank Dolson, "Mauch, Allen Differ on Story of Benching," *Philadelphia Inquirer*, June 12, 1968, 38.

42 Jules Childs, interview with author, May 16, 2013.

43 Allen and Whitaker, *Crash*, 72–73.

44 Neal Russo, "Richie Says It with Homers in Philly Return," *Sporting News*, June 6, 1970, 3.

45 Murray, "Richie Allen—Now There's a Case for You."

46 Conlin, interview with author.

47 Allen Lewis, "Phillies Fire Mauch, Pick Bob Skinner as Manager," *Philadelphia Inquirer*, June 16, 1968, 1.

48 Allen Lewis, " 'Shocked' Carpenter Fires Reply to Skinner's Salvo," *Sporting News*, September 13, 1969, 19.

49 Stan Hochman, "Mauch Fired, Phils Tried to Trade Allen," *Philadelphia Daily News*, June 17, 1968, 52.

50 Ray Kelly, "Players Think Mauch Said: 'Allen or Me,' " *Philadelphia Evening Bulletin*, June 16, 1968, 1.

51 Dolson, "Views on the Life and Times of Richie Allen."

52 Jim Barniak, "Allen's Like Vietnam War," *Philadelphia Evening Bulletin*, May 22, 1970, 33.

53 Allen and Whitaker, *Crash*, 178.

54 Banks, "'I'm My Own Man,'" 89.

55 Jim Brosnan, "Dick Allen: New Boss in Chicago," *Sport* (December 1972), 71.

56 Blount, "Swinging in His Own Groove."

57 Bill Conlin, "Ryan Miffed at Benching," *Philadelphia Daily News*, July 15, 1969, 49.

58 Stan Hochman, "Allen's Tip Generous to a Point," *Philadelphia Daily News*, April 15, 1969, 73.

59 Michael Sisak, interview with author, July 5, 2013.

60 Ibid.

61 Sandy Padwe, "A Man Ahead of His Times," *Philadelphia Inquirer*, August 11, 1969, 18.

62 Sandy Padwe, "Rich the Rebel Is No Hypocrite," *Philadelphia Inquirer*, July 24, 1969, 32.

63 Koenig, "Dick Allen Reflects on Career with No Regrets."

64 A. S. Doc Young, "Rich's Walk," *Chicago Daily Defender*, March 23, 1972, 32.

65 A. S. Doc Young, "Allen's Sox Beef," *Chicago Daily Defender*, March 27, 1972, 29.

66 Norman O. Unger, "Allen Back to His Old 'Tricks,'" *Chicago Defender*, November 13, 1974, 34.

67 "Richie Allen, Phillies Slugger, Still Having Big Problems," *Chicago Defender*, May 11, 1968, 15.

68 A. S. Doc Young, "Legend in Reverse," *Chicago Defender*, June 24, 1968, 24.

69 A. S. Doc Young, "Missed by Critics," *Chicago Defender*, September 9, 1968, 24.

70 A. S. Doc Young, "Open Letter to Richie," *Chicago Defender*, September 11, 1969, 40.

71 Claude Harrison Jr., "Allen Leads Phils in Everything But Cheers from Fans," *Philadelphia Tribune*, May 20, 1969, 20.

72 Claude Harrison Jr., "Baseball Hurt Itself Many, Many Years Ago," *Philadelphia Tribune*, June 22, 1968, 22.

73 Claude Harrison Jr., "Richie Allen Wins Mauch Battle So Now He Must Produce for Fans," *Philadelphia Tribune*, June 18, 1968, 1.

74 Mike Rathet, "Richie Allen: He's Loved and Hated," *Los Angeles Times*, May 20, 1969, B1.

75 Stan Hochman, "Disneyland East: From Impossible to Intolerable," *Philadelphia Daily News*, August 8, 1969, 57.

76 Conlin, "For One Great Ballplayer, Philadelphia Was a Perpetual Traffic Jam."

77 "Slugger Richie Allen Becomes Target," *Philadelphia Tribune*, June 25, 1968, 9.

78 George Kiseda, "Dick Allen?" *Baseball Digest* (December 1964), 66.

79 A. S. Doc Young, "A Visit with Dick," *Chicago Defender*, September 26, 1972, 24.

80 "Rich Allen Tells Phils to Swap Him," *Philadelphia Tribune*, August 27, 1968, 14.

81 Bill Conlin, "Phillies, Tribe Talk Allen," *Philadelphia Daily News*, October 17, 1968, 59.

82 Allen Lewis, "Plate Skid Adds ??? to Allen's Philly Enigma," *Sporting News*, September 28, 1968, 17.

83 Allen Lewis, "Carpenter Planning Shakeup of Phillies," *Sporting News*, October 19, 1968, 19.

84 Conlin, interview with author; Bill Jenkinson, "Career Home Run Log of Dick Allen" (on file with the author).

85 Bill Conlin, "Phils Finding Rich the Apple of Many Teams' Eye," *Philadelphia Daily News*, October 9, 1968, 52.

86 Allen Lewis, "Is Allen-Quinn Hostility Subsiding?" *Philadelphia Inquirer*, December 3, 1968, 42.

87 Bill Conlin, "Skinner: I Like Allen," *Philadelphia Daily News*, December 5, 1968, 64.

88 Stan Hochman, "A Sizeup of Richie's Hat," *Philadelphia Daily News*, July 24, 1968, 64.

89   Bill Conlin, "Good Sign for Phils: Richie," *Philadelphia Daily News*, February 28, 1969, 55.

90   Bill Conlin, "Where's Richie?" *Philadelphia Daily News*, March 6, 1969, 66.

91   "Quinn Bumps into Richie," *Philadelphia Inquirer*, March 9, 1969, Section 3, p. 1.

92   Frank Dolson, "Truant Finds the Officer," *Philadelphia Inquirer*, March 10, 1969, 29.

CHAPTER 8

1   John Brogan, "A Happy Allen Gives His Fans a Few Tips," *Philadelphia Evening Bulletin*, April 15, 1969, 61.

2   Hochman, "Allen's Tip Generous to a Point."

3   Brogan, "A Happy Allen Gives His Fans a Few Tips."

4   Wolf, "Let's Everybody Boo Rich Allen!" 52.

5   Ray Kelly, "Richie Allen Fined $1,000," *Philadelphia Evening Bulletin*, May 4, 1969, Section 3, p. 1.

6   Frank Dolson, "Allen a Tortoise Even in Jet Age," *Philadelphia Inquirer,* May 4, 1969, G1.

7   Frank Dolson, "Allen Makes It—Going Back," *Philadelphia Inquirer*, May 5, 1969, 34.

8   Steve Klessel, "Rough Day for Allen at the Races," *Philadelphia Daily News*, May 14, 1969, 77; "Allen Scuffler Handed $50 Fine," *Chicago Defender*, May 28, 1969, 29.

9   Stan Hochman, "Time to Admire, Not Analyze?" *Philadelphia Daily News*, April 8, 1969, 55.

10   Claude Harrison Jr., "Skinner Admits He's an Allen Man," *Philadelphia Tribune*, March 29, 1969, 18.

11   Claude Harrison Jr., "Skinner Says Rich Allen Could Become Best Hitter in Major Leagues," *Philadelphia Tribune*, May 10, 1969, 25.

12   Allen Lewis, "Phils Warn Allen Must Obey Rules," *Philadelphia Inquirer*, June 26, 1969, 1.

13   Wolf, "Let's Everybody Boo Rich Allen!" 52.

14   Banks, "'I'm My Own Man,'" 92.

15   Murray, "Richie Allen—Now There's a Case for You."

16   Sandy Padwe, "Allen Misses Game Again, Is Suspended Without Pay," *Philadelphia Inquirer*, June 25, 1969, 1.

17   Conlin, "For One Great Ballplayer, Philadelphia Was a Perpetual Traffic Jam."

18   Stan Hochman, "Rich Allen's Latest Escapade May Be His Last," *Philadelphia Daily News*, June 25, 1969, 59.

19   Conlin, "For One Great Ballplayer, Philadelphia Was a Perpetual Traffic Jam."

20   Padwe, "Allen Misses Game Again."

21   Stan Hochman, "Funny Route to Funny Farm," *Philadelphia Daily News,* June 30, 1969, 56.

22   Wolf, "Let's Everybody Boo Rich Allen!"

23   Ray Kelly, "'Through Till They Trade Me,' Allen Says After Suspension," *Philadelphia Evening Bulletin*, June 25, 1969, 1.

24   Sisak, "Rich Allen Admits He's '100 Percent Wrong.'"

25   Kelly, "'Through Till They Trade Me,' Allen Says After Suspension."

26   "Allen Stages Game's First Revolt," *New Pittsburgh Courier*, July 12, 1969, 19.

27   Conlin, interview with author.

28   Quoted in Bill Conlin, "Maybe Rich Allen Would Be Wise to Consult a Doctor," *Philadelphia Daily News*, June 25, 1969, 60.

29   Bill Conlin, "Phillies' Ugliest Tug of War," *Philadelphia Daily News*, June 26, 1969, 55.

30 Sandy Grady, "Allen's Latest Trip Might End in Trade," *Philadelphia Evening Bulletin*, June 25, 1969, 65.

31 Conlin, "For One Great Ballplayer, Philadelphia Was a Perpetual Traffic Jam."

32 "Richie Allen: 'Out of Sight,'" *Chicago Daily Defender*, June 30, 1969, 31.

33 Allen and Whitaker, *Crash*, 74.

34 Ibid., 76.

35 Stan Hochman, "Jenkintown Is Ready Whenever Allen Shows," *Philadelphia Daily News*, February 12, 1975, 66.

36 "IRS Slaps Lien on Richie Allen," *Chicago Daily Defender*, July 3, 1969, 34.

37 Claude Harrison Jr., "I'll Play Somewhere, Maybe in Japan, Richie Allen Asserts," *Philadelphia Tribune*, July 5, 1969, 1.

38 Sandy Grady, "Allen Remains 'Indefinite,'" *Philadelphia Evening Bulletin*, July 11, 1969, 25.

39 "Allen Phillies' Problem—Kuhn," *Chicago Daily Defender*, July 12, 1969, 35.

40 "Mauch Suggests Richie Should Hang Up Spikes," *Sporting News*, July 26, 1969, 42.

41 Stan Hochman, "Nixon Can Rest Easy—Rich Allen's Back," *Philadelphia Daily News*, July 24, 1969, 52.

42 Conlin, "For One Great Ballplayer, Philadelphia Was a Perpetual Traffic Jam."

43 Stan Hochman, "Phillies Bring Allen to Earth with Typical Finesse," *Philadelphia Daily News*, July 21, 1969, 47.

44 Allen Lewis, "'Skinner Pushed Panic Button . . . So Did I,' Says Richie," *Sporting News*, August 9, 1969, 15.

45 Wolf, "Let's Everybody Boo Rich Allen!" 52.

46 Conlin, "For One Great Ballplayer, Philadelphia Was a Perpetual Traffic Jam."

47 Frank Dolson, "Allen Re-Enters on Historic Day," *Philadelphia Inquirer*, July 21, 1969, 22.

48 Sandy Padwe, "'Can't See Playing Here Next Year,' Allen Says," *Philadelphia Inquirer*, July 22, 1969, 28.

49 Ibid.

50 Wolf, "Let's Everybody Boo Rich Allen!" 53.

51 "Richie Allen in Fold; 26-Day Suspension Over," *Chicago Daily Defender*, July 21, 1969, 24.

52 Sandy Grady, "'They Ruined Allen,'—Skinner," *Philadelphia Evening Bulletin*, August 8, 1969, 25.

53 Hochman, "Time to Admire, Not Analyze."

54 Sandy Grady, "Richie Allen Has Lost More than Money This Time," *Philadelphia Evening Bulletin*, June 26, 1969, 29.

55 "Who's in Charge Around Here?" *Sporting News*, August 23, 1969, 14.

56 Leonard Koppett, *The Rise and Fall of the Press Box* (Toronto: Sport Classic Books, 2003), 193.

57 "An Acid Test for Bowie," *Sporting News*, August 30, 1969, 14.

58 Allen and Whitaker, *Crash*, 185.

59 Wright, "Another View of Dick Allen," 5.

60 Robert Ray, Report of Signing, Carpenter Collection, Box #1, Hagley Museum and Library, Wilmington, DE.

61 Mickey Bowers, Report of Manager Bob Malkmus, Carpenter Collection, Box #1, Hagley Museum and Library, Wilmington, DE.

62 Frank Dolson, "Richie Prefers Closet to Company of Fellow Phillies," *Philadelphia Inquirer*, July 30, 1969, 31.

63 Conlin, "For One Great Ballplayer, Philadelphia Was a Perpetual Traffic Jam."

64 Izenberg, "Richie Allen in St. Louis: Can the Love Affair Last?" 47.

65 Dolson, "Richie Prefers Closet to Company of Fellow Phillies."

66 Wolf, "Let's Everybody Boo Rich Allen!" 53.

67 Allen and Whitaker, *Crash*, 79.

68 Wolf, "Let's Everybody Boo Rich Allen!" 53.

69 Sandy Padwe, "Rich Wanted to Sit Out Year," *Philadelphia Inquirer*, August 9, 1969, 22.

70 Allen Lewis, "Skinner Quits Phillies, Assails Front Office in Dispute Over Allen," *Philadelphia Inquirer*, August 8, 1969, 1; Sandy Padwe, "Bob's Explosion Was Powerful," *Philadelphia Inquirer*, August 8, 1969, 27.

71 Lewis, "'Shocked' Carpenter Fires Reply to Skinner's Salvo."

72 "Who's in Charge Around Here?"

73 Bill Conlin, "Skinner's Spectacular Finale: Courageous Man Walks Tall," *Philadelphia Daily News*, August 8, 1969, 57.

74 Ray Kelly, "'Quitter,' Allen Says of Skinner," *Philadelphia Evening Bulletin*, August 8, 1969, 25.

75 Claude Harrison Jr., "Does Richie Allen Have an 'In' with Phils' Owner Bob Carpenter?" *Philadelphia Tribune*, August 12, 1969, 16.

76 Claude Harrison Jr., "All Allen Owes Fans Is a Hard Day's Work," *Philadelphia Tribune*, August 19, 1969, 17.

77 Banks, "'I'm My Own Man,'" 92.

78 Bill Conlin, "Extra Rations for Myattmen," *Philadelphia Daily News*, August 9, 1969, 29.

79 Conlin, "For One Great Ballplayer, Philadelphia Was a Perpetual Traffic Jam."

80 Allen and Whitaker, *Crash*, 80.

81 Wolf, "Let's Everybody Boo Rich Allen!" 53.

82 Allen Lewis, "Allen Faces Public on TV, Vows to Put Show on Road," *Philadelphia Inquirer*, August 19, 1969, 26.

83 "Phils Openly Accused of Racial Prejudice," *Philadelphia Tribune*, October 30, 1971, 8.

84 "Allen's Footwork Out of Step to Phils," *Sporting News*, August 23, 1969, 7.

85 Conlin, interview with author.

86 "Allen's Footwork Out of Step to Phils."

87 Stan Hochman, "Allen's Sandy Scrawls Open New Vistas for Graffiti," *Philadelphia Daily News*, August 5, 1969, 52.

88 Lewis, "A Con Man with Muscles."

89 Padwe, "A Man Ahead of His Times."

90 Barnett Wright, "Dick Allen Reflects on His Controversial Career," *Philadelphia Tribune*, August 26, 1988, 6C.

91 "Allen in Night-Club Act—Invites Patrons to Boo," *Sporting News*, January 4, 1969, 53.

92 Jack Kiser, "Boos Turn to Cheers as Rich Allen Sings," *Philadelphia Daily News*, January 10, 1969, 26.

93 Wolf, "Let's Everybody Boo Rich Allen!" 53.

94 "Unhappy Richie Allen Faces Movie Cameras," *Chicago Daily Defender*, August 30, 1969, 29; Claude Harrison Jr., "Phils Admit They Are Ready to Trade Richie Allen," *Philadelphia Tribune*, August 26, 1969, 10.

95 "Mrs. Rich Allen to Tell of Threats Against Family on Television Show," *Philadelphia Tribune*, September 16, 1969, 18.

96 Bill Conlin, "An Era Ends: Rich Allen's Last Exit," *Philadelphia Daily News*, September 29, 1969, 53.

97 Durslag, "A Non-Love Affair"; Ray Kelly, "A Pat, a Wave, a Kiss: Rich Allen Says Goodbye," *Philadelphia Evening Bulletin*, September 29, 1969, 30.

98 Stan Hochman, "Ex-Phils Know: A Broom Is What Carpenter Needs," *Philadelphia Daily News*, October 8, 1969, 59.

99 Allen Lewis, "Callison Trade Hinges on Flood's 1970 Plans," *Sporting News*, October 25, 1969, 24.

100 Neal Russo, "Richie Seen as Hepped-Up Cardinal," *Sporting News*, October 25, 1969, 20.

101 Allen Lewis, "Allen Traded to St. Louis; Phils Expect Flood to Play," *Philadelphia Inquirer*, October 9, 1969, 1.

102 Russo, "Richie Seen as Hepped-Up Cardinal."

103 Claude Harrison Jr., "Curt Flood Balks at Joining Phillies; Cards Vow to Keep Rich Allen," *Philadelphia Tribune*, October 11, 1969, 21.

104 Stan Hochman, "Flood's Business Is Booming, Urge to Play Isn't," *Philadelphia Daily News*, November 19, 1969, 61.

105 Flood, *The Way It Is*, 176.

106 Ibid., 188.

107 Ibid., 190.

108 Ibid., 181.

109 Miller, *A Whole Different Ball Game*, 185, 186.

110 Flood, *The Way It Is*, 15.

111 Ibid., 174.

112 Norman Unger, "Flood and Allen, Like 'Two Peas in a Pod,'" *Chicago Defender*, September 17, 1974, 24.

113 Sandy Padwe, "What Allen Wants," *Philadelphia Inquirer*, March 31, 1972.

114 Russo, "Richie Seen as Hepped-Up Cardinal."

115 "Richie (HR and 2 Doubles) Credits Mauch, Raps Phils," *Philadelphia Daily News*, April 9, 1970, 61.

116 Durslag, "A Non-Love Affair."

117 Frank Dolson, "The New Rich Allen IS Friendly, Even Effusive," *Philadelphia Inquirer*, March 19, 1970, 29.

CHAPTER 9

1 Izenberg, "Richie Allen in St. Louis: Can the Love Affair Last?" 48.

2 Murray, "Richie Allen—Now There's a Case for You," 21.

3 Izenberg, "Richie Allen in St. Louis: Can the Love Affair Last?" 50.

4 Sandy Padwe, "It Was Liberation Day for Allen," *Philadelphia Inquirer*, October 9, 1969, 32.

5 Flood, *The Way It Is*, 171–72.

6 Bob Broeg, "Redbird Owner Busch Admits, 'I'm Disillusioned,'" *Sporting News,* March 28, 1970, 5.

7 Brosnan, "Dick Allen: New Boss in Chicago," 128.

8 Broeg, "Redbird Owner Busch Admits 'I'm Disillusioned.'"

9 "Allen Reportedly Asking $150,000," *Los Angeles Times*, February 24, 1970, B1.

10 Broeg, "Redbird Owner Busch Admits 'I'm Disillusioned' "; Bob Broeg, "Busch Ultimatum to Allen: Produce First," *St. Louis Post-Dispatch*, March 11, 1970, 1E.

11 Broeg, "Busch Ultimatum to Allen: Produce First."

12 Bob Broeg, "'I'm No Angel, But I'll Play Ball,' Says Allen," *St. Louis Post-Dispatch*, March 13, 1970, 1B; "Disagreement over Fringe Benefits for His Mother Delayed Allen's Signing with Cards," *Philadelphia Tribune*, March 21, 1970, 22.

13 Joseph Durso, "Allen Agrees to Play After Cardinals Issue an Ultimatum on $90,000 Pact," *New York Times*, March 12, 1970.

14 Flood, *The Way It Is*, 193.

15 Curt Flood, interviewed in *Journey of the African American Athlete* (New York: HBO Films, 1996).

16 Joseph Durso, "Carlton Rejects Cardinals' 'Final Offer' as Allen Signs for $90,000," *New York Times*, March 13, 1970.

17 G. Michael Green and Roger D. Launius, *Charlie Finley: The Outrageous Story of Baseball's Super Showman* (New York: Walker & Co., 2010), 133–34.

18 "Richie Allen Says: Managers Can Be Brutal," *Cleveland Call and Post*, July 4, 1970, 12B.

19 Allen and Whitaker, *Crash*, 120.

20 Durso, "Carlton Rejects Cardinals' 'Final Offer' as Allen Signs for $90,000."

21 Leggett, "A Bird in Hand and a Burning Busch."

22 Green and Launius, *Charlie Finley*, 127–28.

23 Durso, "Carlton Rejects Cardinals' 'Final Offer' as Allen Signs for $90,000"; Broeg, "Busch Ultimatum to Allen: Produce First."

24 See Bob Broeg, "Cards Order Allen, Carlton to Report," *St. Louis Post-Dispatch*, March 6, 1970, 1C; the *Globe Democrat*'s response is mentioned in "Allen Reportedly Asking $150,000."

25 Bill Nunn Jr., "Change of Pace," *New Pittsburgh Courier*, March 7, 1970, 10.

26 "Disagreement Over Fringe Benefits for His Mother Delayed Allen's Signing with Cards," *Philadelphia Tribune*, March 21, 1970, 22; Broeg, " 'I'm No Angel, But I'll Play Ball,' Says Allen."

27 Sandy Padwe, "Allen Oks Cardinal Contract," *Philadelphia Inquirer*, March 12, 1970, 25.

28 Blount, "Swinging in His Own Groove."

29 Neil Offen, "Allen Smiles (Stay Tuned)," *New York Post*, March 13, 1970, 89.

30 C. C. Johnson Spink, "We Believe . . . ," *Sporting News*, March 28, 1970, 5; Bob Broeg, "Allen Discovers Baseball Is a Fun Game After All," *Sporting News*, March 28, 1970, 5; Izenberg, "Richie Allen in St. Louis: Can the Love Affair Last?" 49.

31 Broeg, "Allen Discovers Baseball Is a Fun Game After All."

32 Ibid.; Broeg, " 'I'm No Angel, But I'll Play Ball,' Says Allen."

33 Dolson, "The New Rich Allen IS Friendly, Even Effusive."

34 Broeg, "Allen Discovers Baseball Is a Fun Game After All"; Bob Broeg, "Allen at 3b, Temporarily," *St. Louis Post-Dispatch*, March 31, 1970, 4B; Bob Broeg, "Happy Allen Gives Cards Rich Reward," *St. Louis Post-Dispatch*, March 20, 1970, 1C; Ed Wilks, "Allen Wins Friends, Influences Birds with Bat," *St. Louis Post-Dispatch*, May 13, 1970, 1E.

35 Banks, " 'I'm My Own Man,' " 89.

36 Stan Hochman, "Parents Don't Write Allen," *Philadelphia Daily News*, March 27, 1970, 52.

37 "Dick Allen Will Come Back, Kelly Says," *Philadelphia Daily News*, September 16, 1974, 58.

38 Richard Dozer, "Allen's Advice Pays Off for Cardenal," *Sporting News*, August 9, 1974, 17.

39 Jose Cardenal, interview with author, May 6, 2013.

40 Bill Nunn Jr., "Change of Pace," *New Pittsburgh Courier*, March 21, 1970, 31.

41 Izenberg, "Richie Allen in St. Louis: Can the Love Affair Last?" 50.

42 Bob Motley and Byron Motley, *Ruling over Monarchs, Giants & Stars: True Tales of Breaking Barriers, Umpiring Baseball Legends, and Wild Adventures in the Negro Leagues* (2007; reprint, New York: Sports Publishing, 2012), 92–93.

43 Allen and Whitaker, *Crash*, 84–85.

44 Murray, "The Hard-Hat Blues."

45 "Allen Booed, Hits Homer in First Game," *Philadelphia Daily News*, March 19, 1970, 70.

46 Neal Russo, "Tardy Allen Hits 4 Homers in 4 Days," *Sporting News*, April 4, 1970, 21.

47 See Jenkinson, "Career Home Run Log of Dick Allen."

48 Neal Russo, "When Richard the Stone Heart Almost Wept," *Sporting News*, April 25, 1970, 5.

49   Quoted in ibid.

50   Ed Wilks, "At Last, Allen Is Home," *St. Louis Post-Dispatch*, April 12, 1970, 3B.

51   Russo, "When Richard the Stone Heart Almost Wept"; Jenkinson, "Career Home Run Log of Dick Allen."

52   Izenberg, "Richie Allen in St. Louis: Can the Love Affair Last?" 50.

53   Neal Russo, "Allen Debut: Loud Bangs," *St. Louis Post-Dispatch*, April 9, 1970, 3C.

54   Milton Richman, "Cardinals See Allen as an Asset," *Norfolk Journal and Guide*, April 4, 1970, 12.

55   Sandy Padwe, "Fans Cheer, Jeer Allen on Return," *Philadelphia Inquirer*, May 22, 1970, 25.

56   Ray Kelly, "Allen's Still Honeymooning in St. Louis," *Philadelphia Evening Bulletin*, May 12, 1970, 46.

57   Frank Dolson, "'Another Game' Big One to Allen," *Philadelphia Inquirer*, May 13, 1970, 29; Bob Broeg, "Allen Puts Stop to Bunning's Kid Stuff," *St. Louis Post-Dispatch*, May 12, 1970, 9A.

58   Ray Kelly, "Allen Welcomes the Phillies with a Three-Run Blast," *Philadelphia Evening Bulletin*, May 12, 1970, 45.

59   Bill Conlin, "Taylor-Made RBI Single Proves Rich-ly Deserving," *Philadelphia Daily News*, May 22, 1970, 76.

60   Russo, "Richie Says It with Homers in Philly Return."

61   Ibid.; Bob Broeg, "Some Stand for Rich, But Birds Fall for Phils," *St. Louis Post-Dispatch*, May 22, 1970, 1C.

62   Barniak, "Allen's Like Vietnam War."

63   Ibid.; Conlin, "Taylor-Made RBI Single Proves Rich-ly Deserving."

64   Stan Hochman, "Rich Allen's a Card and the Deck's Still Loaded," *Philadelphia Daily News*, May 22, 1970, 76.

65   Frank Dolson, "Saturday's Hero Is Bum on Sunday," *Philadelphia Inquirer*, May 25, 1970, 19.

66   Ray Kelly, "Allen's 'Twin' Booed," *Philadelphia Evening Bulletin*, May 24, 1970, Section 3, p. 1.

67   Nesfield, "New Team. New Town. New Richie?" 63.

68   Kisner, "Dick Allen: Baseball's Big Drawing Card," 54.

69   "With Richie Allen," *Los Angeles Sentinel*, October 15, 1970, B1.

70   Blount, "Swinging in His Own Groove."

71   Ross Newhan, "Allen Finds Life (as Dodger) Can Be Beautiful," *Los Angeles Times*, February 22, 1971, G1.

72   Blount, "Swinging in His Own Groove."

73   Green and Launius, *Charlie Finley*, 135.

74   "Richie Allen Says: Managers Can Be Brutal."

75   Robinson, "The Importance of Being Dick Allen," 196.

76   Cardenal, interview with author; Bob Broeg, "Allen Expected Trade, Denies He Hurt Morale," *St. Louis Post-Dispatch*, October 6, 1970, 1C.

77   Brosnan, "Dick Allen: New Boss in Chicago," 128.

78   Jerome Holtzman, "Why Allen, McLain and Conigliaro *Really* Were Traded," *Sport* (February 1971), 38, 86.

79   Melvin Durslag, "Allen Isn't Dealing with a Ninny," *Sporting News*, October 31, 1970, 44.

80   Holtzman, "Why Allen, McLain and Conigliaro *Really* Were Traded," 86.

81   Ibid., 90.

82   A. S. Doc Young, "Allen's Emancipation," *Chicago Defender*, April 27, 1971, 28.

83   Neal Russo, "St. Louis; Allen Was No Problem to Media," *Philadelphia Daily News*, May 12, 1975, 55.

84 Cardenal, interview with author.

85 Neal Russo, "Redbirds Played Albatross Role in Cub Demise," *Sporting News*, October 10, 1970, 17; Neal Russo, "Allen May Miss Rest of Season," *St. Louis Post-Dispatch*, August 28, 1970, 1C.

86 Bill Conlin, "Farewell Allen HR Leaves 'Em Talking," *Philadelphia Daily News*, September 9, 1970, 56.

87 Ibid.

88 Ibid.; Bob Broeg, "Rich Returns in Farewell," *St. Louis Post-Dispatch*, September 9, 1970, 18A.

89 Conlin, "Farewell Allen HR Leaves 'Em Talking."

90 A. S. Doc Young, "The Richie Allen Trade," *Chicago Defender*, October 13, 1970, 24.

CHAPTER 10

1 Brosnan, "Dick Allen: New Boss in Chicago," 128.

2 A. S. Doc Young, "The Trading Game: Black Athletes Learned Early That a Contract Was No Guarantee of Tenure," *Ebony* (April 1971), 139, 146.

3 Holtzman, "Why Allen, McLain and Conigliaro *Really* Were Traded," 38.

4 Nightingale, "The Human Side of Richie Allen."

5 Young, "The Richie Allen Trade."

6 A. S. Doc Young, "Richie's Welcome Mat," *Chicago Defender*, November 11, 1970, 32.

7 Leggett, "A Bird in Hand and a Burning Busch."

8 Frank Dolson, "Were Cards Stacked Against Allen?" *Philadelphia Inquirer*, October 6, 1970, 23.

9 Ibid.

10 Durslag, "Allen Isn't Dealing with a Ninny."

11 Dolson, "Were Cards Stacked Against Allen?"

12 Herman's story was discussed in "Allen: Was No Problem as Cardinal," *Chicago Tribune*, October 7, 1970, D5; "Stories Conflict on Allen Deal," *Philadelphia Evening Bulletin*, October 6, 1970, 51.

13 "Allen: Was No Problem as Cardinal," *Chicago Tribune*, October 7, 1970, D5; Bob Broeg, "Allen Expected Trade, Denies He Hurt Morale," *St. Louis Post-Dispatch*, October 6, 1970, 1C.

14 Cardenal, interview with author.

15 Charles Maher, "Why They Got Allen," *Los Angeles Times*, October 8, 1970, E2.

16 Broeg, "Allen Expected Trade, Denies He Hurt Morale"; Neal Russo, "Cards Give Fast Shuffle to Allen," *Sporting News*, October 17, 1970, 24.

17 Ross Newhan, "Allen's Misplay in 9th Leads to Cards' Win," *Los Angeles Times*, May 19, 1971, G4.

18 A. S. Doc Young, "Did Dodgers Make a Good Deal in '70?" *Los Angeles Sentinel*, October 8, 1970, B3.

19 "Richie Allen Anxious to Play for LA Dodgers," *Philadelphia Tribune*, November 7, 1970, 19.

20 Nesfield, "New Team. New Town. New Richie?" 31.

21 Durslag, "Allen Isn't Dealing with a Ninny."

22 Bob Hunter, "'I'll Hit 'Em Out of Your Park,' Allen Assures Dodger Mates," *Sporting News*, November 7, 1970, 45.

23 "Allen Is a Rich Dodger," *Los Angeles Sentinel*, November 26, 1970, B3.

24 A. S. Doc Young, "Richie Meets Press," *Chicago Defender*, November 17, 1970, 24.

25 John Wiebusch, "Allen: 'Don't Expect Homer Every Time,'" *Los Angeles Times*, November 11, 1970, F1.

26   Nesfield, "New Team. New Town. New Richie?" 70.

27   "31,000 Acclaim Richie at Dodgers' Practice," *Los Angeles Times*, February 15, 1971, D7.

28   Newhan, "Allen Finds Life (as Dodger) Can Be Beautiful."

29   Nesfield, "New Team. New Town. New Richie?" 63.

30   Ross Newhan, "Allen Feels the Pressure in Dodger Camp," *Los Angeles Times*, March 21, 1971, C3.

31   Ross Newhan, "Allen Hurt in Freak Mishap During Workout," *Los Angeles Times*, March 26, 1971, C1.

32   Bob Hunter, "Richie Is Dodger Reply to Puny Homer Output," *Sporting News*, October 24, 1970, 15.

33   Ross Newhan, "Allen's First Homer Helps Dodgers Win, 4–3," *Los Angeles Times*, April 13, 1971, D4; Jenkinson, "Career Home Run Log of Dick Allen."

34   Prugh, "The Summer of Dick Allen's Content."

35   Ross Newhan, interview with author, July 9, 2013.

36   Young, "Allen's Emancipation." Young was a syndicated columnist based at the *Los Angeles Sentinel* in 1971.

37   "Will Dodgers Cut Maury Wills' Salary?" *Los Angeles Sentinel*, February 18, 1971, B1.

38   Newhan, interview with author.

39   Peter O'Malley, interview with author, February 28, 2014.

40   Prugh, "The Summer of Dick Allen's Content."

41   Ross Newhan, "Hustling Allen Lifts White Sox over Angels, 3–1," *Los Angeles Times*, May 20, 1972, D1.

42   Bill Conlin, "Allen Hasn't Been Horsing Around—He's Ready," *Philadelphia Daily News*, March 19, 1976, 59.

43   Young, "A Visit with Dick."

44   A. S. Doc Young, "Grumbling 'bout Richie," *Chicago Daily Defender*, August 3, 1971, 25.

45   Miller, *A Whole Different Ball Game*, 212.

46   Bill Shirley, "Steve Garvey Is Just Too Good to Be True," *Los Angeles Times*, July 27, 1974, D1.

47   Allen and Whitaker, *Crash*, 134.

48   Nightingale, "The Human Side of Richie Allen," 22.

49   Ross Newhan, "Horses in the Heart of Dodgers' Allen," *Los Angeles Times*, April 4, 1971, G3.

50   "Allen Tells 'My Side' of Bad Press Image," *Chicago Defender*, May 1, 1971, 30.

51   Newhan, "Horses in the Heart of Dodgers' Allen."

52   John Husar, "'Thorobred' Allen Always Had Heart in Horses," *Los Angeles Times*, April 3, 1973, C1.

53   Nesfield, "New Team. New Town. New Richie?" 63, 70.

54   "Hank Allen: From the Diamond to the Derby," *Los Angeles Times*, May 1, 1989, K8.

55   Bill Christine, "At 41, Dick Allen Is Still a Vagabond—and a Horse Lover," *Los Angeles Times*, November 4, 1983, G1.

56   "People," *Sports Illustrated*, January 2, 1967.

57   Newhan, "Horses in the Heart of Dodgers' Allen."

58   Kisner, "Dick Allen: Baseball's Big Drawing Card," 54.

59   "Allen: I'm Not Hard to Get Along With," *Los Angeles Times*, March 29, 1974, B10.

60   Franz Lidz, "What Ever Happened to . . . : Dick Allen," *Sports Illustrated*, July 19, 1993.

61   Milton Gross, "Rich Allen Is Afraid of Dogs," *Philadelphia Evening Bulletin*, March 29, 1967, 56.

62   Hochman, "Allen's Tip Generous to a Point."

63   Kelly, "Allen's Still Honeymooning in St. Louis."

64 Husar, "'Thorobred' Allen Always Had Heart in Horses."

65 Brosnan, "Dick Allen: New Boss in Chicago," 128.

66 "Dick Allen: 'Still My Own Man,'" 83.

67 Hochman, "Time to Admire, Not Analyze?"

68 Newhan, interview with author.

69 Ross Newhan, "Russell Subs for Allen, Paces Dodgers' 4–3 Win," *Los Angeles Times*, June 7, 1971, C1.

70 Murray, "The Hard-Hat Blues."

71 Newhan, interview with author.

72 "Alex Johnson Must Continue to Wait," *Los Angeles Sentinel*, September 2, 1971, B1.

73 "Are the L.A. Dodgers for Real?" *Los Angeles Sentinel*, August 12, 1971, B1.

74 Ron Rapoport, "Allen's Four RBI Paces Dodgers' 9–5 Triumph," *Los Angeles Times*, August 21, 1971, C1.

75 Blount, "Swinging in His Own Groove."

76 Melvin Durslag, "Richie Can Understand," *Sporting News*, October 9, 1971, 20.

77 Murray, "The Hard-Hat Blues."

78 Brock Brockenbury, "Allen Tells It Like It Is," *Philadelphia Tribune*, October 2, 1971, 22.

79 Skip Myslenski, "The Allen Years Anything But Boring," *Philadelphia Inquirer*, May 8, 1975, C1.

80 Ron Rapoport, "Dick Allen, White Sox Fans in Season-Long 'Love Affair,'" *Los Angeles Times*, September 28, 1972, D1.

81 A. S. Doc Young, "Are 1972 L.A. Dodgers a Basket Case?" *Los Angeles Sentinel*, July 6, 1972, B1.

82 A. S. Doc Young, "The Gospel Truth . . . ," *Chicago Defender*, March 14, 1973, 29.

83 "Dodgers and Dick Allen," *Los Angeles Times*, November 18, 1972, B3.

84 Ross Newhan, "L.A. Dumps Allen, Adds F. Robinson," *Los Angeles Times*, December 3, 1971, G1. In an interview for this book, O'Malley denied making that statement to Newhan.

85 "Richie Allen, Meet the Los Angeles Double Standard," *Columbia Journalism Review* 11 (November/December 1972), 36.

86 Padwe, "Rich Wanted to Sit Out Year."

87 Christenson, interview with author.

CHAPTER 11

1 Roland Hemond, interview with author, July 5, 2013.

2 Ibid.

3 Holtzman, "Chisox Crowing Over Allen-Melton Power Duo."

4 Joseph Durso, "New at Bat for White Sox, Dick Allen," *New York Times*, January 23, 1972.

5 Hemond, interview with author.

6 Allen and Whitaker, *Crash*, 136.

7 Nightingale, "The Human Side of Richie Allen," 18.

8 Edgar Munzel, "Chisox Draw Blank on Allen Search," *Sporting News*, February 12, 1972, 42.

9 Holtzman, "Chisox Crowing Over Allen-Melton Power Duo."

10 Nightingale, "The Human Side of Richie Allen," 18.

11 Padwe, "What Allen Wants."

12 "Allen Still Unsigned," *Chicago Daily Defender*, February 23, 1972, 28.

13 "Richie, Sox in Accord," *Chicago Defender*, February 24, 1972, 32.

14 Hochman, "Horses Gentle on Allen's Mind."

15 "Allen Arrives; Leaves," *Chicago Defender*, March 15, 1972, 28.

16   George Langford, "Allen Exits Sox Camp, Asks for Trade," *Chicago Tribune*, March 15, 1972, C1.

17   George Langford, "Tanner's Sure Dick Will Play," *Chicago Tribune*, March 15, 1972, C1.

18   Cooper Rollow, "Melton Doesn't Blame Allen for Being AWOL," *Chicago Tribune*, March 12, 1972, D3.

19   Ted Damata, "Stranger than Fiction: The Richie Allen Story," *Chicago Tribune*, March 23, 1972, C1.

20   Ron Rapoport, "White Sox Call for Richie Allen; Get No Answer," *Chicago Tribune*, March 24, 1972, F1.

21   Green and Launius, *Charlie Finley*, 149.

22   Langford, "Allen Exits Sox Camp, Asks for Trade."

23   "How Much Is a Player Worth?" 152.

24   Art Spander, "Blue and Finley Still Not Talking," *Oakland Tribune*, February 29, 1972.

25   "How Much Is a Player Worth?" 152.

26   Spander, "Blue and Finley Still Not Talking."

27   "How Much Is a Player Worth?" 154.

28   "Blue and Allen Only Unsigned Major League Stars," *Philadelphia Tribune*, April 1, 1972, 20.

29   Dave Anderson, "Vida Blue Signs Film Pact Without a Reserve Clause," *New York Times*, April 4, 1972.

30   Green and Launius, *Charlie Finley*, 150.

31   Stuart Banner, *The Baseball Trust: A History of Baseball's Antitrust Exemption* (New York: Oxford University Press, 2013), 221.

32   Bill Melton, interview with author, October 15, 2013.

33   George Langford, "No April Fool, Allen Deadline the 1st," *Chicago Tribune*, March 25, 1972, 1.

34   Robinson, "The Importance of Being Dick Allen," 194.

35   Edgar Munzel, "'You Made Me a Human Being,' MVP Allen Tells Chisox Fans," *Sporting News*, December 2, 1972, 40.

36   George Langford, ". . . And Allen Walks In!" *Chicago Tribune*, April 1, 1972, A1.

37   Jerome Holtzman, "Allen in Chat with Holcomb," *Chicago Sun-Times*, April 1, 1972.

38   George Langford, "Hitting Star Sees End to 'Gypsy Life,'" *Chicago Tribune*, April 2, 1972, D1.

39   George Langford, "White Sox Scatter, But Allen Practices," *Chicago Tribune*, April 2, 1972, D8.

40   Nightingale, "The Human Side of Richie Allen," 24.

41   Wright, "Another View of Dick Allen," 11.

42   A. S. Doc Young, "Prayer for Richie," *Chicago Defender*, May 4, 1972, 36.

43   Fimrite, "Big Fish in Turbulent Waters."

44   "Dick Allen: 'Still My Own Man,'" 84.

45   Fimrite, "Big Fish in Turbulent Waters."

46   Rapoport, "Dick Allen, White Sox Fans in Season-Long 'Love Affair.'"

47   Melvin Durslag, "An Outrageous Waste," *Sporting News*, February 16, 1974, 34.

48   Melton, interview with author.

49   Henderson, interview with author.

50   Hemond, interview with author.

51   Melton, interview with author.

52   Henderson, interview with author.

53   Norman O. Unger, "Dick Allen Tells It All—Sox Were Wrong," *Chicago Defender*, June 21, 1975, 19.

54   Henderson, interview with author.

55   Robinson, "The Importance of Being Dick Allen," 194.

56   George Langford, "Dick Allen Has Few Complaints (White Sox Have None)," *Chicago Tribune*, July 4, 1972, A1.

57   George Langford, "Tanner Tries to Explain Allen," *Chicago Tribune*, March 25, 1974, C2.

58   "Dick Allen: 'Still My Own Man,'" 84.

59   "Tanner on Allen: 'I'm Positive He Will Not Return to Baseball,'" *Los Angeles Times*, September 17, 1974, D1.

60   Stan Hochman, "Dick Allen: The Play's the Thing," *Philadelphia Daily News*, October 11, 1976, 62.

61   Langford, "Allen: 'What Have I Done Wrong?'"

62   Newhan, "Hustling Allen Lifts White Sox over Angels, 3–1."

63   Rapoport, "Dick Allen, White Sox Fans in Season-Long 'Love Affair.'"

64   "Allen and White Sox: A Happy Deal," *New York Times*, June 4, 1972.

65   Kevin Kernan, "Goose and the Candor," *New York Post*, July 27, 2008; "Goose Gossage 2008 Baseball Hall of Fame Speech," http://www.fanbase.com/article/goose-gossage-2008-baseball-hall/2285/.

66   Mark Liptak, "Flashing Back . . . with Stan Bahnsen," www.whitesoxinteractive.com (accessed January 19, 2013).

67   Henderson, interview with author.

68   "'I Am Now a Human Being' Allen Tells Chicago Fans," *Cleveland Call and Post*, December 9, 1972, 16A.

69   Nightingale, "The Human Side of Richie Allen," 24.

70   Robinson, "The Importance of Being Dick Allen," 199–200.

71   "Allen: I'm Not Hard to Get Along With."

72   Newhan, interview with author.

73   Richard Dozer, "Dick Allen Starts His Workday Early," *Chicago Tribune*, March 4, 1973, B4.

74   Husar, "Dick Allen Is 'Funny Dude,' Soul of Sox."

75   "Allen Tapes Give Wood the Flutters," *Philadelphia Daily News*, May 4, 1974, 34.

76   Hemond, interview with author.

77   Brosnan, "Dick Allen: New Boss in Chicago," 130.

78   Ibid.

79   Ibid.

80   Robinson, "The Importance of Being Dick Allen," 196.

81   Nightingale, "The Human Side of Richie Allen," 18.

82   "Oft-Traded Allen Finds Home in Chisox Uniform," *Sporting News*, May 6, 1972, 23.

83   George Langford, "Allen—Mr. Clutch," *Chicago Tribune*, June 6, 1972, C1.

84   See Jenkinson, "Career Home Run Log of Dick Allen."

85   Ed Garver, "Dick Allen and the Team That Saved the White Sox," http://sabr.org/latest/dick-allen-and-team-saved-white-sox.

86   Jay Johnstone, interview with author, April 30, 2014.

87   Langford, "Dick Allen Has Few Complaints (White Sox Have None)."

88   A. S. Doc Young, "The Week's Wash," *Chicago Daily Defender*, October 3, 1972, 29.

89   Hemond, interview with author.

90   Melton, interview with author.

91   Henderson, interview with author.

92   Robinson, "The Importance of Being Dick Allen," 199.

93   Blount, "Swinging in His Own Groove."

94   Richard Dozer, "Tanner on Allen: Best Season Ever," *Chicago Tribune*, September 15, 1972, C1.

95 "Dick Allen to Take Rest of Season Off," *Los Angeles Times*, September 30, 1972, OC_A2.

96 "Dick Allen Wins MVP Award," *Chicago Defender*, November 16, 1972, 44; "Richie the Leader," *Black Sports* (November 1972), 51.

97 "Richie the Leader."

98 Rapoport, "Dick Allen, White Sox Fans in Season-Long 'Love Affair.'"

99 "Ex–Bad Boy Dick Allen Named Most Valuable Player in AL," *Los Angeles Times*, November 16, 1972, D1.

100 Munzel, "'You Made Me a Human Being,' MVP Allen Tells Chisox Fans."

101 Garver, "Dick Allen and the Team That Saved the White Sox."

102 Munzel, "'You Made Me a Human Being,' MVP Allen Tells Chisox Fans."

103 "Dick Allen Wins MVP Award."

CHAPTER 12

1 "Richie Allen: Most Valuable Player," *New Pittsburgh Courier*, November 25, 1972, A25.

2 Hemond, interview with author. The official titles of Holcomb and Hemond were a perpetual source of confusion. At times Holcomb was referred to as the club's general manager and at times he was referred to as its president. Hemond was sometimes referred to as the club's director of player personnel and sometimes as its president.

3 David Condon, "Holcomb Discloses Feud with Tanner," *Chicago Tribune*, July 28, 1973, A4.

4 Richard Dozer, "Allen's 3-Year Pact—675G!" *Chicago Tribune*, February 28, 1973, E1.

5 "Dick Allen Back in the Spotlight," *Chicago Tribune*, March 2, 1973, C3.

6 A. S. Doc Young, "Dick Does It All," *Chicago Defender*, May 22, 1973, 24.

7 Melton, interview with author.

8 Jerome Holtzman, "Don't Weep for Allyn," *Sporting News*, March 17, 1973, 31.

9 Richard Dozer, "White Sox Cut Johnstone, Spiezio," *Chicago Tribune*, March 8, 1973, C2.

10 Rick Talley, "Sox Repay Spiezio with $1 Price Tag," *Chicago Tribune*, March 11, 1973, B3.

11 Holtzman, "Don't Weep for Allyn."

12 Richard Dozer, "Time for Final Commentary on Sox 'Affair,'" *Chicago Tribune*, August 3, 1973, C3.

13 Edgar Munzel, "Allen's Leg Fracture Gives Sox New Case of Staggers," *Sporting News*, July 14, 1973, 5.

14 Liptak, "Flashing Back . . . with Stan Bahnsen."

15 John Husar, "Stan Got $$, Rick Got Gate, Stu Got the Heat," *Chicago Tribune*, July 7, 1973, A1.

16 Condon, "Holcomb Discloses Feud with Tanner."

17 George Langford, "Most of Sox Players Like Stu's 'Decision,'" *Chicago Tribune*, July 28, 1973, A4.

18 George Langford, "Reichardt, Andrews Regret Departure from Sox," *Chicago Tribune*, July 29, 1973, B4.

19 Blount, "Swinging in His Own Groove."

20 Edgar Munzel, "Tanner Nixes Exclusive DH Role for Allen," *Sporting News*, February 3, 1973, 39.

21 Anthony Blackwell, "Allen's Big Decision," *Chicago Defender*, September 28, 1974, 20.

22 Jim Murray, "Lame Duck Flies High," *Los Angeles Times*, March 2, 1973, G1.

23 Richard Dozer, "Dick Allen Returns Here for Checkup," *Chicago Tribune*, June 30, 1973, A5.

24 George Langford, "Allen Still on Sidelines," *Chicago Tribune*, July 26, 1973, C1.

25 Wright, "Another View of Dick Allen," 9–10.

26 George Langford, "Allen Might Be Out for Season," *Chicago Tribune*, August 5, 1973, B4.

27 George Langford, "Anybody See Dick Lately?" *Chicago Tribune*, August 10, 1973, C1.

28 George Langford, "Allen Thru for Rest of Season," *Chicago Tribune*, August 26, 1973, B1.

29 "White Sox' Dick Allen Finished for '73 Season," *Los Angeles Times*, August 26, 1973, C1.

30 Robert Markus, "Bad Raps Stalking Dick Allen Again," *Chicago Tribune*, August 28, 1973, B3.

31 Ibid.

32 Blount, "Swinging in His Own Groove."

33 Jerome Holtzman, "Allen Shirked Duty, Medic Charges," *Sporting News*, March 2, 1974, 32. Dr. Loftus declined an invitation to comment on the record for this book.

34 John Husar, "Ex-Sox Doctor Says Allen Could Have Finished Year," *Chicago Tribune*, February 8, 1974, C4.

35 George Langford, "Dick Allen Shows Up Early for Sox Training Camp," *Chicago Tribune*, February 28, 1974, C6.

36 Will Grimsley, "Dick Allen: An Enigma Reports to Camp," *Los Angeles Times*, March 19, 1974, B1.

37 George Langford, "Allen Makes Lineup . . . But Not Ballpark," *Chicago Tribune*, April 2, 1974, C5.

38 Jeff Prugh, "In Chicago, Love Means Never Having to Say: 'I'm Quitting,'" *Los Angeles Times*, April 8, 1974, D1.

39 George Langford, "Sox Sink Again; Allen 'Main Leak,'" *Chicago Tribune*, April 15, 1974, C1.

40 Jerome Holtzman, "Well-Paid Allen Just Goes Through Motions," *Sporting News,* June 8, 1974, 22.

41 Hemond, interview with author.

42 Melton, interview with author.

43 George Langford, "Sox Lose 2–1; Allen Tardy, Santo Starts at 1st Base," *Chicago Tribune*, June 15, 1974, C1.

44 Jerome Holtzman, "Chisox' Allen Swings Hot, Heavy Bat," *Sporting News*, June 29, 1974, 22.

45 "Allen Still Rapped by Writers, Fans," *Chicago Defender*, July 20, 1974, 20.

46 Langford, "Allen: 'What Have I Done Wrong?'"

47 A. S. Doc Young, "Aw C'mon, Now . . . !" *Chicago Defender*, August 1, 1974, 36.

48 George Langford, "Sour Bite for Chuck in Allen 'Citric' Debut," *Chicago Tribune*, March 23, 1974, A2.

49 David Condon, "Harry Sounds Off on Tanner," *Chicago Tribune*, November 5, 1974, C1.

50 Clifford Terry, "'Fans, It's So Hot on the Field Today That Our Third Baseman Is Melton!'" *Chicago Tribune*, August 3, 1975, H 12. In the article, the *Tribune* quoted Caray as saying that Tanner was "a horse—— manager."

51 Terry, "'Fans, It's So Hot on the Field Today That Our Third Baseman Is Melton!'"

52 "Dick Allen Happy with the Chicago White Sox," *Philadelphia Tribune*, May 13, 1972, 20.

53 Robert Markus, "Allen Almost Quit Friday, He May Yet," *Chicago Tribune*, April 7, 1974, B1.

54 Jim Barniak, "Allen Keeps All-Stars Guessing," *Philadelphia Evening Bulletin*, July 24, 1974, 31.

55 Frank Dolson, "Allen Makes It to the Game on Time—Barely," *Philadelphia Inquirer*, July 24, 1974, D1.

56 Richard Dozer, "Allen Defended by Tanner on 'Late' Arrival," *Chicago Tribune,* July 25, 1974, C2.

57 Dolson, "Too Many Pro Stars Take But Don't Give."

58 Roger Angell, *Five Seasons: A Baseball Companion* (New York: Simon and Schuster, 1977), 203.

59 Sam Lacy, "Dick Allen to Try His Second Love," *Baltimore Afro-American*, September 28, 1974, 9.

60 Cardenal, interview with author.

61 Unger, "Dick Allen Tells It All—Sox Were Wrong."

62 Marty Bell, "You Can Go Home Again," *Sport* (August 1975), 53, 56–57.

63 Merchant, interview with author.

64 Richard Dozer, "Allen Faces Last Rites of Spring," *Chicago Tribune*, March 12, 1978, C1.

65 Although Marvin Miller, in *A Whole Different Ball Game*, recalls a moment during a 1969 Players Association meeting when Dick stood up and spoke of the importance of the players sticking together (p. 103), this appears to have been if not an isolated occurrence then at least an unusual one. None of the individuals interviewed for this book (some of whom were active in union activities themselves) recalled Dick as being particularly active in the union and the author was unable to uncover any additional documentation that would suggest otherwise.

66 Richard Dozer, "Allen Bids Adieu to Chisox Fame, Fortune," *Sporting News*, September 28, 1974, 29.

67 Quoted in Fimrite, "Big Fish in Turbulent Waters."

68 Markus, "Allen Almost Quit Friday, He May Yet."

69 "$225,000 Won't Make Rich Allen Return in 1975," *Philadelphia Tribune*, September 17, 1974, 1.

70 Unger, "Flood and Allen, Like 'Two Peas in a Pod.'"

71 Unger, "Dick Allen Tells It All—Sox Were Wrong."

72 Tony Blackwell, "Allen Plays New Role, But Still Aids Phils," *Chicago Defender*, September 17, 1975, 28.

73 Wright, "Another View of Dick Allen," 10.

74 Dozer, "Allen Bids Adieu to Chisox Fame, Fortune."

75 Ibid.

76 Henderson, interview with author.

77 Markus, "Allen Almost Quit Friday, He May Yet."

78 "Dick Allen: 'Still My Own Man.'"

79 Robinson, "The Importance of Being Dick Allen," 199.

80 Lacy, "Thanks to Gov. Faubus and Little Rock."

81 Bell, "You Can Go Home Again," 55.

82 Bill Conlin, "Dick Allen's All-Around Ability Knocked the Sox off Hemond," *Philadelphia Daily News*, February 14, 1975, 78.

83 Unger, "Dick Allen Tells It All—Sox Were Wrong."

84 Dozer, "Allen Faces Last Rites of Spring."

85 Dave Nightingale, "Chicago: Manager Tanner Threw in Towel," *Philadelphia Daily News*, May 12, 1975, 55.

86 Hochman, "The Book Closes on Dick Allen." Hochman interviewed Wolf for his column.

87 Dozer, "Allen Bids Adieu to Chisox Fame, Fortune."

88 Allen and Whitaker, *Crash*, 157.

89 Jerome Holtzman, "Chisox Glad to Be Rid of Allen," *Sporting News*, October 12, 1974, 22.

90   "White Sox Decide They Can Make It Without Dick Allen," *Los Angeles Times*, December 4, 1974, G1.

91   Norman O. Unger, "Braves Hope to Lure Dick Allen," *Chicago Defender*, December 4, 1974, 1.

92   Rick Talley, "White Sox Don't Want Dick Allen," *Chicago Tribune*, October 8, 1974, C3.

93   Stan Hochman, "You Gotta Bereave?" *Philadelphia Daily News*, September 19, 1974, 44.

94   Robert Markus, "Allen Says He Cheated Chicago Fans," *Chicago Tribune*, June 17, 1975, C3.

CHAPTER 13

1   Spander, "Allen Marches to Own Drummer."

2   Red Smith, "Dick's Designated Runners," *New York Times*, December 25, 1974.

3   "Dick Allen Will Have to Play—It's a Matter of Horsesense," *Los Angeles Times*, December 7, 1974, C2.

4   Hochman, "Horses Gentle on Allen's Mind."

5   "Dick Allen Announces Retirement from His Retirement," *Los Angeles Times*, November 12, 1974, D2.

6   Hochman, "Horses Gentle on Allen's Mind."

7   Larry Keith, "Philadelphia Story: Act II," *Sports Illustrated*, May 19, 1975.

8   Bell, "You Can Go Home Again," 56.

9   Conlin, "Dick Allen's All-Around Ability Knocked the Sox off Hemond."

10   Bell, "You Can Go Home Again," 56.

11   Bill Conlin, "It's Now Braves' Problem to Get Allen to Play," *Philadelphia Daily News*, December 4, 1974, 78.

12   Frank Dolson, "Only One Take for Allen at $5,000," *Philadelphia Evening Bulletin*, December 4, 1947, 65.

13   Conlin, "It's Now Braves' Problem to Get Allen to Play."

14   Bill Conlin, "Allen Feeling His Oats, Balks at Trade," *Philadelphia Daily News*, December 5, 1974, 71.

15   Unger, "Braves Hope to Lure Dick Allen."

16   Unger, "Allen Tells It All—Sox Were Wrong."

17   Bell, "You Can Go Home Again."

18   Frank Dolson, "Phils' New Slogan: Give Him a Chance," *Philadelphia Inquirer*, May 8, 1975, C1.

19   Charles Price, "Dick Allen's Attitude," *Atlanta Daily World*, February 20, 1975, 4.

20   "Braves to Allen: Retire," *Chicago Tribune*, February 6, 1975, C5; Rick Talley, "Wherever Dick Allen Goes, It'll Be with Fanfare," *Chicago Tribune*, February 7, 1975, C3.

21   Allen Lewis, "Kuhn Investigating Phils for Tampering with Allen," *Philadelphia Inquirer*, February 5, 1975, D1.

22   Richard Dozer, "Allen's 'Threat' Ignores Rules," *Chicago Tribune*, March 15, 1975, H5.

23   Norman O. Unger, "An Apology Could Bring Dick Allen Back," *Chicago Defender*, April 26, 1975, 1.

24   "Sox Shut Door on Allen," *Chicago Defender*, March 22, 1975, 21.

25   "Richie Allen Wants to Play This Year, But Not with Braves," *Atlanta Daily World*, March 28, 1975, 5.

26   "Sox Shut Door on Allen"; Richard Dozer, "Sox Will Not Claim Allen, Nor Seek Return," *Chicago Tribune*, April 30, 1975, E1.

27   Richard Dozer, "Miller Backs Sox Management in Allen Quarrel," *Chicago Tribune*, March 17, 1975, E1.

28   Frank Dolson, "Mets Tune Out Richie Allen, Fear Lack of Harmony," *Philadelphia Inquirer*, March 4, 1975, D1.

29   Bell, "You Can Go Home Again," 55.

30   Ibid.

31   Russ Harris, "Allen Set to Play But 'Won't Beg,'" *Philadelphia Inquirer*, March 26, 1975, D1.

32   Ibid.

33   Markus, "Allen Says He Cheated Chicago Fans."

34   "Love Him—1531, Leave Him—887," *Philadelphia Daily News*, February 19, 1975, 72.

35   Allen Lewis, "Phils Secretly Trying to Lure Dick Allen off the Farm," *Philadelphia Inquirer*, February 4, 1975, C1.

36   Bill Conlin, "Phillies in Stew Over Allen," *Philadelphia Daily News*, February 5, 1975, 68. Conlin recounted the Lewis-Carpenter conversation in his column.

37   Ibid.; Lewis, "Kuhn Investigating Phils for Tampering with Allen."

38   Conlin, "Phillies in Stew over Allen;" Lewis, "Kuhn Investigating Phils for Tampering with Allen."

39   Ibid.

40   Stan Hochman, "Phillies Can Dream of Allen But Does Allen Dream of Phils?" *Philadelphia Daily News*, February 11, 1975, 75.

41   Bill Conlin, "Phils Walk Softly to Allen," *Philadelphia Daily News*, February 27, 1975, 52.

42   Ibid.

43   Bill Conlin, "Owens Plans to 'Waive' Hello to Allen," *Philadelphia Daily News*, April 28, 1975, 52.

44   Frank Dolson, "Richie Allen: Phillies Could Go to Top—or to Pieces—with Him," *Philadelphia Inquirer*, March 2, 1975, F1.

45   "Phils Call Off Deal for Allen," *Philadelphia Daily News*, March 13, 1975, 57.

46   Frank Dolson, "That Was a Smile on Ozark's Face . . . ," *Philadelphia Inquirer*, March 14, 1975, E1.

47   Conlin, "Owens Plans to 'Waive' Hello to Allen."

48   Stan Hochman, "Is Allen a 'Foolish Pleasure'?" *Philadelphia Daily News*, May 6, 1975, 60.

49   Frank Dolson, "Deal for Allen All But Finalized," *Philadelphia Inquirer*, May 7, 1975, C1.

50   Norman O. Unger, "Allen OK's Phillies Deal," *Chicago Defender*, May 8, 1975, 40.

51   Dolson, "Deal for Allen All But Finalized."

52   Keith, "Philadelphia Story: Act II."

53   "Dick Allen Just Wants to Contribute," *Los Angeles Sentinel*, May 15, 1975, B1.

54   John Rhodes, "Allen Vows to Make Phillies a Winner and End Gang Wars," *Philadelphia Tribune*, May 10, 1975, 1.

55   A. S. Doc Young, "Allen of the Phillies . . . ," *Chicago Defender*, May 19, 1975, 30.

56   A. S. Doc Young, "Dick Allen Is Back . . . ," *Chicago Defender*, May 14, 1975, 28.

57   John Rhodes, "Will Allen Get a Second Chance?" *Philadelphia Tribune*, May 17, 1975, 25.

58   Dolson, "Richie Allen: Phillies Could Go to Top—or to Pieces—with Him"; Bill Conlin, "Here's How to Welcome Allen," *Philadelphia Daily News*, May 2, 1975, 74; Stan Hochman, "Allen's Return a Time to Forgive, Time to Forget," *Philadelphia Daily News*, May 7, 1975, 78.

59   Bill Lyon, "Allen Continues His Long Search," *Philadelphia Inquirer*, September 18, 1974, C1, 2.

60   Hochman, "Is Allen a 'Foolish Pleasure'?"

61   Hochman, "Dick Allen: 'I'm No Messiah.'"

62　Dolson, "Phils' New Slogan: Give Him a Chance."

63　David Condon, "Allen: Chicago Treated Me the Best of Any Town," *Chicago Tribune*, May 15, 1975, C3.

64　Dolson, "Phils' New Slogan: Give Him a Chance."

65　Bill Conlin, "Allen's Anger Turns to Strength," *Philadelphia Daily News*, June 19, 1975, 64.

66　Stan Hochman, "Allen Starts New Love Affair," *Philadelphia Daily News*, May 15, 1975, 68.

67　Allen Lewis, "New Enthusiasm Marks Allen's Return as Phillie," *Philadelphia Inquirer*, May 13, 1975, D1.

68　Hochman, "Dick Allen: 'I'm No Messiah.'"

69　Lewis, "New Enthusiasm Marks Allen's Return as Phillie."

70　Bill Conlin, "Hutton Finds Allen Tough Act to Follow," *Philadelphia Daily News*, May 15, 1975, 66.

71　Frank Dolson, "The Boos Turn to Cheers for Richie Allen," *Philadelphia Inquirer*, May 15, 1975, D1.

72　Jim Barniak, "Dick Helps Mow 'Em Over . . . with His Old Bat," *Philadelphia Evening Bulletin*, May 15, 1975, 29.

73　Ellen Karasik, "Richie's Back . . . to 3 Standing Ovations," *Philadelphia Inquirer*, May 15, 1975, A1.

74　Conlin, "Hutton Finds Allen Tough Act to Follow."

75　Hochman, "Allen Starts New Love Affair."

76　Barniak, "Dick Helps Mow 'Em Over."

77　Bell, "You Can Go Home Again," 58.

78　Prugh, "The Summer of Dick Allen's Content."

79　Bill Conlin, "Does Allen Make Phils a Superteam?" *Philadelphia Daily News*, May 8, 1975, 82.

80　Keith Burke, "Dick Allen for Better or Worse," *Philadelphia Tribune*, June 17, 1975, 10.

81　"He's Not Hitting, But Allen Winner with Teammates," *Los Angeles Times*, June 6, 1975, OC_A17.

82　Ibid.

83　Bell, "You Can Go Home Again," 55.

84　"Allen Is Happy; Phils Let Him Do His Thing," *Los Angeles Sentinel*, June 26, 1975, B4.

85　Burke, "Dick Allen for Better or Worse."

86　Dolson, "Phils' New Slogan: Give Him a Chance."

87　"Philly Fans Choose to Cheer Allen Now," *Chicago Tribune*, June 10, 1975, C4.

CHAPTER 14

1　Mark Carfagno, interview with author, May 9, 2014.

2　Stan Hochman, "Everyone Worries But Allen," *Philadelphia Daily News*, July 2, 1975, 78.

3　Stan Hochman, "Ozark Stings Allen's Pride," *Philadelphia Daily News*, September 18, 1975, 71.

4　Ray Kelly, "Guess Who's Early for Spring Drills? Mr. Allen," *Sporting News*, March 20, 1976, 34.

5　Bill Conlin, "Allen Should Take a Cut or Get Cut . . . for Good," *Philadelphia Daily News*, January 20, 1976, 51.

6　Kelly, "Guess Who's Early for Spring Drills?"

7　Conlin, interview with author. Conlin recalled a conversation he had with Allen on this subject.

8   Ibid.

9   Ibid.

10   Johnstone, interview with author.

11   Christenson, interview with author.

12   Conlin, interview with author.

13   Kelly, "Guess Who's Early for Spring Drills?"

14   Bill Conlin, "Allen's 'Father' Dies," *Philadelphia Daily News,* March 30, 1976, 35.

15   Kelly, "Guess Who's Early for Spring Drills?"

16   Bill Conlin, "Dick Allen: A One-Man Draft," *Philadelphia Daily News*, November 9, 1976, 62.

17   Johnstone, interview with author.

18   Bill Conlin, "A $200,000 Platooned Allen? Ozark Says (Er . . . Cough) Yes," *Philadelphia Daily News*, May 14, 1976, 78.

19   Ray Kelly, "Un-Brotherly Love Gags Phil Scribes," *Sporting News*, May 15, 1976, 8.

20   Frank Dolson, "Ozark's Composure Shatters Noisily . . . ," *Philadelphia Inquirer*, May 19, 1976.

21   Kelly, "Un-Brotherly Love Gags Phil Scribes."

22   Ibid. The *Sporting News* reported that Ozark said, "You can take it to the bleeping commissioner or anybody else."

23   Kelly, "Un-Brotherly Love Gags Phil Scribes."

24   Conlin, interview with author.

25   Bill Conlin, "Dick and Danny: Silence Is Not Golden," *Philadelphia Daily News*, May 18, 1976, 62.

26   Allen Lewis, "Allen's Pride Is Hurt: Bats 7th," *Philadelphia Inquirer*, May 19, 1976, D1.

27   Bill Conlin, "Allen Showers Criticism on Ozark," *Philadelphia Daily News*, May 19, 1976, 82.

28   Johnstone, interview with author.

29   Frank Dolson, "Phillies Album: Dick Allen," *Philadelphia Inquirer*, September 12, 1976, D10.

30   Ray Kelly, "Saint or Sinner, Allen Makes Things Happen," *Sporting News*, October 23, 1976, 23.

31   Carfagno, interview with author. Carfagno noted that he witnessed this event personally.

32   John Rhodes, "Dick Allen Says: 'World Series Too Far Down the Road,'" *Philadelphia Tribune*, June 26, 1976, 17.

33   Carfagno, interview with author.

34   Ibid.

35   Christenson, interview with author.

36   Carfagno, interview with author.

37   Ibid.; "Allen's Big Hitter . . . and a Bigger Hit," *Los Angeles Times*, June 26, 1976, C4; Ray Kelly, "Philly Gives Allen Bicentennial Salute," *Sporting News*, July 10, 1976, 16.

38   For the details of Allen's status with the club throughout late July and early August 1976, see Ray Kelly, "'What's All the Fuss?' Asks Dick the Deserter," *Sporting News*, August 21, 1976, 18; "Dick Allen Fined $2,200 by Phils for Going AWOL," *Los Angeles Times*, July 30, 1976, E1; Bruce Keidan, "Phillies' Dick Allen Is Among the Missing Again," *Philadelphia Inquirer*, July 30, 1976, A1; Ray Kelly, "Anyone Here Seen Dick Allen?" *Philadelphia Evening Bulletin*, July 30, 1976, 39; Bill Conlin, "Where's Dick Allen This Time?" *Philadelphia Daily News*, July 30, 1976, 82; Ray Kelly, "Mystery Deepens, Allen a No-Show," *Philadelphia Evening Bulletin*, July 29, 1976, 25; Keidan, "Today's the BIG Day That Allen Comes Back."

39   Kelly, "'What's All the Fuss?' Asks Dick the Deserter."

40   Stan Hochman, "It's Getting Late for Dick Allen," *Philadelphia Daily News*, September 17, 1976, 82; Bruce Keidan, "Allen Return Postponed: 'Still Sore,'" *Philadelphia Inquirer*, August 11, 1976, D1.

41   "Dick Allen Fined $2,200 by Phils for Going AWOL."

42   Bruce Keidan, "Dick Allen Returns to Play Again Another Day," *Philadelphia Inquirer*, July 31, 1976, A1.

43   Keidan, "Allen Return Postponed: 'Still Sore.'"

44   Keidan, "Today's the BIG Day That Allen Comes Back."

45   "Dick Allen Signs '76 Contract," *Philadelphia Inquirer*, September 3, 1976, C1; Ray Kelly, "Sudden Skid Surprises and Bewilders Phillies," *Sporting News*, September 25, 1976, 7.

46   Hochman, "It's Getting Late for Dick Allen."

47   Ibid.

48   Frank Dolson, "Allen Now a Rich Spectator," *Philadelphia Inquirer*, September 20, 1976, C1.

49   Bill Conlin, "Allen's Return Is a Big Hit," *Philadelphia Daily News*, September 22, 1976, 98.

50   John Rhodes, "Dick Allen Sees Future on West Coast," *Philadelphia Tribune*, October 9, 1976, 17.

51   Ibid.

52   Bill Conlin, "If Taylor Sits Out, So Will Allen," *Philadelphia Daily News*, September 25, 1976, 44.

53   Jim Barniak, "Has Dick Allen Mouthed Himself Off Phillies?" *Philadelphia Evening Bulletin*, September 26, 1976, Section 2, p. 1.

54   Conlin, interview with author; Bruce Keidan, "Allen Declines to Join in Phils' Fun," *Philadelphia Inquirer*, September 27, 1976, C1.

55   Ray Kelly, "Internal Rift Has Racial Overtones," *Philadelphia Evening Bulletin*, September 30, 1976, 29; Allen and Whitaker, *Crash*, 166.

56   Frank Dolson, "Phillies Bewildered in a Tower of Babel," *Philadelphia Inquirer*, October 1, 1976, D1; Allen and Whitaker, *Crash*, 166; Conlin, interview with author.

57   Bill Conlin, "Dissension Brewing on Phillies?" *Philadelphia Daily News*, September 29, 1976, 78.

58   Conlin, interview with author.

59   Bruce Keidan, "Phillies Are Resting Uneasily as Ozark Hides Hurt and Anger," *Philadelphia Inquirer*, September 30, 1976, C1.

60   Kelly, "Internal Rift Has Racial Overtones."

61   Ron Fimrite, "Two Big Red Machines," *Sports Illustrated*, October 11, 1976, 28.

62   Rich Ashburn, "Phillies' Problems Don't Include Racism," *Philadelphia Evening Bulletin*, October 3, 1976, Section 2, p. 5.

63   Allen and Whitaker, *Crash*, 163; Bill Conlin, "Phils Feuding Over Allen's Flight?" *Philadelphia Daily News*, September 30, 1976, 58.

64   Conlin, "Phils Feuding over Allen's Flight?"

65   Dolson, "Phillies Bewildered in a Tower of Babel."

66   Ibid.

67   Fimrite, "Two Big Red Machines."

68   David Condon, "Allen Up to His Old Tricks Again," *Chicago Tribune*, October 1, 1976, C3.

69   Bill Conlin, "Allen Flips 'On' Switch," *Philadelphia Daily News*, October 1, 1976, 90.

70   Ray Kelly, "Allen Still Upset, Mom to Miss Playoffs," *Philadelphia Evening Bulletin*, October 7, 1976, 32.

71   Ray Kelly, "Allen's Bat Answers Boos," *Philadelphia Evening Bulletin*, October 2, 1976, 11.

72 Dolson, "Phillies Bewildered in a Tower of Babel."

73 Kelly, "Allen Still Upset, Mom to Miss Playoffs."

74 Hochman, "Dick Allen: The Play's the Thing."

75 Bruce Keidan, " 'They Grew Up in a Few Days,' Ozark Declares," *Philadelphia Inquirer*, October 14, 1976.

76 Frank Dolson, "Rose Could Teach Allen Sweaty Smell of Success," *Philadelphia Inquirer*, October 12, 1976, C1.

77 Ray Kelly, "Dick Allen Exits Quickly: Prelude to His Final Exit," *Philadelphia Evening Bulletin*, October 13, 1976, 49; Bill Conlin, "Ozark In, Allen Out," *Philadelphia Daily News*, October 13, 1976, 76.

78 Conlin, "Ozark in, Allen Out."

79 Ibid.

CHAPTER 15

1 "Suppose They Gave a Draft for Allen and Nobody Came," *Los Angeles Times*, November 7, 1976, C2.

2 Bill Conlin, "Dick Allen: A One-Man Draft," *Philadelphia Daily News*, November 9, 1976, 62.

3 "Only Finley Shows Interest in Dick Allen," *Los Angeles Times*, November 13, 1976, C1.

4 Green and Launius, *Charlie Finley*, 258.

5 Stan Hochman, "Who Says Free Agent Draft Will Make Rich Get Richer?" *Philadelphia Daily News*, November 23, 1976, 51.

6 "Only Finley Shows Interest in Dick Allen."

7 "Cash Suggests Expos Make Bid to Get Allen," *Los Angeles Times*, December 14, 1976, E4.

8 Talley, "Sox, Cubs Interested in Signing Allen."

9 Ibid.

10 Rhodes, "Dick Allen Sees Future on West Coast."

11 Green and Launius, *Charlie Finley*, 159.

12 Ibid., 198.

13 Ibid., 192–93.

14 Johnstone, interview with author.

15 Green and Launius, *Charlie Finley*, 259.

16 Dave Anderson, "The Free Agents Santa Claus Forgot," *New York Times*, December 25, 1976.

17 Rick Talley, "Finley Hopes His Chili Has Won Dick Allen for A's," *Chicago Tribune*, February 23, 1977, C3.

18 "Allen-Finley Pffft," *Chicago Tribune*, March 2, 1977, C1.

19 "Allen's Gone Once Again," *Baltimore Afro-American*, July 30, 1977, 9.

20 Herm Rogul, "A's Dick Allen Set to Have Fun," *Philadelphia Evening Bulletin*, March 11, 1977, 43.

21 "Allen Agrees to Contract with A's," *Philadelphia Inquirer*, March 11, 1977, C2.

22 "Allen Joins A's," *Philadelphia Daily News*, March 11, 1977, 78.

23 Rick Talley, "Allen Makes It Official: He's Joining the A's," *Chicago Tribune*, March 11, 1977, C1.

24 Tom Weir, "Allen Joins A's and Everybody's Happy," *Sporting News*, March 26, 1977, 23.

25 Tom Weir, "Allen Pens Bye-Bye Note, Hints He'll Play in Japan," *Sporting News*, August 6, 1977, 11.

26 Tom Weir, "McKeon Learns Too Late Allen Exempt as A's DH," *Sporting News*, April 30, 1977, 23.

27 Dave Anderson, "The A's Confusion Continues," *New York Times*, May 6, 1977.

28 Weir, "McKeon Learns Too Late Allen Exempt as A's DH."

29 Tom Weir, "Disciplinary Collapse Led to McKeon's Exit," *Sporting News*, June 25, 1977, 19.

30 Ibid.

31 "Dick Allen: All Wet," *Philadelphia Daily News*, June 21, 1977, 60.

32 Tom Weir, "Chump Charlie Asks Jumper Dick to Take Hike," *Sporting News*, July 9, 1977, 13.

33 Scott Ostler, "Blue and Allen Speak Kindly of Their Boss," *Los Angeles Times*, March 11, 1978, C1.

34 Weir, "Chump Charlie Asks Jumper Dick to Take Hike."

35 "A's Lift Allen Ban But He Fails to Show," *Los Angeles Times*, June 29, 1977, F1.

36 Tom Weir, "Finley Bats .000 in Search for Allen," *Sporting News*, July 16, 1977, 13.

37 Dozer, "Allen Faces Last Rites of Spring."

38 Weir, "Allen Pens Bye-Bye Note."

39 Rick Talley, "Allen Offered to Cubs," *Chicago Tribune*, July 4, 1977, C1.

40 Weir, "Allen Pens Bye-Bye Note."

41 Bill Conlin, "Dick Allen in a Japanese Baseball Training Camp?" *Philadelphia Daily News*, August 16, 1977, 39.

42 Ostler, "Blue and Allen Speak Kindly of Their Boss."

43 Green and Launius, *Charlie Finley*, 276.

44 Ibid., 268.

45 Ibid., 278.

46 Ibid., 280–81.

47 Dozer, "Allen Faces Last Rites of Spring."

48 Dave Anderson, "Lolich, Allen Spring Eternal," *New York Times*, March 11, 1978.

49 Ibid.

50 Ostler, "Blue and Allen Speak Kindly of Their Boss."

51 Dozer, "Allen Faces Last Rites of Spring."

52 Ostler, "Blue and Allen Speak Kindly of Their Boss."

53 "Dick Allen Is Cut from A's Roster," *Los Angeles Times*, March 29, 1978, E2.

54 Eddie Jefferies, "Allen's Drumbeat Comes to an End," *New Pittsburgh Courier*, August 6, 1977, 24.

EPILOGUE

1 Allen and Whitaker, *Crash*, 179.

2 "Dick Allen's Home Destroyed by Fire," *Philadelphia Tribune*, October 12, 1979, 1.

3 Joe Falls, "Heaven Can Wait on Richie Allen," *Sporting News*, April 3, 1982, 9.

4 Ibid.

5 Murray Chass, "Dick Allen Returns to the Batting Cage," *New York Times*, February 26, 1982.

6 Craig Wright, interview with author, November 27, 2012.

7 Chass, "Dick Allen Returns to the Batting Cage."

8 Wright, interview with author.

9 Chass, "Dick Allen Returns to the Batting Cage."

10 Falls, "Heaven Can Wait on Richie Allen."

11 Wright, interview with author. See also Falls, "Heaven Can Wait on Richie Allen."

12 Falls, "Heaven Can Wait on Richie Allen."

13 Wright, interview with author.

14 Ibid.

15 Ibid.

16 Christine, "At 41, Dick Allen Is Still a Vagabond—and a Horse Lover."

17 Bill Christine, "Dick Allen Puts Baseball in Past," *Sporting News,* January 16, 1984, 55.

18 Jerome Holtzman, "Dick Allen Walking Softly," *Chicago Tribune*, March 4, 1986, C1.

19 James, *The Politics of Glory.*

20 Klein, "A Slugger's Story."

21 John Brazington, "Obituary: Terri Lynn Allen, Daughter of Former Phils' Player," *Philadelphia Tribune*, June 11, 1991, 2B.

22 Koenig, "Dick Allen Reflects on Career with No Regrets."

23 Lidz, "Whatever Happened to . . . Dick Allen."

24 John Diamos, "Baseball: The Belle of the 70's Praises the Belle of the 90's—Belle," *New York Times*, July 9, 1996.

25 Koenig, "Dick Allen Reflects on Career with No Regrets."

26 Diamos, "Baseball: The Belle of the 70's Praises the Belle of the 90's—Belle."

27 Scott Cacciola, "On Rays, Spear and Boar Meet Bat and Ball," *New York Times*, August 19, 2013, D3.

28 Stan Hochman, interview with author, October 28, 2014.

29 William Rhoden, "Weighing the Complexity of a Hall Candidate and His Times," *New York Times*, December 7, 2014, Sports Sunday, 9.

30 Mike Oz, "Dick Allen Falls One Vote Short of Hall of Fame, Leaves Friend Crushed," *Yahoo Sports*, December 8, 2014.

Bibliography

Allen, Dick, and Tim Whitaker. *Crash: The Life and Times of Dick Allen.* New York: Ticknor and Fields, 1989.

Angell, Roger. *Five Seasons: A Baseball Companion.* New York: Simon and Schuster, 1977.

Banks, Lacy J. "'I'm My Own Man.'" *Ebony* (July 1970), 88–95.

Banner, Stuart. *The Baseball Trust: A History of Baseball's Antitrust Exemption.* New York: Oxford University Press, 2013.

Bell, Marty. "You Can Go Home Again." *Sport* (August 1975), 53–58.

Blount, Roy, Jr. "Swinging in His Own Groove." *Sports Illustrated*, September 10, 1973.

Bonventre, Peter. "Dick Allen: 'Still My Own Man.'" *Newsweek*, August 21, 1972, 83–84.

Bouton, Jim. *Ball Four.* New York: Wiley, 1990.

Brosnan, Jim. "Dick Allen: New Boss in Chicago." *Sport* (December 1972), 70–73, 28–30.

Bryson, Bill. "How Screen Door Nearly Kept Allen from Phils." *Baseball Digest* 65 (December 1964), 65–66.

Cain, Susan. *Quiet: The Power of Introverts in a World That Can't Stop Talking.* New York: Broadway Paperbacks, 2013.

Charness, Neil, Michael Tuffiash, Ralf Krampe, Eyal Reingold, and Ekaterina Vasyukova. "The Role of Deliberate Practice in Chess Expertise." *Applied Cognitive Psychology* 19 (2005): 151–65.

Conlin, Bill. "For One Great Ballplayer, Philadelphia Was a Traffic Jam." *Jock* (January 1970).

Cope, Myron. "The Cheerful World of Richie Allen." *Sport* (September 1964), 38, 81–83.

Du Breuil, Linda. *The Greengage Affair.* New York: Tower Publications, 1969.

Fimrite, Ron. "Big Fish in Turbulent Waters." *Sports Illustrated*, April 29, 1974.

———. "Two Big Red Machines." *Sports Illustrated*, October 11, 1976, 28.

Flood, Curt, and Richard Carter. *The Way It Is.* New York: Trident Press, 1971.

Fussman, Cal. *After Jackie: Pride, Prejudice and Baseball's Forgotten Heroes: An Oral History.* New York: ESPN Books, 2007.

Green, G. Michael, and Roger D. Launius. *Charlie Finley: The Outrageous Story of Baseball's Super Showman.* New York: Walker & Co., 2010.

Gregg, Robert. "Personal Cavalries: Sports in Philadelphia's African-American Communities, 1920–60." In *Ethnicity, Sport, Identity: Struggles for Status*, ed. J. A. Mangan and Andrew Ritchie. London: Routledge, 2004, 71–92.

Hall, Donald, with Dock Ellis. *Dock Ellis in the Country of Baseball.* New York: Simon and Schuster, 1976.

Hano, Arnold. "A Week with the Phillies." *Sport* (December 1964), 33–35, 82–85.

Hoberman, John. *Darwin's Athletes: How Sport Has Damaged Black America and Preserved the Myth of Race*. New York: Houghton Mifflin, 1997.

Hoebeke, Tim, Annelore Deprez, and Karin Raeymaeckers. "Heroes in the Sports Pages." *Journalism Studies* 12, no. 5 (March 2011), 658–72.

Holtzman, Jerome. "Why Allen, McLain and Conigliaro *Really* Were Traded." *Sport* (February 1971), 38–41, 86, 90.

"How Much Is a Player Worth?" *Ebony* 27, no. 8 (June 1972), 152–54.

"Is Allen Just Horsin' Around?" *Black Sports* (August 1974), 10–11, 38.

Izenberg, Jerry. "Richie Allen in St. Louis: Can the Love Affair Last?" *Sport* (July 1970), 44–50.

Jacobson, Matthew Frye. " 'Richie' Allen, Whitey's Ways, and Me: A Political Education in the 1960s." In *In the Game: Race, Identity and Sports in the Twentieth Century*, ed. Amy Bass. New York: Palgrave Macmillan, 2005, 19–46.

James, Bill. *The Politics of Glory: How Baseball's Hall of Fame Really Works*. New York: Macmillan, 1994.

Jenkinson, Bill. *Baseball's Ultimate Power: Ranking the All-Time Greatest Distance Home Run Hitters*. Guilford, CT: Lyons Press, 2010.

Jiobu, Robert M. "Racial Inequality in a Public Arena: The Case of Professional Baseball." *Social Forces* 67, no. 2 (December 1988), 524–34.

Keith, Larry. "Philadelphia Story: Act II." *Sports Illustrated*, May 19, 1975.

Kisner, Ronald E. "Dick Allen: Baseball's Big Drawing Card." *Jet* 42 (August 3, 1972), 52–56.

Koppett, Leonard. *The Rise and Fall of the Press Box*. Toronto: Sport Classic Books, 2003.

Kuklick, Bruce. *To Every Thing a Season: Shibe Park and Urban Philadelphia, 1909–1976*. Princeton, NJ: Princeton University Press, 1991.

Lamb, Chris. *Conspiracy of Silence: Sportswriters and the Long Campaign to Desegregate Baseball*. Lincoln: University of Nebraska Press, 2012.

Leggett, William. "A Bird in Hand and a Burning Busch." *Sports Illustrated*, March 23, 1970.

———. "The Rookie from Wampum, Pa." *Sports Illustrated*, April 20, 1964.

Lidz, Franz. "What Ever Happened to . . . Dick Allen." *Sports Illustrated*, July 19, 1993, 84.

Melville, Herman. *Bartleby, the Scrivener: A Story of Wall Street*. 1853.

Miller, Marvin. *A Whole Different Ball Game: The Inside Story of the Baseball Revolution*. 1991. Reprint, Chicago: Ivan R. Dee, 2004.

"More Blacks Will Wear Nats Uniform, Says New Owner." *Jet* (April 24, 1969), 54.

Motley, Bob, and Byron Motley. *Ruling over Monarchs, Giants & Stars: True Tales of Breaking Barriers, Umpiring Baseball Legends, and Wild Adventures in the Negro Leagues*. 2007. Reprint, New York: Sports Publishing, 2012.

Nathanson, Mitchell. *The Fall of the 1977 Phillies: How a Baseball Team's Collapse Sank a City's Spirit*. Jefferson, NC: McFarland, 2008.

———. *A People's History of Baseball*. Urbana: University of Illinois Press, 2012.

Nesfield, Carl. "New Team. New Town. New Richie?" *Black Sports* (July 1971), 30–31, 62–70.

Nightingale, Dave. "The Human Side of Richie Allen." *Baseball Digest* (July 1972), 16–24.

Olsen, Jack. "The Cruel Deception." *Sports Illustrated*, July 1, 1968.

Primm, Eric, Summer DuBois, and Robert Regoli. "Every Picture Tells a Story: Racial Representation on *Sports Illustrated* Covers." *Journal of American Culture* 30, no. 2 (June 2007), 222–31.

Rampersad, Arnold. *Jackie Robinson*. New York: Alfred A. Knopf, 1997.

Razer, Bob. "The Black Traveler: Dick Allen and Little Rock Baseball, 1963." *Pulaski County Historical Review* 61, no. 2 (2013), 2–10.

Regoli, Robert M., Eric Primm, and John D. Hewitt. "Where O' Where Did My Baseball Cards Go? Race, Performance, and Placement in the Topps ERA, 1956–1980." *Social Science Journal* 44 (2007), 742–50.

Rhoden, William C. *Forty Million Dollar Slaves: The Rise, Fall, and Redemption of the Black Athlete*. New York: Three Rivers Press, 2006.

Bibliography

"Richie Allen, Meet the Los Angeles Double Standard." *Columbia Journalism Review* 11, no. 4 (November/December 1972), 36.

"Richie Allen: Pride of the Phillies." *Sepia* 13 (September 1964), 52–55.

Riva, Sarah. "Desegregating Downtown Little Rock: The Field Reports of SNCC's Bill Hansen, October 23 to December 3, 1962." *Arkansas Historical Quarterly* 71, no. 3 (Autumn 2012), 264–82.

Robinson, Louie. "The Importance of Being Dick Allen." *Ebony* 27 (October 1972), 192–99.

Ronner, Amy D. *Law, Literature and Therapeutic Jurisprudence.* Durham, NC: Carolina Academic Press, 2010.

Ronner, Amy D. "The Learned-Helpless Lawyer: Clinical Legal Education and Therapeutic Jurisprudence as Antidotes to Bartleby Syndrome." *Touro Law Review* 24 (2008), 601–96.

Shecter, Leonard. "Richie Allen and the Use of Power." *Sport* (July 1967), 67–72.

Seligman, Martin E. P. *Helplessness: On Depression, Development and Death.* New York: W. H. Freeman & Company, 1992.

"Training Tricks Help Wampum Swamp 'Em." *Life* 44, no. 1 (January 6, 1958), 47–48.

Vass, George. "Baseball's Five Most Over-rated Players." *Baseball Digest* (February 1970), 14–16.

Vilensky, Lee. "Ode to Dick Allen." *Elysian Fields Quarterly* 20, no. 3 (2003).

Wolf, David. "Let's Everybody Boo Rich Allen!" *Life* 67, no. 8 (August 22, 1969), 50–53.

Wright, Craig. "Another View of Dick Allen." *Baseball Research Journal* 24 (1995), 2–14.

Young, A. S. Doc. "The Trading Game: Black Athletes Learned Early That a Contract Was No Guarantee of Tenure." *Ebony* (April 1971), 139–46.

Young, Dick. "Behind Baseball's Fights and Fines." *Sport* (November 1965), 52, 104–5.

Wasserman, Robert. "What Signatures of Players and Ex-Stars Reveal." *Baseball Digest* (December 1980), 90–94.

WEB SITE SOURCES

"Amis Robert Guthridge (1908–1977)." *The Encyclopedia of Arkansas History and Culture.* www.encyclopediaofarkansas.net.

Baseball-Reference.com.

Curtis, Bryan. "In Memoriam: Sportswriting Iconoclast Stan Isaacs." www.grantland.com, April 4, 2013.

Garver, Ed. "Dick Allen and the Team That Saved the White Sox." http://sabr.org/latest/dick-allen-and-team-saved-white-sox.

"Goose Gossage Hall of Fame Acceptance Speech." http://www.fanbase.com/article/goose-gossage-2008-baseball-hall/2 285/.

Liptak, Mark. "Flashing Back . . . with Stan Bahnsen." www.whitesoxinteractive.com.

Retrosheet.org.

Sabr.org.

"Wampum High Gymnasium—Wampum PA." In *Lawrence County Memoirs.* www.lawrencecountymemoirs.com.

NEWSPAPERS

Atlanta Daily World
Baltimore Afro-American
Chicago Daily News
Chicago Defender
Chicago Tribune
Cleveland Call and Post
Los Angeles Herald Examiner

Los Angeles Sentinel
Los Angeles Times
Milwaukee Journal
Nassau Guardian
New Amsterdam News
New Pittsburgh Courier
New York Clipper
New York Newsday
New York Post
New York Times
Norfolk Journal and Guide
Oakland Tribune
Philadelphia Daily News
Philadelphia Evening Bulletin
Philadelphia Inquirer
Philadelphia Tribune
Pittsburgh Courier
Sporting Life
Sporting News
St. Louis Globe Democrat
St. Louis Post-Dispatch
USA Today
Wall Street Journal

Index

Allen, Dick (*continued*)
222, 265, 278–79, 309–11, 337–38; as
role model, 192, 212; and rules,
120–21, 136, 222, 263–64, 267–69, 292;
spring training (opinion of), 94, 185,
186, 208, 234–36, 242, 295; team
captaincy, 119, 240–41; Frank Thomas
fight, 79–91; and Tony Taylor, 36–37,
295, 296, 300, 306–7, 310; upending
baseball's salary structure, 73–76, 105,
106–11, 232, 314; and videotape (game
preparation through use of), 242–43;
wearing batting helmet in the field, 154
Allen, Dick, Jr., 124
Allen, Era, 25–27, 29, 48–49, 124, 190,
199, 233, 311–12, 325; and the Allen-
Thomas fight, 81, 85; and Dick Allen's
upbringing in Wampum, 19–21; and
baseball as a business, 60–61; and spat
with Conlin, 128–30
Allen, Hank, 28–30, 35, 247–48, 249, 252,
259, 274, 278, 294, 325; and horses,
215–16
Allen, Ron, 25–26, 161, 174
Allyn, John, 251–54, 268–69, 272–76
Alston, Walter, 205, 206–7, 210, 219–24,
271; and horses, 214–15
Amaro, Ruben, 70, 82
Anderson, Mike, 284
Anderson, Sparky, 281
Andrews, Freddie, 308
Andrews, Mike, 253, 255
Aparacio, Luis, 228
Ashburn, Richie, 151, 165, 176, 198; and
Allen's 1975 return to the Phillies, 282;
and broom closet incident, 309
Autry, Gene, 315

Bahnsen, Stan, 241, 253–55
Bailey, Jim, 37, 43–45, 49–50
Bair, Doug, 326
Baker, Dan, 290
Bando, Sal, 317
Bannister, Alan, 284, 285
Barber, Red, 165
Bartleby the Scrivener, 7–8
Bavasi, Peter, 315–16

Bell, Cool Papa, 195
Belle, Albert, 335
Bench, Johnny, 281
Bernstein, Ralph, 115–16, 298
Berra, Yogi, 281
Bilovsky, Frank, and the Allen-Thomas
fight, 85
Blavat, Jerry, 179
Blount, Roy, Jr., 6
Blue, Vida, 231–33, 264, 321, 326
Blyleven, Bert, 243
Bonnell, Barry, 285
Boozer, John, 173
Bosetti, Rick, 300
Bostic, Joe, 14
Briggs, Johnny, 80, 167
Brock, Lou, 36, 197
Brown, Ollie, 308–9
Browne, Byron, 180
Buck, Jack, 201
Bunning, Jim, 63, 94, 108, 197, 284
Burrell, Stanley (MC Hammer), 327
Busch, Gussie, 181–82, 185–90, 204, 281
Bush, Kenny, 173–74, 290, 298, 301

Callison, Johnny, 63, 77, 80–81, 86, 118,
119, 173, 213
Campanis, Al, 205–10, 222, 227, 251, 252
Campbell, Bill, 121, 197
Candelaria, John, 303
Capozzoli, Clem, 22, 127–28, 142, 154,
156, 174, 314; and Allen's 1969
suspension, 163, 166; death of, 296–97;
and horses, 217–18
Caray, Harry, 231, 243, 262
Cardenal, Jose, 192–93, 198, 201, 206,
267, 270
Carew, Rod, 248
Carfagno, Mark, 293, 300–302, 336
Carlton, Steve, 186–87, 190, 198, 204,
225, 284, 300
Carpenter, R. R. M. (Bob), 176–77,
263–64, 288, 311; and Allen's 1969
suspension, 166–67; and Allen's salary,
63; and Allen's trade to St. Louis,
180–81; and contract negotiations with
Allen, 77, 109–112, 132; and the firing

Greer, Thom, 90
Guthridge, Amis, 47–48

Haller, Tom, 182
Hano, Arnold, 67–69
Hansen, Bill (of SNCC), 42–43
Harrison, Claude, 104–5, 159, 175, 181;
    and Allen's salary, 106–7, 127; and the
    Allen-Thomas fight, 82, 85–86; and
    Tony Curry, 12; his support of Allen,
    148–49
Hayes, Marcus, 90
Heidman, George (of Jenkintown Steel),
    164
Hemond, Roland, 250, 273, 280; and
    Hank Allen, 247; and Allen's 1972
    holdout, 230; and Allen's 1973 leg
    injury, 257; and Harry Caray, 243; and
    compassion for Allen, 239–40, 249,
    261–64, 267; and ire toward (from
    Allen), 271–72; and Stu Holcomb,
    251–52, 255; and trade for Allen,
    226–28; and trade of Allen to Atlanta,
    276–78
Henderson, Ken, 94, 101, 114–15, 237,
    238–39, 241, 247, 271; on Allen as a
    baserunner, 102
Hennon, L. Butler, 24–25, 234
Henry, Orville, 49
Herman, Jack, 206
Hermann, Ed, 231, 246
Herrera, Pancho, 10–11
Hoak, Don, 55–56
Hochman, Stan, 30–31, 69, 108, 138, 146,
    147, 165, 166, 180, 274, 287, 290, 305;
    and admiration of Allen, 289, 336; and
    Allen's 1969 suspension, 161–62; on
    Allen's clothing, 59–60, 68, 289; and
    booing, 121; on Clem Capozzoli, 128;
    on dirt doodling, 178; on the firing of
    Gene Mauch, 145
Hodges, Gil, 153
Hoerner, Joe, 158, 180
Holcomb, Stu, 227, 262, and contract
    negotiations with Dick, 228–34,
    251–52; and departure from the White
    Sox, 253–56

Holtzman, Jerome, 200, 204, 253, 254,
    260, 261–62, 273
Howard, Elston, 183
Hughes, Ron, 23, 100
Huntz, Steve, 227
Hutton, Tommy, 290, 302

Isaacs, Stan, 163

Jackson, Grant, 165, 166
Jackson, Larry, 136
Jackson, Reggie, 188–89, 200, 212–13,
    225, 261, 264, 321; and facial hair, 317
James, Bill, 4, 334
Javier, Julian, 196
John, Tommy, 222, 227, 228
Johnson, Jerry, 180
Johnson, Judy, 28, 125–26
Johnstone, Jay, 253, 255, 295–97,
    299–300; and Allen's "chili dog"
    homer, 245–47; and Charlie Finley,
    319

Keidan, Bruce, 50, 304
Kelly, Pat, 230
Kelly, Ray, 56, 88, 98, 136, 139, 180, 296,
    311; and Allen's 1969 suspension, 162;
    and Allen's salary, 107
Kennedy, John, 17–18
King, Clyde, 278
King, Hank, 291
King, Willie, 19, 23
Kissell, George, 197
Koppett, Leonard, 169
Kuhn, Bowie, 165, 166, 169, 182, 282–83;
    and Charlie Finley, 319, 326

Lacy, Sam, 52, 267, 271
Lane, Frank, 180–81
Lang, Jack, 195
Langford, George, 258
Lee, Leron, 199
Lewis, Allen, 50–51, 75, 88, 141–42, 168,
    180, 282–83; and Dick Allen not a
    superstar, 117–20; on dirt doodling,
    178; and truce with Allen, 289
Loftus, Gerald, 257, 259

Wise, Rick, 202
Wolf, Dave, 32, 272
Wood, Wilbur, 243

Young, A. S. "Doc," 201, 205; and Allen's
1975 return to the Phillies, 285, 286;
and the Allen-Thomas fight, 90; and
Dick vs. Richie, 152; and his criticism
of Allen, 113, 148, 222–23; and praise
of Allen, 205, 210, 213, 247, 252–53,
262; and *Prayer for Richie*, 236; and the
Reserve Clause, 205, 207; and Tommie
Davis, 204
Young, Dick, 86–87

Zimmer, Don, 331–32

Acknowledgments

WHEN, IN THE early stages of this project, one of Dick Allen's representatives informed me that Dick would not be accepting my invitation to sit down for an interview for this book, I suffered a brief crisis of confidence. I brushed that aside, for the moment at least, as I delved into the yard-high stack of newspaper and magazine articles piled on my floor that contemplated his career as it was taking place. It wasn't long before my confidence returned. Here was the story, I realized. Here lay the pieces of the puzzle that made sense of everything that otherwise seemed so senseless as I looked back on Dick's career from my twenty-first-century perch. Here lay the foundation of the book you now hold in your hands.

As I marched onward, I reached out to others who had known Dick as a youngster, as a minor leaguer, as a major leaguer. Some of these people responded favorably to my request for an interview; others declined. Through the course of these interviews one thing became apparent: despite a lengthy career spent as baseball's supreme outlaw, Dick appeared to have no detractors circa 2013 and 2014. Save one person (who then thought better of his comments and requested that he not be quoted directly), nobody would even admit to having thought badly of him way back when. Very quickly I realized that if I was seeking insight as to how and why things happened the way they did, I would need to travel a different route to get there. And once again, I found it within the heap of mainstream and black papers of the era piled alongside my desk. Newspapers can't help but fall short if expected to provide historical context, given that they exist in the midst of the moment rather than beyond it, but few sources are more effective at conjuring up the mood of the times. And it was this mood I was most interested in.

What do people conclude when they ponder Dick Allen today? That's easy—most everybody seems to, at a minimum, admire not only his talent but his outspokenness as well (albeit some more begrudgingly than others). What does Dick Allen have to say as he looks back upon his career? Again, that's easy—*Crash* traverses that territory. But what about the thoughts and feelings of people—Dick Allen and others—as the events that enveloped his career were unfolding? The man himself, as I wrote within the body of the book, has proven to be an unreliable source. "Dick Allen is not his own best historian," Stan Hochman observed in 1975, and in many respects I found that to be true. (The passage of an additional four decades since then only further complicates things.) But his words, as he spoke them at the time to both the white and black press, do a remarkable job of conveying what he thought day in and day out. They, along with the words of his supporters and critics, provided the narrative I was looking for.

Of course, the interviews I conducted were invaluable as supplementary resources, and I am eternally grateful to those who responded favorably to my requests. Invaluable as well was the help offered up by those who responded to my litany of questions on SABR's listserv and elsewhere concerning statistical minutiae and other hard-to-find information concerning Dick's career and the era in which he played. My thanks to John Allyn Jr., Jon Arakaki, Jim Bailey, Jose Cardenal, Mark Carfagno, Louise Carroll, Jules Childs, Larry Christenson, Bill Conlin, Rory Costello, Richard Crepeau, Guy Demaio, Chuck Dombeck, Gary Fink, Frank Fitzpatrick, Ron Galbreath, Gary Gillette, Sandy Grady, Dallas Green, Arnold Hano, Marcus Hayes, Roland Hemond, Ken Henderson, Stan Hochman, Ron Hughes, Bill Jenkinson, Jay Johnstone, Willie "Sonny" King, Charles Korr, Kit Krieger, Gerald Loftus, MD, Frank Lucchesi, Dr. Mike Marshall, Ron Mazzano, Bill Melton, Larry Merchant, Rod Nelson, Ross Newhan, Peter O'Malley, Bob Razer, Dick Rosen, Michael Sisak, Mark Whicker, Bill White, and Craig Wright.

I would also like to extend special thanks to my research assistant, Dominic Origlio, who spent countless hours poring through microfilm in search of those references to Dick Allen that had heretofore escaped the digitization process (as it turned out, that would be the overwhelming majority of them). Amy Spare and Benjamin Carlson at the Villanova University School of Law library were likewise helpful to me in this regard, as were several librarians at Villanova University's Falvey Library who came and went before I was able to get their names. And, of course, my heartfelt thanks to Bob Lockhart at the University of Pennsylvania Press, whose editorial suggestions helped shape the manuscript and tighten its focus.

Reflecting upon those in the working press who tried to chronicle his life and career as they were unfolding, Dick once said, "Some of what was written about me was true. Some of it was not." I suspect he'd say the same thing about this book. Regardless, all of it has been documented, with a variety of sources confirming everything that is detailed within these pages; if nothing else, Dick Allen did not want for press coverage. When accounts of various events differed, I have included the divergent takes—not with an eye toward resolving the inconsistency but in the hope of illuminating just how and why Dick Allen became the medium through which so many attempted to make points that extended far beyond the diamonds on which he played. In the process, it is my hope that the tenor of the times emerges and, with it, at least some clarification of all that consumed his playing days. "Injuries and turmoil, my career had it all," he added. An understatement if ever there was one.